Fourth Edition

TEACHING CHILDREN DANCE

Susan Flynn, MA
College of Charleston

Emily Enloe, EdD
Oakbrook Middle School

Theresa Purcell Cone, PhD
Rowan University, Professor Emeritus

Stephen L. Cone, PhD
Rowan University, Professor Emeritus

Library of Congress Cataloging-in-Publication Data

Names: Flynn, Susan, 1958- author. | Enloe, Emily, 1987- author. | Cone,
  Theresa Purcell, 1950- author. | Cone, Stephen Leonard, author.
Title: Teaching children dance / Susan Flynn, Emily Enloe, Theresa Purcell
  Cone, Stephen L. Cone.
Description: Fourth edition. | Champaign, IL : Human Kinetics, [2024] |
  Includes bibliographical references.
Identifiers: LCCN 2023028452 (print) | LCCN 2023028453 (ebook) | ISBN
  9781718213159 (paperback) | ISBN 9781718213166 (epub) | ISBN
  9781718213173 (pdf)
Subjects: LCSH: Dance for children--Study and teaching. | BISAC: EDUCATION
  / Teaching / Subjects / Arts & Humanities | EDUCATION / Schools / Levels
  / Elementary
Classification: LCC GV1799 .P87 2024 (print) | LCC GV1799 (ebook) | DDC
  792.8083--dc23/eng/20230705
LC record available at https://lccn.loc.gov/2023028452
LC ebook record available at https://lccn.loc.gov/2023028453

ISBN: 978-1-7182-1315-9 (print)

Copyright © 2024 by Susan M. Flynn, Emily I. Enloe, and Stephen L. Cone
Copyright © 2012 by Theresa Purcell Cone and Stephen L. Cone
Copyright © 2005, 1994 by Human Kinetics, Inc.

Human Kinetics supports copyright. Copyright fuels scientific and artistic endeavor, encourages authors to create new works, and promotes free speech. Thank you for buying an authorized edition of this work and for complying with copyright laws by not reproducing, scanning, or distributing any part of it in any form without written permission from the publisher. You are supporting authors and allowing Human Kinetics to continue to publish works that increase the knowledge, enhance the performance, and improve the lives of people all over the world.

The online learning and video content that accompanies this product is delivered on HK*Propel*, **HKPropel.HumanKinetics.com**. You agree that you will not use HK*Propel* if you do not accept the site's Privacy Policy and Terms and Conditions, which detail approved uses of the online content.

To report suspected copyright infringement of content published by Human Kinetics, contact us at **permissions@hkusa.com**. To request permission to legally reuse content published by Human Kinetics, please refer to the information at **https://US.Human Kinetics.com/pages/permissions-information**.

The web addresses cited in this text were current as of March 2023, unless otherwise noted.

Acquisitions Editor: Bethany J. Bentley; **Developmental Editor:** Jacqueline Eaton Blakley; **Managing Editor:** Melissa J. Zavala; **Copyeditor:** Francesca Moisin; **Proofreader:** Joyce H.-S. Li; **Permissions Manager:** Laurel Mitchell; **Graphic Designer:** Joe Buck; **Cover Designer:** Keri Evans; **Cover Design Specialist:** Susan Rothermel Allen; **Photograph (cover):** © Human Kinetics; **Photographs (interior):** © Human Kinetics; **Photo Asset Manager:** Laura Fitch; **Photo Production Specialist:** Amy M. Rose; **Photo Production Manager:** Jason Allen; **Senior Art Manager:** Kelly Hendren; **Illustrations:** © Human Kinetics; **Printer:** Versa Press

We thank Oakbrook Middle School in Ladsdon, SC, and Memminger Elementary School in Charleston, SC, for assistance in providing the locations for the photo and video shoot for this book.

Printed in the United States of America

10 9 8 7 6 5 4 3 2 1

The paper in this book is certified under a sustainable forestry program.

Human Kinetics
1607 N. Market Street
Champaign, IL 61820
USA

United States and International
Website: **US.HumanKinetics.com**
Email: info@hkusa.com
Phone: 1-800-747-4457

Canada
Website: **Canada.HumanKinetics.com**
Email: info@hkcanada.com

E8617

Theresa Purcell Cone—a gifted and caring professional and my beautiful wife—passed away on September 27, 2019. While she lived with amyotrophic lateral sclerosis (ALS) and contributed to many clinical trials, we continued to travel and share life with family and friends. She was the foundation for this book, and I miss our collaborations.

—Stephen L. Cone

Contents

Preface viii | Acknowledgments x

Part I A Framework for Teaching Children's Dance — 1

1 Understanding the Importance of Teaching Children's Dance — 3

What Is Children's Dance?	4
Why Teach Children's Dance?	9
What Are the Benefits of Children's Dance?	11
Applying 21st-Century Skills to Teaching Dance	20
Meeting the Whole Child Through Dance	21
Linking the Physical Activity Guidelines to Dance	22
Summary	22

2 Presenting Essential Content for Dance — 25

The Body	26
Body Shapes	27
Space	28
Time	30
Force	31
Flow	32
Relationships	32
Dance Forms	34
Summary	38

3 Designing a Dance Program — 39

Planning a Yearlong Dance Program	40
Planning a Dance Unit	42
Planning the Dance Lessons	44
Sample Unit and Lesson Outline	50
Interdisciplinary Connections	52
Summary	55

4 Creating a Dance Education Setting 57

Class Size 57
Equipment and Teaching Materials 58
Facilities 62
Class Frequency and Length 63
Community Characteristics 63
School Policies 64
Program Advocacy 64
Summary 66

5 Making Teaching Effective 67

Helping All Students Learn 67
Using Various Teaching Styles and Strategies 69
Motivating Learners 72
Establishing Protocols and Rules 73
Creating a Safe Learning Environment 75
Presenting Demonstrations 75
Providing Feedback 76
Engaging Students in Performances 77
Observing and Responding to Dance 78
Summary 80

6 Assessing Children's Learning in Dance 81

Teacher Assessment of Program 84
Teacher Assessment of Students 86
Peer Assessment 87
Student Self-Assessment 90
Assessment Instruments 93
Summary 96

7 Including All Children in Dance 97

Knowing Your Students With Disabilities 97
Creating an Inclusive Environment 98
Implementing Inclusive Teaching Strategies 99
Inclusive Dances 103
Double Circle Mixer 104
Greet and Meet Dance 104
Freeze Dance 105
Shape Get-Together 106
Scarf or Streamer Dance 106
Going for a Drive Dance 107
Bandanna Dance 107
Olympic Sport Dance 108
Summary 109

Part II Learning Experiences   111

8 Learning Experiences for Kindergarten, First Grade, and Second Grade   113

Neighborhood Friendship Streamer Dance	115
Floating Clouds and Rain Showers	118
Run, Hop, Jump, Skip	122
The Playground	127
Ocean Waves and Swimmers	130
Spaghetti Dance	133
Balloon Dance	137
Percussion Instrument Dance	140
The Hungry Cat	143
Circus Dance	146
Connect the Spots	150
Frog Dance	153

9 Learning Experiences for Third Through Eighth Grades   157

Dancing Homework Machine	159
Creative Square Dance	163
Action Words	167
Baseball Dance	171
Birthday Celebration	174
Partner Dance	178
Three Sport Dances: Sport Add-On, Sport Web, and Sport Pictures in Action	181
Dance Maps	187
Create Your Own Hip-Hop Dance	191
Funky Shape Museum	195
Stick Figures Come Alive	197

10 Learning Experiences in Popular, Fitness, and Social Dances   203

Overview of Popular, Fitness, and Social Dances	203
Teaching Strategies for Choreographed Dance Lessons	205
Basic Social and Popular Dance Movements	210
Learning Experiences	213
Jumping Steps Line Dance	215
16-Step Contra Dance	217
Disco Fever Dance	219
Funky Cowboy Line Dance	222
Grapevine Slide Dance	224
Hey Baby Line Dance	227

The Hit Man Contra Dance	229
Honky Tonk Line Dance	232
Honky Tonk Circle Dance	234
Rockin' Shuffle	236
Rock This Party Line Dance	238
Baba Hou Fitness Dance	240
T Fitness Dance	243
Cha-Cha Plank Fitness Dance	244
Circle Jam Fitness Dance	248
Tabata Dance	250
Salsa	252
Swing	255
Cha-Cha	258
Create Your Own Fitness Dance	261
Create Your Own Popular Dance	263
Sample Rubrics	265

11 Learning Experiences in Folk and Cultural Dances — 267

American Square Dance	269
Bele Kawe	272
Appalachian Big Circle (Elementary Version)	274
Appalachian Big Circle (Secondary Version)	276
Kinderpolka	279
La Raspa	281
Mayim, Mayim	284
Samoan Sasa	286
Tanko Bushi	289
Tinikling	291
Virginia Reel	295

References 299 | About the Authors 302

Preface

The fourth edition of *Teaching Children Dance* retains everything you have loved about previous editions while adding to and updating it for future generations. Susan Flynn and Emily Enloe have joined the author team to carry the work of Theresa Purcell Cone and Stephen L. Cone into the future. Most of the original content remains and is now enhanced with new learning experiences, new ideas, new photos, and new resources for instructors, students, and professionals. As in previous editions, the goal of this text is to make the teaching of dance accessible to educators and future educators. Whether you are a physical education teacher, a dance teacher, a grade-level classroom teacher, or a student, we hope that your interest in dance is expressed in the enthusiasm you bring to students when you offer dance in your program. Dance remains popular as a result of a recent flood of television shows, commercials, and online media that share the process of learning and performing and the strong message of dance as a means of expression and communication. An increasing number of students are talking about dance, dancing during recess, and using dance as a way to stay fit. Dance is now the cool activity to do. Students enjoy recreating new moves they see on television and in videos. They view dance as a way to have fun and celebrate with friends and family. This opens the door for dance to be a welcomed activity in the school curriculum.

This edition of *Teaching Children Dance* brings a new perspective focused on dance as an inherent component of a student's education. Since our 2012 edition, educational issues have refocused on students' gaining knowledge and skills that can be applied to all aspects of their lives. Dance is one mode for learning that involves using the body and senses to gather information, communicate, and demonstrate conceptual understandings. Teachers are interested in gaining new strategies for assessing what students learn in dance. They want inclusive approaches to designing lessons for students with disabilities, and they want to develop learning experiences that encourage creativity, positive social interactions, and development of motor skills.

The revisions in this edition include updates to discussions on dance and the whole-child education initiative; 21st-century skills that promote creative thinking, collaboration, communication, global awareness, and self-direction; and the link between dance and the 2018 Physical Activity Guidelines. Two new chapters have been added to explore choreographed dances that teachers can easily learn and adapt to teach a variety of students: Chapter 10 features 21 new learning experiences for popular, fitness, and social dances that focus on both the fun and health-related aspects of learning dance. Chapter 11 includes 11 new learning experiences for folk and cultural dances based on traditional movements and songs from around the globe.

This edition is packaged with new online resources to support instructors, students, and professionals. For instructors, suggested answers to the reflection questions, PowerPoint presentations, and a test package are available to supplement lectures and instruction. For students and professionals, HK*Propel* Access provides assessments, tables, and other forms that can be used as is or adapted for classroom application, as well as instructional videos of dances from the new chapters. Icons denote material from the book that is available in HK*Propel*.

As in the third edition, this edition is divided into two parts. Part I contains the foundational content and strategies for developing dance learning experiences. We have updated our references to dance works and added new photos, figures, and tables. You will find ideas for planning a yearlong program, a dance unit, or a single lesson. We also include suggestions for class management, advocacy, assessment, and interdisciplinary teaching. At the end of each chapter, you will find revised questions for reflection that are applicable to both teachers and university students enrolled in dance courses.

Part II includes two chapters of creative dance learning experiences and two chapters on choreographed learning experiences. In this edition, we have updated the creative learning experiences with newer reference material and suggestions for use with middle-school-aged students. The instructions for each dance learning experience are similar to the dialogue you would use with your students. As you read the instructions, you can imagine yourself in your teaching space with your students. Each learning experience includes learning outcomes; equipment needed; ideas for the introduction, development, and culminating dance; and assessment suggestions that are directly linked to each outcome. There are suggestions for interdisciplinary teaching and ideas for varying the learning experience to meet your students' abilities and interests. The two new chapters provide detailed explanations of choreographed learning experiences in popular, fitness, social, folk, and cultural dances to share with students from kindergarten to high school.

One of our challenges in writing this edition was to provide a clear description of the essential dance content and instructional strategies that are feasible and can lead to your success in teaching both creative and choreographed dances. Our hope is that, as a result of this book, more students will gain the opportunity to learn, create, perform, and respond to dance and that more educators will include dance as a cultural, social, and creative form in their programs. If you have used the previous editions of *Teaching Children Dance*, we know you will find this edition expanded and more comprehensive. If this is your first copy, we know this book will help you find the joy of teaching dance and help your students find the joy of learning dance.

Acknowledgments

Susan and Emily would like to thank Theresa Purcell Cone and Steve L. Cone for entrusting us with their outstanding book. It has been a pleasure to continue this work on their behalf and update their work in this newest edition. We hope our contributions continue the legacy of teaching children dance and assisting educators in their journey the two of them began many years ago.

The authors would also like to thank the following for their contributions and support:

- The students, staff, and administration at Oakbrook Middle School, Memminger Elementary School, and N.E. Miles Early Childhood Development Center for their contribution to the images and videos in this edition.

- Michael G. Flynn, Ph.D.; William Zeigler; and Amanda Flynn for their technical and moral support of Susan and Emily during the writing process.
- The many dance and physical education teachers who provided support and contributions to some of the new dances in this edition.

Most importantly, we would like to thank Human Kinetics and the *Teaching Children Dance* team for this opportunity and the commitment to completing this new edition. We are thankful to have been a part of the process and have learned much from everyone along the way.

PART I

A Framework for Teaching Children's Dance

What is children's dance? Why should it be taught? How does one design and assess a dance program? Educators ask these foundational questions frequently when developing dance programs. We hope that in the following seven chapters, you find the information that will help you understand children's dance and develop the skills to enhance or initiate dance as part of a physical education or arts education curriculum.

Chapter 1, Understanding the Importance of Teaching Children's Dance, addresses the essential content for teaching dance. It provides a description of what is considered children's dance and explains the significance and benefits of a children's dance program. Included in this edition is information on how dance addresses the 2018 Physical Activity Guidelines, 21st-century skills, and whole-child education initiatives.

In chapter 2, Presenting Essential Content for Children's Dance, the elements of dance are described: the body, space, time, force, flow, and relationships. Also explored are the forms of children's dance and how they contribute to a comprehensive dance program.

Chapter 3, Designing a Dance Program, provides the nuts and bolts of program construction and delivery. We include examples for planning a yearlong program and a dance unit and lesson outline. The section on making interdisciplinary connections between dance and other subject areas continues to be an important component, and specific subjects are identified at the end of each learning experience in part II.

Chapter 4, Creating a Dance Education Setting, includes a discussion on tailoring a dance program to fit various teaching settings. Teachers are frequently faced with justifying to their students, parents, administrators, and other colleagues why dance should be included in the curriculum. To make such justification easier, we include advocacy strategies for maintaining and developing a program.

The way you teach is as important as what you teach. In chapter 5, Making Teaching Effective, we discuss how teaching and learning styles affect the success of a dance experience. Also included are strategies for establishing protocols and expectations that lead to a safe and productive learning environment and strategies for student feedback, demonstrations, and observations.

Assessment is essential to all learning experiences. In chapter 6, Assessing Children's Learning in Dance, we include examples of assessment in dance and a menu of assessment instruments for teacher, peer, and student self-assessment.

Chapter 7, Including All Children in Dance, focuses on teaching children with disabilities.

This chapter focuses on the importance of creating an inclusive teaching environment that recognizes the abilities of all students. Teaching strategies for success are included, along with descriptions of dances that can be used in an inclusive dance class as well as a self-contained dance class.

CHAPTER 1

Understanding the Importance of Teaching Children's Dance

Imagine a class of young children running as fast as they can, waving red streamers over their heads, then spinning around and slowly descending to the floor with the streamers floating down beside them. Through these dance movements, children might be expressing their interpretations of a fast-burning flame slowly flickering out, or they might be pretending to sprinkle red paint all over a room. Now, imagine yourself as the teacher who designed and presented this dance idea to the class. The children responded with great enthusiasm, and you feel successful for sharing this experience with them. It would be wonderful if every dance experience resulted in this feeling of success for both the student and the teacher. The goal of this book is to provide you the content needed to design and present a successful dance experience to students. All the learning experiences in this book have been taught by the authors, and many others have been adapted by those studying dance pedagogy or by experienced educators in dance or physical education. The success of a dance learning experience is in making relevant and developmentally appropriate content choices combined with a passion for teaching. The first step is to decide what you want students to learn and what benefits they will gain from the opportunity to participate in a dance learning experience. Clarifying the final outcome will guide you in selecting, planning, and implementing a meaningful learning experience for you and the students.

Teaching children dance may be a new area of study or an area in which you would like to improve your current knowledge and skills. It does not require being an accomplished dancer or knowing everything about every dance form; however, some experience with dance is helpful. Everyone has had the opportunity to experience dance either as a participant or a spectator. Think about the times you heard a piece of music, and you could not resist the urge to move. Perhaps you have been at a social gathering where everyone is having fun dancing, and you are drawn into the energy of the group and find yourself moving your feet, laughing, and enjoying a moment of friendship and fun.

Teaching dance does require an educator who is dedicated to delivering high-quality dance lessons in the dance unit or program and who believes that dance is essential to students' overall education. Even if you agree that dance is important, you may not be sure where to start. We ask you to consider the experiences, knowledge, and skills you already have and use them as a foundation for teaching dance, whether you are taking your first steps or reaching for the next level.

As a dance educator or physical educator, you enjoy physical activity in many forms. You like creating new possibilities for movement, such as developing a new game strategy, exploring how to express a poem through movement, or developing a new line dance. You value creativity and view it as a skill that students need in order to learn problem-solving and critical-thinking skills. Your enthusiasm for physical activity and positive attitude about exploring various ways to move provide you with a strong foundation for planning and teaching dance.

You can also rely on your teaching and dance experiences as a background for selecting the types of dance activities that are appropriate for students. Find out about students' dance experiences. Begin by asking them where they have participated in or watched dance. This information can help you anticipate their acceptance of the dance experiences you have planned. Your experiences interacting with students have taught you that students enjoy creating new ways to move and that they are eager to share their accomplishments. You acknowledge that each student needs to learn in a caring and nonthreatening atmosphere. You may have already planned and implemented successful movement experiences, and you know that if one idea does not work, you may need to try another and maybe even another. These movement experiences with students, in a variety of settings, apply easily to teaching dance; all you may need are some ideas for lessons and a planning process.

Be confident in the knowledge and skills you bring to the dance learning experience, and be open to students' suggestions for dance content. Students' involvement in the content selection will increase their motivation to participate. Learning to teach dance begins with a willingness to try something new, take a risk, and persist so you can improve. Teaching will present challenges—you may encounter reluctant students, require new teaching materials, or need additional professional development. But you can also make your teaching career full and exciting—why not try? Be open and willing to accept the challenges of learning something new, just as you ask your students to do every day.

WHAT IS CHILDREN'S DANCE?

Dance is a unique form of moving that holds various meanings for each of us, depending on how and why dance is a part of our lives. It is purposeful, intentionally rhythmic, and culturally patterned. It goes beyond ordinary motor activity because it also reflects one's aesthetic values (Hanna 1987). In the elementary school setting, dance has many purposes and can exist in a variety of forms. Children enjoy learning cultural dances, social dances, aerobic dance, square dances, and line dances as well as composing their own dances through creative dance. No single specific dance form should be taught exclusive of others. We recommend that students have an opportunity to experience many dance forms throughout their education.

In the secondary school setting, students continue to enjoy learning a variety of dance forms and styles. In addition to the aforementioned forms, students at the middle and high school levels enjoy more challenging dance sequences and are more likely to have the attention span for longer, more in-depth learning of specific techniques. All dance forms are equally important to teach to secondary students as well. These students also enjoy the social aspect of dancing as much as their younger counterparts.

Children's dance is a way of knowing that fully integrates all aspects of being human. Kinesthetically, intellectually, socially, and emotionally, children learn about themselves and others through the medium of dance. Ruth Lovell Murray (1963), a pioneer educator of elementary school dance education, noted the following in the second edition of her book *Dance in Elementary Education*:

> *Perhaps the best interpretation [of dance] is one that emphasizes not only body mastery and discipline in movements but even more the use of such movement for expressive and imaginative purposes. Dancing may borrow from and lend to many other kinds of movement activities. It is when the ultimate concern is with the meaning of movement that the term dancing is accurately applied. (pp. 7-8)*

In the elementary curriculum, dance can be taught as a discrete subject, as a component of the physical education or arts program, or as a component that is integrated with another subject area (e.g., science or language arts). In all of these contexts, regardless of the type of dance that is taught, dance exists simultaneously as an art form and a movement form (see figure 1.1). Dance becomes the means through which children develop, express, and communicate their life experiences. As a result, they gain an aesthetic awareness about how the body and its movements are connected to meaning and intention.

In the secondary school curriculum, dance can also be taught as component of an existing program or as a discrete subject. In any format, it builds on elementary skills with a focus on social interaction, communication, and creativity. As students are more aware of how their bodies work, they can begin to construct and use dance to express ideas about themselves, their communities, and global issues. They learn how to develop their movement skills and use them to communicate and connect with the world around them.

When dance is part of the physical education curriculum, it provides students an expressive way to use movement in addition to fulfilling the functional purposes of games, sport, fitness, and gymnastics. Dance is the only form of moving that meets people's innate need to communicate thoughts, feelings, understandings, and ideas through movement. All other types of movement in the physical education curriculum are functional—students acquire skills, such as throwing or kicking a ball, to improve their motor skills and ultimately use the skill in a game to perhaps score points (see figure 1.2a). In gymnastics, students may learn the principles of balance to perform a handstand (see figure 1.2b). Although similar movements may appear in a dance, they are detached from their functional purpose (e.g., raising the arms high to catch a ball or get a stretch through the body) and instead become movements that illustrate or express an idea, thought, understanding, or feeling, such as the feeling of reaching toward the sky (see figure 1.3). Both functional and expressive movements are necessary so students can use them to express and communicate ideas and feelings in addition to developing healthy, active lifestyles.

Children's dance involves more than exploring various ways to make a shape or learning a series of steps to use; it is a way of expressing understandings and feelings. This ability to use movement to express and communicate differentiates creative movement from creative dance. The purpose of creative movement is to explore movement possibilities and discover new

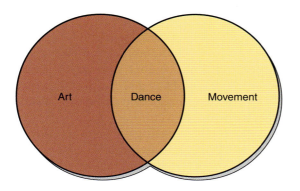

Figure 1.1 Dance, as a discrete subject, is simultaneously a movement and an art form.

Figure 1.2 Functional movement: (a) shooting a basket; (b) supporting body weight in a handstand.

Figure 1.3 Expressive movement: Children stretch their arms up to express the feeling of reaching toward the sky.

ways to change movement. Creative dance uses the exploratory process in coming up with new movements; however, it takes the process further. After exploration, learners make aesthetic choices about movements and the qualities of those movements that will best express their ideas, feelings, or understanding of a concept. These movements are then organized into a movement sequence or a dance. Students practice, refine, rearrange, and finally perform their dance individually as part of the whole class dancing, or they share dancing with a partner or small group. A dancer can be compared to an artist's paintbrush as it moves on a canvas, transforming an idea or feeling into a tangible form. Dance movements and the applied elements of dance are like the colors, lines, shapes, and textures a painter uses to express ideas. The dancing space becomes the canvas. Just as every painter might interpret a sunset, flower, or the feeling of anger differently, children will also demonstrate their own unique interpretation of an idea, dance movement, or feeling using the body and its movements as their expressive tools.

Dance at the elementary level allows for personal decision-making; the exploration of new ways of moving; and the development of new ways of knowing, creating, and learning. Dance learning experiences are based on teacher- or student-selected outcomes that promote achievement in the psychomotor, cognitive, and affective domains. These outcomes can guide curriculum development and help identify the benefits that students will gain as a result of participating in a dance program, unit, or lesson. Through physically learning and performing dances and creating, observing, and responding to dance, students develop their ability to physically move in different ways and understand how to create and adapt movement, and they discover how movement can be a means of learning about others and collaborating with others to accomplish a goal.

Dance at the secondary, or middle and high school, level continues to build on the basic foundation set in elementary school. Students explore new ways of moving and find their own personal preferences. Dance learning experiences are based on both teacher- and student-selected outcomes, with students developing their own artistic voices in the process. By continuing to learn and perform dances, students find new ways to challenge their growing bodies and physical abilities. In creating, observing, and responding to dance, students continue to develop their own understanding about dance and how to use movement as a way to express ideas and feelings. They also build collaboration skills and develop leadership abilities by working with others toward a common goal.

Through participating in various learning experiences that include dance as a social, cultural, and creative movement form, students accomplish the following:

- Develop the knowledge and skills to use dance for self-expression and communication of ideas, concepts, understandings, and feelings.
- Increase their ability to observe and reproduce movement accurately.
- Develop their ability to use movement exploration to create new movements or find different ways to perform a specific movement.
- Increase their understanding of how dance represents social and cultural traditions, values, heritage, and ways of living.
- Acquire collaboration skills and demonstrate respect for others.
- Develop an understanding and appreciation for dance as a movement form and art form.
- Understand how the elements of dance—the body, space, time, force, flow, and relationships (see chapter 2)—are used in

learning, performing, creating, observing, and responding to dance.
- Recognize how dance can be a learning strategy for acquiring knowledge and skills in other arts and subject areas.
- Develop locomotor and nonlocomotor skills.
- Increase their coordination, balance, strength, flexibility, and cardiorespiratory endurance as well as develop their knowledge of fitness.

For many children, the elementary school dance program may be their first encounter with dance. Children may bring perceptions and opinions about dance that influence their level of participation. By offering a variety of dance forms throughout the school year, children can become more comfortable with the different ways movement is used as a basic means of expression and communication.

Secondary school dance programs may also be the first time a student encounters dance. These older students are often more socially aware than their elementary school peers, making them more sensitive to the pressures of dancing and performing with others. This might make dancing in front of peers stressful for some students. However, by continuing to work with secondary school students in a variety of dance forms while remaining aware of their social needs, you help older learners become more comfortable dancing and using movement to express their ideas and feelings. Fitness dances are one great way to introduce dance and provide relevance to its importance. When you introduce dance through the lens of fitness, students focus on concepts such as increasing heart rate, building bone or muscular strength, and repeating steps with specific music cues. This may relieve some pressure new dancers feel in more traditional dance settings, which often focus on specific shapes, techniques, or steps. With the focus on fitness, students can enjoy the learning experience of dance and working toward individual goals of improving physical health. Other ways of making older students feel more comfortable include practicing dance steps as part of a warm-up to build confidence, using contemporary music, or allowing students to practice in small groups.

Awakening New Perceptions

Every time children experience dance, whether as dancers, observers, or creators, they gain new perceptions about themselves and their world. Through dance, children learn more about who they are, how they move, what they think, how they feel, and how they relate to others. They also learn that there are multiple ways to express the same idea. For example, as a result of participating in a cloud dance where the children used their own body shapes and movements to express clouds they saw in the sky, the children expanded their insights into how clouds move and observed their classmates' unique interpretations of cloud shapes and movements.

Awakening new perceptions and understandings is an aesthetic experience. Through manipulating the elements of dance, students make aesthetic choices about what movements to use and the quality of those movements. In the cloud dance, the following explorations might be suggested to help shape students' aesthetic choices: "Find a way to use your arms to create a long cloud shape. What pathway will you use to travel across the room in your cloud shape? Change your speed to show how slow and how fast the clouds move. How can you and another person connect your cloud shapes and move together?" (See figure 1.4.)

All dance movement is the result of a series of qualitative decisions about how the elements of dance will be used to express an idea. The way the dance movement appears, using body, space,

Figure 1.4 Young children holding hands in a circle to demonstrate the shape of a cloud.

time, force, flow, and the relationships of the dancers to each other, is the result of purposeful decision-making. This decision-making is applicable to all types of dance. Traditional cultural dances were designed in a specific way to reflect a particular aspect of a culture. The formations, dance steps, clothing, and music all reflect what a group of people hold as significant representations of their history, traditions, values, and beliefs. Social dances evolve from the needs of people to move together as a community, to share in celebrations, meet others, and maintain connections. Creative dances are also based on individual or group decisions about how to manipulate movement to express an idea or feeling.

Dance in both the elementary and secondary school curriculum provides students with a variety of dance experiences. These experiences allow them to create their own dance movements and learn dances created by others. Creating and learning dances help learners make meaning of what happens in their lives as well as in the lives of others.

Creative Dance

In creative dance, children generate, vary, and manipulate movement using the elements of dance (body, space, time, force, flow, and relationships; see chapter 2) through the process of improvisation. Creative movement is the product of improvisation and becomes the first step used in developing ideas for a creative dance. Children may select improvised movements and arrange them into a sequence or choreographic structure to form a dance. The teacher or the children generate the initial idea for the dance. The following are examples of creative dance:

- A kindergarten class creates a dance about the animals and people they recently saw at the circus. They dance about lions jumping through hoops, elephants balancing, tightrope walkers moving forward and backward, acrobats swinging on the trapeze, and clowns juggling colorful balls.
- A 1st-grade class is studying a science unit on bubbles. They form a list of vocabulary words that describe how bubbles move and then create dance movements to illustrate those words. Next, the children develop a three-word sequence such as *pop*, *float*, and

burst to create a dance that reflects the word sequence.

- The opening of baseball season is the main story in the news. A 3rd-grade class creates a dance that reflects the movements that occur in a baseball game. They include movements that represent various ways to run, catch, strike, and throw.
- A 4th-grade class creates a large-group dance sculpture representing straight, twisted, and curved shapes. They focus on how to collaborate while changing from one shape to another using various tempos.
- A 6th-grade class has collaborated to write several poems. They select a poem they would like to express through dance. The class breaks into three groups, and each group creates a dance to represent the selected poem.
- A 10th-grade class, organized into groups of three, creates dances that use movements from everyday life such as brushing teeth, riding a bicycle, petting a dog, eating a sandwich, or reading a book. They discuss how many popular or social dances were created by using everyday movement as a starting point. Then they make their movements more abstract and perform to various types of music to develop their own social dances.

Traditional and Choreographed Dances

Traditional, cultural, square, and social dances are dance forms created by people in a specific culture or during a specific time period, as are dances choreographed by a professional choreographer, the teacher, or another student. These types of dances can be handed down from one generation to the next; they can be recorded digitally or in a written form; they can be performed live onstage or live-streamed online; or they can simply exist within the mind and body of the person who composed it. The following are some examples of cultural, social, and choreographed dances:

- A dance choreographed by one student or a group of students with designated move-

ments and a repeatable sequence that is taught to other students
- A dance choreographed and taught by the teacher (see figure 1.5)
- A traditional cultural dance such as la raspa, troika, or Virginia reel
- A popular dance from a particular time period such as the twist, electric slide, or lindy
- A children's social dance such as the hokey pokey, alley cat, or bunny hop
- A square dance such as the Texas star or Oh, Johnny
- A contemporary popular line dance such as the cha-cha slide or cupid shuffle
- A choreographed dance by a professional choreographer in dance forms such as modern dance, jazz, ballroom, hip-hop, ballet, or tap

WHY TEACH CHILDREN'S DANCE?

Dance is an essential component of a high-quality, comprehensive physical education or arts education program. Students at the elementary and secondary levels need to have the opportunity to develop their abilities to use movement for both functional and expressive purposes. They should participate in a full range of experiences to learn the many possibilities for movement. In the *National Dance Education Standards Framework*, dance is defined as an art form that communicates meaning and understanding through movement (National Dance Society 2020).

Dance addresses the needs of children to express and communicate their ideas, understand and know themselves and their world, and expand their own movement abilities. Using movement to express ideas is already familiar to children. Along with their language development, they use locomotor and nonlocomotor movements to support and emphasize what they want to say. This natural use of movement for expression and communication becomes a foundation for learning dance. Children's life experiences, culture, physical and intellectual abilities, and understanding of themselves also influence how they perceive and integrate dance into their lives.

Expressing and Communicating Ideas, Feelings, and Understandings

Dance addresses children's need for expression and communication in the following ways:

- Allows children to use their natural creative instincts to make a statement about their world
- Encourages children to reach beyond the conventional response to a movement task and discover new ways to move, feel, perceive, and understand themselves and others in their environment
- Teaches an avenue of expression and communication in addition to writing, speaking,

Figure 1.5 Learning dances created by others expands a student's movement vocabulary.

the visual arts, music, and theater (literacy in all these areas is important for increasing the quality of interaction with others)

- Develops imagination, creativity, critical thinking, and the ability to make decisions through creating new dance movements
- Provides opportunities to share the experience of creating and learning with others
- Increases opportunities for children to create, perform, observe, and respond to movement they have learned or viewed

Starting at birth, children use movement as a way to express and communicate their needs. As they grow and develop, they naturally combine movement and language to share with others what they want or have experienced. Dance fosters children's innate need for movement and offers the opportunity to expand their knowledge and skills in using movement as a way of learning about themselves, others, and their world. In many school environments, writing, reading, and math are emphasized as ways to learn. Movement—specifically dance—is a natural and essential means for learning and sharing information and experiences.

Knowing and Understanding Yourself and Your World

Dance enables children to understand themselves and the world around them in the following ways:

- Reinforces learning about the elements of the body, space, time, force, flow, and relationships, which are common to all movement activities in the physical education and dance education curriculum
- Recognizes the significance of all cultures through learning traditional cultural dances
- Increases understanding of how dance represents the history, traditions, beliefs, and values of a culture
- Enhances the skills of perception, evaluation, problem-solving, observation, and concentration
- Defines and clarifies ideas, thoughts, understandings, or feelings
- Plays a significant role in a student's total education by integrating cognitive, psycho-

motor, affective, and aesthetic development in each learning experience

- Increases knowledge about various ways to move
- Develops self-concept, self-esteem, and self- and group identity
- Helps students recognize similarities and differences among people
- Changes the way people perceive their world

A major outcome of education is to ensure that each student gains the knowledge and skills to live a successful, meaningful life. Understanding how to create, learn, collaborate, and apply new ideas and learnings is essential to being productive and enjoying all aspects of life. Through dance, students learn to explore new experiences and discover what they can do and what they want to do. They learn the process of creating, making something new, solving a problem, evaluating a product, and sharing their perspective; all these attributes are required for success in any area a student wants to pursue. Success leads to positive self-esteem and a feeling of empowerment, which contribute to further opportunities to learn about themselves, others, and their world.

Developing Movement Abilities

Dance contributes to students' development of their movement abilities in the following ways:

- Increases their ability to perform locomotor and nonlocomotor movements and patterns or sequences of movements while applying the dance elements of the body, space, time, force, flow, and relationships in a variety of ways
- Develops their strength, flexibility, cardiorespiratory endurance, coordination, speed, and balance
- Adds to the number of experiences that promote learning about the infinite ways the body is capable of moving
- Enhances motor learning through repetition and practice of dance movements
- Teaches them to safely move as they express and communicate ideas, feelings, and understandings

Dance is experienced primarily through the body and its movements. Children learn to dance by observing a movement and then reproducing the movement based on their ability to perceive the details of how the movement occurs and their actual physical ability to perform the movement. They also demonstrate their ability to create through movement. The more experiences children gain in the various ways to dance, the more background they will have to draw on when they learn new movements and patterns or make movement choices. Motor skills, fitness levels, and a variety of movement experiences all contribute to a child's ability to use dance to express and communicate ideas and feelings.

Children who participate in a variety of dance experiences use their ability as kinesthetic learners to discover many ways to move. As they develop physically, cognitively, emotionally, and socially throughout their elementary and secondary education, they continue to increase their motor skills and expand their understanding of how to use their bodies as instruments of expression and communication. They find joy in moving to a repetitive rhythm, running across a space and leaping into the air, or spinning around as their physical, cognitive, and creative abilities are integrated in a moment of dancing alone or with others. Secondary-level lessons should continue to build the students' confidence and comfort as the lessons ease into advanced creative movement dance skills. The greatest barrier to teaching dance at the secondary level is a lack of comfort with dance on the part of teachers and students. For most students, moving with music is comfortable and provides an immediate boost of energy and enjoyment. For others, dance and moving freely can bring stress and fear. This book provides resources and videos to guide teachers as they plan their dance unit or program.

WHAT ARE THE BENEFITS OF CHILDREN'S DANCE?

The chapter's opening dance scenario illustrates the joy children experience as they interpret the movement of a red streamer. Although enjoyment and celebration are apparent when children dance, they are also learning. The primary goal of dance education is for children to learn how to use movement as a means of exploring, expressing, and communicating an idea, understanding,

concept, or feeling, whether a movement is initiated by them or by others. For the teacher, what students are learning can be clearly evident and easily assessed, yet for children, there are intangible benefits that are unique and personal and cannot be measured or observed. Children who view the world primarily through movement rely on kinesthetic thinking, in which the images and feelings that emerge are best understood when a symbolic language, such as dance, is used to provide a concrete experience to transform knowledge (Payne and Costas 2021). Children who love to move and who learn best through movement welcome dance experiences because they feel dance is a natural and fun way to learn. These children seek out movement experiences and, as a result, gain the related psychomotor, cognitive, affective, and social benefits. Yet all children gain many benefits from dance. Children learn motor skills through the psychomotor domain and knowledge through the cognitive domain, and they gain an understanding of their feelings and preferences and learn how to interact positively with others in the affective domain.

Psychomotor Benefits

The dance component in a physical education or arts education curriculum provides children the opportunity to develop and improve their fitness and motor skills, which form the kinesthetic foundation children rely on to express and communicate through dance. Understanding basic motor skills, coordination, and development not only is essential for one's life but also provides important information for effective teaching and learning (Goodway, Ozmun, and Gallahue 2019) Physical literacy is essential to success in learning and creating dances. It also contributes to all physical activities that children pursue. Dance learning experiences are characterized by learning multiple ways to move the body through space, in time, with force, flow, and relationships. Children run, jump, twist, leap, wiggle, crawl, and roll in many directions and pathways, using different tempos with varied amounts of force. They learn to move the whole body or its parts in isolation in a safe and effective manner. The ability to move from one shape into another or perform a combination of locomotor movements that require body control is developed through exploration and repetition. Children gain strength, improve balance, and increase flexibility and coordination through creating movements or learning new movements. They learn to reproduce and refine movement patterns, increase their spatial and body awareness, and develop the ability to coordinate their movements with the movements of others. Dance learning experiences, taught throughout the school year, provide children with opportunities to continue their development of motor skills and expand the use of these skills in their lives. Children become better at controlling the transfer of weight when performing locomotor movements, combinations of locomotor and nonlocomotor movements, and transitioning from moving to stillness. They are able to demonstrate body control at changing levels, directions, amounts of energy, and speed. This sense of learning to master the infinite movement possibilities that dance provides enhances children's self-perception that they are capable movers. They feel comfortable trying new physical activities and understand the value of practice and persistence in learning something new.

Cognitive Benefits

The cognitive benefits of dance include learning about one's body and how it moves and relates to others and the environment. Children gain knowledge about themselves and their world through active interaction; that is, they learn best by doing. Ultimately, the way children think and construct their knowledge is influenced by the types of experiences they have (Barone and Eisner 2012). Through dance, children better comprehend the concepts of direction, range, pathways, levels, tempo, shape, force, and flow by experiencing these concepts through being physically active in the learning process.

Dance nurtures cognitive development with each task in a learning experience. Children demonstrate their conceptual understanding when they move. We refer to this as a *kinesthetic answer* to the task presented by the teacher. For example, when the teacher instructs the child, "Using your hand and arm, draw a curved line in the air in front of your body," the child needs knowledge of body parts, of the concept "curved," and of the frontal plane of the body; the child also needs the ability to synthesize these concepts into one movement. If the child does not demonstrate the anticipated response, knowledge of one of the components of the task may be missing. The teacher will need to analyze the task, investigate what knowledge is missing, and then adjust the task to help the child learn the concepts. Offering a variety of dance experiences will increase children's knowledge of their bodies and a body's infinite movement possibilities. Learning to dance requires children to recall terms and movement sequences, identify movement similarities and differences, demonstrate the application of concepts, analyze how the elements of dance are used in a dance, and evaluate their own and others' performances.

Critical thinking and creative thinking are other cognitive abilities used in learning, performing, creating, observing, and responding to dance. As children create, perform, or observe dances, they make an objective or subjective analysis and evaluation about the movement. An objective evaluation is clearly observed and reported in a factual manner. For example, you may ask students to observe their partners holding their bodies in a balanced shape and count how many body parts are touching the floor. Asking questions that require personal reflections, opinions, or analysis as part of the response will elicit subjective evaluations. You may ask students, "What idea do you think the dancer was expressing in the dance?" or "What was the most exciting part of the dance for you?"

Through dance, children gain an understanding of their own aesthetic preferences as well as the preferences of others. Aesthetic understanding involves how the elements of dance are manipulated into meaningful patterns of body movements that express an idea or feeling. When children laugh while viewing a dance, they may be amused by the movements, rhythm, or use of space in the dance. As children reflect and describe what happened in the dance that made them laugh, they gain an understanding of their own aesthetic preferences.

The process of making a dance also involves cognitive development through using the imagination to create or rearrange movements in new ways to express ideas and feelings. Children instinctively use imaginative thinking in their everyday play environments. They create new characters, act out inventive scenarios, and use everyday objects in new ways to support a play concept. We encourage you not only to attend to correct replication of movement patterns but also to offer the opportunity to stimulate innovation and imagination by providing a classroom where students feel safe to experiment with creative ideas (Stauffer 2019).

Finally, assessment of a student's cognitive abilities—recall, comprehension, application, and evaluation—can take the form of a spoken, written, or movement response. For example, after creating a dance about the rejection and acceptance of friends, students can be asked to verbally describe a sequence of movements they created to draw the shapes used in the dance or to demonstrate a movement from the dance that used strong or light energy. The assessment of a learning experience can be most challenging, yet physical educators and dance educators are familiar with using observation and analysis to see how the students respond to a task. They know from watching children dance that the movement needs to be clarified, repeated in a different way, or changed to enhance effectiveness or safety. Children show what they know as they listen to, process, and respond to what the teacher presents. Dance is one of the only content areas in the curriculum where children can demonstrate their understanding through movement. For those children who are kinesthetic learners, dance classes are the ideal learning environment.

Affective and Social Benefits

Children need to feel successful about the experiences they pursue and accomplish. They also have a need to express their joy, fear, anger, frustration, and excitement and to communicate their understanding about their world. Dance recognizes and fulfills these needs. Through dance, children discover who they are, how they move, where they can move, how it feels to move in different ways, what movements they like to do, and how those movements are different from and similar to others. They learn to make decisions, develop their imaginations, express ideas and feelings, and share with others. Dance learning experiences, whether positive or negative, contribute to a child's self-concept and self-esteem.

Dancing can make children feel proud of the way they move; however, it can also make them feel vulnerable. Children who are unsure of themselves will say, "I can't do it" or "I don't know how." Children are immediately aware of what they can and cannot do as they begin to move, and they know that others are also aware of how they are moving. As a teacher, you will need to recognize children's discomfort and encourage them gently and with sensitivity to their feelings.

The body and its movements are the medium that reveals how a child feels inside. The ways in which children move through space, use time and force, and relate to others and their environment reveal these feelings. Modern dance pioneer Martha Graham said, "Movement is the one speech that cannot lie" (de Mille 1991, p. 22). How we feel at any moment is revealed in our actions, body shape, and facial expression. Dance provides children the means to express and communicate what they really feel and know about themselves and their world. For example, children can express feelings of anger by stamping their feet and pounding their hands. These movements can then be explored further and inspire a dance that demonstrates angry feelings.

Socially, children enjoy interacting with others through movement. They laugh and talk with each other while sharing an experience that is fun and personally rewarding. Dance in the school environment usually occurs as part of a whole-class experience, with the teacher facilitating the session. Children participate in dances as individuals, partners, members of a small group, or part of the whole class dancing in unison. While dancing in a small group, children assume various leadership roles, learn to share ideas, practice moving together, and develop a group identity. They experience the perspectives of others and see that an idea can be expressed in a multitude of ways. The dance lesson provides children with the opportunity to participate as learners, creators, and observers. In these roles, they are taught to respect different movement preferences and learn to accept or positively negotiate ideas with other students. They learn how to cooperate with a partner or small group, solve conflicts peacefully, motivate others to stay focused, and provide support for others in the process of creating or performing a dance.

Students enjoy interacting with each other through dance.

The teacher plays an important role in ensuring that the dance experience is positive and successful for all children. Each learning experience must be designed to match the developmental level of the student. Dance learning experiences for 5-year-old children, for example, are very different in content and presentation than experiences designed for 9-year-old children. Furthermore, learning experiences designed for 9-year-old children are very different from those created for 13-year-old or 17-year-old students at the secondary level. However, all students need frequent positive reinforcement from the teacher and from peers. Most learners want the teacher to watch them and respond with a positive comment. Young children frequently make comments such as "Watch me," "Watch how I can do it," and "Look at me." They depend on the teacher for approval, and the positive feedback helps motivate them to stay focused on the learning experience. Positive comments followed by a specific description of what the teacher observed reinforce that the child's effort is acceptable and has value. For example, a teacher commenting on a turn may say, "That was wonderful." The teacher might then continue, "That turn was very high off the floor, your head stayed up, and you landed with control." The teacher can continue to question the child: "What did you do that helped your landing to be so smooth?" In another example, two children have designed a repetitive movement to reflect the movement of a machine part. The teacher may use the following positive comment to clarify for students what they are doing well and support their collaborative effort: "Your movements are very clear, and both of you can keep the rhythm going at the same time. The way you both work together is great."

Older students at the middle and high school levels continue to seek the teacher's approval, though it may show itself in different ways than in elementary school. Secondary school students are more socially aware than their elementary school peers and often seek to gain approval from their same-aged peers before their teacher. This may look like joking and laughing during an exploratory movement exercise to ease the awkwardness and ensure that their friends do not think less of them for dancing oddly before fully attempting the movement to impress the teacher. The teacher may embrace this situation by beginning class with a word about how everyone is going to look different, and that is okay. As older students move through the exercise, the teacher may make positive comments about the risks some students are taking, such as, "I see some brave dancers who are using the floor to experiment and move in new ways," or "Some dancers are using wonderful, sharp, heavy movements that look like monsters, and it is exactly what I was looking for." Teachers may continue to offer positive comments and use the social nature of older students by engaging them in discussions after the dance, in order to allow time for students to express their feelings of awkwardness or anxiousness. This lets students understand that they are not alone in experiencing movement in new ways while also giving the teacher an opportunity to praise students both individually and as a group for some of the choices they made.

Teachers make a difference in the attitudes that children develop about dance. Commitment to prepare and present a dance experience that is exciting, relevant, and developmentally appropriate is essential for effective and meaningful teaching. Teaching with enthusiasm and a sincere desire to make the dance experience a positive learning moment is essential. The lesson needs to ensure that children feel comfortable taking risks, trying new ideas, and sharing their ideas with others. Extending what you already know about teaching dance will be challenging but will also bring personal and professional rewards, and a positive attitude will affect your students' feelings of success.

Learning Outcomes

The content of a dance experience for students reflects the characteristics unique to each age level. Every child comes to school with a unique set of life experiences and needs. A dance curriculum that encourages and celebrates what each individual brings to the learning experience recognizes these differences. Students may meet the same outcomes; however, there may be different ways for students to demonstrate what they know and are able to do. This differentiated approach to learning recognizes the strength of each child and the areas for continued development. The dance learning outcomes describe what a student should know and be able to do as a result of participating in a kindergarten through fifth-grade (K-5) dance program, a middle school dance program (6-8), and a high school dance program (9-12). We offer a set of outcomes as an example of guiding statements for a dance program (Cone and Cone 2003). The outcomes are divided into four levels: kindergarten through 2nd grade, 3rd through 5th grade, 6th through 8th grade, and 9th through 12th grade.

Learning Outcomes for Grades K-2

Children in kindergarten through second grade should have the following cognitive skills as a result of the dance education program:

- Describe their movements using elements of dance terminology. For example, children may describe a shape by saying, "I am making a big shape," or they may describe

a level when they are moving on the floor by saying, "I am moving at a low level."

- Describe the movements of others using terminology related to the elements of dance. For example, a child may say, "Briana is skipping in a circle" or "Josh is wiggling very fast."

- Recognize that dance is a way to express an idea or a feeling using movement.

- Identify various locomotor and nonlocomotor movements, body parts, and shapes used in creating and performing dances.

- Understand that an idea or feeling can be expressed through dance in many ways. For example, when the sun is the topic for a dance, some children may walk slowly in a curvy pathway and slowly fall to the floor to express how the hot sun feels and how it drains their energy, while other children jump quickly with strong energy from spot to spot to demonstrate how they feel when moving on a hot floor warmed by the sun.

- Understand that different cultures develop and perform dances for different reasons. In the traditional Japanese dance tanko bushi, the dancer's movements represent the work actions of coal miners. These dancers perform this when celebrating the importance of coal mining in Japanese life. Another example is the German kinderpolka, which demonstrates young children's hand games and makes fun of adults scolding children with pointed fingers. Other dances celebrate a plentiful harvest, the crowning of a king, or the work actions of a shoemaker.

- Acknowledge that dance can be used in learning or reflecting learning in other arts and school subjects.

- Comprehend that dance is a physical activity that builds strength and flexibility and improves balance and coordination.

- Recognize that dance is a way to enjoy creating and performing with others.

- Understand how technology is used in viewing and recording dances.

- Understand how to move safely in a variety of dance spaces.

These basic understandings are essential content that is unique to dance. The knowledge is gained primarily through learning, performing, creating, observing, and responding to dances whether they are a traditional cultural dance, a fun social dance, or a creative dance about animals.

Children in kindergarten through second grade should be able to do the following as a result of the dance education program:

- Demonstrate various movements that exemplify one or more elements of dance. For example, when children are asked to make a round shape or jump in a forward direction, they respond to the task with the corresponding movement.
- Perform the basic locomotor and nonlocomotor movements.
- Reproduce their own and others' movements, movement patterns, and shapes.
- Cooperate with a partner or small group to create and perform a dance.
- Improvise and generate movements to express an idea or feeling.
- Observe others' dances and respond to those observations by drawing, writing, or talking about the dances.
- Perform age-appropriate dances from a variety of cultures and time periods.
- Create a dance that expresses or interprets a concept from another subject area (e.g., dance about how the planets revolve around the sun).
- Create a dance using a self-selected idea.
- Demonstrate respect for the dances created and performed by others.
- Demonstrate the ability to move safely to avoid bodily injury.
- Use technology in viewing and recording dances.

Dance is learned by physically engaging in the movements and shapes that are part of a cultural, social, or creative dance. Children learn to collaborate with others by sharing ideas for movements, learning movements from others, and practicing together to perform a dance. Learning in dance is best accomplished by actual dancing because young children are eager to use movement to express and communicate their ideas.

Learning Outcomes for Grades 3-5

Children in third through fifth grade should have the following cognitive skills as a result of the dance education program:

- Describe their movements by applying several terms of the elements of dance. For example, children may describe a shape by saying, "I am making a stretched shape that is low to the floor" or "I am running forward using a zigzag pathway."
- Describe the movements or combinations of movements of others by applying several terms of the elements of dance. For example, a child may say, "Julio is rising up slowly and softly" or "Madeleine turned on one foot, then skipped backward, and froze in a curved shape."
- Observe dances created and performed by others and describe their perceptions of the dance using dance terminology such as naming the formation, dance steps, gestures, costumes, and props or describing how the elements of dance are applied.
- Recognize dance as an art form that uses the elements of movement as the tools to express and communicate an idea or feeling.
- Learn the terminology and movements specific to a form or style of dance.
- Acknowledge that dance is representative of a variety of cultures and historical and social contexts.
- Understand that dance can be integrated with other art forms and other subject areas as a way of learning.
- Comprehend that dance is a physical activity that can improve strength, balance, coordination, cardiorespiratory endurance, and flexibility.
- Understand that cooperation is needed for performing or creating dances with others.
- Understand how to use the elements of dance to generate movement variations.
- Learn about choreographic structures such as AB, ABA, chance, or narrative.
- Understand how to access technology as a tool for learning creative, cultural, and social dances.

- Understand how dance as a physical activity can contribute to a healthy and active lifestyle.

Children in third through fifth grade are capable of understanding and applying dance terminology to describe a dance sequence or a complete dance. They are able to understand the process of composing a dance related to an idea and have a greater understanding of their physical abilities in performing alone or with others. These children are very familiar with technology as a learning tool and can offer ideas for viewing, recording, and choreographing using technology.

Children in third through fifth grade should be able to do the following as a result of the dance education program:

- Perform combinations of the basic locomotor and nonlocomotor movements using changes in space, time, and force.
- Demonstrate safe technique in movement to avoid bodily injury.
- Demonstrate respect for dances created and performed by others.
- Create and perform a dance with a clear beginning, middle, and end using a self-selected idea.
- Create and perform a dance that represents a concept from another art form or another subject area.
- Reproduce the movements, sequences, rhythmic patterns, energy, and use of space with age-appropriate dances.
- Create a dance using one or more choreographic structures such as AB, ABA, chance, or narrative.
- Perform age-appropriate dances from another culture or time period.
- Apply the elements of dance to create multiple movement variations and revisions to created dances.
- Apply technology skills to learning and performing creative, cultural, and social dance.

Children at these grade levels can learn and perform more complex dances and explain the meaning of the movements. They can collaborate in small groups to compose and perform dances based on self-selected ideas and integrate technology into their choreography and performance.

Learning Outcomes for Grades 6-8

Students in middle school, or sixth through eighth grade, should have the following cognitive skills as a result of the dance education program:

- Describe their movements by applying several terms of the elements of dance as well as specific dance terminology. They can also connect their reason for their creations in more abstract ways while using this terminology. For example, older students may describe a shape by saying, "I am traveling in a spiral shape from low to medium to high levels to show the way a flower grows and twists toward the sun," or "I chose sautés and jetés to show how a frog would jump high in the air."
- Describe the movements or combinations of others by applying several terms of the elements of dance as well as specific dance terminology. They can also make inferences about why others may have made these movement choices while using this terminology. For example, an older student may say, "Maria is using different directions while turning sharply to show us the force she hears in the music," or "Derek chose lots of low, twisted shapes while traveling across the floor, which made me think of a snake in the woods."
- Observe dances created and performed by others and describe their perceptions and interpretations of the dance using dance terminology, describing how the elements of dance are applied, and analyzing how effectively the steps and elements conveyed the choreographer's intent.
- Recognize dance as an art form that uses the elements and specific dance steps as a way to express and communicate ideas, feelings, and abstract ways of thinking.
- Learn, remember, and replicate the terminology and movements specific to a form or style of dance.
- Acknowledge that dance is representative of a variety of cultures and historical and social contexts. Be able to explain the various elements and steps used in various cultural dances, as well as acknowledge similarities among them.

- Understand and create dances integrated with other art forms or subject areas as a way of learning. For example, dancers at this age should be able to use a piece of artwork as the starting point for creating a dance, possibly focusing on the shapes, colors, and perspective of the artwork to develop movement ideas. Students can also use journaling or written expression to defend their reasons for creating a dance, integrating art, dance, and language arts into a single choreography.

- Comprehend that dance is a physical activity that can improve balance, strength, flexibility, and coordination. Dancers at this age can learn about the various body systems, such as skeletal, muscular, and cardiovascular, and understand how they work together during physical activity.

- Understand and demonstrate cooperation and compromise as a necessary part of creating and performing dances with others.

- Learn, remember, and create dances using a variety of choreographic structures such as AB, ABA, theme and variation, narrative, or rondo.

- Understand and use technology as a tool for learning creative, cultural, and social dances.

- Understand and evaluate how dance as a physical activity can contribute to their own personal healthy and active lifestyle by describing choices, their effects, and ways to improve.

Students in sixth through eighth grades are continuing to build on their basic understanding of dance from elementary school to use dance and its terms in more abstract ways. They are able to understand the process of creating, performing, responding, and connecting a dance related to an idea or concept, as outlined in the dance standards developed by the National Coalition for Arts Standards (2014). Older learners also have a greater understanding of their physical abilities in their growing bodies and are eager to explore more challenging ways of moving, both alone and with others. These students are often familiar with a variety of technology tools and can implement new ideas for using them within their own choreography.

Students in sixth through eighth grades should be able to do the following as a result of the dance education program:

- Create dances from a variety of stimuli such as social events, personal experiences, or literary works and justify the choices they made.

- Demonstrate an expanded movement vocabulary with both the elements of dance as well as specific dance terminology when performing or discussing dance works.

- Create dances using one or more choreographic devices or structures in an original work—such as AB, ABA, theme and variation, narrative, or rondo—and articulate to others the reason for their choices.

- Demonstrate an understanding of dance terminology and its documentation through words, drawings, symbols such as the Movement Alphabet from Language of Dance (Hutchinson Guest 2006), or other technology tools.

Students in middle school can learn, remember, and apply dance terminology in both learned and self-created dances. They can think more abstractly than their elementary school peers, engaging in conversations about how dance movements represent various ideas and concepts. They can be self-directed in collaborating with peers or working on their own to create complex dances, and integrating technology into choreography and performance comes naturally.

Learning Outcomes for Grades 9-12

Students in high school, or 9th through 12th grade, should have the following cognitive skills as a result of the dance education program:

- Describe their movements with the elements of dance and specific terminology and also construct artistic statements about their intent in creating choreography. For example, high-school-aged dancers may describe a section of movement by saying, "I wanted to demonstrate the hardships of personal loss, so I used sharp, forceful movements to show the weight of these feelings," or "I examined how jazz dance began from everyday pedestrian movements to evolve into codified steps and created three new steps from watching the everyday movements of my peers."

- Describe the movements and dances of others by applying and synthesizing both the elements of dance and specific dance terminology. They can also analyze others' movement choices using this terminology to explain why one was effective in their artistic intent. For example, an older student might say, "Janessa's dance demonstrated the playfulness of childhood through her use of light, free-flowing sautés and chassés; it felt like a small child running around outside and having fun" or "Elijah chose to dance heavy, bound, closed-body shapes to airy classical music; this contrast made me believe he wanted to show the audience the struggle he faces with wanting to grow up to be an adult while also enjoying the freedoms of childhood."

- Observe dances created and performed by others and describe their perceptions and interpretations of the dance using dance terminology, describing how the elements of dance are applied, and analyzing how effectively the steps and elements conveyed the choreographer's intent. Students can compare and contrast personal choreographic choices to peers and well-known choreographers.

- Recognize and analyze dance as an art form that uses the elements and specific dance steps as a way to express and communicate ideas, feelings, and abstract ways of thinking.

- Replicate and analyze the terminology and movements specific to a form or style of dance.

- Acknowledge that dance is representative of a variety of cultures and historical and social contexts. High-school-aged students can compare and analyze the elements and steps used in various cultural dances as well as explain how the dance communicates cultural values.

- Investigate and analyze dances integrated with other art forms or subject areas. For example, dancers at this age should be able to research a topic of interest and col-

laborate with others to solve movement problems related to the topic. Students can describe orally or in writing their artistic intent and knowledge gained from the research as well as connect their learning from this project to other situations.

- Evaluate and develop a plan for improving balance, strength, flexibility, and coordination. High-school-aged students can apply anatomical principles and an understanding of the various body systems to a range of technical dance skills to support healthy living.

- Understand and demonstrate leadership qualities during class and performances through skills such as cooperation, dependability, commitment, and responsibility.

- Create and analyze dances using a variety of choreographic structures such as AB, ABA, theme and variation, narrative, or rondo. Students can justify the reason for their choices and how they support the artistic intent of their choreography.

- Understand and use technology as a tool for learning, analyzing, and evaluating creative, cultural, and social dances.

- Understand and evaluate how dance as a physical activity can contribute to their own personal healthy and active lifestyle by researching healthful practices and modifying personal choices based on findings.

Students in 9th through 12th grades are developing their artistic voices in dance and becoming more aware of the world outside of school. They are able to think at higher cognitive levels to analyze and synthesize information in order to develop their own personal understanding of dance. They enjoy collaboration and working on leadership skills. They are familiar with various types of technology tools and can offer their own opinions about how to use them to record, edit, and evaluate various types of dance.

Students in 9th through 12th grades should be able to do the following as a result of the dance education program:

- Synthesize a variety of content to experiment and create original dance sequences and explain their artistic intent.

- Demonstrate an expanded movement vocabulary as well as expanded personal movement choices when performing or discussing dance works.

- Demonstrate fluency in using one or more choreographic devices or structures in an original work—such as AB, ABA, theme and variation, narrative, or rondo—and articulate to others the artistic intent of their choice.

- Document a dance using a recognized system of words, drawings, symbols such as the Movement Alphabet from Language of Dance (Hutchinson Guest 2006), or other technology tools.

- Revise and refine choreography using self-reflection and feedback from others, justifying the changes made.

Older students at the high school level can work beyond replicating others' dance movements to discover their own artistic voice and preferred ways of moving. They can show leadership qualities in collaborating with others and can show that they are able to work in a self-directed manner with minimal direction from their teacher. They can discuss dance at higher levels of thinking by evaluating, analyzing, and synthesizing information to justify the choices made in their artistic works. These older learners can also make connections to careers, technology, and healthful living, demonstrating how dance affects their learning in other areas.

National Dance Education Standards Framework (National Dance Society 2020) describes how dance education standards can be practically applied and assessed in the school setting. These standards describe the basic knowledge and skills necessary for developing an effective dance program. They focus on the content applicable to any dance program and do not dictate methodology or a specific curriculum design. Many states have referred to the national standards as a guide in developing state-level dance standards. We suggest that you obtain a copy of the national dance standards or your state dance or arts education standards to use as a reference in planning the content of your dance program. When dance is included as part of the physical education curriculum, you can also refer to SHAPE America's National Standards & Grade-Level Outcomes for K-12 Physical Education (2013) as a guide in developing a comprehensive dance program. These standards describe the essential concepts and skills for participating in a variety of movement forms, interacting with others, and using movement for self-expression, enjoyment, and maintaining a healthy and active lifestyle. Also, check with your school district for the physical education or arts education standards that may need to be addressed.

APPLYING 21ST-CENTURY SKILLS TO TEACHING DANCE

Also called "soft skills" or "learning skills," 21st-century skills are the nonacademic skills students learn in the classroom and beyond. The best news about the educational buzz surrounding the 21st-century skills is that creativity, collaboration, critical thinking, self-direction, problem-solving, and global awareness are taking center stage in education. These skills are inherent to dance education. They form the foundation for content and pedagogy. Future employment and products will rely on the creative capacity of people to think in new ways and create new solutions that improve our lives. Through dance, children have the opportunity to explore diverse ways of moving, find multiple ways to express an idea and feeling, and use their imaginations and creative-thinking skills to create a dance. Our current students will create the future we will inhabit. Developing their abilities to use critical reflection about what they have learned and created will guide them to see multiple perspectives and be able to discover alternative outcomes. Young people growing up in the 21st century need to manage the complexity and diversity of everyday living and their careers. They will need to be more fluid, flexible, globally aware, and innovative. Every time a teacher asks students to find various ways to make a round shape with their bodies or move across the space using various directions and levels, the students engage in creative thinking to discover solutions to the task. As the students make the shape and move across the space, they evaluate the success of their solutions and increase their knowledge of the ways the body can move to express and communicate a concept. This self-directed moment builds on previous creative experiences and develops the students' understanding that many solutions exist through using the exploration process.

When students dance together, they collectively share in the cognitive process of remembering a movement sequence and collaborating to create or perform a dance. Dancers learn that each group member can offer new ideas that benefit everyone. This generation of students has opportunities to observe, create, and perform dance through new technology that did not exist a few years ago. They can see dance at any time through Internet sources from around the globe. New ideas, dances, moves, and forms of dance are created and available for viewing, and they invite interaction. Static, traditional definitions of dance are challenged as the body and technology blend to birth a new generation of dances and dancers. Dance educators who encourage students to voice their own ideas, embrace cultural diversity, and view dance as a conduit to teaching innovation provide learning experiences that prepare learners to be productive members of society. The body and its movements are what we all share as humans. Knowing how to collaborate with others, seek fresh insights, and value ingenuity are achievable outcomes in a dance curriculum that offers authentic learning experiences and challenges students to think beyond the conventional response.

MEETING THE WHOLE CHILD THROUGH DANCE

Every child deserves an education that addresses all the ways in which learning can occur. The arts, and specifically dance, offer children an opportunity to be active participants in their learning. Through dance, children acquire the psychomotor and cognitive skills required for expressing their understandings, ideas, and feelings. While dancing with others, they learn how they are similar to and different from others and how multiple perspectives can contribute to how children experience the world. The whole-child initiative is focused on five components that lead to success in school: Children need to be healthy, safe, engaged, supported, and challenged (ASCD 2015). A whole-child-oriented curriculum reflects an interdisciplinary approach with multiple ways to demonstrate acquired knowledge and skills. Pedagogy and content address children's varied interests, the ways they learn and respond to instruction, and learning experiences in all the multiple intelligences. *Crosswalk for SHAPE America National Standards & Grade-Level Outcomes for K-12 Physical Education and CASEL Advancing Social and Emotional Learning* (SHAPE America 2019) will guide you in developing the unit objectives and outcomes. Social and emotional learning is an integral part of learning and human development. Dance establishes learning environments and experiences that reinforce such skills as self-awareness, collaborative relationships, and responsible decision-making.

Dance education is whole-child education. Through dance, children are physically active as they learn and perform dances and create new movements. As a result, they can demonstrate development of body coordination, balance, strength, endurance, muscle memory, agility, and flexibility. Children learn that dancing is an activity that can contribute to a healthy and active lifestyle—and a healthy child is a better learner. A dance educator who presents developmentally appropriate content and encourages students to believe in their ability to learn provides a safe learning environment where all students are respected. In this educator's learning space, students are supported for their imagination, creative thinking, and collaboration with peers. Children who learn to create, perform, and observe dance learn to recognize the many ways an idea or feeling can be expressed through movement. These children are engaged in making decisions about their aesthetic preferences, learning to remember movement sequences, and developing critical- and evaluative-thinking processes that are applicable to learning in all subjects. Emotionally, they are supported by an atmosphere of respect for taking risks and are encouraged to experience how a range of feelings can be explored through dance. When children are empowered to explore their ideas, make sense of their experiences, and know that their ideas and talents matter, they feel they are recognized for their ability and acquire a better understanding of themselves and others (Farrington et al. 2019). Addressing the whole child requires you as the dance educator to be knowledgeable in dance content, education theory, child development, and current education issues; to be able to integrate dance with other curricular areas; and to be able to collaborate with other faculty members.

LINKING THE PHYSICAL ACTIVITY GUIDELINES TO DANCE

In 2018, the United States Department of Health and Human Services issued *Physical Activity Guidelines for Americans, Second Edition*. The scientifically based guidelines in this publication help Americans ages six and older improve their health through appropriate physical activity. The guidelines describe the types and amounts of physical activity that offer substantial health benefits and include a tool kit of resources on the health-related components of fitness plus suggestions for activities. The guidelines state that when children and adults participate in regular physical activity, they can reduce their risk of many adverse health outcomes. The guidelines recommend that children and adolescents participate in 60 minutes a day of physical activity, which includes moderate or vigorous aerobic physical activity, muscle-strengthening activity, and bone-strengthening activity. Dance is mentioned as an activity that children and adolescents can enjoy doing alone or with friends and family members. Three types of activities, as noted earlier, that contribute to a healthy and active lifestyle for children and adolescents are defined in the guidelines.

Aerobic activities involve moving the large muscles using locomotor and nonlocomotor movements in space with varying amounts of force. In dance, children can learn and repeat dances that include running, skipping, sliding, galloping, leaping, jumping, and hopping. When children and adolescents repeat the dances several times during a class session, they can increase cardiorespiratory fitness. Cultural dances such as the mayim and troika use running, grapevine, and hopping steps in quick-tempo repeated patterns. As dancers repeat these dances, they use a lot of energy, resulting in increased blood flow and oxygen consumption. A dance learning experience can include a moderate aerobic warm-up followed by exploration or learning experiences that require traveling through the space at different tempos and conclude with a complete dance that includes extended movement sequences that can involve cardiorespiratory fitness.

Muscle-strengthening activities use the muscles to engage in large movements that are rhythmic and repetitive. Learning, creating, or performing a dance uses the whole body and requires that students use strength and balance as they travel in the space and hold still shapes. Through dancing, students gain awareness of how the muscles are used and can be developed by participating in the many types of dance. For example, when students learn a hip-hop movement, they may be supporting their weight on their hands and feet while changing levels. Repeating this movement several times can strengthen the muscles in all body parts. Stopping and starting a dance movement or demonstrating a smooth transition between movements also requires strength to control coordination and balance.

Bone-strengthening activities occur when the body movements produce a force on the bones. All locomotor movements require the body to use force in takeoff and landing, which increase bone development. When children use locomotor movements in a social, cultural, or creative dance, they are participating in weight-bearing activities. For example, in a creative dance that expresses the actions of a frog, children will explore various amounts of energy, range, and levels as they demonstrate a jumping frog exploring life in a pond. In another example, children crawl and roll on the floor to express a dance about the ocean waves as they move toward and away from the beach. Older students might experiment with partner work during a creative movement exercise that requires bearing each other's weight to create group shapes or complete a fun line dance such as the cha-cha slide while in plank position. As these examples illustrate, bone-strengthening activities can also be aerobic and muscle strengthening.

Dance is an activity that promotes fitness, social interaction, and cultural understanding and provides children with the skills and knowledge to pursue dance as a lifetime activity. One of the many benefits of learning and creating in dance is the opportunity to increase fitness levels.

SUMMARY

All children and adolescents need to express their thoughts, understandings, ideas, and feelings. Dance fulfills this need when presented in developmentally appropriate learning experiences. These experiences should include movement that is natural for their developmental level yet teaches new movements that expand their movement vocabulary and develop skills. Dance complements the acquisition of motor skills in performing a function by teaching movement for expression and communication. Participation in dance promotes motor skill development and self-discovery, builds self-esteem, engages children in a positive opportunity to interact socially, and increases cultural understanding.

As an integral component of the physical education or arts education curriculum, dance experiences should offer opportunities for students to create dances, learn dances created by others, observe dance, and respond to dance. Planned outcomes for a dance program guide you as the teacher in developing learning experiences that address what students should know and be able to do as a result of participating in a dance program. In this way, learning is meaningful and relevant. For success in teaching any type of dance, you and the students must enter the learning experience together with enthusiasm, a positive attitude, and the willingness to allow the joy of dancing to envelop you.

  ## Questions for Reflection

1. What role does dance play in your life? Artistically? Socially? Culturally?
2. What is your definition of dance? How do others define dance?
3. What perceptions do you think your students will have about dance? What do you think influences their perceptions?
4. How do you think creative dance differs from creative movement? How are they similar?
5. What skills and knowledge about movement and teaching do you have that can be applied to teaching dance?
6. Throughout children's education, students participate in many experiences that contribute to their physical, intellectual, emotional, and social development. What unique contributions does dance make to a child's development?

CHAPTER 2

Presenting Essential Content for Dance

This chapter presents a description of the content for dance within the physical education or arts education curriculum. In both program areas, teaching children and adolescents to move and to use movement as a way to learn is the primary goal. Including dance as a significant component of the curriculum ensures that students have the opportunity to integrate their capacity to think with their bodies and to analyze its movements as a means of expressing and communicating what they know and experience. Through dance, young people expand their movement abilities and use critical-thinking skills to learn, perform, create, and respond to dance.

The elements of dance—the body and its movements, space, time, force, flow, and relationships—are the foundation for the dance curriculum. All the elements are part of every movement we perform; however, dance manipulates and emphasizes specific elements in expressing an idea or feeling. Compare, for example, a box of crayons to the elements of dance. Using different crayon colors in various combinations can produce an infinite number of drawings and pictures; using different elements of dance in various combinations will produce many different dances. The specific way the elements of dance are combined depends on the intended meaning of the dance. For example, a dancer can illustrate the wind by running with fast, light, and small steps or with slow, strong, and large steps, each producing a unique feeling. In a creative dance about the solar system, students may choose dance elements that emphasize slowly turning round shapes or movements that rotate quickly with strong energy. Many social and cultural dances have predetermined ways of using the elements of movement. The twist, a popular dance from the 1960s, moves the upper body and lower body in a strong, fast, side-to-side twisting movement. As soon as the music for the twist is played, everyone performs a similar twisting movement. However, a dancer can personalize the basic twisting movement by adding other dance elements to vary the level or speed. Many cultural dances delineate how the elements of dance are applied to reflect particular cultural values, traditions, or beliefs. Variations to a cultural folk dance may represent a regional style or a group preference yet still contain basic characteristics of the traditional form.

In this chapter, we offer our version of the elements of dance based on the work of Rudolf Laban (1976) and other dance educators (Gilbert 2015; Wall and Murray 1990; Zakkai 1997). We have organized the elements of dance into six categories—the body, space, time, force, flow, and relationships (see table 2.1). Each element is individually defined; however, all the elements typically work in combination in every movement we make.

Table 2.1 Elements of Dance

Body parts isolated, combined, leading, supporting	Body actions and movements		Body shapes: still (static), moving (dynamic)
Head, face, neck, shoulders, elbows, hands, fingers, forearms, chest, arms, upper arms, wrists, back, hips, waist, abdomen, legs, thighs, knees, shins, calves, ankles, feet, toes, heels	**Locomotor** Walk, run, jump, hop, skip, leap, slide, gallop, crawl, roll, move on different parts	**Nonlocomotor** Twist, shake, bend, stretch, turn, wiggle, swing, collapse, sway, rock, push, pull, vibrate, pivot, bounce, curl, press, float, punch, dab, flick, slash, glide, wring, kick, gesture with hands or feet	Balanced, off balance, straight, curved, twisted, wide, narrow, angular, symmetrical, asymmetrical, round, elongated
Space	**Time**	**Force or energy**	**Flow**
Personal and general space **Levels** High, medium, low **Size or range** Big, medium, small, far, near **Directions** Forward, backward, sideward, up, down, diagonal, clockwise, counterclockwise **Pathways (in air and on floor)** Straight, curved, zigzag, circular, angular, spiral, arch Straight, curved, zigzag, circular, angular, spiral, arch	**Tempo or speed** Fast, sudden, slow, sustained, accelerated, decelerated **Rhythm** Even beat, uneven beat, percussive, patterns	**Strong** Heavy, firm, hard, powerful, explosive **Light** Soft, fine, gentle, delicate, smooth	**Free** Ongoing, unrestrained, uncontrolled, continuous, relaxed **Bound** Stoppable, restrained, controlled, tense
RELATIONSHIP TO OTHERS, OBJECTS, AND THE ENVIRONMENT				

Who	How	Where	Formations	What
Individuals, partners, groups (small and large)	Contrast, copy, echo, follow, connect, mirror, lead, shadow, unison, alternate, call and response	Above, below, apart, together, behind, in front, side by side, meeting, parting, over, under, between	Scattered, lines (short, long), circles, curves, square, semicircle, triangle, rows, rectangle, X-shape	Objects, furniture, props, equipment, walls, ceiling, ground, floor

THE BODY

In dance, we can construct infinite variations of movements to express and communicate ideas, feelings, concepts, perceptions, and meaning. The body and the mind act jointly to create, perceive, and perform each movement that emerges in a dance experience. Eddy (2016) describes this mind and body connection as *somatic education*, in which dance communicates both emotions and ideas through an integration of the body and the mind. Through dance, students explore, discover, and gain knowledge of all the infinite possibilities for movement. They increase control over their movements while developing body awareness. They learn the names of body parts, identify where they are located, and learn the ways the body parts can move in isolation or as a coordinated whole.

Locomotor and Nonlocomotor Movements

Body movements are categorized into two basic types: locomotor movements and nonlocomotor movements. Locomotor movements are movements in which the body travels from one place to another in the space. Usually, we think about traveling on the feet as in running, jumping, walking, skipping, sliding, hopping, galloping, or leaping; yet other body parts can also be used for traveling (see table 2.1).

Nonlocomotor movements describe the actions of the whole body or its parts (see table 2.1). They are performed while the body is stationary or combined with a locomotor movement. For example, the whole body or only one arm can shake while stationary, or both arms can shake while combined with skipping. Other nonlocomotor movements include twisting, bending, stretching, curling, turning, swinging, rocking, pushing, pulling, kicking, punching, pressing, rising, and sinking. Two or more nonlocomotor movements can be combined to create a new movement such as swinging the arms from side to side as the torso twists. Also, locomotor and nonlocomotor movements frequently are combined to form more complex movements that allow for a greater interpretation of an idea, thought, or feeling. Picture a student running and leaping to express the idea of a leaf blowing in the air. Yet, when the student adds a swinging arm movement to the leap, this increases the movement complexity and further defines the shape of the leaf or the path of the wind as the leaf floats in the air. Combining locomotor and nonlocomotor movements increases students' movement vocabulary beyond what they already know while challenging them to create, learn, and practice new ways of moving.

Actions of Body Parts

Body parts are involved in movement in three ways: in isolation, leading a movement, and supporting the weight of the body. Isolated movements occur when one body part is moving and the rest of the body is still. This type of movement, which appears quite simple, is actually difficult for young children. Balance, strength, and concentration are required to keep the body still while a single body part moves. When a body part leads a movement, it will initiate the movement and the rest of the body will follow with the same movement. A body part can also lead the rest of the body through space, as in running forward with the arms reaching forward. The third way is when a body part supports the body weight.

In many cultural and social dances, the feet primarily support the body weight. Yet in some dance forms such as break dancing, capoeira, and creative dance, other body parts such as the hands, head, back, knees, and shoulders can be used to support the body weight.

BODY SHAPES

The body is capable of forming an infinite variety of shapes. The body always takes a shape, whether moving or in a still position. Most body shapes used in everyday life are for functional purposes, such as sitting at a computer or standing in the shower. Certain body shapes send powerful messages, however, such as pointing a finger at someone, slumping in a moment of sorrow, or hugging a loved one.

Shapes that are created or reproduced in a dance experience are classified into three general categories: straight, curved, and twisted (see figure 2.1). Straight shapes can be formed with the whole body or its parts. By bending the elbows, knees, wrists, fingers, or spine, the body can make an angular shape composed of many smaller straight shapes. The second shape category is curved. In this type of shape, the body can be rounded through curving the spine forward, backward, or sideward. Also, arms and legs can be individually curved or curved as part of the whole body shape. Other words frequently used to describe a curved shape are *rounded*, *squiggly*, *curled*, *wavy*, *arched*, or *spiraled*. The third category describes twisted shapes in which the body rotates in two opposing directions at the same time. Most twisted shapes begin at the waist with the legs and the hips twisted in one direction and the upper body twisted in the opposite direction. A single body part can form a twisted shape by rotating in an opposing direction to the rest of the body, such as twisting an arm away from the torso or both legs twisted around each other.

Two additional shape categories are symmetrical and asymmetrical. Symmetrical shapes in dance are positions in which the left and the right sides of the body are in exactly the same shape. Asymmetrical shapes are positions in which the two sides of the body are in different shapes.

Shapes can be expressed through stillness, like a stone sculpture or a frozen statue. Shapes are also inherent in all locomotor movements.

Figure 2.1 In creative dance, students explore various ways to make straight, twisted, and curved shapes.

Some shapes appear naturally as the body travels, and other shapes are intentional. For example, a straight, symmetrical arm shape may be combined with a jump, or a curving shape of the back may be combined with a skip.

SPACE

We are always moving in space, mainly for functional purposes (e.g., walking forward to turn on a light switch). In dance, a person moves in space as the result of a series of choices that express an idea or a feeling. Changing levels from high to low can represent the action of a wave moving toward the beach. Skipping forward on a curved path may express the wind blowing from side to side, or it can express happiness. Space for a dancer can be compared to the canvas of an artist. As dancers move in various directions, levels, pathways, and ranges, they create a spatial design. In many cultural or social dances, the space is designed in circles or lines to represent a community of people sharing an experience together. When we engage in a creative dance experience, we develop new spatial designs that reflect our meaning of the movement. The element of space is further delineated through its six interrelated components: personal space, general space, levels, directions, pathways, and range.

Personal Space

The term *personal space* describes the space immediately surrounding the body—that is, the space that is always around us everywhere we move and when we are stationary. Although the size of one's personal space changes with each dance activity, it is generally thought of as an adequate amount of space around the front, back, top, and sides of the body so the student can move without touching another person or object. The image of a giant bubble around the body is an effective way to describe personal space. We can find the limits of our personal space by reaching out with our hands and feet in the immediate space around the body and sensing that we have adequate space for movement.

General Space

General space refers to all the space outside of personal space that is available for movement; everyone shares this space. In a dance where students are running and leaping, each student leaps in the shared general space, but an individual's leap occurs within the limits of that individual's personal space. Dancers carry their personal space with them as they move in the general space. Whether students are creating their own dances or learning a dance from another person, the general space has a defined boundary. As a teacher, you may designate the boundary by the lines on the floor or cones marking an outside space. In a cultural or social dance, the general space is usually determined by the formation required for the dance, such as a circle, square, or single line.

Levels

The term *level* in dance implies three different heights—low, medium, and high—in which the body moves and makes shapes. A low level is considered close to or on the ground—that is, the space below the knees. Movements such as crawling, rolling, or stretching on the floor occur at a low level. The medium level is the space midway between high and low or generally between a person's knees and shoulders. Movements such as walking or running can occur at a medium level. The space above the shoulders is considered a high level. When students are asked to reach for the sky, raising their arms above their shoulders, or to jump and leap, they are using space at a high level.

Directions

When students dance, their bodies move in six general directions in space:

- Forward, defined as the front of the body leading the movement
- Backward, where the back of the body leads the movement
- Sideways to the right or left, in which the right or left side of the body leads the movement
- Up and down, defined as moving the body up toward the sky or down toward the ground

The first four basic directions (forward, backward, right, and left) can be combined with the up and down directions in many ways, some of which form a diagonal direction (e.g., forward and to the right). A student can move forward and up as in a leap or forward and down by lowering the body to the ground. The same movement performed in each of the different directions will have a different feeling and communicate a different idea. For example, reaching forward and up with the hands and arms can illustrate reaching toward the sun to express how wonderful the warm sun feels after a cold winter season, whereas the same reach in a sideward and down direction can demonstrate reaching to help someone who has fallen.

Dancers demonstrate shapes at low, medium, and high levels.

Pathways

Pathways describe the way space is shaped as the body moves in space. Two types of pathways occur in dance. The first type, floor pathways, is created by traveling movements (such as running in a circle or skipping in a straight line), and the second type, air pathways, is created by a body part or parts moving in the space around the body (as in drawing a zigzag line in the air with an elbow). If a student stepped in a puddle of water and then ran in a circle, the result would be a pathway of footsteps that describe the shape of where the body traveled. All pathways are composed of straight and curved lines or a combination of both. In dance, the student makes a decision about the pathway for movement or learns a specific pathway that has already been designed for a dance. Examples of floor and air and pathways are illustrated in figure 2.2.

Range

Range defines the size of a movement. Another word used interchangeably with range is *extensions*. Descriptions about how large or small, long or short, or wide or narrow the movements are all relate to size. The steps to a cultural dance may

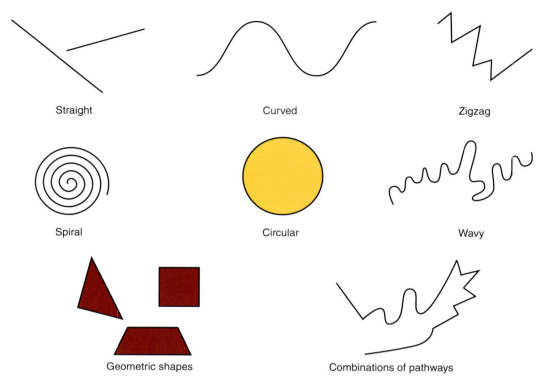

Figure 2.2 Students can choose from several floor and air pathways when creating a dance.

require the students to take large running steps in a circle, whereas in another dance the students might perform small, swinging arm movements.

TIME

The time element in dance refers to the tempo and the rhythm of the movement. Time also refers to the duration of the pauses between movements. Dance is composed not only of movement but also of the stillness between movements. For example, in a dance that explores different ways to jump, the student may hold a still shape for a long time between a repeated series of three quick jumps. The next sections describe further details of the time elements tempo and rhythm.

Tempo

Tempo is the pace of a movement (that is, how fast or slow the movement occurs). In the action of clapping hands using a steady beat, the tempo may be fast or slow. Walking can also demonstrate a steady beat—the beat of the steps can be fast or slow, and the number of steps can be short in duration (with only a few steps) or longer in duration (walking for 30 seconds). Tempo can change abruptly from fast to slow or vice versa, and tempo can change gradually through acceleration and deceleration. The increase or decrease in speed can occur over a long duration or very quickly. In the familiar social dance the alley cat, the foot pattern accelerates toward the end of the dance to challenge the dancers to repeat the pattern faster and faster. The dance ends with a deceleration of the pattern to the original speed. Another familiar social dance, the chicken dance, also accelerates at the end of the song to challenge dancers to repeat the hand-arm-twist-clap movement pattern faster and faster. In a creative dance that interprets a rainstorm, the movement may begin at a slow speed to demonstrate the beginning of a rainfall. The speed of the movement may then accelerate to illustrate a strong rainstorm and end with a deceleration of speed to represent the final raindrop.

Rhythm

Dance movements are organized through rhythm in much the same way that sounds in music are organized. Rhythm is the organization of music in time, using sounds and silences (Sarrazin 2016). The most basic rhythm is a beat (pulse), which occurs at regular intervals. This beat is what we feel in the body when we hear a piece of music. Movement, whether it is the bouncing of the head or tapping of the feet, translates the sound we hear into a kinesthetic and visual response. The pulse becomes the foundation for a dance, supporting other even or uneven rhythms. Rhythm is also the combination of long and short sounds or slow and quick movements, such as a dance using the rhythm slow-slow-quick-quick-quick. Cultural dances have rhythms inherent to the culture from which the dance originated. These rhythms represent ways in which people move in that culture or how they work, play, worship, celebrate, and express their ideas. As students learn various cultural dances, they discover that some of the rhythms in the dance movements feel comfortable, whereas other rhythms may be difficult to perform. We all grow up in cultures that have their own rhythms. Learning the rhythms of another culture can be challenging, but it can lead to an understanding of the similarities and differences between and among cultures.

One aspect of rhythm is accent. Accent is an emphasis placed on a beat. As the emphasis is repeated in a series of beats, a rhythmic pattern of stronger and weaker beats is established. A regular accent (called the *downbeat*) falls at the beginning of a pattern, whereas a syncopated accent (or *upbeat*) is placed on the weaker beats in the pattern. In dance, an accent becomes evident by a change in the movement or quality of the movement. The accent can be represented through a movement that is stronger, bigger, higher, or faster. An accented dance step may move in a different direction, or the accent may appear as a movement of an isolated body part. For example, a folk dance may call for a strong stamp on the first beat of a pattern of steps, or a short dance composed of 12 beats may require reaching into the air on the 1st and 4th beats. Students will notice the accented movement in a dance; it will feel different and perhaps be exciting to express or challenging to coordinate.

In music, the organization of strong and weak beats, often in repeating patterns, are referred to as a *meter* (Sarrazin 2016). Dance also uses these terms to describe a phrase of movements that contains a certain number of beats. In many cultural and social dances, the pattern of dance movements corresponds to the rhythmic measures in the music. Creative dance uses regular, repeating rhythmic patterns as well as rhythmic patterns that are not regularly structured. For example, an 8-beat repeating rhythmic pattern of movement can be R-step, hop, L-step, hop, R-run, L-run, R-step, and L-leap. In another case, a dance may begin with a measure of 4 beats, then follow with a measure of 7 beats, and continue with a measure of 2 beats.

FORCE

Force is the amount of energy expended in a movement. It can be strong, as exhibited in a punch, or light, as expressed in a floating movement. When we move about our daily routines, we use force to be efficient and effective. Scrubbing a burned pan requires a different force than washing out a crystal glass. We have learned to use the appropriate amount of muscular energy to complete a task. In dance, too, we learn to use different amounts of force depending on the intention of the movement. Using strong force with tense, firm muscles results in a powerful movement that may express the movement of a stalking lion. Using light force with loose, relaxed muscles results in soft, gentle movements that can capture the feeling of stepping on a cloud.

In a cultural dance, the dancers may perform a pattern that uses several strong foot stamps and then several quick, light kicks. A social dance like the hokey pokey may use a strong movement to emphasize placing a body part in or out of the circle followed by a soft turning movement with arms and fingers moving lightly from side to side. Children in a creative dance unit can use strong force to illustrate the powerful sound of a thunderstorm or light force to express a story about a butterfly visiting a garden of flowers. Older students choreographing their own dances may use variations in force to demonstrate changes in emotion, such as light, loose movements for a carefree attitude or a heavy, drooping shape to show heartbreak.

FLOW

Flow refers to how force is controlled in a movement. The two words commonly used to describe flow are *free* and *bound*. In free flow, the mover is not completely in control of the energy of the movements and may feel out of control, unrestrained, or unable to stop. This use of force implies taking some risks with balance and experiencing some uncertainty in how space is used. Students may create a dance that has a section where the movement feels out of control and then returns to a sequence of defined dance steps. Bound flow denotes controlling the energy of the movement. The student can stop the movement at any time. For example, in a dance using eight slides to the right and eight slides to the left, the students will need to use bound flow to change from the eighth slide to the right to the first slide to the left. Many dances use bound flow when changing the direction of a movement, pausing in a shape, ending the dance, or dancing with another person.

RELATIONSHIPS

Dance includes various types of relationships. Relationship terms include *near, close, far, away, over, under, through, in front, in back, alongside, around, between, inside, outside, above, below, together,* and *apart*. The definition of this element includes three parts: the relationship of a person's body parts to their other body parts; the spatial and temporal relationship of individuals organized into partners and groups; and the relationship of one's body to props, equipment, and the dance environment.

Body Parts

As children move their body parts into various relationships, they make various body shapes. A hand may be held over the head or behind the back in a cultural dance, or the head is placed close to the knees to depict the curled shape of a caterpillar. Each body part is capable of many movements that occur in the personal space around the body and in relation to other body parts. When students perform a dance in which they gallop and swing their hands in front of and behind their bodies, they are using body-part relationships. In a creative dance where the students begin as small flower seeds under the earth, their body parts would be close to each other in a small, round shape. As the seeds begin to sprout, their hands and feet will begin to reach away from their torsos to demonstrate the plant growing toward the sun.

Partners and Groups

When students dance with a partner or as a member of a group, they relate to each other in space and time. Partners or groups can move in a spatial relationship to each other such as side by side, facing each other, back to back, one behind the other, or side to back (see figure 2.3). They can also move in a temporal relationship to each other: in unison (moving exactly at the same time) or with a time delay between one person's movement and the other person's movement. The following movement relationship descriptions characterize a variety of uses of space and time.

- Shadow (also known as follow or copy): One student is behind another and follows the first student, performing the same movement at the same time. The right and left sides of the body move in the same way as the leader (see figure 2.3, one in front and one behind).

- Mirror: In this relationship, students face each other and perform the same movement as if they are looking in a mirror. When the leader moves the left arm, the follower moves the right arm using the same movement. The movements of the follower occur at the same time as the leader's movements. A slow tempo is recommended to allow the follower to stay in unison with the leader (see figure 2.3, facing each other).

- Echo: The leader performs a movement, and the follower observes the leader and then repeats the same movement after a very short delay between the movements. When a group does a sequence of echo movements, the effect is like falling dominoes or the wave. Dancers can use any spatial relationship.

- Unison: Two individuals or a group all perform the same movement at the same time. Dancers can use any spatial relationship.

Chapter 2 Presenting Essential Content for Dance 33

Figure 2.3 Partner spatial relationships can include side by side, facing each other, back to back, one behind the other, or side to back.

- Call-and-response: This relationship is similar to having a conversation with words, where one person speaks and the other person responds. One person or a group makes the first movement, considered the call, and then the other person or group makes a movement, the response. The movements of the caller and the responder are usually completely different or a variation of each other movements. Dancers can use any spatial relationship.
- Contrast: Students perform a movement or make a still shape that is opposite to the movement of a partner or another group. A stretched-out movement can be contrasted with a closed and rounded movement, a forward movement can be contrasted with moving backward, or strong movements can be contrasted with light movements. The contrast can also appear in the use of time; for example, one person can be moving rapidly while the other moves slowly. Dancers can use any spatial relationship (see figure 2.3, one stretched tall and one curved to the side).
- Connected: Two or more students move or make a still shape connected by one or more body parts. Dancers can use any spatial relationship.
- Supported: One or more students hold some or all of the body weight of another student, as in leaning on another person or lifting someone into the air. Dancers can use any spatial relationship (see figure 2.3, students back to back with support).
- Meeting and parting: This relationship describes how students move toward and away from each other in space. Dancers can use any spatial relationship.

Spatial Formations

The formation of the dancers in the space reflects the intent of the dance. In traditional cultural and social dances, students frequently dance in circles, squares, and line formations. These formations may express the feeling of unity as the dancers move using the same steps to the same rhythm. This type of dance fosters a feeling of acceptance and identity with a group. Other dances use formations that are like the spokes of a wheel, an X, or a cross shape. Creative dance also uses these formations in addition to scattered and geometric formations (see figure 2.4). One formation can be used for the entire dance, or the formation can change with different rhythmic patterns or to express different ideas in a dance.

Props, Equipment, and the Dance Environment

The relationship element is used here to describe the spatial relationship of an individual or group to a prop, piece of equipment, or the dance environment. A dancer relates to a prop by moving it in the personal space surrounding their body, to equipment by moving in the space surrounding the equipment, and to their environment by moving toward or away from the perimeter or center of the room or dance space. Children dancing with scarves in a creative dance experience, for example, can explore the space in front of or behind their bodies, over their heads, between their legs, or around their waists. In another lesson using a piece of equipment such as a chair or a cardboard box, students may explore ways they can move around, over, or under the equipment. A cultural dance may use long, colorful ribbons held between the hands of dancers in a circle while other dancers move under and over the ribbons. The dance environment can be used imaginatively and become the sky as students run around the perimeter, or a circle taped in the center of the space can be used as a place to dance inside of, outside of, around, or to move toward and away from.

DANCE FORMS

This section of the chapter describes the dance forms that are included in a dance curriculum: dances created by the students, defined in this book as creative dance, and dances created by others, such as social and cultural dances. A complete and inclusive dance program will provide students with experiences in creative dance, cultural dances, and social dances. Students will also have an opportunity to learn and create dances as individuals, in partnerships, and as members of a group.

Creative Dance

In creative dance, students generate their own dances to reflect or interpret an idea, thought, or feeling. Through the process of improvisation, students can manipulate movements using the elements of dance and then select and arrange the movements into a sequence to form a dance (see figure 2.5). Creating new dance movements is often a challenge for both the student and the teacher. Students must rely on their personal backgrounds to create something new. This process is not always easy for them. Young children may not have an extensive vocabulary of ideas and movements to use. They may look to you as the teacher to provide examples of movements until they develop a stronger vocabulary. Alternatively, some children have a wealth of movement experiences and are always eager to offer new ideas. Older students with a richer resource of life experiences may also encounter difficulty creating new movements. They may feel self-conscious and concerned about what their peers will think. Students need clear tasks that define what is expected yet are open-ended to allow for a creative response. The challenge for you as the teacher is to design a learning experience and establish a supportive atmosphere that encourages creativity and risk-taking, where students are willing to share their ideas.

For students with limited dance experience, a specific-task approach is recommended. This approach gives students a clear understanding of what the task requires and still leaves room for personal decision-making. For example, in the task "Find a way to do three consecutive jumps, each one moving in a different direction," a student can choose the shape of the jumps, the direction of each jump, the height of the jumps, and the force of each jump. The task can be more specific if you require that all the jumps be high with strong energy and use a designated rhythm.

The term *personal dancing* refers to the experience of students creating their own dance movements based on a teacher-presented task. The task may be broad, such as "Make up your own way of moving to this slow music," or specific, such

Chapter 2 Presenting Essential Content for Dance 35

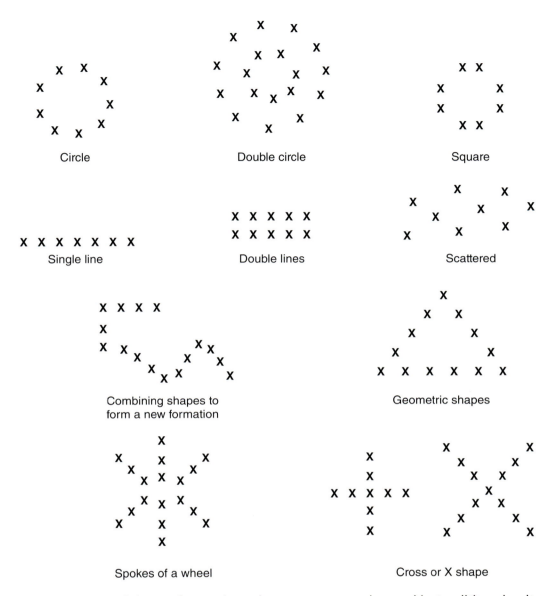

Figure 2.4 A variety of dance formations that are commonly used in traditional cultural and social dance.

Figure 2.5 Creative Process Used in Creating a Dance

1. Explore movements using the elements of dance.
2. Select movements from those explored.
3. Choose a movement sequence.
4. Decide where the movements will happen in the space.
5. Practice the sequence and make changes.
6. Practice the new sequence.
7. Perform the completed dance.

as "Find a way to rise slowly from the floor using a turn." Students make personal decisions about what movements they will use and how they will perform the movements within the guidelines of the task. They use their creativity, points of view, and resources to move in new ways to express a feeling or idea (see figure 2.6).

Personal dancing offers students the opportunity to discover what movements they like doing, what movements they may feel comfortable doing, how well they can do a movement, and what movements they would like to perform better. An example of personal dancing in a large-group experience is the floating clouds and rain showers dance experience (see chapter 8). This dance experience begins with a discussion about various cloud shapes and how clouds move in the sky. The students might describe cloud shapes as long, wide, puffy, big, or round and cloud movements as slow, floating, fast, or light. Next, each student creates a personal dance in response to the following task: "Think about the words you used to describe the clouds, and make shapes with your body that demonstrate cloud shapes. How many cloud shapes can you make with your body? Begin moving your body in its cloud shapes around the space. Move your shape forward and backward and turn it as you travel. Keep changing to different shapes as you float in the sky." In this dance experience, each student develops a personal dance even though the whole class responds simultaneously to the same task.

It is not only important to provide the opportunity to create individually but also critical to learn to create with others. Students spend most of their time in school interacting with others. They cooperate on science projects, eat lunch together, tutor each other, participate in the school band, and play together at recess. Working together to create a dance, whether with a partner or a group, requires cooperation and active involvement. Not all students are ready for this type of interaction. As a teacher, you need to keep in mind the motor-skill level of each age, the cognitive level of the students, and their ability to cooperate with others socially. Clearly defined tasks that include assigned roles will help the students be successful. Young children need to gain some control and understanding of their own bodies before they can interact with other students their age. Young learners work more easily with a partner than in a group. Older students who are more coordinated and have a broad range of movement experiences are capable of creating partner and small-group dances when they are given a clearly defined task that encourages creating in a cooperative atmosphere. You need to make sure, however, that students have the social and collaborative skills they will need to create and perform dances (see figure 2.7). This means that teaching children how to work together is as important as teaching the dance content.

Traditional and Choreographed Dances

In these types of dances, the student is focused more on being a learner or performer of dances created by others. Students can learn and perform the following types of dances:

- Personal or group dances created by another student or the teacher and taught to others in the class
- Dances created by a professional choreographer
- Social dances, such as the twist or chicken dance, that may reflect a particular time period
- Cultural dances that represent a particular country or ethnic population (sometimes referred to as folk dances)

A description of each type of dance follows.

Dances Created by the Students or the Teacher

Student- and teacher-created dances can be created by an individual or a group and then taught to other individuals or groups. They are new

Figure 2.6 A creative dance that reflects the shape of a leaf.

> ### Figure 2.7 Collaborative Skills for Creating a Group Dance
>
> Give everyone a turn to share their ideas.
>
> Listen to one another's ideas.
>
> Agree on a group idea through consensus or vote.
>
> Compromise and blend ideas.
>
> Encourage group members through the use of positive comments.
>
> Remain focused on the task and practice together.

dances created as a result of an idea presented and developed during a learning experience. The student or the teacher organizes the movements into a sequence with a definite beginning, middle, and end. The dance is taught in a way that is developmentally appropriate and ensures a positive learning environment. The dances can be recorded in a variety of forms including recorded digitally, as a written record, or in a series of pictures.

Dances Created by a Professional Choreographer

Students may have the unique opportunity to study dance in their school with a professional choreographer or dancer, a guest artist, or an artist in residence. Complete dances or excerpts of dances from the dancer's or choreographer's repertoire can be taught to the students and adapted to meet the students' developmental level.

Social Dances

These types of dances emphasize using dance as a means of experiencing the joy of moving with others. Social dances exist within a cultural and historical context and represent one of the ways in which people share, celebrate, and experience life as a community. They are dances that have become popular through sharing, both in person and online. They are performed at many social occasions in groups or shared via online media for others around the world to see and replicate. Examples include the cupid shuffle, lindy, twist, hip-hop dances, salsa, and electric slide. Students are always ready to teach a new dance that is popular, and they enjoy learning dances from other eras.

Cultural Dances

These dance forms focus on how dance represents events, traditions, and cultural heritage. Through these dances, students learn about what is important to another culture—its traditions, values, beliefs, history, and lifestyles. The dances are like stories passed down from one generation to another. They hold history and heritage in every movement and formation. Students need to learn more than the sequence of steps; they should be informed about the cultural background of the dance. It is important to teach about the environment and the people from which these dances emerged to promote appreciation and respect for that culture. In this book, for example, American square dance is considered a cultural dance because it reflects how the diversity of cultures in various geographical areas of the United States contributed to the evolution of square dance.

Choosing dances created by others requires thoughtful selection of developmentally appropriate dances. Many cultural dances require dancers to perform movements in unison, in structured formations, or in time to a specific piece of music or rhythm. Young children may not be able to accurately reproduce the movements in the correct rhythm as a large group. As the teacher, you will need to find dances that are suitable for the ability of your students or adapt a dance while maintaining the integrity of its movements and formations. When possible, teach traditional cultural dances as they were originally intended. If you make numerous changes to the steps, gestures, and formations, the characteristics that make it representative of a culture can be compromised, and the authenticity of the dance is lost. As you teach dances from a variety of cultures, be aware that your personal culture will influence your presentation. The best situation is to have someone from the cultural group teach the dance; however, this is not always possible. You can research information on the Internet, in a library, through pictures or recorded videos, and via artifacts that will make the teaching and learning experience accurate and meaningful.

SUMMARY

Children's dance, as a medium of expression, is manifested through the body and its infinite variations of movement. The elements of dance—the body, space, time, force, flow, and relationships—have an impact on how the movement is designed and performed. Movement in dance has meaning—it expresses an idea or the intention of the performer or creator. When students participate in creative dance, they explore, improvise, and discover new ways to move. They also learn dances created by others—another student, the teacher, a professional choreographer—or dances from a specific historical period or ethnic population. The three forms of children's dance—creative, social, and cultural—make up a comprehensive dance program that provides students with opportunities for learning to create, perform, and respond to dance.

Questions for Reflection

1. How many ways to walk can you create using the elements of dance? For example, walk forward quickly using a curvy pathway or walk slowly taking big steps. What additional ideas can you think of?

2. If you were creating a dance about the water cycle, how would you use space, time, and force to create movements that represent evaporation, condensation, and precipitation?

3. Teaching dance within a cultural and historical context provides students with an understanding of how the dance movements and formations reflect traditions, values, beliefs, and ways of living. What are some strategies you would use to teach a cultural dance? How can technology be integrated into your teaching?

4. Think of several instances in which you participated in a cultural dance or a social dance. What did you enjoy about the experience? Who was dancing? What types of movements did you perform or observe?

CHAPTER 3

Designing a Dance Program

Teaching dance is both challenging and rewarding. Deciding on the best way to organize and present a learning experience or a unit of study is a constant learning process. In every lesson you teach, you learn something new about the content, the task sequence, and the response from your students. You are constantly evaluating your teaching and making changes for the next session. In this chapter, we offer ideas for developing a yearlong program, specific units of study, and the individual lesson. Your school may already have a dance curriculum to guide your teaching, or you may be starting a new curriculum. In either situation, planning is essential. Begin by getting to know your students, understanding the school's goals, and determining what is critical to the dance program. Review national, state, or local education standards that are required for your program. These standards provide a guide to the content that students should be able to do and know, as a result of learning in a dance education program. You will not be able to teach everything in depth, and some content may not be addressed each year. You will need to make decisions about what students need to know and experience.

What is important, however, is that students have the opportunity to learn, perform, create, and observe dances as well as respond to their own performances or dance creations and the dances of others. The components of the artistic process form the foundation of a comprehensive dance program that addresses the psychomotor, cognitive, and affective domains inherent in all dance learning experiences. Teachers choose the appropriate content that meets their learning outcomes and incorporate two or more artistic processes into the unit or lesson development and implementation. For example, in a unit on cultural dances of the South Pacific region, the first lesson would be on learning about the history, customs, traditions, and characteristics of those people. Students then observe a video, a teaching artist, or the dance teacher who presents the movements of a traditional dance. Next, students learn to reproduce the dance movements, rhythms, and formations through repetition and practice. The lesson concludes with the students performing the dance to traditional music. Additionally, students can observe each other performing the dance and then respond through a discussion about what parts of the dance were most successful.

Here are the five components of the artistic process:

- *Learning* requires observation, reproduction, and repetition of movements through practice.
- *Creating* refers to generating new movements or movement variations through improvisation and exploration and also composing dances.
- *Performing* involves physically demonstrating dance movements or complete dances.

39

- *Observing* includes watching dances performed live and on recorded video or online sources.
- *Responding* engages students' critical-thinking skills to reflect on their performance, a dance they created, or an observation of a dance performed by others. Students can respond through discussion, writing, demonstration, or drawing.

PLANNING A YEARLONG DANCE PROGRAM

The dance content taught in the span of a school year for each grade level may be determined by the school district's curriculum for dance education. When a predetermined curriculum is not available, the dance educator or physical educator may be responsible for designing and implementing the dance program. Planning a dance program can be an overwhelming task. Knowing what type of dance to teach and how to organize the learning experiences requires combining knowledge of how students learn with knowledge of the dance content. Each dance learning experience focuses on several outcomes that emphasize some or all of the artistic components of dance—that is, learning, creating, performing, observing, and responding. These outcomes are met through a sequence of lessons that develop and refine the knowledge and skills that students need in order to express and communicate ideas, thoughts, and feelings through dance. The specific theme for the learning experience, such as traditional West African dance or creating dances about the planets, must be relevant to the students in order to make their participation personal and meaningful.

As a full-time dance educator, you might teach the same classes for the entire school year, or you might be scheduled to teach different classes that rotate every few weeks. The amount of time available determines the amount and depth of the content you will teach. In an elementary school where the children attend a dance class once a week for 45 minutes, you might plan 5 to 10 units delivered in 4 to 8 lessons per unit. The units can be different lengths depending on the content and age of the children. We recommend that children have the opportunity to learn about dance from creative, social, and cultural perspectives within the yearlong program. In a secondary school program, students might attend dance class every day throughout a semester or year. This could require several more units than an elementary program or allow you more time to dive further into each unit's content. Younger secondary students, such as middle school students, might have shorter or less in-depth units than older, high-school-aged students. Even for secondary school students, the amount of time available with each class will determine the amount and depth of the content. It is also still recommended to have these students learn about dance from various perspectives, including creative, social, and cultural.

When dance is part of the physical education program, it may be delivered in one or more units during the school year. This requires you as the teacher to make some tough decisions about what to teach within the time allotted for dance. Even with a limited amount of time, children need to experience dance as a creative, social, and cultural form of expression. We recommend that dance be taught several times throughout the school year for both elementary and secondary school students.

One approach to developing a yearlong program is to design one or more units for each grade level in each of the dance forms: creative, social, and cultural. In this approach, grade levels could be clustered for units such as kindergarten to first grade, second to third grades, and fourth to fifth grades. It is also possible to separate or cluster units for secondary school students with sixth grade learning creative dance, seventh grade learning cultural dance, and eighth grade learning social dance. High school students may have mixed grade levels in a single class, but the level of the class could determine the dance form to teach. An example of a dance program in the elementary or middle school physical education curriculum might be as follows:

- Creative dance could involve a four-lesson unit focused on exploring and creating a dance about various water forms. In the first lesson, students identify five water forms such as a river, the ocean, a waterfall, a rainstorm, and a stream; they then explore movements that represent the characteristics of each water form. In the second lesson, students organized in pairs select two water forms and create a dance that demonstrates a change in levels, pathways, and tempos using the movements they learned in the first session. The third lesson is focused on small groups of students collaborating to select one water form; they create a dance that includes a beginning group formation, uses locomotor movements in different directions, and ends in a group formation. In the final session, each group begins the class by practicing and refining their dance and then shares their dance with other groups while you conduct the assessment.

• Social dance could involve a three-lesson unit focused on learning social dances from the 1950s and 1960s. In the first lesson, students learn three dances from the 1950s. The second lesson presents three dances from the 1960s. In the third lesson, students in small groups choose three of the six dances they learned, practice them together, and then record themselves for a self-assessment or show their dances to another group.

• Cultural dance could be a unit focused on learning three dances from Uganda connected to a social studies unit taught by the classroom teacher. The unit contains four lessons in which a dance artist, hired by the school, teaches the first two sessions. During these sessions, the students learn three traditional dances from various parts of Uganda. In the third session, you set up three dance stations, one for each dance learned in the first two sessions. The students, organized into three groups, visit each station and practice the dance identified with that station. In the fourth session, the students perform the dances for another class and write about how the movements reflect the Ugandan culture.

A second approach to a yearlong program, applicable for the dance and physical education program, is to present units that include all three dance forms. These units are centered on a theme or one or more elements of dance. In this way, students gain a comprehensive understanding of how the theme or elements can be addressed from creative, social, and cultural perspectives (see figure 3.1). For example, a unit based on the outcomes that children demonstrate respect toward others and increase body coordination can include two lessons on learning popular social dances, two lessons on learning dances from a culture not represented in their school, and two lessons on creating dances about friendship. Respect is taught through learning to cooperate and dance with others, and coordination is increased when children learn and repeat patterns of movement that are present in all the dance forms taught in the unit.

A third approach is to choose a dance form as the primary focus and include another form as an extension. The extension provides a more in-depth study and demonstrates how the dance forms are interrelated. For example, in a five-lesson unit focused on social dance, the students learn four line dances in the first three lessons. In the fourth and fifth sessions, creative dance is used as an extension in which the students create their own line dances (Johnson 2002). Another example in a three-lesson unit focused on the dances of the Southwest Native Americans is to teach two social circle dances performed by those groups of people during celebrations in the first lesson. During the second lesson, you can add a creative element by performing the dances using a different formation, and in the third lesson you can use creative dance in extending the social dances by having the students create two new dance steps to add to the dances they already learned.

Figure 3.1 Sample Theme-Based Dance Unit

Theme: Birthdays

Creative	Social	Cultural
Students create partner dances about making a birthday cake	Students learn a line dance to the song "Happy Birthday."	Students learn a cultural dance performed at a birthday celebration.

A fourth approach is to plan teaching one dance form for the entire year to all grade levels. Each grade level or grade cluster would learn different dances that represent the selected dance form. For example, if social dance is selected for the yearlong plan, the unit could consist of three lessons for kindergarten and first grade, four lessons for second and third grades, and five lessons for fourth and fifth grades. A similar pattern could occur for middle school students who have limited time in dance or physical education throughout the year with three lessons for sixth grade or beginning level, four lessons for seventh grade or intermediate level, and five lessons for eighth grade or advanced level. Example content for the social dance units for each elementary grade cluster could include the following:

Kindergarten and First Grade

Lesson 1: hokey pokey, chicken dance, and seven jumps with a partner

Lesson 2: meet and greet dance (see chapter 7), the bunny hop, and the animal dance

Lesson 3: one new dance, the woodland get-together based on Boynton's (2021) *Woodland Dance!*

Students select their four favorite dances and perform each dance.

Second and Third Grades

Lesson 1: meet and greet dance using locomotor movement variations, friendship mixer dance (Cone and Cone 2011), and bandanna dance (see chapter 7)

Lesson 2: partner dances combining social and creative dance using mirroring, shadowing, echoing, and call-and-response

Lesson 3: three teacher-selected simple line dances

Lesson 4: students organized in small groups agree on one favorite dance and practice and share it with their peers.

In this lesson, the students can perform the dance for peers or lead their peers in performing the dance together.

Fourth and Fifth Grades

Lesson 1: cha-cha slide, cupid shuffle, and a line dance selected by you

Lesson 2: double circle mixer (see chapter 7), a review of one dance from lesson 1, and a line dance selected by you

Lesson 3: dances from the 1950s, '60s, and '70s

Lesson 4: review of selected dances taught in the first three lessons

Lesson 5: students teach new popular social dances and select dances taught in the first three lessons and create a variation to the formation or add new dance steps

In this approach, the following school year could focus on cultural dances that are appropriate for each grade level. Finally, in the third year, creative dance would be the focus of the yearlong plan. In this way, over three years, the students have had the opportunity to learn dance in all three forms.

Finally, as part of the planning process, consider the following criteria as a checklist to ensure that you have designed a comprehensive, developmentally appropriate, and meaningful dance learning experience:

❏ The annual plan, units, and lessons are aligned with national, state, or local standards.

❏ Each unit and each lesson contains clear outcomes and assessments.

❏ The selected content is relevant to the age and interests of the students.

❏ The collection and organization of teaching materials are feasible.

❏ Cultural dance units and lessons are integrated with accurate and relevant information about the culture.

❏ Lesson tasks follow a sequential progression that builds skills and knowledge.

❏ The dance space is appropriate for students' learning and safety.

PLANNING A DANCE UNIT

A unit of study in dance is a series of lessons that focus on a set of instructional outcomes (see chapter 1). The unit outcomes describe what students will know and be able to do as a result of participating in the lessons. Each lesson contains more specific outcomes that can be achieved in a single session, but single-lesson outcomes still relate to the broader unit outcomes. There are many ways to plan and implement a unit; however, what is common to all units is a thoughtful and meaningful design that provides for skill development, social interaction, attainment of knowledge, and understanding of a culture. For example, if pathways have been selected as the topic for a creative dance unit, the unit outcomes will state that students learn to identify various types of pathways and create ways to move using pathways. The unit is planned to occur in four dance lessons, and specific lesson outcomes are as follows:

- Session 1: Children explore locomotor and nonlocomotor movements using straight, curved, and zigzag pathways on the floor and in the air.

- Session 2: Children explore locomotor and nonlocomotor movements using straight, curved, and zigzag pathways on the floor and in the air that represent numbers and letters of the alphabet.

- Session 3: Children and the teacher collaborate to create a whole-class alphabet dance that uses pathways on the floor and in the air.

- Session 4: Children collaborate with a partner to create a dance about letters or numbers that uses two types of pathways that demonstrates a change in direction, tempo, or level.

Using the elements of dance as a topical theme for a creative dance unit is one strategy for selecting a unit topic. Numerous other interesting topics can be selected (see table 3.1) depending on the ages and interests of the students.

Table 3.1 Topics for Learning Experiences in Creative Dance

Theme	Topics
Literature	Poems, novels, picture storybooks, folktales, and stories (both published and those written by students)
Holidays	National, cultural, and religious holidays
Special events	Birthdays, graduation, getting a driver's license
Machines	Car wash, homework machine, computer
Day-to-day activities	Getting ready for school, family dinners, playing games
Media	Films, television programs, online videos
School activities	Eating in the lunchroom, recess, walking in the halls
Feelings	Sadness, fear, joy, anger, excitement
Seasons	Fall leaves, snow and ice, spring flowers, summer fun at the beach
Friendship	Name dances, partner dances, dances about acceptance and helping one another
Circus	Horses, tightrope walkers, acrobats, clowns, lions
Animals	Bears, dogs, birds, fish, monkeys
Weather	Tornadoes, clouds, wind, rain, lightning, a sunny day
Action words	Wiggle, burst, float, punch, press, melt
Sports	Basketball, soccer, tennis, swimming, football, baseball, hockey
Environments	Mountains, water forms, desert, rainforest, icebergs
Social issues	Rejection, acceptance, fighting, discrimination, bullying
Historical events	Baseball World Series, inauguration of a governor, war
Life experiences	Losing a tooth, welcoming a new student into the class, a first date
Current events	Major headlines, sports news, popular culture
Dance maps	Designing pathways and movements
Other academic subjects	Science, social studies, math, language arts, music, visual arts, theater, foreign languages, technology

When planning a unit, decide what dance form will be taught, the broader outcomes of the unit and specific lesson, and how to assess learning. Then plan the progression of tasks for each lesson (see figure 3.2). This process is called a backward-design planning process (Wiggins and McTighe 2005). Wiggins and McTighe, educational researchers and consultants who developed the popular Understanding by Design curricular development process, suggest that teachers identify the desired results, determine what evidence demonstrates learning, and then design the activities. For example, planning a dance unit for first-grade students that is focused on pathways would begin with identifying the outcome: Students will learn to identify various types of pathways and be able to create movements that travel on pathways. Next, the type of assessment is determined. A teacher observation checklist can be used in noting whether students can move on various pathways when asked to by the teacher, or students may draw pathways to demonstrate their understanding. Additionally, students can write the names of the movements or draw pictures of themselves moving on the pathways. Another assessment strategy requires students to verbally describe a pathway danced by a peer or demonstrate and identify a pathway they created.

The next step in unit design is to delineate how the content will be presented. How many teaching sessions are needed, or how many sessions are available? Next, an outline or a detailed description for each lesson is developed. Remember, as you plan, include sufficient time for students to fully engage in the processes of learning, performing, creating, observing, or responding to the dance content. Students' performances and assessment of their work can occur at any point in the unit; however, these activities are sometimes used as a closure activity. Before the unit starts, collect or order music, props, equipment, costumes, or other required materials. At the beginning of the unit, communicate your expectations to the students, and be clear about what they will be learning. Your planning should reflect a thoughtful sequence of learning tasks that facilitates meaningful and successful learning.

Finally, after you have presented a dance unit, take time to reflect on the teaching experience. Reflective teaching (Brookfield 2017) is a critical analysis of students' responses, the framework of the unit, and what the teaching experience was like for the teacher. What parts were most frustrating, satisfying, unexpected, or challenging? The insights gained from reflection will help to refine your teaching practice and offer you an opportunity to reflect on your own attitudes, beliefs, assumptions, behaviors, and perceptions. Ongoing self-observation and self-evaluation help you make changes and deepen the rationale for content selection, design, and teaching techniques.

PLANNING THE DANCE LESSONS

Once you have identified the dance form, content, instructional outcomes, and assessment of the dance unit, you can design the lessons and tasks that will occur in each dance lesson. A similar planning process is appropriate for teaching creative, social, or cultural dances. Each dance lesson includes four main sections: introduction, development, culminating dance, and closure activity. These sections are discussed next. The dance lesson also emphasizes one or more specific outcomes that relate to the broader outcome of the unit. Generally, lessons may be completed comfortably in one session; however, you can decide based on how your students respond to the content if more time is needed. If appropriate,

---

Figure 3.2 Unit Planning Outline

- Identify grade level.
- Review national, state, or local dance standards.
- Determine the dance form.
- Select a dance topic or theme.
- Develop a unit outcome.
- Identify the number of lessons in the unit.
- Develop outcomes for each lesson.
- Decide on the assessment type and instrument.
- Plan the content and progression.
- Collect instructional materials, music, or props.

use a second session or even a third to complete the lesson, giving students a chance to fully explore the concept. This may result in adjusting the amount of content you can teach in the unit.

Introduction

The introduction serves as a transition for students between the activities they have just experienced (perhaps a math lesson or lunch) and the dance learning experience. You can offer several approaches to these first moments of class. One option is to provide an instant activity where students, as they enter the space, are immediately engaged in practicing skills, viewing posted instructions, or obtaining materials to be used in the lesson (Graham, Elliott, and Palmer 2016). This teaching technique allows time for a transition as well as time for students to talk informally with you. During this time, you can play the music that will be used in the lesson to familiarize students with the music's tempo, mood, and style. Another way to begin a lesson is to gather the students in a designated listening spot and start the lesson with a brief verbal introduction.

Here, you tell the students what they are going to learn, why you chose the topic or theme, and how it relates to them. One way to begin is by asking the students what they know about the topic or theme. As a result, you gain insights into their understanding and experience regarding the topic or theme. Another part of the introduction can include a review of skills and concepts taught in a previous lesson or a question about what students remember. In this way, students develop an understanding about how lessons are related to one another as part of a planned sequence. It is also appropriate to accompany the verbal introduction by showing a movement that will be taught, an object, video, book, map, or pictures related to the topic.

The introduction for teaching a cultural dance should include background information on the origin of the dance and its relationship to the culture or ethnic group. The information presented can be supported with a video, pictures, maps, clothing, artifacts, books, newspapers, music, artwork, crafts, food, the language, religion, or other materials that provide context for the dance. Communicate how the values, traditions, lifestyle, environment, and history of the culture influence the movements, music, and formations of the dance. Avoid stereotyping a culture or making biased comments, and present accurate information based on reliable resources.

The beginning of a social dance lesson can emphasize concepts of respect, responsibility, cooperation, leadership, kindness, or being helpful to others. Students can talk about their understanding of what these words mean to them and how they can demonstrate these concepts through dance. This type of introduction sets the expectation for the learning outcome and places the enjoyment of socializing through dance in a broader context. When possible, include historical information about the social dances and discuss the types of social gatherings where they occur.

You can introduce a creative dance lesson in many ways. You can begin with a story, photo, prop, book, or perhaps a news event. When students ask, "What are we going to do today?" the first response sets the tone for the day. Be enthusiastic. For example, to introduce the spaghetti dance (see chapter 8), you might say, "Today we are going to dance about straight and curved shapes. I chose these two shapes because they are everywhere in our world. Let's begin to find these shapes by looking at our clothes." As the students are looking at their clothes and pointing to shapes, you can quickly assess whether they can identify shapes. You can use a prop, such as a rope, to illustrate the straight and curved shapes, or you can draw the shapes on a poster or whiteboard.

After the verbal introduction, a body warm-up follows. The warm-up is directly related to the type of movements students will be doing in the dance lesson and prepares the body for safe and active participation. The warm-up can be a series of movements that warm up the muscles and increase the body's blood flow. The students can begin with locomotor movements such as walking, galloping, or skipping in the space and then continue with nonlocomotor movements such as stretching, bending, twisting, or swinging the whole body or its parts. If the students will be running, leaping, twisting, and bending during the dance learning experience, the warm-up should include movements that prepare the body for those actions. Movements in the warm-up should be whole-body actions that include both locomotor and nonlocomotor movements.

A warm-up for a cultural dance may include moving to the music used in the dance or performing specific movements from the dance. Students can move body parts in isolation, such as moving the head from side to side, the shoulders up and down, and the hips in a circle; bouncing through the knees lightly; reaching the arms up and out to the side; stepping in place with the feet; and twisting the torso from side to side. Warm-ups for a social dance can follow a format similar to that of a cultural dance. To emphasize the social aspect, students can do the warm-ups with partners or in small groups and then change to another warm-up group. A warm-up for a creative dance can include a short aerobic section; isolated body part movements; and bending, stretching, and twisting movements. If the lesson is on pathways, you can incorporate the words and types of pathways into the warm-up. In the spaghetti dance (see chapter 8), for example, the warm-up may include instructions related to shape making: "Walk around the room and look for straight and curved shapes. Where can you find them? Look high and low. When you find a shape, imitate the shape with your body. Find another shape and another." Here, the students are using walking as the whole-body movement and making shapes with their bodies. To summarize, through the introduction, the dance topic is presented, students' prior understanding of the selected topic is revealed, topic relevancy is established, and the students are prepared physically to participate.

Development

During the development section, students experience new ways to move, whether through patterned movements from a cultural or social dance or a series of movements they have created. You can create a sequence of tasks, which is a coherent progression that leads the students to learn and create movements relevant to the lesson outcomes. Students learn, explore, improvise, and create movements that express and communicate concepts, ideas, thoughts, and feelings. During a lesson on learning a cultural or social dance, students would be learning the sequence of movements and the formations inherent in the dance. Usually, this is presented using the part–whole or whole–part teaching strategy (see chapter 5). If the lesson focus is on a creative

Students use their bodies to form a snowflake shape in a creative dance.

dance, the task sequence needs to be relevant to the topic. Just asking students to make up a dance or dance to the music is too general and does not provide for focused learning. However, this general task does have value if you want to see what the students could create, and you can use it as an assessment for students to demonstrate a specific skill or concept (Fencl 2014). When the focus is on an element of dance such as contrasting fast and slow tempos, students will explore a variety of movements using the different tempos. The tasks can be specific ("Find a way to walk eight steps forward using a fast tempo, then walk eight steps backward as slowly as you can.") or more open-ended ("How can you change levels, alternating between a fast and a slow tempo?"). This task may evolve into a dance or a selected sequence of movements that represent an idea, or the lesson can focus on a topic, such as a circus, a sport, a poem, or celebrating a birthday. The students explore movements that interpret the actions, events, or feelings relevant to the topic or theme. Here, the elements of dance are applied to the topic as tools in developing the type and quality of movements. Instead of saying, "Act like a lion, or be a seed," extend the imagery to provide rich descriptions of the movement in order to enhance the creative choices of students (Karin and Nordin-Bates 2020). Change it—act like a lion to move low and slowly, like a lion stalking its prey. In this way, the movement quality is the focus and students can increase their variety of movement responses to the task. For example, in a dance about zoo animals, you would ask each student to choose an animal. You then present the following as exploratory tasks related to the elements of dance (EOD; see table 2.1). The tasks guide students as they create their movements:

- Demonstrate three ways your animal moves. Does the animal walk, run, jump, gallop, swing, twist, stretch, slither, wiggle, shake, or kick? (EOD: body actions)
- Show me how your animal moves its arms, head, shoulders, back, legs, and feet. (EOD: body parts)
- Have your animal move using very small steps . . . now huge steps. (EOD: space, range)

- Find a way your animal can move in different directions. Can it move forward, backward, and sideward? (EOD: space, directions)
- Find a partner. One of you be a leader and the other a follower, and slowly mirror your partner's animal movements and then switch roles. (EOD: relationships)
- Show me how slowly your animal can move. Can your animal begin moving slowly and then increase its speed? (EOD: time, tempo)
- Create three still shapes that show different actions your animal does. Is your shape twisted, round, or straight? (EOD: body shapes)
- Demonstrate how your animal moves very lightly and then moves with strong energy. (EOD: force)
- Decide if your animal moves smoothly and slowly or sharply and quickly, and then practice the movement. (EOD: force, time)
- Find a way for your animal to move on a straight pathway. Now change to a curvy pathway. Change the pathway to a zigzag. (EOD: space, pathways)

By exploring the creative dance topic through the elements of dance, students broaden their movement vocabulary. They learn to find multiple ways to express movements that go beyond their initial action. The next step would involve creating a dance about animals. In this way, students are performing a sequence of movements that can be repeated and refined. The dance may follow a short story designed by you, or the students may suggest an idea for the animal dance. The students would then choose movements they have explored in the dance. For example, in this teacher-designed dance, the animals begin by sleeping in a shape low to the floor; then they slowly wake up and move in general space to meet other animals. They play follow-the-leader with a partner and finally return to where they started and fall asleep again. Although the students follow the sequence of your story, they are choosing the type and quality of the movements their animal makes.

The development section is an important component of the learning and creative process and it relates directly to the culminating dance or final product and outcome of the unit or lesson. This section is the journey students take as they create, learn, practice, and refine new movements. Bucura and Brashier (2021) tell us that students grow in their learning "when provided space to make sure of what they have learned. Such space includes time and places to practice, a sense of inquiry, and an openness to creative ventures of their own choices and interests" (p. 4). Knowing the desired result—whether it is a specific line dance, a creative dance about force, or the words of a poem expressed through a dance—is a key element to planning meaningful tasks. In some creative dance experiences, the exact form and sequence of the culminating dance may be unknown until after the students explore and improvise movements; however, a general framework or outline of the final outcome should be planned. Here, Wiggins and McTighe's (2005) concept of backward design in unit planning, described earlier, can also be applied to each lesson.

The sequence of tasks in the development section is presented in what Mosston and Ashworth (2008) refer to as guided discovery. The tasks are designed and sequenced to prepare and lead the students to create and learn movements that are evident in the culminating dance. One approach to developing an appropriate sequence of tasks is to analyze how the elements of dance are used in the culminating dance. The following questions guide the analysis of the culminating dance:

- What movements of the whole body and its parts are used in the dance?

- How are levels, pathways, range, and direction used?

- What is the speed and rhythm? Are there accents in the movements? Will the movements accelerate or decelerate? Is there a pause in the movements? Will everyone be moving on the same beat? Is there a contrast in speed? Do the rhythms change?

- What type of force is used? When are the movements strong or light? Do they change force?

- Is the flow of the movements free or bound? Does the flow change?

- How will the students be organized—as individuals, with partners, or in small groups? Will they follow each other, connect, support, or mirror? What formations will they use? Will the relationships and formations change during the dance?

Chapter 8 includes a description of the culminating dance for the spaghetti dance lesson, which focuses on making straight and curved shapes and movements with the body. From reading the description, you can anticipate the sequence of movements, changes in quality, and formations used in the dance. During the development section, the presentation of the tasks uses the guided discovery strategy to lead students to experience and create the types of movements that are included in the culminating dance. In the culminating spaghetti dance, children begin in a straight shape and travel on a straight pathway to a pot of water. During the development section, children explore making straight shapes with their bodies and find various ways to travel on a straight pathway. Through the exploration process, you guide the children to experience movements that are used in the culminating spaghetti dance.

A similar analysis for task construction can be applied to cultural and social dance, in which you have prepared the culminating dance. The following example demonstrates the first two tasks presented while teaching the Russian troika dance during the development section of the lesson.

- Task 1: "Each person will take 4 running steps forward and stop. Now try it again, beginning on the right foot, and take the 4 running steps moving diagonally to the right." This task teaches the first 4 steps of the culminating dance. The elements of movement to be emphasized are running, direction, and moving in a specific rhythm and tempo.

- Task 2: "I will organize you into groups of 3. Join hands and practice the 4 steps diagonally right, then left, and then take 8 steps forward." In this task, the students are learning to move in unison while connected by their hands. These 16 steps make up the first section of the culminating dance of the troika. The elements of dance highlighted are running, a connected relationship, tempo, rhythm, and direction.

Each task prepares the students for the way they will move in the culminating dance and emphasizes one or more elements of dance.

Culminating Dance

The culminating dance brings together the movements experienced in the development section. In this part of the lesson, structure is given to the movements that were created and learned. Students select, organize, and perform movements individually, in small groups, or as one large group. The dances may follow a choreographic structure much like simple music structures, such as round, narrative, ABA, AB, chance, and theme and variation (see figure 3.3) (Kassing and Jay-Kirschenbaum 2021). Keep in mind that it may be appropriate for young children to participate in large-group culminating dances until they are ready to work more independently to create their own dances. Large-group dances are also appropriate for older students with little dance experience, because they often feel more comfortable if everyone is doing the same dance at the same time. The large-group culminating creative dance is similar to everyone performing a cultural or social dance as a group.

Culminating dances usually have a recognizable beginning, middle, and end. The dance may be a narrative form or it may express a range of feelings. It may be a sequence of movements that show how a round shape can change size, move at different tempos, or travel in different pathways. The dance can begin and end in a formation such as a circle, a line, or scattered around the perimeter of the space. In the middle section, students may maintain a formation or they may change to one or more formations. In addition to formation changes, the rhythm, movements, force, flow, and relationships of the dancers can change. Another approach for creating the culminating dance may be a spontaneous performance of movements experienced during the development section. For some young children, the act of spontaneously creating dance movements is their dance. They do not make a definitive distinction between the process of creating and the final dance (Cone 2002). In a spontaneous culminating dance, there is no set choreographic structure; instead, the dance is more organic in nature, where the dance is created from moment to moment while the children are dancing. The dance may end when the children decide they are tired, or they may keep dancing until you tell them the dance is over.

As the teacher, you may want to create your own new culminating dance for a creative dance instead of using a previously created dance like the spaghetti dance. In this situation, you would outline your vision of the dance through a written description or through drawings and notes. You may envision a dance about fall leaves and develop a dance that expresses the action and qualities of the leaves as they fall from the tree and blow around the field. Then, you can analyze

Figure 3.3 Choreographic Structures Used in Dance

AB—A two-part composition. *A* represents a movement, and *B* represents another movement.

ABA—A three-part composition. The *A* movements are performed, then the *B* movements are performed, and the *A* movements are repeated.

accumulation—A dance that begins with one movement, then another is added, then another, each time repeating all the movements from the beginning before another movement is added.

chance—A dance that is composed spontaneously with random movements.

narrative—A dance that tells a story or series of events.

rearrange—A dance that has the dance movement sequence changed to a different order.

retrograde—A dance that is performed in reverse order.

round—A dance that is like an echo. The same dance is performed, but it is started by another dancer at a different time shortly after the first dancer begins.

theme and variations—A movement that is changed but is still related to the original movement.

the anticipated movements, changes of quality, and use of space, and plan a series of tasks for the development section that will guide students toward this culminating dance.

Consider the following questions when developing your own culminating dance:

- What do you want students to gain as a result of learning this dance?
- What is the image, theme, story, piece of literature, idea, or feeling that will be expressed in the dance?
- What is the sequence of movements in the culminating dance?
- What specific elements of dance can be emphasized to support the movements of the dance?
- What formations will be used? Lines? Circles? Scattered?
- How will the dance begin?
- Where and how will the students move in the middle of the dance?
- How will the dance end?

To create the spaghetti dance, we began with the idea that we wanted students to learn how to make straight and curved shapes with their bodies and to travel on straight and curved pathways. Making different shapes and finding different ways to travel would be suitable for exploring the concept; however, we believed children would understand the concept better if we created a story about what happened to a box of spaghetti. We knew the image of spaghetti was familiar to the students, and they would find humor and interest in dancing the imagined event of the spaghetti as it cooks. The culminating dance expresses the events of the story. In this dance, the students travel as straight pieces of spaghetti on a straight pathway from an imaginary box to a pot of water and then jump in. They change from straight to curved shapes as they cook and move around in the pot among the other pieces of spaghetti. A giant bubble appears and pushes the spaghetti out of the pot. The spaghetti runs and leaps in a curved shape as it flies around the kitchen and becomes stuck in a curved shape on the wall. Finally, the curvy cooked spaghetti slowly moves off the wall, walks in a curved pathway, steps onto the dinner plate, and ends lying down on the plate in a curved shape. The students experience a change of levels while cooking, flying around the kitchen and falling onto the dinner plate; a change of tempo; a change of shape; and a change in relationship, moving close together and farther apart. The entire class dances the sequence at the same time, yet they all use their own unique ideas about how to express straight and curved shapes and pathways.

Closure Activity

A closure activity is appropriate at the end of each lesson as well as the end of the unit (Graham, Elliott, and Palmer 2016). The activity may be a performance of culminating dances, a review of all the dances learned during the unit, a written response or drawing of the experience, or a discussion focused on what the students learned. This activity brings a conclusion to the lesson or unit and is one way in which you can assess students' learning and check for understanding. Students should have a moment to reflect on and recall what they experienced during the lesson or unit and think about what knowledge and skills they acquired. The nature of the ending can vary, but you should provide time for a meaningful closure activity. Remember that how you end is as important as how you begin.

SAMPLE UNIT AND LESSON OUTLINE

We offer an outline of an initial planning document for a creative dance unit. This unit is taught during the fall season to correspond with the falling leaves and the science teacher's unit on environmental changes.

Grade Levels: Kindergarten and First Grade

National Dance Education Standards (National Dance Society 2020) are as follows:

- 3: Creative and artistic communication in dance
- 4: Choreography, performance, and production
- 6: Dance, arts, and media literacy for integrated learning

The National Dance Standards are reprinted from the National Dance Society and Human Kinetics (2020).

Dance form is creative dance.

Dance topic is leaves in the fall season.

Unit outcome is that children will create and perform a dance that represents leaf shapes and movements.

Number of lessons in the unit is three.

Outcomes for Each Lesson

Lesson 1: The children will create still shapes to represent the various leaf shapes and use various locomotor movements to demonstrate how the leaves fall from the trees and blow in the wind.

Lesson 2: The children will create a personal dance that uses three still leaf shapes and three locomotor movements.

Lesson 3: The children will perform a dance story created by the teacher about the fall leaves.

Unit assessment: The checklist used in lesson 2—assess the personal dances that include three still shapes and three locomotor movements.

Lesson 1 Outline

Introduction and warm-up: The teacher shows leaf shapes gathered from school property and the book *Full of Fall* (Sayre 2017).

For the warm-up, the students walk around the space; on a signal, the students freeze in various shapes designated by the teacher.

Development: The students explore making their bodies into the shapes of the leaves while using levels and range.

The students explore rocking and turning movements in various directions and ranges using their leaf shapes to represent the leaves swaying in the wind while attached to the tree.

The students explore locomotor movements using various pathways to express the leaves blowing in the space.

Culminating activity: The students dance a sequence of movements designed by the teacher—such as balance in leaf shape 1, leaf shape 2, and leaf shape 3—then slowly rock forward and backward to express the

leaf blowing in the wind. Then they run on a curvy pathway to show the leaf flying around the yard and freeze in leaf shape 1 to end the dance.

Closure: The students discuss their favorite leaf shapes and locomotor movements.

Lesson 2 Outline

Introduction and warm-up: The students are asked to relate the movements in the previous lessons. "What do you remember we danced about in lesson 1?"

For the warm-up, the students walk around the space; on the teacher's signal to freeze, the students freeze on a leaf shape they created in lesson 1. This is repeated several times.

Development: Each student chooses three leaf shapes and practices making the three shapes. The teacher adds counts to hold the shapes still. The students practice. The teacher adds a count number to change from one shape to the next. The students practice.

The teacher reviews the locomotor movements and pathways used in lesson 1, and the students practice. The teacher sets a specific number of steps for each locomotor movement.

The students choose three locomotor movements and choose the order and practice.

The students create a dance that uses the three still shapes followed by the three locomotor movements.

The teacher conducts the assessment while the students practice their dances.

Culminating activity: In pairs, the students show their dance to their partners.

Closure: The teacher asks half of the class to demonstrate their dance while the other half observes, and then the groups switch roles. The teacher can complete the assessment if needed.

Lesson 3 Outline

Introduction: The teacher tells the students they will collaborate to create a story about the falling leaves.

In the warm-up, the students repeat the warm-up used in lesson 2. The teacher adds counts to the still shapes and includes the rocking movement.

Development: The teacher and students create a story about the falling leaves. Key words in the dance are recorded on a flip chart. The students and the teacher create movements for each key word and form a dance.

Culminating activity: The teacher tells the story while the students dance. Each time, a different piece of music is used. One piece of music is slow and soft, and another is fast and energetic.

Closure: The teacher asks the students how it felt to dance to different types of music.

INTERDISCIPLINARY CONNECTIONS

Many terms are used to describe an integrated learning experience, such as *interdisciplinary, connected, correlated, cross-curricular, transdisciplinary,* or *multidisciplinary*. These terms refer to a progressive view of education in which students are the center of learning, developing 21st-century skills through teaching that link inquiry and multiple subjects together (Drake and Reid 2020). Interdisciplinary learning acknowledges the integrity and uniqueness of each subject area yet recognizes the interrelationships of one subject to another. Separating disciplines allows systematic attention to mastery of content and is necessary for knowledge acquisition, but students also need to see the interconnectedness of problems, issues, and knowledge (Kaittani, Kouli, Derri, and Kioumourtzoglou 2017). These authors, in their article on interdisciplinary teaching in physical education, say, "It helps the learners to integrate school, lesson and life with one another. Furthermore, it helps learners to realize their own thinking and learning style, enabling them to think and learn effectively" (p. 96). Learning experiences are less fragmented and foster multiple perspectives on a theme or topic. Knowledge and skills in one subject area are viewed as applicable to learning in another subject area and promote creative and divergent thinking.

Dance integrates easily with other content areas. It offers students who are kinesthetic learners (Gardner 2011) the opportunity to use movement as a means of understanding and communicating their life experiences by using their own unique perspectives. For all students, the body and its movements are a means of attaining and expressing knowledge and skills. As Maloney Leaf and Ngo (2017) found in their study, youth learn confidence, commitment, and a sense of purpose in addition to the craft of dance. Educators who believe that dance is an essential mode of learning not only address the goals of a dance education program but also provide students with the knowledge and skills applicable to all aspects of their lives.

Although dance has a discrete body of knowledge, the topics students dance about are frequently related to other subject areas. In a dance about spring flowers, for example, information about how flowers grow is essential when creating a dance that interprets the growing process. Cultural dances represent aspects of how people live, what they value, their traditions, histories, and beliefs. These are also concepts taught in the social studies curriculum. Dance is embedded in cultures for a variety of reasons, and thus integrating dance and social studies becomes a viable teaching strategy for each discipline. In many classrooms, the teacher selects a common theme such as community, change, patterns, conflict and resolution, or respect. The theme is explored through various subject areas, creating learning from multiple perspectives. In this thematic approach, dance plays a role in adding a kinesthetic, creative, and aesthetic dimension to learning. Students can express their understanding of a particular theme through learning or creating dances that represent various aspects of the theme (see figure 3.4).

Many of the learning experiences in chapters 8, 9, and 10 are applicable for integration. Suggestions for interdisciplinary connections are included at the end of each learning experience. For additional lessons that integrate dance with other subject areas, we encourage you to check the suggested readings section of this book to review the work of Ostersmith and Jeffs (2023); Benzwie (2011, 2002, 2000, 1987); Brehm and McNett (2015); Cone (2000); Cone, Werner, and Cone (2009); Donnelly (2002); Gilbert (2002); Kaufmann and Dehline (2014); Newman and Feinberg (2015); Overby, Post, and Newman (2005); Rovegno and Bandhauer (2017); and Stinson (1988). These educators

Chapter 3 Designing a Dance Program 53

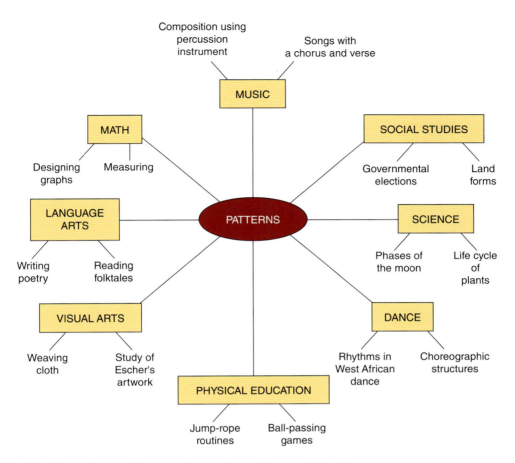

Figure 3.4 Students learn about patterns in various subject areas.

offer many wonderful ideas for integration. Here are some other suggested strategies that can lead to developing opportunities for interdisciplinary connections:

- Visit the classrooms of your students to see what they are learning with other teachers.
- Talk with the classroom teacher, school librarian, music specialist, and art specialist, and find a way to connect what you are teaching in dance with what they are teaching in their classrooms.
- Ask teachers to place a note in your mailbox about upcoming units of study.
- Invite teachers into your class to see your program in action.
- Attend grade-level meetings or set up a monthly meeting to share ideas.
- Review curriculum guides for information about the content of various subject areas.

This information is helpful when planning to integrate concepts and skills from another subject with dance.

The process of integrating content from other subject areas requires an examination of the discrete skills and concepts of each subject area and, specifically, the content you are interested in for an interdisciplinary learning experience.

We suggest considering three models of interdisciplinary teaching that function on a continuum from simple to complex. These models are connected, shared, and partnership (Cone, Werner, and Cone 2009). The models clarify your intent and objectives and make the learning experience meaningful to the students as well as the teacher (see figure 3.5). In the connected model, the skills, topics, and concepts of the dance curriculum are the primary focus of the learning experience, and the content from another subject area is used to enhance, extend, or supplement the learning experience. For example, you are teaching European cultural dances, and you show the students a map to indicate where the countries are located and share pictures of people in traditional dress performing the dance as a means of connecting to social studies. The shared model integrates two or more subjects through presenting similar skills, topics, or concepts that are part of the content of the integrated subjects. In this model, the dance or physical education teacher would coordinate with other subject-area teachers to look for common areas that can be taught at the same time. A dance lesson might be shared with a math lesson on fractions. In dance, the students are learning about quarter, half, three-quarter, and full turns, and in the math class children are introduced to the concept of fractions. The third model, partnership, is an equal representation of two or more subject areas that are taught simultaneously. The line between the subject areas is completely blurred, and the learning activities fuse content seamlessly. For example, the dance, visual arts, and music teachers collaborate to teach a partnership unit focused on hip-hop culture. All three teachers teach the unit as a united team. They use their expertise in their respective subject areas to create common outcomes and assessments. During the experience, students learn and create music, dance, and visual arts and discuss other cultural artifacts associated with the topic. This model requires considerable planning and a willingness to view content from a new and different perspective.

As educators, we seek to make connections between what students experience in their lives and the content of dance. Teaching from an interdisciplinary perspective offers an opportunity to deliver knowledge and skills holistically to help students transfer what they learn in one subject area to another. Interdisciplinary learning experiences recognize and promote multiple ways of knowing a concept or a skill and enlarge our view about what we can experience in our world. Opportunities for exploration and expanded experiences can provide students the ability to stretch their imagination, grow creatively, and find new ways to generate ideas (Stauffer 2019). Teachers are responsible for providing learning

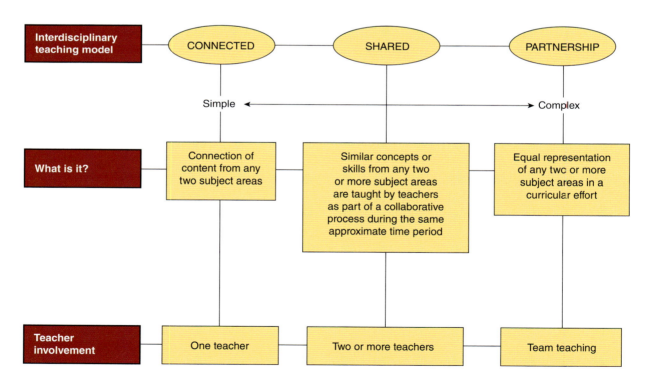

Figure 3.5 A comparison of three selected interdisciplinary teaching models.

Adapted by permission from T.P. Cone, P. Werner, S.L. Cone, *Interdisciplinary Elementary Physical Education,* 2nd ed. (Champaign, IL: Human Kinetics, 2009), 11.

SUMMARY

A successful dance learning experience is the result of planning an appropriate sequence of tasks that leads students to learn how movements can communicate an idea, a tradition, or a feeling. You will choose an idea for the learning experience that is relevant to the students, has meaning in their lives, and emphasizes the elements of dance.

Each learning experience can make a significant impact on the way students view dance. The learning experience must be well crafted so that students can develop an idea that is logical and well planned. This process begins with a verbal and physical introduction to the idea; it provides time to explore, learn, or create movements related to the idea; and it ends with composing or performing a completed dance. The culminating dance belongs to the students as they become fully engaged and find personal meaning in the movements.

Dance should play a vital role in the school's curriculum. It can be taught as a single learning experience that occurs frequently throughout the school year or as several units that focus on a particular theme. Both creative dance and dances created by others need to be included in the dance program each year at the primary, intermediate, and secondary levels. Providing students with the opportunity to create, learn, observe, perform, and respond to dances offers them a comprehensive program that includes all dimensions of dance as an art and movement form.

experiences that challenge conventional methods of learning and embarking on a journey with their students to explore the world through a myriad of paths.

Questions for Reflection

1. Where do you obtain your ideas for a unit of study? Are they prescribed in the curriculum, or do you design your own units within a framework of school outcomes?
2. What parts of a unit are easy to plan? Why? What challenges do you encounter when planning a dance unit? How do you resolve those challenges?
3. How would you prioritize the content you will teach for a yearlong plan in dance?
4. The components of a lesson described in this chapter are one way to organize and develop the content. What ideas can you add to the lesson design?
5. What do you see as the significance of teaching an interdisciplinary unit that integrates dance with another subject area? What other curricular areas can you integrate with dance?

Creating a Dance Education Setting

Teaching would be much easier if we could teach in what we consider an ideal environment. Then, our planning and implementation would easily fall into place. The fact is that your teaching situation most likely does not have everything you need and you adapt your ideas to make student learning meaningful, safe, and effective. We all share some similarities . . . and some definite differences! These differences include class size; frequency of class meetings; length of class period; facilities; equipment and materials; community; and a broad range of ages, abilities, and special needs within the same class of children (Bevans et al. 2010). In 1995, the National Dance Association, in collaboration with the Consortium of National Arts Education Associations, published the *Opportunity-to-Learn Standards for Dance Education*. These standards, updated through the National Dance Education Organization (Faber 2018), describe the physical and educational conditions necessary for enabling students to learn and achieve in dance. Topics addressed in the standards include curriculum, scheduling, materials, equipment, facilities, and staffing. As guidelines for developing a dance program, the standards present criteria for providing an environment that facilitates effective teaching and learning. This chapter presents strategies for planning and delivering dance content in various teaching situations to best meet the needs of your students and heighten their enjoyment of learning.

CLASS SIZE

Although the Society of Health and Physical Educators (2010) recommends that physical education or dance classes contain the same number of students as the classrooms (e.g., 25 per class), some schools and school districts schedule 2 or 3 classes at the same time. This means a physical education teacher or a dance teacher might teach 60 or more students during one session. Although this makes teaching a challenge, you can find ways to deliver the content to provide positive learning experiences. For example, the use of stations or learning centers is an efficient way to organize large groups. Each station can contain written instructions, pictures, or diagrams about how to perform a specific movement of a line dance or a traditional cultural dance. After visiting each station, the students can put all the steps together in the correct sequence. Another set of stations can focus on tasks that explore an element of dance. A station about the element of time might include the following tasks:

- Find a way to walk in a circle as quickly as you can.
- Next, walk in a circle as slowly as you can, or begin walking in a circle slowly and accelerate to running and then decelerate to walking.
- Find a partner and practice mirroring each other's movements.

57

Props such as scarves can enrich the dance learning experience.

Safety is an important consideration when many students are moving at one time. The students can keep themselves from bumping into others or into objects in the space by being aware of their personal space (the space immediately surrounding their bodies; see chapter 2). You must teach and reinforce this concept in each dance lesson. Another way to organize a large class is to place the students into lines. Keep the number in the line to a minimum to reduce waiting time and increase activity. Creating a balance between allowing for movement that is fully expressive and ensuring that all can move without injury requires careful planning and a willingness to make the appropriate modifications to the lesson.

Teaching a large group will be more effective when your voice is amplified so the students can hear the instructions. Also, it's a good idea for students to use a microphone when asking and answering questions. In this way, the entire class can hear without your needing to repeat the comments. To present instructions and information needed for the lesson, consider using posters, a whiteboard, a projector, or other electronic projection-type devices.

EQUIPMENT AND TEACHING MATERIALS

The addition of equipment and materials such as music, props, and costumes can enrich the dance learning experience. These items can be used as the stimulus for creating dances or as the accompaniment to a dance. Music and dance are frequently partnered in a learning experience. The voice, percussion instruments, and recorded music support the rhythm of the movement and set an environment for dancing. Props help illustrate the meaning of the movement, exaggerate the movement, or create a visual component that complements the dance. Most props are light, handheld objects that students manipulate while moving through space. Sometimes students dance around, over, or under larger objects; these larger objects help establish an environment for dancing. Costumes are also a wonderful addition to a dance. Students enjoy dressing up as a character, an animal, a tree, a monster, or any other idea from their imaginations. Every dance program should have access to a variety of teaching materials. Music, books, photos, posters, and computers or tablets for accessing websites, applications, and videos can be the catalysts for new dance ideas, present information on cultural and social dances, and support the dance concepts that are emphasized in the learning experience.

Music

Most dance experiences use music to accompany the movement, whether it's through the use of voice, percussion instruments, or live or recorded music. Music can stimulate ideas for dance, support the tempo and rhythm, provide a mood or atmosphere, or provide structure to a dance. The voice is one instrument that we always have with us. It can generate sounds and words that express the qualities of a movement. Even the way the voice is used when giving instructions can make a difference in how students respond. To illustrate this point, think of how these action words can be expressed differently to elicit a specific way to move. You can say "splat" in a loud, fast, and sharp voice; "press" in a loud and sustained voice; and "fall" in a voice that begins at a high pitch and ends at a low pitch.

Students can also use their voices to sing songs as accompaniments for dances. Consider using a familiar song, such as "Row, Row, Row Your Boat," as the accompaniment for a dance structured on a round (also known as a *canon*). Students can create movements for each section of the song and then, in small groups, sing and perform the movements to create a dance round. Another possibility is to make up a song that describes a movement sequence. For example, in a dance about planting a garden, you and the students sing, "Seed, seed, cover up with dirt, and jump, jump." On the words "seed, seed," the children pretend to place a seed in the ground. Next, on each syllable of the phrase "cover up with dirt," the students use their feet to stamp quickly while pretending to bury the seeds. A big jump on each "jump" word completes the phrase. This phrase is repeated several times with the students singing and moving simultaneously. You can also vocalize rhythms by making a variety of sounds with the voice. In a dance about a machine, for example, students can create sounds with their bodies or voices to accompany the machine's movements. Words, poems, and stories read out loud can all involve the voice as accompaniment.

Develop a collection of percussion instruments as a readily available resource to accompany dance. Most percussion instruments can be carried easily while teaching or dancing. When planning a dance experience, consider what movements could be supported by the strong, percussive beat of a drum; the light, sustained sound of a triangle; or the quick, vibratory sounds of the maracas (see the percussion instrument dance in chapter 8). Also, consider making instruments to create interesting and unusual sounds (see table 4.1). You don't have to be an accomplished musician to use instruments in dance. Take time to become familiar with the instruments, and explore ways to play them by hitting, rubbing, or shaking them with your hands. Ask the school's music teacher to help you

Table 4.1 Percussion Instruments

Traditional instruments	Nontraditional or found instruments
Drums of various sizes	Pot lids
Triangle	Spoons
Maracas	Glasses filled with water at different levels
Gong	Plastic garbage cans
Chimes	Plastic or metal cans
Rain stick	Round oatmeal boxes
Bells	Wooden spoons
Sticks	Metal or plastic garbage can lids
Woodblock	Rocks scraped or tapped together
Guiro	Plastic buckets
Cymbals	Containers filled with beans
Xylophone	Paper bags

learn to play a few basic rhythms. Investigate the possibility of borrowing instruments, or look for them in music stores, toy stores, museum shops, yard sales, and school catalogs.

Finding the appropriate recorded music for a dance experience is always a challenge. There is such a variety of music that it is hard to know where to begin to look. One option is to purchase music that is prepackaged with ideas for dance lessons. These types of recordings can be a way to begin to develop a personal library of music. Another option is to set some time aside to listen to music, and then record selections that could be used for dance. Label the selections with ideas for future use, and then try the music with the students. Include in your collection music that

- has a definite even beat;
- offers varying tempos for slow and sustained as well as fast and percussive movements;
- has various rhythms for skipping, running, or jumping;
- produces various moods, such as feeling peaceful, anxious, or powerful;
- evokes images and feelings (e.g., sounds like music for strange creatures landing on the earth);
- represents other cultures; and
- denotes a specific time period.

Be sure to include a variety of music that represents a wide range of styles and cultures. Students may prefer music that is popular and familiar to them; however, use the dance experience to present many types of music to broaden the students' exposure to and knowledge of music. Your list can include classical, jazz, pop, rap, reggae, hip-hop, new age, rock, gospel, opera, a variety of vocal music, movie soundtracks, sounds of nature, children's songs, and traditional and contemporary music from various countries and cultures. Different types of dances can be paired with different types of music. African music can be used in a dance about a rainstorm, for example, or ragtime music can be used to accompany a dance about baseball. Traditional cultural dances usually require a specific piece of music as accompaniment and can help make the experience more authentic. The music teacher can be a valuable resource for selecting music and can offer assistance with identifying rhythms and musical structures.

Once you have chosen your music, be sure to become thoroughly familiar with the selection. Play the music in the space where the dance experience will occur so you can ensure the volume is appropriate and the audio equipment functions properly. Always acknowledge the composer, the name of the music piece, and the performer when introducing music into the dance session.

Having the proper audio equipment can make a significant difference in the quality of music used in the learning experience. Purchasing state-of-the-art equipment is not always possible; however, using a portable Bluetooth speaker and playing music from your phone is an easy, affordable option. When you have the opportunity to purchase new equipment, consider the following wish list:

- A stereo system with options such as a USB connection, a remote control, a CD player, or Bluetooth capability and speakers that will project into the space. The remote control or Bluetooth functionality enables you to position yourself easily for effective teaching.
- A portable or battery-powered stereo system with similar features as a stationary system if you plan to teach outdoors or in multiple spaces throughout the day.
- A portable microphone and speaker. A wireless lavalier microphone can allow you to teach in any space and move with the students. You also have the ability to speak over the music to provide instructions.
- An MP3 player with playlists created using a music app.
- Cords for all MP3 or Bluetooth devices.
- Storage for all audio equipment and MP3 players. Proper storage will eliminate damage.

Props

Dance learning experiences frequently require equipment or handheld props to accompany the dance. Students may manipulate streamers, hoops, elastic strips, balloons, wands, ropes, and pieces of material or scarves as they dance. Or they may use equipment such as chairs, mats, cones, or tables to move around, over, under, on, or between. Ideally and when appropriate, each student should have their own prop. When there aren't enough of the same type of prop available for each student, they can share or trade props. For example, in a lesson on making different shapes, one group uses an elastic rope, the next group uses wands, and another group makes shapes with long pieces of yarn. When choosing equipment or props, consider each student's developmental abilities to handle the equipment or prop safely. Can the student move the prop easily? If the prop falls out of the student's hand, is there a potential for injury? Do students have adequate space in which to move with the prop?

Props are used to initiate, extend, or accompany movement. Cultural dances may use scarves, sticks, ropes, flowers, or baskets as part of the movements or to express a character or cultural artifact. In a learning experience focused on creating straight and curved lines, students can lay ropes on the floor in straight and curved lines and then match their bodies to the rope shapes. Streamers or ribbons held in the hand can be imaginary brushes with which to paint letters in the air, and scarves can be flames, leaves, or flower petals (see figure 4.1). Partners and small groups can share a prop and discover ways to move together. Students can hold hoops as imaginary doorways into outer space or to connect students as rays of the sun. Curtains or long pieces of material are easy for a small group of students to use as a floating cloud, a swirling river, or the wind of a tornado. Most schools have a playground parachute that can be turned into a giant monster when a group holds one side of the parachute and runs in the space with the parachute floating in the air. There is no end to the ways props can be part of a dance experience. When you ask the question, "What else could it be?" about any prop, students will enthusiastically offer many new ideas.

You can also use props to illustrate a concept or element of dance. Students often need a concrete object to help them visualize the words and concepts presented in the learning experience. For example, the concept of roundness can be illustrated by showing a ball or a globe, the concept of increasing and decreasing size is best illustrated by inflating and deflating a balloon, and the feeling of strong and light force can

Figure 4.1 Children dancing with streamers to express the movements of a flame.

become vivid when you wring a towel or float a piece of tissue paper. Using props to create an environment for a dance magically transforms the space and stimulates ideas for creating movements. Imagine a room filled with red and orange streamers scattered on the floor. The students immediately pretend they are dancing on the sun as they run and leap over the streamers. You can also use hoops to move in and out of as if they were different worlds, such as the fast world, the shaking world, or the frozen-shape world. Ropes tied to volleyball poles can form a web for a spider dance, chairs arranged in lines could depict a dance about traveling on a train or a bus, and taped lines on the floor can be used for pathways. An environment created by props encourages students to use their imagination and helps make an abstract idea real. Here are some additional ideas for creative props:

- Pom-poms (cover a paper-towel tube with contact paper, cut 8-inch [20 cm] strips of plastic, and staple 8 to 10 strips together on one end of the tube)
- Large sheets of plastic cut into various shapes (plastic tablecloths work well)
- Sheer curtains, sheets, and other pieces of material
- Stuffed animals or dolls
- Tissues or paper napkins

- Juggling scarves
- Stretchable plastic bands or pieces of elastic
- Long pieces of ribbon
- Beanbags
- Deck rings (streamers can be attached)
- Paper bags
- Rolls of toilet paper
- Beach balls
- Umbrellas
- Lummi sticks (7- to 12-inch wood sticks) and wands

Costumes

Students, especially young children, welcome the opportunity to create and wear costumes while dancing. Costumes can be as simple as a scarf tied around a wrist, a piece of material draped over a shoulder, or streamers taped to a shirt. Adding a costume to a dance can help define a character, a mood, a time period, a culture, or an animal. Aluminum foil can be wrapped around the arms or molded into a headpiece as a costume in a dance about lightning bolts. Monster costumes can be made of large plastic garbage bags with a hole cut out of the bottom for the head and the sides cut into long strips. When designing costumes, consider ease of movement and safety. Make sure the costume is fastened securely and that headpieces allow the students to see and breathe.

FACILITIES

Although some teachers have adequate indoor and outdoor space, others are less fortunate. In fact, some teachers have no indoor space whatsoever. In some schools, dance may be taught in the children's classroom, outside on the blacktop, in the lunchroom, on a stage, in the foyer of the school, or on an outside grassy area. Following are some suggestions for how the content in this book can be adapted for limited indoor or outdoor space.

You can teach dance learning experiences both outdoors and indoors. Teaching dance outdoors can be inspiring, especially when using the outdoor environment as a theme for the learning experience (see figure 4.2). The challenge is to find a way to accompany the dance with music. We suggest using a battery-operated, portable stereo system or running a long extension cord outdoors. Percussion instruments work well outdoors because they are portable and can be handheld; however, some of the sounds may not carry well in a large, open space. Before you begin to teach, test your voice and musical accompaniment in the outdoor space to determine what adjustments may be needed. To keep students focused and safe in an outdoor area, you need to set spatial boundaries for the dance. Cones or ropes laid on the ground are useful as markers to define the space. Be sure the outdoor space is free from objects that children can slip on, such as loose gravel, glass, or oily spots.

Figure 4.2 After observing the wind blowing the leaves, children create strong, stretched movements to express the feeling of being blown around by the wind.

Most gymnasiums are well suited for indoor dance. However, a classroom or a hallway is sometimes the assigned space for the dance session. These situations are not ideal. Define the boundaries of the space clearly, and check for objects that may cause injury. Not all floor surfaces are suitable for dancing, and adaptations will be necessary. Excessive jumping on concrete, turning on a carpet, or moving on a waxed tile floor can lead to injury for you and the students. You are always responsible for the safe participation of your students. Be aware of the limitations of the environment, and plan lessons that are meaningful, appropriate for the available space, and safe for active movement.

Whether teaching inside or outside, use a wall or portable easel to display dance concepts, photos, students' work, articles, or drawings. A whiteboard in the space will allow you to display the lesson plan, list vocabulary words, or draw pathways and diagrams of formations. Storage space is essential for audio and video equipment, instruments, props, and other instructional materials. Also, students learn best when the facilities have good lighting, ventilation, and access to drinking fountains and bathrooms.

CLASS FREQUENCY AND LENGTH

Schools differ in the number of days per week that the students attend physical education or dance classes and the length of those classes. As one might expect, students who have physical education or dance every day for 30 minutes will learn more content and enjoy more of the physical benefits of regular exercise than students with less contact time. Realistically, the goals that can be achieved in the dance program are determined by the total amount of time students participate in dance during the school year. When planning, keep in mind school vacations, class trips, assembly programs, and special events that affect the regular school schedule. One approach is to obtain an annual school schedule and note how many sessions are available and the time frame for each marking period. Then plan units that fit into the available time.

Dance, as part of the physical education curriculum, can be presented in several units of concentrated experiences or in single class sessions several times throughout the school year. Sometimes, a single learning experience can be completed in a 30-minute session; at other times, it may be necessary to continue in additional sessions. Students may need more time to learn and practice a dance or to complete the process of creating a dance. When a learning experience is continued over several sessions, students will need time to review what happened in the previous session. This connection between sessions is important for a meaningful experience to occur. Consider that a high-quality experience may be more important than staying on a set schedule. Having students feel a sense of accomplishment in the learning experience will lead to increased understanding of the value of the dance experience. This understanding builds positive attitudes toward dance in the physical education and dance curriculums.

COMMUNITY CHARACTERISTICS

The characteristics of the community in which you teach are important elements to consider when planning and delivering a dance program. A community includes not only the city or town but also the school community. Every town, city, and regional area has its own culture, traditions, history, and ways in which the community functions. The values and beliefs of a community have a direct impact on the people who grow up in that community.

As a teacher, you should know the community in which you teach. Learn about how and what the community celebrates, where your students live, what types of recreational activities are available, what religious institutions are located in the community, and what languages are spoken. Become familiar with what it is like to live in the area. As a teacher, you must be sensitive to the communities in which you work, especially if the customs and traditions of a community are not part of your background. Sensitivity implies understanding the socioeconomic and ethnic composition of the community as well as what the community values in education. Each community has a vision for its students, and this vision is reflected in the schools' goals. You need to be aware of these goals and ensure that your dance program is in alignment.

As a means of expression and communication, dance helps students understand the unique composition of their community and how it relates to other communities around the world. A specific cultural population in the community may request that students have the opportunity to learn dances from their cultural heritage (see figure 4.3). Reach out to the community as a resource if you are not sure how to teach these dances. Parents are usually willing to share their cultural customs and dances with the class. Religious values of the community are another consideration. Dancing and specific topics for dance that focus on celebration are not part of every religion. You may need to eliminate or change certain dances so students do not feel they must compromise their own beliefs in class. Look to parents and other community members as a resource for cultural and social information that will help you understand what is appropriate, and make your dance experiences meaningful to the students.

SCHOOL POLICIES

Every school has policies and procedures for dealing with a variety of situations. This means the school has planned how to address unexpected situations or has carefully anticipated what emergencies could occur and planned accordingly. As a responsible teacher, you must know the school policies and protocols and be prepared to act when necessary. This information may be available in a school handbook or provided by the administration. All schools have requirements to practice fire drills, school lockdowns, and evacuations. Review the procedures and discuss and practice with your students the appropriate behaviors for complying with an emergency event. There are three parts of a school's emergency plan that you should know (Tanis and Hebel 2016). During the crisis, you should first know how to make contact when help is needed, how to address a student's injury, and who should be involved in decision-making. The second part occurs after the crisis and is related to completing accurate reports; gathering evidence of the event or injury; and communicating with parents, administrators, and school staff. In the third part, you evaluate the incident and assess whether procedures were followed and make recommendations for changes in policy and procedures if needed.

Have a plan for students who are injured in your class. The initial response to an injury requires a careful but speedy assessment followed by safe and appropriate action to help the student. Seeking the advice of the school nurse about procedures for dealing with injuries before someone gets hurt is essential. To ensure a safe learning environment, the nurse should also inform you about students with life-threatening allergies or other medical conditions, such as diabetes, asthma, or epilepsy.

PROGRAM ADVOCACY

You may already be teaching in a school where dance is considered an integral part of the curriculum, or you may be asked to initiate a dance program. Both situations call on you to use your knowledge about dance to communicate the benefits of offering a dance component to the physical education or arts education curriculum. Your efforts to maintain or start a dance program require you to become an advocate for dance. Serving as an advocate means you must become the voice of support for dance in the school curriculum.

Advocacy is a planned approach to making your views count in the decision-making process. It is actively supporting a cause or idea while using purposeful communication to influence

Figure 4.3 Folk dances can offer students the opportunity to learn about their own or others' cultural heritages.

decisions and the opinions of people or organizations (Buckley 2018). You must always be ready to clearly and concisely express the importance of dance in a child's education. Dance can be a vulnerable area of the curriculum because in many schools it is not considered part of the core curriculum and is often subject to budget cuts; thus, opportunities for children to participate in dance experiences are often minimal. Here are some tips to help you in your advocacy role. To be an effective advocate you need to be

- well informed about the benefits of dance for children;
- willing to solve problems and collaborate with others;
- open to listening to other perspectives;
- prepared when speaking to an individual or a group;
- sincere, optimistic, and passionate about your goals; and
- ready to seize opportunities to discuss dance with your colleagues, school administrators, and parents.

Advocacy in dance can be proactive or reactive. In the proactive situation, advocacy efforts are ongoing throughout the school year. Following are ideas for ongoing advocacy efforts:

- Submit an article, written by you or your students, about the dance program to the school newspaper or the local newspaper, or post on social media.
- Contact a newspaper photographer or reporter to cover a dance class or performance featuring your students.
- Collaborate with another teacher in the school to integrate dance with another subject area.
- Publicize dance events in the weekly or monthly school calendar.
- Invite parents or your administrator to observe a dance class.
- Prepare a fact sheet about the dance program for distribution to parents on back-to-school night.
- Present an in-service workshop on dance education to faculty members in your school or district.

- Send letters of invitation, with complimentary tickets, to members of the board of education, school administrators, and community leaders for the school's dance performances.
- Organize a special event, such as a family dance night, to promote dance as a social activity.
- Invite community members or parents with expertise in a specific dance form to share their knowledge and skills with your students.
- Attend a conference, workshop, or convention on dance education to keep updated on current issues, research, and practices.
- Inform parents, administrators, and colleagues of your program goals, and include the skills and knowledge that students gain as a result of participating in the dance program.
- Emphasize to your students what they are learning. Clearly articulate your goals, clarify your assessment strategies, and keep your students actively involved in learning during the class.
- Create a bulletin board to highlight what students are learning in the dance class; include pictures, students' drawings, or essays.

If you find yourself in a reactive situation, one in which the dance program might be reduced or eliminated, you will want to develop a plan of action. Begin planning by asking yourself the following questions:

- What do I see as the outcome? What do I want to occur?
- Why should this issue be addressed?
- What message about dance do I want to communicate?
- Who is the target audience or whom do I need to influence?
- What strategies can I use to reach my target audience?
- Who can help me deliver the message?

The best way to advocate is to deliver a solid program founded on standards and goals. A good program will be relevant to the students, have clear objectives, present information in multiple ways, and contain multiple forms of assessment. Students can be very influential in what they say to their teachers, the school administrator, and their parents about their dance learning experiences. Consider their voices as a means of advocating for the dance program. When they experience a sense of accomplishment and success, they will know how meaningful dance can be to their lives and be willing to share their excitement with others.

SUMMARY

Numerous factors influence the teaching and learning environment. You may find yourself teaching a small group of children on a carpeted floor in the classroom or teaching 50 children in one part of a large gymnasium while another class meets in a different section of the gym. The best strategy for making the most of a less-than-ideal situation is to focus on your goals for the learning experience and the children you are teaching. The facilities, equipment, schedule, and class size certainly influence your planning and implementation; however, teaching is a learning experience, and the challenges you face open new possibilities for a creative teaching opportunity. There are a variety of ways to teach dance regardless of the environment. Your responsibility is to be realistic in what you can achieve, considering the educational parameters of your environment, and to continually seek effective teaching methods. Students and colleagues can be valuable resources for ideas to help you deliver your program. Ask them to help you find alternative solutions. This collaborative effort can lead to increased support for dance, especially when students are asked to contribute their ideas. Finally, dance is an invaluable learning experience for children. As a teacher of dance, you are responsible for advocating for your program and ensuring that children have the opportunity to discover the relevance of dance in their lives.

Questions for Reflection

1. Think about a time when you needed to make a last-minute change in your teaching facility or schedule. How did you handle it? What worked best? What could you have done differently?
2. How would your teaching strategies change according to the size of the class?
3. What do you see as a benefit of using props or equipment in a dance lesson?
4. Think about different spaces in which you might teach dance. How would you adapt a lesson to work in several different spaces?
5. What do you know about the community in which you teach? How is the community where you live similar and different?
6. The safety of children is of utmost importance in teaching. Are you familiar with the procedures to follow in case of an emergency such as fire, bomb threat, injury, or breach of security? What are your plans?
7. What do you think your students would tell their parents about their dance learning experiences? What would you like your students to say?
8. Why is it important to advocate for dance in your school? Have you considered the various people you would need to contact? What are some steps you might take to be an effective advocate for dance in education?

CHAPTER 5

Making Teaching Effective

Effective teaching begins with planning a learning experience based on knowledge of students' growth and development, the ways in which students learn, the content in the dance program, and lesson development and implementation. The goal is to provide a meaningful learning experience that integrates the needs of students with the content of the dance program. This chapter offers strategies for making the dance experience positive for both the student and you as the teacher.

HELPING ALL STUDENTS LEARN

Every student is unique. They all learn differently, which requires you to adapt content and pedagogy to help all people be successful learners. Krasnoff (2016) notes, "Students in the United States and its territories come from a large and increasing number of racially, ethnically, culturally, and linguistically diverse families" (p. 1). Although you should welcome this diversity in learning, it poses a challenge for you as a teacher. Dance and physical education classes include students with a range of abilities; for some, movement is one of the best ways for them to express ideas and feelings. These learners are familiar with using movement as a means of communicating and they respond eagerly to the sounds and rhythms of music. Not all students, however, respond to movement as comfortably or as easily. Meeting students' educational needs begins with learning about their physical, cognitive, emotional, and social characteristics. This knowledge helps you differentiate instruction through providing variations in content, teaching style, and outcomes to meet the needs of each individual (Tomlinson 2014). Observe students in their classes and talk with their teachers to identify their strengths and learning styles as well as what instructional strategies seem to be the most effective. Also, talk with the students to learn about their interests and needs. How do they feel about dancing, what are their previous experiences with dance, and what kind of dance would they enjoy? Most important, be flexible and willing to adapt your learning experiences to ensure success for all students in the class (see figure 5.1). The Opportunity-to-Learn Standards for Dance from the National Dance Education Organization (2018) notes, "Dance, in particular, is an art form that addresses physical health and well-being in an enjoyable, aesthetic, cognitively challenging and non-competitive environment. All students can achieve self-confidence through self-expression in dance" (p. 2). Teaching students with a broad range of abilities and learning styles presents challenges that can result in gaining new insights about teaching dance.

In addition to ability level, teachers need to be aware of students' cultural, ethnic, linguistic, and social backgrounds. The whole-child approach requires that you honor cultural traditions and understand that students' lives may be different from yours. The way students learn, behave, and feel about learning is culturally influenced

Figure 5.1 Students bring their own background of movement experience and creative potential to the dance learning experience. As the teacher, you offer information about the elements of movement and the process of learning about dance.

by their families' values and experiences. One strategy is to let parents and guardians know that you want to maintain frequent communication about the students' progress. In this way, parents hear the good news about achievement as well as share concerns if they arise. Invite family members to your class to observe and share their dances, music, and cultural heritage. When students have the opportunity to share family celebrations and events, they become empowered and view their ideas as equally valuable to others' ideas. Most important is that you have established a learning environment that is respectful and safe for everyone. Set high expectations for all learners. Believe that all students can learn, be leaders, help others, take responsibility, and have a perspective that needs to be acknowledged. McCarthy-Brown (2017) relates the importance of culturally relevant dance education as follows: "In instances where students are unable to see themselves in the curriculum content, they often feel as if they do not belong and disengage from their learning. There must be an awareness that what is ordinary for the instructor may be out of the ordinary for students. From that place of understanding, instructors can find ways to build bridges to their course objectives" (p. 23). There is no one-size-fits-all approach to teaching. If you view each lesson as a learning moment for you and your students, they will see how your acceptance of other ways of living—and specifically dancing—is an essential concept to learn. Notice the types of pictures, videos, music, and books you use to support teaching dance. Teach dances from cultures around the world, use music from many cultures in creative dance lessons, and use music from different time periods. Are multiple gender identities and cultures represented? Can students relate to your teaching materials as well as learn new perspectives? Use culturally diverse and relevant teaching materials and pedagogical approaches, and use feedback that is culturally responsive to your students.

You may have students who are not able to physically participate in class because of a temporary medical condition or injury, or they might not be prepared for class. Some activities and lessons can be adapted for these situations, as we discuss in more detail in chapter 7 on including all children in dance. However, there are times when a student may be physically unable to participate in a lesson even with modifications. These students still need to be engaged in learning the content in a way that is appropriate. If the student's physical participation is highly restricted or unable to be physically modified, you can plan in each lesson an activity that addresses cognitive and affective learning. Students can listen to your instructions, observe their peers' dances, or contribute ideas to a group dance. You can develop observation forms that enable students to focus on the movements and formations or how the elements of dance are used. Students can be peer assessors for parts of the lesson: They can list dance terms they hear used in the class and share their lists with other students at the end of the lesson. They can draw or make pipe-cleaner shapes they see their peers using or draw shapes they would use if they were physically participating. Sometimes students who are not dancing can help with the music player or they can play a percussion instrument for accompaniment. The most important thing is that the students learn. In this way, they will feel included and able to engage with the content.

USING VARIOUS TEACHING STYLES AND STRATEGIES

Skillful educators know and use a variety of teaching styles that may be different from the way they personally learn. You must see learning from your students' perspectives and develop content that is developmentally appropriate and meaningful to the students. You should also understand that there are common strategies that can be applied that are appropriate for many students (Ball and Forzani 2011). Choosing the best teaching style to present a dance movement or complete a dance depends on what you want to accomplish in the lesson. A teaching style that is appropriate for presenting a social dance or a cultural dance that has established movements and formations may be different from a creative dance lesson where exploration and spontaneous movement are involved. It may be appropriate to use several teaching styles within a single learning experience to address the task and students' individual learning styles.

One common teaching style that is effective for teaching social, cultural, or aerobic dance or doing a set warm-up is the command style. In this style, you lead all the movements and the students follow, reproducing the movement. You decide on the movements, how they are performed, the sequence, and the number of repetitions. This style is useful when teaching movements in which everyone is dancing the same step at the same time. A natural follow-up to command-style teaching is practice style (Mosston and Ashworth 2008). After you demonstrate the movements or the complete dance, you ask the students to practice the movements or the complete dance while you circulate among the students to offer corrective or affirmative comments.

You can use a problem-solving teaching style when asking the students to create or rearrange dance movements. Graham, Elliott, and Palmer (2016) describe this style as divergent problem-solving, in which there are many ways to solve the problem. This style is important for the instruction of creative dance because of its emphasis on problem-solving and engagement in creative and higher-level thinking skills (Kassing and Jay-Kirschenbaum 2021). Students make decisions about how to move within the limits of the task. Exploration and improvisation are frequently associated with problem-solving. Exploration is a thoughtful response to a task in which the student finds a variety of answers. In the task "Find various ways to move on your hands and feet," for example, students think about a way to accomplish the task, try out the movement, then think of another way, try that idea, and continue to think about and perform different answers to the task. Improvisation is a spontaneous response to a task, evoking an immediate physical action. In the task "Move in a way that expresses the word *splatter*," the students immediately respond by moving their bodies with the first idea that comes to mind.

When using the problem-solving teaching style, be open to students' responses. Even if you can anticipate some of the responses, you may be surprised when the students try out something new and unexpected. You can elicit a variety of responses from students by repeatedly asking them to find another way to accomplish the movement task. When you first present the task, students will move in ways that are familiar to them, but as you continue to ask for different responses, they will begin to explore and create new alternatives. This is when creative thinking occurs.

Presenting a task with a specific solution and allowing the students to discover the solution for themselves is called convergent problem-solving (Graham, Elliott, and Palmer 2016) or guided discovery (Mosston and Ashworth 2008). This teaching style leads the students to a specific solution through a sequence of planned questions. You know the solution beforehand and choose this method to provide students with a more in-depth understanding of how to arrive at the solution. For example, the following sequence of questions leads students to discover how to achieve a balanced position with another person when exercising: "Stand facing your partner with your toes touching, and grip each other's hands at the wrists. Now, slowly begin to lean away from each other until your arms are straight. Can you both stay balanced on your feet? How are you using your energy in the pull? Repeat the same balance with one partner pulling more than the other. What happened? When you felt yourself falling off balance, how did you change the energy of the pull to maintain a balanced position? You are now experiencing counter-tension. What do you think makes it work?"

When students understand the concept and principles of using counter-tension, switch to a problem-solving task that requires them to demonstrate their understanding through application. For example, direct the class as follows: "Find another way to balance with your partner using counter-tension. What other body parts can you pull with instead of your hands? Create a counter-tension balance that uses four people." Students can share their solutions to the problem with others and use the imitation teaching style themselves to present their solutions to other groups for duplication.

The following additional teaching strategies serve as a menu from which you can choose a variety of approaches to present dance. You can apply the strategies to small- and large-group teaching, to teacher- or student-led presentations, or when integrating technology.

- *Modeling.* You demonstrate the dance movement. Students observe and reproduce the movement. Modeling is also used in demonstrating a process or step-by-step plan for creating a dance. The students observe and follow the process when creating their own dances. This process is frequently supported with printed instructions.

- *Part-to-whole add-on.* You can teach the dance movements one at a time and then combine them into the correct sequence. You demonstrate the first movement, and then the students observe and practice along with you or on their own. Then, you demonstrate the second movement and the students practice it. Next, the students combine the first and second movement and practice. Then you demonstrate the third movement, and the students practice it and then add it to the first two movements. This procedure continues until you have taught the movements of the entire dance.

- *Show all first.* You demonstrate the entire dance before teaching the individual movements. In this way, students see the end result and understand how the individual movements they will learn fit into the dance. After demonstrating the entire dance, you teach each movement using the part-to-whole add-on strategy.

- *Big screen.* You project a video of a dance onto a wall or screen so that all students can see the dance. Students follow and perform the dance movements along with the performers in the video.

- *Observe and join in.* You or a student demonstrates the movements or a complete dance and continues to repeat the movements or dance several times. When the observing students think they are ready to try some or all of the dance movements, they join in and practice the dance along with you or a student demonstrator. This strategy allows students to work at their own pace for learning a dance. This strategy is often used when students are at a social event and want to join in a dance they see others doing.

- *Peer teaching.* This strategy introduced by Mosston and Ashworth (2008) is also known as reciprocal teaching. Students are organized into partners or small groups. They collaborate to help each other review and practice the movements or dance that were presented in class.

- *Photograph sequence.* A photograph of each movement is placed on the wall in the correct sequence. Students view the photographs and reproduce the movements. The photos can be used as a visual reference to help students remember the dance sequence. A printed description can be added under each photograph to further clarify how the movement is performed.

- *Stations.* Stations are set up in the space, which include one dance movement or one complete dance. Each station has a poster with printed instructions, a video, a photograph, a diagram, and the accompanying music when appropriate. Students organized into small groups spend a few minutes at the station learning and practicing the movement or the dance and then rotate to a new station. The rotation continues until the students learn all the dance movements or the selected dances. Then all the students join together to practice the dance or dances in the correct sequence. One idea for a social dance unit is to design stations that focus on a dance from another decade. Students rotate to the stations and learn dances or steps from four or five decades.

- *Student leaders.* A small group of students learn the movements or the complete dance before it is presented to the class. During the class session, these student leaders teach the dance to their classmates. When teaching a line dance that faces the four walls, leaders can be located around the perimeter of the room so that when the dancers turn to face a different wall, they have a leader to follow.

- *Student video performance.* A small group of students learn the movements or the complete dance before it is presented in class and record themselves performing the dance. You show the video during the lesson as an instructional tool using the big screen or stations strategy.

- *Symbols sequence.* A symbol is created for each movement and organized in the correct sequence. The symbols can be used as a visual reference to help students remember the dance sequence. This may look like a music score or a dance notation.

- *Recorded video as teacher.* Have students watch the complete dance or part of the dance and then stop the video. Ask the students to remember what they observed and then reproduce the movements. Next, show the video again and ask students to observe and see if they are missing movements. Students observe and practice the dance again. This strategy is appropriate for individuals or small groups. When small groups observe the dance, each group member can contribute what they remembered; as a result, the groups can collectively put the dance sequence together.

- *Background information using video.* You can use video to present historical and cultural information for cultural and social dances. Students learn about the history, customs, geographic location, political scene, or local traditions and rituals. This information is critical to teaching cultural dances and social dances that represent a culture or historical period.

- *Line switch.* When students are learning a dance where they are organized in multiple lines facing in the same direction, some students will be in the back of the space and some will be in the front. You can switch the lines to allow all students to dance in the front line and have a better view of you.

- *Direction readers.* Provide students with the printed instructions for performing a dance. In partners or small groups, they take turns reading instructions and collaborate to interpret the instructions, then practice and perform the dance.

- *Contextual teaching.* When you present a dance to the students, include historical, social, or cultural information that supports the dance steps, formation, rhythms, and meanings of the movements. The information can include books, articles, online information, pictures, videos, personal stories, press releases, artifacts, props, clothing, maps, or music.

- *Jigsaw.* This is a cooperative teaching approach that uses small groups organized in two ways to learn movements and collaborate to create a dance. First you assign each group a letter identification, such as A, B, or C. In the letter group, each person is assigned a number beginning with 1, then 2, and so on, until everyone has a number. Each letter group creates or is assigned a specific movement to learn and practice. This can be a step from a cultural or social dance or a movement they generate for a creative dance. Next, all the students with the number 1 form a new number group named number group 1. This procedure continues until all the letter groups have been reformed into number groups 1, 2, 3, and so on. As a result, each person in the number group knows a different step or movement they learned or created as part of the letter group. Then students from the letter group teach the other members of their number group the step they learned when they were part of the letter group. Now, all students have learned all the new steps and movements that can be organized into a complete dance.

- *Mental rehearsal.* After students have learned or created a dance, they close their eyes and see an imaginary video of the dance being played in their minds. The students visualize the steps, sequence, and formation. This strategy helps students improve their memories and prepare to perform the dance.

- *Verbal cueing.* While teaching the dance, you call out the key phrases or words to help students remember the dance sequence. You can eliminate the cues when students become familiar with the dance.

A small group of students can learn a dance and help teach the dance to their classmates.

MOTIVATING LEARNERS

All teachers have students who are reluctant to try a new activity—particularly dance. The thought of presenting a dance learning experience that some students might not receive with enthusiasm can deter you from attempting to teach dance. However, there are students in each class who do enjoy participating in a dance experience and welcome the opportunity to do so. You need to take these students into consideration as well. Engage students in the learning experience through specific feedback and allowing choice in the activities and experience (Davies et al. 2015). Ensure that students feel their effort and voice are valued and that the content is relevant to their lives. When planning, be sensitive to students' conceptions of the subject matter.

Although you may ignite enthusiasm in many of your students, you will also find that there are reluctant learners who are hesitant to participate in dance. Wells, Jones, and Jones (2014) noted resistance to learning is likely to surface when one does not enjoy, respect, or value ideas or people. Addressing the issue and finding various strategies to solve the resistance is the responsibility of the teacher. One approach to addressing students' reluctance is to acknowledge the feelings of students who say, "Why do we have to dance? I don't like dancing. Dance is not for me. I can't dance." You can respond, "I hear what you're saying. I understand that dance is not your favorite activity. I know that dancing makes you feel very uncomfortable," or "I know that you feel that you're not very good at dancing, but all the movements in today's lesson are movements you already know how to do." Then ask the students to try the dance, and set time aside at the end of the session for them to talk more about their feelings. Students may find all or part of the experience enjoyable, but some will continue to feel reluctant and may not change their minds for the entire school year.

Here are some other strategies for addressing the concerns of reluctant students:

- Acknowledge that there are many definitions of dance and that all are valuable representations of the way people incorporate dance into their lives.
- Be generous with honest praise for all students during the dance experience. The praise can help alleviate some of the "I can't" feelings. Students want to trust that you will help them.

- Take time at the end of each session to talk about the experience. Discuss with students what parts of the lesson were uncomfortable, what worked well, what could be changed for the next time, and what could be added to make the experience more challenging. This type of questioning allows the students who enjoyed the experience, as well as the reluctant students, to voice their opinions.

- Listen carefully to what students tell you. Talk with students individually about their feelings outside of the session, either in a formal conference or casually as you meet them in the hallway. In this way, you can show that you are sincerely interested in their feelings and that you want to help them feel comfortable with learning dance while honoring their various differences and backgrounds. According to McCarthy-Brown (2017), "Student dancers who currently do not see their culture reflected in the curriculum would experience a more affirming education if they understood and believed that the goal was to add to the cultural knowledge they already possess as opposed to trying to overcome or change it" (p. 24).

- Find hooks. Have the music or a video of the dance playing when students enter the room. Add a pictorial display that represents the content or topic, dress in a relevant costume such as a sport shirt when teaching sport-themed dances, or ask students to arrive dressed for a theme or bring a prop, such as a stuffed animal or favorite toy.

- Teach by invitation (Graham, Elliott, and Palmer 2016). This strategy allows students to make choices. You could say, "You can choose to add percussion instruments to accompany your dance or create the dance without any accompaniment."

- Set a positive atmosphere in the beginning of the learning experience as you would with any area of the curriculum. Students do not want to be viewed as foolish or incompetent in front of their peers. You can tell students that you are trying this lesson for the first time, and you would like their feedback at the end of the session. Then, ask them what parts of the learning experience were the most interesting. What did they learn today about dance? What changes would they suggest for the next session? We stress that students respect the individual differences among their peers. We all bring strengths to the experience, and we can all learn something new about ourselves and how we move. What is challenging to one student may not be as challenging to another. Acknowledge these differences in a positive, accepting atmosphere that helps alleviate the feeling of vulnerability.

- Students seem more reluctant to participate in dance than in other curricular areas. However, when you exhibit sincere enthusiasm as you introduce the learning experience, choose content that is relevant to the students, and ensure a positive atmosphere, your students will begin to understand and value dance as an important part of their experiences.

Frequently, teachers who anticipate reluctance when they use the word *dance* will begin the session by saying, "We are going to create some new movements today," or "This lesson is about moving to a rhythm in the music." They purposely avoid using the word *dance* because some students will immediately turn off from the learning experience because of their preconceptions about dance. Using other phrases or words as a substitute for *dance* in the beginning of a lesson may encourage students to participate. We strongly recommend that at some point, either at the end of the lesson or at the end of the unit, you explain that what the students were doing is called dance. When their experiences are positive, they will link a new meaning to the word *dance*. Students must know that they are dancing and that the learning and feelings of success and joy they experience are a result of a dance experience.

ESTABLISHING PROTOCOLS AND RULES

Most teachers have a series of established protocols and rules they use with their classes. Protocols are usually teacher-designed ways of operating during the class that facilitate efficient class management and allow maximum time for active participation (Graham, Elliott, and Palmer 2016). These include ways to enter and exit the class, obtain and return equipment, stop an activity, and react to fire drills and other emergency situations. Rules establish guidelines for responsible behaviors that foster learning (Brady, Forton, and Porter 2011). Often, students can suggest rules that address respect, good listening, sharing, and cooperation. Dance learning experiences follow similar protocols and rules used in other educational experiences.

One important protocol to establish is the stop signal. Clarify your meaning of *stop*. Explain to students the specific behaviors you expect—the voice is quiet, the body is still, everyone is looking at you, props are placed on the floor, a shape is held still, or hands that are connected are let go. The signal can be you saying "stop" or "freeze," or it can be another specified signal. For example, when using recorded music, you might say, "When the music stops, I want you to stop." When using percussion instruments, you could tell students, "I am going to play a skipping rhythm on the drum. When I hit the drum loudly, like this, stop." Or you might say, "This movement will not be accompanied by music. Stop when you hear me tap the triangle three times, like this: one, two, and three." You can also incorporate a way to stop in the movement task: "Run, leap, turn, and freeze in a stretched shape," or "As you are running in the space, begin to run slower and slower until you come to a complete stop."

Another protocol that supports effective teaching is to establish a way to begin and end the dance session. To begin class, you could have students sit in a circle and take attendance by asking each student to respond with a movement or a clap of their hands. One attendance strategy that allows you to get to know more about students is to choose a category, such as colors, foods, animals, or sports, and when you call a child's name, the child responds with an answer that fits the category. At the end of the class, students can convene to talk about what they learned or to hear about what will happen in the next session. In the book *Teaching Children and Adolescents Physical Education, Fourth Edition* (Graham, Elliott, and Palmer 2016), the authors offer strategies for establishing and maintaining effective class management protocols. Teachers can design a plan, communicate it to the students, and monitor students' reactions. Students need parameters to help them focus on learning, being safe, and respecting others.

Creating rules begins with awareness for you as the teacher and for each student about the goals for learning. Ask students what they hope to learn and what they want to learn. Their comments become the foundation for developing rules that help them reach their goals. The task now is to solicit from the students their ideas for rules. During class, students can offer spoken suggestions, write or draw about rules, or work in small groups on a rule list. Encourage students to frame rules in the positive instead of beginning each rule with "Don't" or "No" (Brady, Forton, and Porter 2011). Consolidate the lists and make the rules global and concise (see figure 5.2). Once the rules are developed, it is time to bring them to life. Practice the rules with students by having them experience what the rules look like and sound like in action. You can ask, "What does respect look like when you are listening to someone talk?" or "What would you say if you are sharing a prop?" Role-play with students about the situations that occur in the dance session. Here, students can connect the rules to actual situations. These moments of practice model for students the acceptable way to behave and further their understanding of the rules. Consequences for choosing to not follow rules or protocols should be logical, maintain the integrity of the students, and offer an opportunity to learn from the situation. Provide learners with problem-solving techniques for settling disputes and with the language to express their feelings in an appropriate manner. There is no question that it takes time to establish rules, practice rules, and discuss consequences; however, establishing classroom protocols is a worthy investment that will establish a positive environment for teaching and learning.

Rules for Dance Learning

Be kind, helpful, and caring.

Respect others and school materials.

Always try your best.

Listen to each other.

Figure 5.2 Sample list of rules for a dance class.

CREATING A SAFE LEARNING ENVIRONMENT

In dance and physical education classes, children are always moving, and the potential for injury is greater than in a classroom where children are more sedentary. Establish a safe environment by communicating the safety protocols and rules to the students and then reinforce appropriate behavior during the session. Before you teach, review the lesson and anticipate where an emphasis on safe behaviors will be needed. For example, when asking children to huddle closely together in a group, you can anticipate that some of the children may push or fall and injure themselves or another child. Before the huddle, explain to the children that they need to move into the huddle slowly, remain still, and then move apart slowly. When children are traveling in the room, they need adequate space to dance freely without bumping into others. Not all children have fully developed agility and perceptual skills to make quick changes of direction and weight shifts to avoid collisions. As a result, you will need to organize the children for safe movement. First, reinforce understanding of the concepts of personal space (the space immediately around the body, whether while stationary or traveling) and general space (all other available space). Developing an awareness of appropriate personal space takes practice. Many children tend to be too close to others, the walls, and objects. It may be helpful to remind them, "Look in front of you, to the sides, and in back of you to see if you have enough space to move without bumping into another person." Also, identify safety lines on the floor that border the dance space and instruct students to stay within the lines to protect them from hitting a wall, furniture, or other obstacles. Check to make sure children are wearing appropriate footwear, such as sneakers or dance shoes, and clothing that allows for easy, safe, and effective movement.

When students are making quick traveling movements such as running or leaping, have all students move in the same direction in the space. They can be organized into lines of three or four and take turns, or they can move in a large circular path around the space, not necessarily in a single circle. With very large groups, taking turns for fast movement may be the best choice for keeping the environment safe. A balance is necessary between the time students spend moving and the time they are waiting for a turn to maintain active participation in a safe space.

You also need to stress personal safety to enable students to perform dance movements without injuring themselves. Teach students appropriate techniques to help them express themselves and avoid injury (Kassing and Jay-Kirschenbaum 2021). Teach students to land softly through their feet when coming down from hops, jumps, and leaps. The toes should touch the floor first, followed by the ball and then the heel of the foot, and the knees should be bent on the landing to absorb the force. When students lower themselves to the floor, they need to use their hands to help control their body weight and avoid dropping directly onto their knees. Require students to be cautious when bending or moving backward, switching weight from one body part to another, or turning and stopping quickly. As the teacher, you are responsible for the students' safety. Anticipate problems, teach safe ways to move, and attend to injuries immediately. Always begin each session with a proper warm-up and end the session with appropriate cool-down movements.

PRESENTING DEMONSTRATIONS

In many learning experiences, movement patterns or sequences require a demonstration by either the teacher or the students. When demonstrating a specific movement or dance step for a large group, you have several choices. Facing the students with the front of the body allows you to see all the students. This requires you to reverse the right and left orientation of the movement. For example, you call for the students to step to the right yet demonstrate a step to your left side while the students step their right side, similar to looking in a mirror. Having your back to the students allows the students to match the movement identically, but it is difficult for you to see if the students are following correctly. Another possibility for demonstrating is to stand beside a student. This works well when demonstrating to one student. The student can match the movement, and you can see the student at the same time. This approach is helpful when teaching specific dance steps that are difficult for students to learn.

You can also demonstrate from the center of a large group where the students face the center of the circle. In this situation, the students will follow the movement in a general way rather than match it exactly. For example, you may say, "I am going to move very slowly. I want you to follow my movements and stop when I stop."

Be sure all students can see the demonstration. The demonstrator can repeat the movement in different places in the room or change the position of the students (Graham, Elliott, and Palmer 2016). Those in the back of the space can move to the front, or those in the center can switch with students on the periphery of the group. When teaching a large class, it may be possible to teach from a raised platform or stage to allow the students to view the demonstration easily.

Besides the appropriate location, how you present the demonstration requires consideration. Sometimes, showing the whole dance or complete sequence of movements gives students the big picture, and they can see how the individual movements are part of the whole. Then you can break down the steps or short phrases of movement. You may need to first demonstrate the movement slowly so that students can follow, and then demonstrate using the appropriate tempo and quality of movement. Finally, accompany the demonstration with verbal focus or cues to help direct students' attention to the movement (Graham, Elliott, and Palmer 2016).

PROVIDING FEEDBACK

Frequent positive and constructive comments to students will maintain motivation and reinforce learning (Graham, Elliott, and Palmer 2016). Because dance can be an area of the curriculum where learners may feel more self-conscious and vulnerable, it is important to acknowledge accomplishments, no matter how small, and also to make corrections when necessary. Both types of comments—acknowledgment and correction—should be specific and descriptive. Acknowledge students' work with comments such as these: "That's great. I see you've used your back and arms to make a round shape." "You are using great control to lower your body carefully to the floor." "Everyone learned the steps very quickly. Your concentration and coordination

are improving." When using corrective comments, acknowledge the positive aspects of the movement first, and then add a comment to help the student improve their performance. Say, for example, "You are moving in the right rhythm, but you need to think ahead about which side you move to first," or "I see that you are moving at a low level. Now can you use only your hands and feet for traveling?" Always look for something positive to say to students. They value your comments and use them to reassure themselves of their progress.

In order for comments to be effective, the students must be able to hear the positive feedback. Students tend to use their voices and can be noisy when moving. To ensure that they hear your comments, move close to them. Sometimes, however, it is appropriate to comment from across the room. Making sure that students hear your positive feedback is valuable and can help them feel good about their movements. It is also helpful to say a student's name first before commenting. Doing so will gain their attention so they are ready to hear the comment. Here is an example: "Tim, I see you are using a jump in three directions to show your popping movement. That's great!"

Students also want the opportunity to talk about their experiences. Allow a few seconds after a dance is performed or a series of tasks is presented for students to talk. Frequently, students share their feelings or describe their experience with their peers when performing or learning. You may hear comments such as "That was so much fun," or "I could not get that step. Did you?" Students need to be quiet when you or another student is speaking to allow everyone to hear the comment the first time. When a student answers a question or makes a comment, you should refrain from rephrasing the comment every time. Doing so can send a message to students that their comments are not valued and that you can say it more effectively. Some do not speak loudly enough to be heard in a big space. It may take extra time to gather the class closer and make sure they can hear someone speaking, yet you must respect the integrity of the speaker. In dance, value is placed not only on the students' abilities to create and learn movement but also on what they think and say about movement.

ENGAGING STUDENTS IN PERFORMANCES

In a dance class, the purpose of performance is to share dance movement that has been created or learned with other students or with you as the teacher. Not all students' work needs to be performed; however, there are times when students' performance is appropriate. Performance provides the opportunity to communicate the intent of the dance to others. When students perform a folk dance, for example, they are communicating an event or custom of a particular culture. A dance about clouds may communicate the shapes of clouds and how they move across the sky. These performance opportunities can occur at various times throughout the learning experience. Often a teacher will ask one or more students to perform a particular sequence of movements. This pinpointing method of performance (Graham, Elliott, and Palmer 2016) is valuable when you need to illustrate accuracy and quality in movement or demonstrate a variety of solutions to a problem-solving task. At other times, the performance will occur near the end of a learning experience to demonstrate the culminating dance that was learned or created.

Generally, you will ask all the students to perform the dance movement at the same time. This is a comfortable approach for students who are hesitant about performing. Many are afraid to make a mistake in front of others or to show their work because they believe that their work will not be accepted, yet they are willing to perform as part of the whole class. Asking them to perform solo when they are not ready or have not volunteered places them in an uncomfortable situation. Do not expect anyone to perform solo unless they request to do so. Also, if anyone refuses to perform, even after your encouraging words, do not demand that they do so; your insistence will only intensify resistance. Respect the student's decision and find a time to talk outside of class to discuss their feelings. Together, you and the student can explore other ways they can share what they have learned.

Designing a variety of performance circumstances will allow students to communicate their dances to others, provide students with an opportunity to observe others dancing, and give you an opportunity to observe how the students complete the tasks. The following are examples of performance opportunities:

Performance allows students to share what they have created and learned in dance class.

- A student readily volunteers to perform for the whole class.
- A student shares a movement or sequence of movements with a group of three or four other students. Each student in the group is encouraged to take a turn.
- Students paired together as partners perform for another set of partners.
- An individual student shares a movement idea or completed dance with one other student.
- Two or three small groups of students perform at the same time for the whole class.
- Half the class performs at one time while the other half observes, and then they switch roles.
- One small group of students performs for another small group, and then the groups switch roles.
- Individual students or small groups perform for you at a time other than during class.
- Students perform for you or other students at a performance station.

For reasons that are understandable, students cannot and should not sit and observe or wait for extended periods for their turn to perform. Keep the performance times short.

When the students are ready to perform, make one or two specific comments that focus the students' attention on how they will perform the dance. Offer comments such as these: "Think about what you want to express in this dance, and make each movement clear." "Be sure to feel the strong energy in your movement, especially when you jump into the air." "Take your time in the turn and fall to the floor, thinking of lightly and slowly melting." "Listen carefully to the change in the music as the cue to change the dance formation." Request that students begin and end their performance with their bodies still. This stillness defines the beginning and end of a specific movement or a whole dance, both for the dancer and the observers. Remind students who are observing to applaud or comment in a respectful manner after the performance. A great way to show support for the performer is to have the observers applaud before as well as after the performance. Starting a performance on such a positive note builds self-esteem and encourages students who are reluctant to be more enthusiastic about performing.

OBSERVING AND RESPONDING TO DANCE

Observing dance, whether it is a professional company or student class work, is a valuable component of the dance program. Frequently, dance observation is overlooked because the emphasis of the lesson is experiential; that is, the students are actively involved in physically learning or creating dances. Observing can give students an appreciation for dance as a means of nonverbal communication and expression. It is a valuable means of learning about dance if you prepare the students beforehand so their response is thoughtful and meaningful. A general statement such as "Tell me what you liked about the dance after the performance" can precede the observation. Additionally, you can state more specific expectations by telling the students what to look for in the dance: "Pay attention to how the dancers use light and strong energy in their locomotor movements." This verbal focus makes observation more meaningful and increases comprehension of the dance.

Other suggestions for directing students' observation include asking the students to look for the following:

- The ways the dancers use straight and curved pathways
- Movements in which dancers go into the air
- How the dance steps match the beat of the music
- How the dances are similar to or contrast with each other
- Whether the dance tells a story
- Movements and shapes that remind you of a specific idea
- How the dance begins and ends
- Feelings expressed by the dancers
- Answers to student-created questions for the observation

After the observation, a discussion should occur in which students respond by expressing their thoughts and perceptions and hear a variety of other viewpoints. Guide the class discussion by asking questions such as these:

- What movements did you see? Describe how the dancers were moving.
- How did the spatial formations change throughout the dance?
- How did the dancers use gestures to convey a character?
- What ideas or feelings might the dancers have been trying to express?
- What does this dance mean to you personally?
- What other possible meanings might the dance have?
- What did you see in the dance?
- What part of the dance was the most exciting and why?
- Describe the ways the dancers related to each other.
- Was there a message in the dance?
- Can you suggest another way to end the dance?
- What part of the dance would you like to dance yourself?
- What do you think about the music used for the dance?
- How did the costumes, props, or setting affect the dance?
- How did the dance relate to the title of the dance?
- What do you feel about what you saw?
- What was original or imaginative about the dance?
- What did the dance tell you about the time period it represents?
- What did the dance tell you about the people and their environment, traditions, or culture?

Students can respond to their observations through drawing pictures (see figure 5.3), writing in a journal (see figure 5.4), writing a review, composing a poem, or demonstrating their responses through movement or discussion. In a large class, it is not always possible to have the time to listen to everyone's response to a question. A strategy that is helpful for sharing verbal responses requires that students be organized into pairs or small groups and take turns sharing their comments with each other. This is referred to as the pair and share response method. Encourage students to use the movement vocabulary from the elements of dance in their comments. In this way, they will be able to extend and clarify their comments beyond stating simply, "I liked the dance," or "It was interesting." Probe for in-depth comments by asking students what they liked about the dance or what, specifically, they found interesting. Asking a follow-up question to a comment engages learners' critical-thinking skills, helps them understand what they observed, and increases their ability to articulate their perceptions.

Figure 5.3 Drawings depict children's responses to an observation.

May 17, 2023

I thought the dance assembly was very entertaining and informing about dance all over the world. The three dancers showed the movements and told us where it originated from. I liked the Brazilian dancers the best. It was fast and colorful. I wonder how the dancers remembered all the movements and dance so well together. I wasn't always interested in dancing, but now I am because of the cool moves.

Figure 5.4 Journal writing about a dance observation.

SUMMARY

From the moment students step into the space to their last step out the door, the dance experience should be engaging, relevant, and enjoyable. You know the needs of the students and plan a unit and lessons that invite them to experience dance in a variety of ways. Students are recognized for their individual perspectives, learning styles, and abilities to learn and create dance movements. As the teacher, you have established protocols and rules that help students learn and grow in a safe, kind, and orderly place. Here, students feel their way of learning is respected and they are willing to take risks as they collaborate with others to create, perform, and observe dances.

Questions for Reflection

1. What are some characteristics of effective teaching in dance? What would it look like and sound like in your classroom?
2. We can all agree that students learn in a variety of ways. What are some of the strategies that you can use to help them be successful?
3. What supportive phrases can you share with students as feedback to their dancing? Create a list of 10 or more comments.
4. What strategies can you use for including students in constructing rules for effective learning?
5. What suggested strategies for reluctant learners do you find appropriate for your situation? What other strategies in other content areas have you used to help stucents feel comfortable and motivated to learn?
6. Students enjoy learning new activities, yet they also need the comfort of a routine. What protocols can you use with your classes that are applicable to teaching dance?
7. Think about your experiences in viewing a dance. What do you look for when you are observing a dance?
8. What precautions do you take to ensure the students' safety during the lesson?

CHAPTER 6

Assessing Children's Learning in Dance

Assessment, as a significant part of a comprehensive dance curriculum, can be conducted in a variety of ways. Most important, the type of assessment selected must be directly related to the outcomes of the learning experience. Current educational settings use the terms *formative assessment* and *summative assessment* to describe the two types of assessment tools teachers use to assess student learning. Formative assessment includes various types of tools used to provide feedback to both students and teachers in order to improve learning, while summative assessment can be described as using data to determine how much a student knows or retained at the end of a learning sequence (Dixson and Worrell 2016). As an essential component of the teaching and learning process, both types of assessment are embedded throughout the dance curriculum. Those who teach dance are continually seeking the best ways to assess students' learning. They look at how creativity, performance, group cooperation, personal growth, and change in attitude and values can be assessed feasibly in a valid and reliable manner. Many assessments used in dance are designed by a teacher and focus specifically on learning that occurs in a particular unit or lesson. These types of teacher-constructed assessments reflect a student's level of skill, acquisition of knowledge, and perception of what they learned. The assessment offers feedback to you and the students about how the outcomes are being met. Assessments can occur before, during, and at the conclusion of a unit.

All collect different types of information that can inform prior knowledge and skills and progress. To complete a comprehensive assessment, you need to access the three learning domains inherent in dance. Psychomotor assessment is one of the primary areas of dance assessment and evaluates how well the student can perform the dance movements. Cone and Cone (2005) explain psychomotor assessment for elementary-level students as follows: "This assessment looks at accuracy and clarity in performing movements; rhythmic coordination; flow from one movement to the next; or ability to change tempo, direction, levels, 'size' [range], pathways, and energy" (p. 10). You can observe how a student uses strength, balance, flexibility, cardiorespiratory endurance, body and spatial awareness, and body control to perform a dance movement or a complete dance. One example of psychomotor assessment in a creative dance about performing three different cloud shapes involves observing a student performing a sequence of three cloud shapes and assessing the student's body control as they hold each shape still for 4 counts, then assessing the student's ability to move from one shape to the next with smooth control (see figure 6.1). Assessment can also involve evaluating whether the student can accurately perform a sequence of dance steps from a cultural dance or perform dance movements to a specific music rhythm. The psychomotor domain is assessed through teacher or peer observation based on clear criteria for achievement. This domain challenges the

81

observer to focus and remember the movements, especially during live performances. With the increase of technology in the classroom, recording and video have become more widely available to use for assessment purposes, allowing teachers to use video or to revisit videos for assessment and evaluation. However, it is not always possible in every dance class, and the assessment relies on your knowledge of the criteria and ability to be in a good viewing position.

Cognitive assessment determines what knowledge students have about the unit or lesson content. The assessments focus on recalling terminology; identifying dance steps or facts about a dance, such as origin, formation, choreographic structure, or order of movements; explaining their perceptions and opinions of their own dance or the dances of others; and analyzing dances for commonalities, differences, or application of the elements of dance. One way knowledge can be revealed for young children is to ask them to give a movement answer to a question. When young students blend movement with language, they have a greater range of responses to use to express their understanding. You can also assess cognitive understanding by administering a written quiz or test, having students write a response to a journal question, or asking students to give a verbal response or draw a picture.

The affective domain involves feelings, reactions, attitudes, preferences, social interactions, and self-concept. Assessment of the affective domain should not be limited to assessment of participation, effort, and attitudes. Evaluating specific social and emotional competencies is also important and includes assessing items such as the ability to follow safety procedures, negotiate conflict constructively, control impulses, understand the perspectives of others, and cooperate with others (Assessment Work Group 2019). Knowing how students feel about the content or about themselves as dancers can help you design lessons that are meaningful and relevant. In many lessons, students collaborate to learn, teach each other, respond to a peer, or create and perform a dance together. This social interaction is a critical component in assessing students' leadership, responsibility to stay focused, willingness to listen to other ideas, demonstration of respect, and positive negotiation and compromise. Information on the affective domain can be collected by teacher observation, student surveys, verbal comments, drawings, and journal writings.

In dance, students learn, perform, create, observe, and respond to dances; thus, various types of assessments are needed. Assessment of how a student performs a dance movement or a completed dance or how a student creates a dance is usually embedded in most dance lessons and units and conducted formally or informally. Be sure to plan time for assessment to occur during the lesson or unit. Assessment may also take the form of a written test using multiple-choice questions or questions requiring short response phrases or paragraphs. Other written assessments can include journal writing in response to

Figure 6.1 Sample Psychomotor Assessment

Criteria

Shapes: yes = included 3 shapes; no = included 1 or 2 shapes

Control: yes = smooth transition from one shape to another; no = hesitated, lost the flow of the movement, or fell down

Students' names	3 cloud shapes	Control
Mina	Yes	Yes
Shawn	Yes	No—hesitated
Thomas	No (only 2)	Yes
Genese	Yes	Yes
Pen Pen	No (only 1)	No—fell down

their own dancing or the dancing of others, constructed books containing descriptions and drawings of dances, and lists of vocabulary words used in the dance lesson. Students can also respond orally to questions, lead a discussion, interview a peer, deliver a presentation on dance, or complete a project. Relying on a single type of assessment will not fit all situations and limits the information that you collect about students' learning. It is not enough to simply measure a student's ability to recall memorized facts or perform an isolated movement; instead, assessment of what students know and are able to do should include a balance of lower- and higher-order thinking skills, as represented in Anderson and Krathwohl's update of Bloom's taxonomy (Anderson and Krathwohl 2001; see figure 6.2).

Figure 6.2 Sample Tasks Reflecting Bloom's Taxonomy

Remembering: Retrieving, Recalling, or Recognizing Knowledge From Memory

Name three movements in square dance.

Demonstrate how to skip forward using a fast speed.

Observe and repeat the three movements I have demonstrated.

Understanding: Constructing Meaning by Interpreting, Summarizing, Comparing, Classifying, or Explaining

Describe the benefits of participating in a social dance.

Express anger using three different shapes.

Show me the difference between a strong reaching movement and a light reaching movement.

Applying: Carrying Out or Using a Procedure Through Executing or Implementing

Practice the dance you learned at two different tempos.

Develop a new line dance using the steps you learned.

Organize the members of your group into a circle formation.

Analyzing: Breaking Material or Concepts Into Parts, and Determining How the Parts Relate or Interrelate to One Another or to an Overall Structure or Purpose

Compare and contrast Samir's dance with Kristen's dance.

Experiment using three pathways for the leaf dance, and select one that best expresses the leaves blowing in the wind.

Watch a video of a cultural dance, and categorize the movements as either locomotor or non-locomotor.

Evaluating: Making Judgments Based on Criteria and Standards Through Checking and Critiquing

After viewing a dance performed by your peers, decide what you think they were expressing in the dance.

After observing a dance video, choose a different way to begin and end the dance.

After performing your sport dance, check to see if you included a change in level and tempo.

Creating: Putting Elements Together to Form a Coherent or Functional Whole; Reorganizing Elements Into a New Pattern or Structure Through Generating, Planning, or Producing

Create a new line dance using five of the steps you learned.

Rearrange the steps to the cupid shuffle to create a new line dance.

Plan a dance map that shows the pathways you will use to move through the space.

Adapted from Anderson and Krathwohl (2001).

Assessing dance presents a challenge because of its ephemeral nature. Dance is a live art form that occurs in a time and space that cannot be exactly replicated. As a form of human movement and art, the dance is embodied in the dancer, and as experience affects the dancer, the dance itself is also affected. This is why conducting a single view of assessment captures only one moment, whereas a variety of assessments can provide a more comprehensive picture of what one knows, understands, and is able to do. Taking a video of students dancing may be considered one way to address this concern; however, although a video can be a useful tool for assessment, it does have its limitations. Dance on video is taken through the view of the person with the video recorder and, as a result, may provide a limited view of the dance.

Subjectivity is another issue in dance assessment. One's background, values, and aesthetic preferences play into the interpretation of what the assessor views. Teachers, alone or in collaboration with students, need to define the criteria for the rubric. The criteria become the description of what is considered an appropriate response, and the rubric delineates the range of possible responses. Rubrics can be analytic, in which different aspects of student performance are considered separately and graded, or holistic, containing several criteria and considered simultaneously (see figure 6.3; Jönsson, Balan, and Hartell 2021). A rubric for six elements of choreography developed by Rovegno and Bandhauer (2017) is a clear example of how an analytic rubric can be used in making assessment less subjective. For each of the six choreographic elements—originality, sequence, transitions, expressing an idea, relationships of body parts, and contrasts and aesthetic highlights—Rovegno and Bandhauer (2017) include a different range of performance levels accompanied by a description of what you would observe at each level. When rubrics are used to guide self- and peer assessment, students become increasingly aware of how to assess their work and set goals for improvement. It is okay to make adjustments in the assessment during the unit because as you teach you will also learn more about how students respond to the content.

Assessment in dance should address students' knowledge and skills as learners, creators, performers, and responders to dance. In this chapter, we address dance assessment from four approaches: teacher assessment of program and effectiveness of a unit or lesson, teacher assessment of individual student learning, peer assessment, and student self-assessment.

TEACHER ASSESSMENT OF PROGRAM

Effective teaching is the result of creative thinking, planning clear outcomes, dynamic delivery, and reflection on the teaching and learning experience. What worked and why, and what can be changed for the next lesson? These questions influence a recurrent cycle of planning, presenting, and reflecting. As an ongoing part of teaching, the dance experience shared by the teacher and the students is evaluated based on a set of outcomes that describe what students should be able to do and know as a result of participating in the dance learning experience. The answers to the following questions provide you with valuable information to use in evaluating your preparation and presentation of a specific learning experience or the total dance program.

Figure 6.3 Holistic Rubric Created by Students

Circle the number that describes how well your group performed the dance.

3	Awesome	Everyone did the whole dance really great.
2	Very good	Two or three people made a mistake, but the dance was still good.
1	Try again	A lot of people made mistakes, and we need more practice.

Questions for Reflection of a Program's Effectiveness

- Did students have experiences in all the artistic processes throughout the program?
- How was dance as a cultural, social, and creative dance form included?
- What types of assessment instruments were used in gathering evidence of learning? How were the results analyzed, and what changes were planned for program improvement?
- What national, state, or local standards were emphasized, and what standards need to be strengthened?
- What new learning experiences were added to the program, and what learning experiences need to be deleted or changed?

Questions for Reflection at the Conclusion of a Dance Unit

During and after the unit and lessons, you reflect on the lesson design and how it was presented to the students.

- Were the unit and lesson outcomes clear, and did they address a set of standards?
- What were students expected to learn in the psychomotor, cognitive, and affective domains?
- How did the sequence of the learning experiences contribute to meeting the outcomes?
- Did the units include new information or a review of previous knowledge?
- How were the assessments implemented during the unit? Were formative and summative assessments used? What type of assessment instruments were used in assessing the psychomotor, cognitive, and affective domains?

Questions for Reflection at the Conclusion of a Dance Learning Experience

Assessment of teaching is an ongoing process. You look at the way the students respond to each task and adjust the tasks during the learning experience to ensure students' achievement of the planned outcomes. The following are questions to consider:

- Did students have time to practice and create dances? Did I rush through the content without providing adequate time for skill accomplishment and knowledge acquisition?
- Was the content too hard or too easy for students? Were students challenged or bored?
- Did the introduction provide background information?
- What did I learn about students' prior experiences with the topic or dance form?
- How did the warm-up relate to the movements used in the dances?
- Was the task progression logical and built developmentally so that students were successful?
- Did I include a culminating dance?
- Did students have time to fully perform the dance with expression and understanding?
- Did I use different ways to close the lessons? Which ways were meaningful to the students? How do I know what they learned?

A more focused approach in assessing a single learning experience is to develop a list of questions that relate to each psychomotor, cognitive, or affective outcome. For example, when teaching a cultural dance, the outcomes can be for students to learn the sequence of steps (psychomotor), understand the cultural background of the dance (cognitive), and dance with enthusiasm and in cooperation with others (affective). Questions for assessment of the learning experience could include the following:

- How many of the students can accurately perform the steps in the dance? (psychomotor)
- How many of the students could remember a sequence of steps and perform them without cues? (psychomotor)
- Are the students able to change direction smoothly? (psychomotor)
- Can they maintain the spatial formation of the dance? (psychomotor)
- Can they describe what the steps represent about the culture in which the dance was designed? (cognitive)
- Are they dancing with a sense of joy in the experience? (affective)

- Are the students able to relate positively to their partners and the group as a whole? (affective)

You can also include the following suggested list of general questions that are appropriate to the overall experience:

- What parts of the learning experience were successful, and why were they successful?
- What outcomes were met by all the students, and what outcomes continue to be addressed?
- What parts of the learning experience could be changed, what indicated that change is needed, and what changes would be made?

At the end of each learning experience, it is helpful to record a few notes about each class, review the written plans, and add or delete tasks for the next learning experience. In addition, review what was successful about the way you taught the lesson. Ask yourself, "Was it the way I demonstrated a movement, how I used my voice, where I placed myself in the space, my addition of a video or picture or diagram, or my energy and enthusiasm for the topic?"

Assessment of teaching effectiveness is a form of teacher self-assessment. The reflective process of thinking about how the unit and lessons were planned and taught and how the students experienced learning challenges you to reconsider prior assumptions, attitudes, beliefs, behaviors, and perceptions and to be open to change. As a result of self-assessment, you are more informed about your teaching and can develop a rationale for better practice (Brookfield 2017; Dervent 2015). You can look at your work objectively and know with some confidence why you believe what you believe and why you do what you do.

TEACHER ASSESSMENT OF STUDENTS

Formative and summative assessment of students' learning can be formal (specifically designed tests) or informal (usually conducted through observation while students are participating in the lesson). In both types, you monitor a student's progress during a single learning experience or over time. Assessing students' learning in dance requires a feasible approach that provides you with the information you need when you see many students in a limited time. Instruments and formats for collecting information of students' learning can include teacher-constructed assessments, standardized norm-referenced state or national assessments, teacher observations using a rating scale or checklist (see figure 6.4), written notes, recorded comments, and video recordings. You can also collect information through tests, quizzes, journal writing, drawings, verbal responses (see figure 6.5), and portfolios.

Teacher assessment of students' performance begins with a discussion of the rubric and criteria. Show students examples of good and not-so-good work and identify the characteristics of each. Articulate the gradations in the rubric, such as

Figure 6.4 Teacher's Checklist for a Single Evaluation

Class: Mrs. G

Dance: Line dance pattern

+ = Child is able to demonstrate

x = Child is unable to demonstrate

Students' names	Correct movements	On the beat	Changes direction
Sharia	+	+	+
Donovan	+	x	+
Robert	+	+	+
Zui	x	x	+

Chapter 6 Assessing Children's Learning in Dance   87

Figure 6.5 Student responding to the teacher's question.

beginning, improving, and excelling, so students can set levels of achievement for themselves. Leisen (2022) suggests, "If we want to place the student experience at the center of the learning process, we need rubrics that are written for students, rather than for teachers." Be clear about the criteria for each rubric level. For example, in a lesson in which students are creating a dance about geometric shapes and pathways, explain what you are looking for specifically as they perform their final dance: "I want to see you begin your dance in a geometric shape, then travel on a geometric pathway, and end in a different geometric shape. Make sure your dance contains at least one change in tempo and one change in levels. A dance with all these parts and clear shapes and pathways will be graded as excellent, a dance missing one of these parts will be graded as satisfactory, and a dance with two or more missing parts will be graded as needs more time to improve." Students understand the levels of achievement and can set goals during their learning and creating. After watching each student's performance, you record on the rubric how well the student's dance met the criteria.

Another student assessment format is to use a form that notes the rubric and criteria and write the student's name in the rubric category (see figure 6.6). Space is also available for writing specific comments. In addition to the performance of the dance, you can assess a student's understanding of how their body represents a geometric shape, for example, by asking the student to draw their body or the shape used in the dance (see figure 6.7). Older students may write about their choreographic process for the dance (see figure 6.8). Be aware that for some students, the ability to communicate their understanding through drawing and writing may be limited by their ability to use those media of expression. Again, it is important to assess students' knowledge and experience in a variety of ways.

PEER ASSESSMENT

Peer assessment provides students with an opportunity to respond to the dancing of their classmates in a one-to-one relationship or as part of a small group. In this form of assessment, students can observe their classmates performing a dance and share what they observed through discussion, reviewing a drawing or written comments, interviewing a student about their process to create a dance (see figure 6.9), or responding to a peer teaching or tutoring situation (Nurmi and Kokkonen 2015). When students develop the assessment criteria and rubric, they take ownership of their learning and set their level of achievement. Peer assessment is a highly effective teaching strategy yet should not be used as part of a student's grade. It should be focused on improvement, not on grading (Double, McGrane, and Hopfenbeck 2019). We have used this type of assessment in a square dance unit for fourth- and fifth-grade students. During the square dance unit, students learned four dances and chose one for their final assessment. Before the assessment, the class constructed the criteria and rubric. This activity helped the students set a goal for their group's practice and performance. Small groups of students assessed one another. The students developed the criteria for the final performance. They chose a holistic rubric (see figure 6.3). Students observed one another and then checked the level of performance they thought the group achieved. They also added a written statement of justification for their score.

Figure 6.6 Recording Sheet With Rubric and Criteria for a Cultural Dance Performance.

Type of Dance: Cultural Dance

Level of performance	Evidence of student's behavior	Student	Teacher comments
Basic	Cannot accurately reproduce all movements Loses rhythm Has steps but not arm or head movement Body parts not coordinated Moves out of formation Not focused during the dance Loses control	Addie	Needs to stay focused on the lesson. Demonstrated difficulty staying in rhythm.
Proficient	Accurately reproduces all movements Loses rhythm but can regain Remembers the dance sequence Stays focused on dance Moves out of formation but can regain Loses coordination on a movement Loses control on a movement	Deon Julio	Remembered the sequence of the dance and recalled the names of the steps. Stayed focused on the lesson. Demonstrated initial difficulty with coordination on the slide step; successful after continued practice.
Advanced	Performs all movements accurately in sequence and rhythm Includes movement details and arm and head movements Demonstrates good balance and strength Stays focused Stays in formation the entire dance Coordinates movements with others	Jackson	Was very helpful to other students and took time to show them slides to the right and left and how to count the steps in rhythm to the music.

Figure 6.7 Student's drawing of a geometric shape.

Chapter 6 Assessing Children's Learning in Dance 89

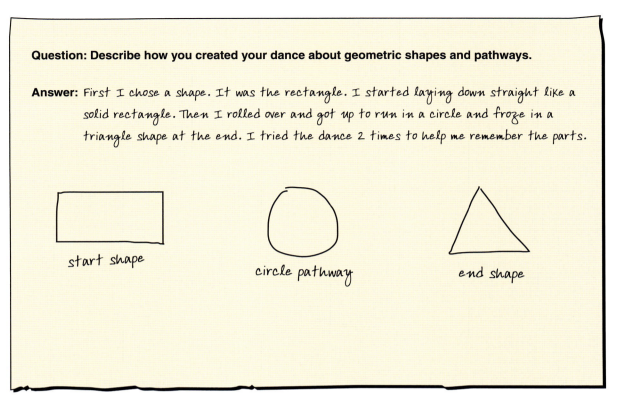

Figure 6.8 Student's writing explaining the student's choreographic process.

Figure 6.9 Student-constructed questions for a peer assessment.

Peer assessment of a creative dance can include both objective and subjective observations and responses. For example, one student chose to create a dance inspired by water evaporation and cloud formation, and another chose to dance about an erupting volcano. After spending a session creating and practicing the dances, students worked in pairs to assess each other's dance. The teacher created two questions to focus the response to the observation: (1) Name three movements you saw the students do in their dance (objective), and (2) What part of the dance was most exciting and why (subjective)? The students wrote down their answers and discussed their comments with each other. Additional questions appear in figure 6.10.

> **Figure 6.10 Teacher-Constructed Questions for a Peer Assessment**
>
> - What movements did the students use to show the dance idea?
> - What direction, speed, or type of force did they use?
> - Was there a change in level?
> - Did the dancer perform the movement the way you expected? In what way?
> - What changes would you recommend? Why?
> - What ideas can you add to the dance?
> - How is this dance the same or different from yours?
> - What question would you like to ask the dancer?
> - How did the dance begin and end?
> - Where did the dancer move in space? Can you draw the pathway?
> - What about the dance did you think was creative?
> - How do you think the music went with the dance?
> - What was the purpose of the props in the dance?
> - What effect did the costumes have on the dance?
> - Did you observe that the dancer or dancers focused on the dance? How so?

Young children who are not proficient in reading and writing a response can draw a pathway or shape that they observed, demonstrate a part they liked, or tell their peer what they remembered about the dance. You can provide a question to focus the observation and facilitate the assessment.

The link between assessment and learning becomes strengthened when students have the opportunity to revise their work after peer assessment (Ndoye 2017). In this way, students can reflect on the assessment and make changes to improve the dance they created or to their performance of a dance. Through peer assessment, students take responsibility for their learning, become autonomous learners, and develop transferable personal skills needed for lifelong learning. This shared activity promotes the interaction of ideas and the discovery of preferences about dance.

STUDENT SELF-ASSESSMENT

In self-assessment, the students evaluate themselves on what they know about dance; how well they learned, performed, or created a dance; and how they feel about dance. This type of assessment increases students' responsibility for their own learning and clarifies their understanding of expectations for achievement. Students can assess their learning through a variety of tools that include completing a questionnaire, writing a journal entry, having a personal conference with the teacher, writing a letter about their experience, drawing a picture, or recording comments. These activities all take considerable time and can occur during or outside of the dance session. If occurring outside of a dance session, you could ask the classroom or content area teacher to help with the writing and drawing portions of the assessment. We find that the students' responses to the self-assessment inform us about what the students were experiencing and learning. They also contributed to our revision of lessons and units. Sometimes the questions are announced at the beginning or end of a unit or lesson, whereas others are asked throughout the lesson. We have developed a question bank as a resource for a variety of self-assessment situations (see figure 6.11). You can select one or two key questions from the bank that will provide you with the information you are seeking and design a tool that is easy for students to read and complete.

Portfolios are an approach that provides students and teachers with a comprehensive view of learning. This assessment tool is a chronological

Chapter 6 Assessing Children's Learning in Dance 91

Figure 6.11 Sample Bank of Questions for Student Self-Assessment

Psychomotor Reflection Questions

1. What movements did you perform best in your dance?
2. What was the most important thing you learned about your body in doing this assignment?
3. What movements did you perform in your dance that used balance?
4. What movements could you practice so they are better the next time?
5. What movements did you perform that took a lot of strength?
6. Did you have enough energy to perform the dance without getting tired? Why or why not?

Cognitive Reflection Questions

1. What did you learn about dance today?
2. Is the dancing you did today like any other dancing you have done before? How is it the same or different?
3. What was the hardest part of this assignment? Why?
4. What was the most important thing you learned in doing this assignment?
5. What new thing did you discover about dance from the lesson today?
6. How would you describe your dance to someone at home?
7. What part of your dance should be changed? How would you change it?
8. Did you choose to use music? If you did, why did you choose that piece of music for your dance? If not, why did you choose not to use music?
9. Explain how you used the prop in your dance.
10. What were three different movements you performed in the dance?
11. What are some reasons that people dance?
12. How did the dancers use directions and levels in the dances?
13. What movements are similar in the two cultural dances we learned today?
14. What's one movement from each dance that you think was strong and powerful?
15. What do the movements in the [name a specific dance] tell us about the culture?
16. Describe the sequence of the [name a specific dance]. How does it begin? What happens next? How does it end?

Affective Reflection Questions

1. What was the most important thing you learned about dancing with a group in doing this assignment?
2. Did you offer ideas to your partner or group? Why or why not?
3. Did you cooperate with your partner as you moved together? Why or why not?
4. What was your favorite part of the learning experience? Why did you like that part?
5. Would you like to do this dance lesson again? Why or why not?
6. What parts of the learning experience were most important to you? Why?
7. Would you like to perform this dance again? Why or why not?
8. What do you like most about dancing? What do you like least? Why?

(continued)

Figure 6.11 *(continued)*

9. How do you feel when you are dancing?
10. Do you feel you can be creative in dance? Why or why not?
11. Do you enjoy dancing with others as part of a small group? Why or why not?
12. Did you feel uncomfortable in any part of the dance learning experience? If so, during what part and why?

collection of students' work gathered throughout the year or throughout several dance units and used in documenting progress and achievement. McTighe (1997) describes portfolios using this analogy: "If a test or quiz represents a snapshot (a picture of learning at a specific moment) then a portfolio is more like a photo album—a collection of pictures showing growth and change over time" (p. 12). A dance portfolio might include writing samples, journal entries, drawings, notations of dances, a list of dance ideas or music, tests, audio recordings, photographs, videos, peer reviews, collections of articles and news items, and artwork. Establish and communicate the purpose of the portfolio to the students and take time to review and reflect on its contents frequently (see figure 6.12). In addition to providing a method of documenting students' work, portfolios provide a tangible way for students to view and celebrate what they have accomplished.

When students take their portfolios home, they can share their work with parents and other adults, which facilitates school-to-home communication about what is learned in the dance program. The management and storage of portfolios can be overwhelming and will take time for review and filing. We suggest that you provide each student with a folder and organize the folders by class in a basket or box. Then, bring the box to the dance session so that students can place their work in it and review the portfolios at the end of each unit. For students or classes that are proficient with technology, there are also virtual or technology-based portfolio systems you can use to organize, update, and share the dance work for each student or class. Choices may depend on what is available in your school or district and what students are already familiar with. Some examples include creating a personal website, using platforms such as Google or Microsoft to create slides and personal pages, or even using an online storage site such as Dropbox to share files and folders with others. With either a traditional or technology-based portfolio, you will gain valuable insights into what your students think and how they can express themselves in a variety of ways.

Figure 6.12 **Reflective Questions for Student Portfolios**

What did you learn about dance this year?

What do you think was the best dance that you performed or created? Why was it your best?

What was the most difficult dance you learned this year and why?

Did you improve your ability to dance or create dances? How so?

Comment on your abilities as a dancer or a choreographer.

What helps you do your best dancing?

What does your dancing say about you?

Did you achieve what you wanted to learn about dance this year? Why or why not?

ASSESSMENT INSTRUMENTS

Gathering assessment information before a lesson or unit is useful in ascertaining students' current skill level, knowledge, experience, or interest. This pre-assessment helps you prepare for adjustments you may need to make in your planned lessons or unit and can also stimulate students' interest in the dance topic. Assessment that occurs during the lesson or unit, known as ongoing or formative assessment, can occur at different times and determines skill development, understanding, and progress in meeting the outcomes. The third time that assessment can occur is at the conclusion of a lesson or unit. This summative assessment determines the extent of learning or provides students an opportunity to reflect on their progress in skill development, knowledge gained, and feelings or attitude about the content (Cone and Cone 2005).

Once the outcomes are established, the next step is to determine what type of assessment will yield the best evidence that the outcomes have been met. You decide when the assessment will occur, the domains that will be assessed, who will conduct the assessment, and the best instrument for collecting evidence. The following is a list of assessment instruments that can be used for psychomotor, cognitive, and affective assessment. Remember that feasibility is important for ensuring that the assessment is easy to administer in a class of students.

- *Checklist.* The checklist is easy to use and contains a two-item rubric, such as yes and no, that evaluates whether the criteria are present. The format usually lists the names of the students down one side of the recording sheet and the skills across the top. Criteria for a yes and a no for the skills are clearly defined (see figure 6.13). This instrument is frequently used for assessing skills in the psychomotor domain.

- *Rating scale.* This assessment identifies three or more performance levels based on criteria described for each level (see figure 6.14). This instrument is an effective tool for assessing ability in performing dance skills.

- *Written test or quiz.* This cognitive assessment is in the form of multiple-choice, matching, fill in the blanks, true or false, or short written answer (see figure 6.15). Be aware of the students' reading and writing abilities, and develop a form that has adequate space for students to write.

- *Exit slips.* This assessment is applicable to the cognitive and affective domains. Students answer a question about the content taught in the lesson or respond to a prompt about how they performed or felt about the dances. They write their answer on a slip of paper and place it in a box as they exit the dance space. The following are examples of prompts: "Write the name of your favorite dance you did in class today" and "Write the name of the movement that was the hardest to learn."

- *Drawing.* This cognitive and affective assessment reveals students' understanding or feelings about the lesson. Because children take time to complete this assessment, you can ask the elementary classroom teacher to provide time during the day to complete the assessment. For example, if the assessment asked students to draw one of the body shapes they used in their cloud dance, the students would draw their body shape and add a descriptive word (see figure 6.7).

- *Peer flash cards.* This psychomotor assessment uses an observer and a performer. Each card represents a symbol that relates to a performance level. For example, a two-card assessment can use one card with a smiley face, which means the dancing is fantastic, and a card with a neutral face (the mouth is a straight line), which means the dancing needs more practice. The observer watches the performer and then holds up the card that represents their assessment. Color cards can also be used. Clearly identify the criteria for each card.

- *Human graph.* This assessment asks students about their preferences. You set up three signs attached to a cone that are lined up side by side. One sign is labeled "Awesome," the second sign is labeled "Okay," and the third sign is labeled "Needs more work." You call out a dance movement or a dance completed in the lesson or unit, and the students line up behind the sign that reflects their preference. A human graph appears as students line up based on their preference. The labels can be changed to represent other evaluative terms or dances.

- *Journal writing.* Students can use journals for writing or drawing their responses to questions that you ask. The questions can be either cognitive or affective. Collect the journals, read them, and make comments for the students. The following are some sample questions: "What part of the lesson did you like the best?" "How did you work together with your group to create the tornado dance?" "Describe a movement you created for your line dance." "Identify one thing you learned today."

• *Dance maps and webs.* This cognitive assessment provides an opportunity for students to draw and write what they learned about creating or learning a dance. The dance map includes a line drawing of the pathways while also noting the movements (see figure 6.16), and the web helps students define terminology or descriptive words about a learned or created dance (see figure 6.17).

• *Video recording.* You or the students can use a video recording of a completed dance that they learned or created. Students can learn to use a video device to record their own or others' dance performances. You can also set up the video device at an assessment station where you record students' verbal responses or dance performances. Examples of video devices may depend on what is available or allowable at your school but could range from a handheld digital video camera, an MP3 player or a phone with a video camera, or a laptop with an embedded camera for recording video.

• *Portfolio.* This assessment is a collection of a student's achievement over a period of time. The portfolio contains written tests, drawings, selected journal entries, dance maps, reports on a dance topic, or photographs. In addition to these items, a digital portfolio can contain video of dance learning and performance, student interviews, and verbal explanations of how a student created a dance or their process in learning a dance. Either portfolio type can be used for parent conferences or for students to reflect on their own learning behavior, processes, and products throughout an entire course of study (Slepcevic-Zach and Stock 2018).

• *Peer teaching.* As a formative assessment of knowledge and physical ability, one student teaches a dance or a movement to one or more peers. The peer teacher explains how to perform the dance or movements and adds a demonstration. In this way, the cognitive understanding and physical ability are integrated. You or the students' peers can develop the criteria for assessing how accurately the peer teacher explains and demonstrates.

• *Zone assessment.* This assessment is used in large classes for assessing a student's ability to perform a dance step, a sequence of a couple steps, or a completed dance. The class space is organized into three or more zones, and six to eight students are assigned to a space zone. You identify the dance content for assessment and then ask all students in the zone to perform the movements. Use a checklist and note the students who are unable to repeat the movement accurately. Move to the next zone and repeat the assessment with the same or a different movement. This continues until all students in the designated zones are assessed.

Figure 6.13 Teacher Checklist for Rockin' Shuffle Dance Steps

Complete four side steps to the right, four side steps to the left, four kicks, and a quarter turn to the left to face the next wall.

Repeat the dance two times.

Yes = on the beat for both dance repetitions

No = off the beat on one or both dance repetitions

Students' names	Rockin' shuffle
Liam	Yes
Aaliyah	No
Christian	Yes
Jun	No

Chapter 6 Assessing Children's Learning in Dance   95

Figure 6.14 Rating Scale for Student Self-Assessment

Name:

Check how well you performed the dance you created.

Skill	I was great	I messed up once	I need a lot more practice
Remembering the moves			
Body control			

Figure 6.15 Written Test Items for a Unit on Cultural Dance

1. Name two dances that used the grapevine step.
2. Identify two dances that used the circle formation.
3. Choose one of the dances and explain how the dance reflects the people's culture.

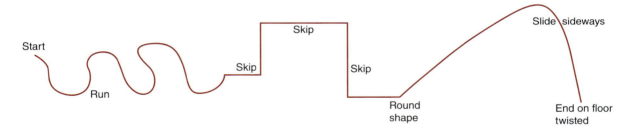

Figure 6.16 Dance map: Peer assessment of pathway in partner's dance.

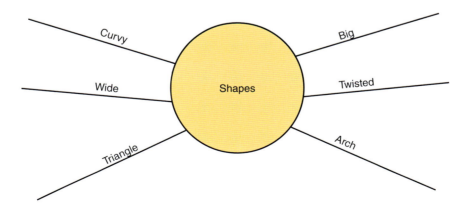

Figure 6.17 Dance web: Student self-assessment.

SUMMARY

Designing and facilitating assessment in dance can be challenging. However, for dance to be viewed as an important component of the arts or physical education curriculum, it must provide evidence of students' learning. Remember that assessments need definitive criteria and practical rubrics to be effective in helping students understand learning expectations. The content and type of assessment we choose convey a strong message to students about what is important for them to learn. Assessment can be addressed using a variety of approaches. We have discussed four approaches: assessing the teaching effectiveness, students' learning, peer assessment, and student self-assessment. Each assessment instrument provides a strength of its own, and in combination they provide a comprehensive view of what students know and can do. Select an instrument that meets the outcomes and provides meaningful evidence of students' achievements. The value of feasible and relevant assessments is evidenced in increased appreciation and understanding of dance as a language for expression and communication.

Questions for Reflection

1. What type of assessments would you use in evaluating a student's ability to perform a dance with a specific sequence of movements, such as a line dance or a cultural dance?
2. Creativity is frequently included as a criterion for a student-choreographed dance. How would you create a rubric that describes three different creative levels?
3. Small groups frequently work together to create a dance. What would be the criteria for assessing a group's final dance?
4. How could you use technology in assessing a student's dance performance?
5. What type of technology is available for you to use to record observations, journal notes, or reflections at the end of a unit or learning experience?

CHAPTER 7

Including All Children in Dance

All people have the need to express and communicate their feelings and ideas, whether it is through speaking, writing, movement, or the visual and performing arts. Through dance, students with disabilities can discover how movement can be a way to express their emotions, expand their range of movements, engage in social interactions, and explore new ways of knowing themselves and their world. As a dance educator, you must be committed to helping each student reach their potential. View the learner through the lens of ability instead of a lens of limitations. Recognize each student's individuality, and avoid viewing the learner as a member of a disability category or as a label. All students are respected for their different learning styles, and success is defined with the use of individualized standards. Individual differences in the classroom should be supported no matter the type or ability level of a student, as dance allows learning to be physical, social, and expressive while also developing body awareness and control (Torzillo and Sorin 2018). Successful educators understand the significance of using multiple strategies to present a concept or a skill. What works for one student may not work for another. Creativity, flexibility, empathy, and passion to make a difference are essential characteristics for effective planning and implementation. Cone and Cone (2011) assert, "Each student's uniqueness contributes to everyone's learning experiences. When students learn that there are many variations of a dance and many different ways to perform a movement then acceptance of differences is valued and stereotypes are dismissed" (p. 24). Teach with an open mind and a curious spirit, and know that students enjoy dancing and being part of a group. They also want to experience success.

KNOWING YOUR STUDENTS WITH DISABILITIES

As an educator, you will be teaching students with physical, cognitive, emotional, and neurological disabilities. These students all have the ability to learn, create, perform, and respond to dances whether they participate in a full class of learners with disabilities or in an inclusive class with their peers who do not have a disability. In either environment, you need to gain information about the student's disabilities and have a strong belief that all people can learn. The list of disabilities is comprehensive, and even if a student is diagnosed with a specific disability, the characteristics are manifested differently in each person. When you teach a student with a disability, understand that each one is unique in ability, personality, interests, and needs. Get to know your students. What is their favorite color, sport team, cartoon character, food, book, or game? (See figure 7.1 for additional questions.) Use this information to motivate students to participate and make the learning meaningful and enjoyable. A student may like the feel of fleece, or the color red, or a poster of a popular

97

cartoon character. Each learner will have sensory preferences. The music may be disconcerting, the lights may be too bright, or the sound of too many voices may be confusing. Be aware of these preferences, and use them to support the lesson content and avoid other sensory stimuli that can be irritating to the student. In addition, know the student's physical range of motion and strength. Dance movements need to be safe. Be aware of contraindicated movements, especially for students who use wheelchairs, crutches, scooters, or braces to support their mobility. Check with the physical therapist or school nurse for information specific to each student in addition to contacting the student's parents or guardians.

The amount of information about any specific disability, whether available online or in professional journals and texts, is tremendous. Use caution and make sure that your sources are reliable. Accessing information and increasing your knowledge about the causes, characteristics, teaching strategies, and resources are essential to becoming an informed and effective educator. Many organizations dedicated to disability advocacy provide information on research and fundraising, personal stories, photos, and videos; these organizations also provide access to other sources of information. Other sources are the parents or guardians, school administrators, child study team, physical therapists, occupational therapists, school nurses, and other educators in the school who hold valuable information about the student and about teaching people with

disabilities. Seek information about laws and regulations regarding the Individuals with Disabilities Education Act (IDEA) and its definition of the 13 categories of disabilities, the operational definition of free appropriate public education and a least restrictive environment (LRE), and the student's individualized education program (IEP). Check the student's IEP and incorporate the goals into the dance lessons.

CREATING AN INCLUSIVE ENVIRONMENT

The smile on your face tells your students that they are welcomed into the teaching space and that you are accepting and eager to help them learn. This simple facial gesture is significant to any learner and especially important to a student with disabilities. The smile also indicates to anyone else in the space, student or adult, that you are caring and willing to make the learning experience meaningful for all. The environment is more than a space; it is an attitude of acceptance that permeates all the activities that occur in a lesson. From the moment a student enters the space, you are there to greet them and acknowledge something personal, such as a new shirt, a necklace, a toy in the child's hand, or a new haircut. This initial connection provides you with information about how the student is feeling physically and socially on that day. Next, you describe the dance activity and mention how the space and equipment are organized for the lesson and help the student to a place where the lesson will begin. You may say, "Today we are going to dance with the scarves that are in a red basket near the wall. Everyone find a place." If the student with a disability has a paraeducator or a peer buddy, that person will also help the student to the space to begin the lesson. Sometimes, you can play music as the students enter the space to set a calming atmosphere or a signal that this is the dancing space.

The dance teaching space needs to comply with the requirements of the Americans with Disabilities Act (ADA) for access (United States Department of Justice 2010). Bathrooms, water fountains, entrances, and exits need to be designed for all students to access. The floor should be clean, and the lighting and temperature should be appropriate. Extra equipment such as

---

Figure 7.1 Questions About Personalities and Preferences

What do you want to learn this year in dance?

What are three things I should know about you?

What are your best subjects in school?

What do you like to do in your spare time?

What would you like to do when you grow up?

What did other teachers do to help you be successful?

Do you have any questions for me?

chairs, bleachers, equipment bins, media players, or devices need to be on carts so they are easily moved when space is needed. The boundaries for dancing need to be clearly marked with tape, painted floor lines, or cones. There needs to be space between the end of the boundary and the wall so children can stop without getting hurt. Keep the wall space clear of excess posters and other visual displays to keep distractions to a minimum, if appropriate, yet place needed information on the wall.

Simple rules for safety and learning should be posted and reviewed periodically. Develop a strategy about how you will help students who wander out exit doors, accidentally run into equipment, or are resistant to participating in the lesson and roam the space. Provide a rest space that is in the dance space but offers a quiet place for students to rest, calm themselves if they are overstimulated, or take a break from the lesson. Most important, ensure that students dance in a safe space that is comfortable and supports learning.

IMPLEMENTING INCLUSIVE TEACHING STRATEGIES

The goal of dance for learners with disabilities is to explore and develop each student's unique movement style. Bilitza (2021) asks educators to address the challenges of creating inclusive environments for education by identifying structures, behaviors, and methods of teaching. The author describes motivated dance educators who "take all physical differences of the participants as creative input for choreographing and creating artistic work" (p. 3). This perspective emphasizes the exploration and learning process as a foundation for the dance experience. While a product may emerge, the experience of learning and creating is primary. Teaching students with disabilities, like teaching all students, requires creativity and adaptability. The lessons should include high-level teaching conditions, differentiated instructions or activities when appropriate, use of teacher proximity to students, and activities at an appropriate skill level (Bertills, Granlund, and Augustine 2019). One of the most effective strategies for making an accommodation is to ask the student how a movement, prop, space, formation, or complete dance can be changed for their inclu-

sion. They have experience in negotiating their environment and making changes for access to be able to function and participate successfully. Most important, maintain the dignity of students with disabilities. Modify the environment, equipment, or lesson as necessary and ensure students embrace these modifications. However, you should also create an environment of integrative dance in which students' differences of movement and exploration are celebrated to maintain a high level of participation from all (DiPasquale 2022). The following are several strategies that are applicable for teaching dance to all students and can be used in a class for all learners with disabilities, an inclusive class, or a class with students who do not have a disability.

• Apply the principle of universal design. This strategy reflects the principle of architecture. The premise is that the design accommodates all people. For example, everyone can benefit from using a ramp to enter a building or from lever door handles. In dance, the circle formation is inherently inclusive because everyone can be seen and has an equal place in the group. A creative dance about exploring straight and curved shapes is appropriate for all students. The task of finding a way to make a straight shape with a part of your body can be answered in a variety of ways. This strategy is especially applicable to classes where students with disabilities participate with a class that includes students who do not have a disability. Everyone can participate in their own way because multiple answers are encouraged. Another application of universal design is using several sign language gestures with all students to support verbal directions. Teachers frequently use words such as *stop, go, line up, good job, no,* or *look at me.* In this way, you use two modes of communication, verbal and gestural, simultaneously to help learners hear and see directions and feedback. Students learn that there are multiple ways to learn and communicate, all of them equally effective.

• Establish a lesson routine. This strategy describes a set activity that occurs in the same space and at the same time (typically at the beginning or end of each dance session). The routine provides a clear, familiar expectation for each student and can help with organization and class management.

- Use designated spots. Each student has a predetermined place to begin and end the lesson and a place to return to for listening to instructions. The designated place can be marked by plastic poly spots, an X taped to the floor, an identifying line, a letter painted on the floor, a hoop, or a taped-down name card.

- Develop dances for beginning and ending the class session. These dances become part of the lesson routine and emphasize rhythmic patterns and repetition of movement. The same dance can be used throughout the school year or changed monthly. One example that welcomes students and encourages verbal communication combined with rhythm and repetition is the "We Are Glad to See You" dance. In this dance, students are seated in a circle on the floor or in chairs. Everyone repeats the following sequence together, which is accompanied by hand gestures. This is repeated for all students. This dance is best for small groups. A student may need help from you or the paraeducator to move their hands or arms, or you can delete the movements and use only the voice.

  - We are (two hand taps on the thighs, one tap on each word)
  - Glad to (two hand claps, one clap on each word)
  - See you (both hands point to a student in the circle)
  - Student's name (hands point to the student)

- Use peer helpers. These helpers are usually peers who do not have a disability who are in an inclusive class or older or same-age peers who help in a self-contained class. These peers are students you have trained in reinforcing instructions and demonstrations, providing feedback, and increasing practice time. Peers should not manipulate a student's body, move students who use a wheelchair, or assist with bathroom needs.

- Offer assistance to paraeducators to support learning. These adults, who are also known as aides, educational assistants, or teaching assistants, may accompany one student or provide support for several students. They may not be familiar with the dance content and may not be sure how to effectively assist the student. One way is to meet before the lesson and discuss specific strategies for helping, such as reinforcing or reading instructions, providing demonstrations, giving feedback, and helping to keep the student focused on the lesson. You can also send an email or a printed description of the lesson before the class or present a task card upon arrival at the session that describes verbal cues, appropriate feedback strategies, and tactical or visual prompts that help the student learn (see figure 7.2).

- Develop a visual schedule. This strategy is a pictorial display of the dance lesson showing the order in which the dance tasks or activities will be presented. The schedule can be placed on a wall near the entrance or near where directions are presented. A number, the picture, and a word describing the picture are included (see figure 7.3). Using the visual schedule allows students to see what will happen in the dance session and helps them feel organized and more secure. After each task or activity, you can return to the schedule and check off what was completed or show what activity is next.

- Use person-first language. When referring to someone with a disability, be respectful by using the name of the person or the type of person first and the disability second. For example, use *student who has autism* instead of *an autistic student*, or the child's name (e.g., *Malik, who has an intellectual disability*) instead of *the mentally challenged student*, or *Jan, who uses a wheelchair* instead of *the*

Figure 7.2 Sample Task Card

Warm-up dance: Cue words: "Kara, hands up and down."

Exploring shapes: Cue words: "Kara, round back." "Twist your waist." "Stretch big."

Cloud dance: Help her hold on to the curtain. Use hand over hand if needed.

Feedback: High fives or "Nice job!"

Chapter 7 Including All Children in Dance 101

Figure 7.3 Visual Schedule

1	Listening spot	●
2	Circle warm-up dance	
3	Shoemaker's dance	
4	Tanko bushi	
5	Listening spot	●
6	Line up	

wheelchair-bound girl. As an educator, you should always see the person first and understand that the disability is only one of their characteristics. Most important, students are not identified by their disabilities; they are viewed as one of the many students you teach who all have their own way of learning and being in the world.

- Establish clear stop and start signals. A stop signal is necessary for stopping the dancing and providing additional directions, changing to a new dance, ending the session, or attending to an emergency. The signal can be a verbal command, the sound of a percussion instrument, a hand signal, or a prop held up for all to see. Using both a verbal and a visual signal is most effective. Be aware of students who are sensitive to certain sounds or need more time to stop to control their bodies. Practice using the stop signal and the start signal, and use the signals consistently.

- Make feedback meaningful. Responding to a student's action can be affirmative or corrective. Words and phrases such as *fantastic, great job, excellent*, or *you did it* affirm a positive action; however, they will be more effective if the initial phrase is followed by a brief description about what the learner did well. For example, the phrase *nice job* is followed by *your arms were raised up very high*. In this way, the student knows what they did well and is more likely to repeat the action. When using a corrective statement, apply the sandwich approach, which begins with a positive statement, follows with the correction, and closes with a positive statement. For example, "Alicia, that turn went all the way around, but you need to keep your head up so you can keep your balance. I know you can do it." You can also use a positive word wall (Cone and Cone 2011) that has the printed affirmative words listed. You or the student can point to how the student performed the activity.

- Set up a personal folder. This strategy helps an individual focus on the sequence of the dance lesson or on the expected behaviors. In a folder is a list of the dance activities and a place to check when the activity is completed (see figure 7.4). The student, a paraeducator, or you can check the items off the list during the session or at the conclusion.

- Change the space, equipment, music, or props. Although many students with disabilities need only minor modifications to a lesson when learning, creating, or performing a dance, some of them will need extra modifications to the space, equipment, music, or props that support their way of learning. You can reduce or divide the amount of space for dancing into parts to help students know where to move. Use lines and arrows to mark directions, pathways, and formations. You can change the texture of the prop or equipment to make it easier to grip or more acceptable to touch, or you can attach props to a wheelchair. (Check with the school administration before using this approach.)

- Use mnemonics and key words as cues to identify a dance. A mnemonic is a memory strategy using letters organized into a word that represents a phrase that relates to something specific, like a dance. For example, GET means *gather everyone together*. You can use *GET dance* as the name of a dance that can be performed as part of a beginning routine. Another example of a beginning dance is the *how are you*, or *HAY dance*. Key words such as *time to go dance* or *good-bye dance* can indicate that this is the dance the class performs at the end of the session.

- Provide instructions in chunks. In this strategy, you divide the instructions into smaller pieces of information; you present one instruction at a time in a series. Check for understanding by observing whether a student complies or asking the student to repeat the instruction. Verbal instructions should be accompanied by a demonstration or supported by pictures or objects to provide multiple means of delivering the content.

Figure 7.4　Personal Folder Checklist

Date:

Dance activity	Completed
Warm-up dance	
Slow and fast movements	
Learning the cat dance	
Showing the cat dance story	
Sharing time	
My behavior	
I followed instructions.	
I did not yell out in class.	

- Wait for a response. After you ask a question or give an instruction, allow a short time for students to process the information and form a response. Some students need time to formulate the words or gestures or use their assistive technology to respond. The waiting time helps everyone think about what and how they want to communicate as an answer or make a comment.

- Apply closed- and open-skill teaching. Closed-skill teaching means that the movements for the dance are taught in isolation or out of the context of the complete dance. The dance movement is repeated in a predictable way to reinforce cognitive understanding and motor patterns. Then the dance movement can be inserted into an open-skill situation or the whole dance. In the open-skill or whole-dance situation, the movement may take on a variation, or there may be an unpredictable moment where the dancing partners change, the space or tempo is altered, or a spontaneous formation occurs.

INCLUSIVE DANCES

You can modify all dances to include students of various abilities. You know the students' developmental abilities, learning styles, and interests and can make adaptations so that everyone can participate. Some learners may not know they like to dance because they have not had the chance to try it or to communicate that they are interested. Others may need additional prompts to stay focused, or they may need time to watch others before they feel confident to join in. Students with hearing loss need to have a clear view of you or the student who is speaking or demonstrating. A student who is blind or has any visual disability needs a clear description of the activity or spatial arrangement, and that student may need help from a peer or paraeducator when moving in the space. Those students with orthopedic disabilities, whether ambulatory or those using wheelchairs, crutches, or walkers, can participate in all dances when they have adequate space and time to perform the movements. Dancing benefits all students. Through inclusion, they know that others care about their learning and want them to be part of their group. They increase their experiences in the many ways to move through learning social, cultural, and creative dances as well as experience the benefits of improved fitness, social interaction, decision-making, and motor development. Most dances can be modified to accommodate a student with a disability.

Cultural and Social Dances

In any cultural or social dance appropriate for elementary-age students, you can change the formation, tempo, skill complexity, and number of movements to meet the learners' abilities. These changes are also possible for any cultural or social dances appropriate for secondary-age students. Although these dances have traditional movements and formations, making changes is appropriate without losing the essence of the dance. For example, students can perform the popular chicken dance in a random formation instead of in a circle, and the four movements representing the beak, wings, tail, and claps that are usually repeated quickly four times can be reduced to one repetition. Students can move at random in the space on the second part of this dance instead of all moving in the same direction in a circle. Your role is to be creative in making changes that all learners can perform. A student with a disability should not be singled out to do a movement that is completely different from the other students' movements. One example of a social dance is the double circle mixer.

Double Circle Mixer

Students dance with many partners, which promotes positive social interaction and acceptance. The students learn a pattern of movement that is repeated many times, and on each repetition, they dance with a new partner.

Organization

Students are assigned a partner. The partners stand side by side facing counterclockwise. This forms the double circle.

Dance Description

All students move forward in the circle formation for 16 counts. Then they stop and turn to face their partners using 8 counts. Next, partners move backward away from each other using 8 counts. They clap their hands 4 times for 8 counts, 2 counts for each clap. Next, they point to the student in the opposite circle who is diagonally to their right for 8 counts. This is their new partner. They move forward toward their new partner and return to the side-by-side position. This takes 8 counts. Now the dance begins again with a new partner. Students can high-five or wave to their new partner as they move forward to meet them. The students can walk, skip, jog, gallop, wheel, or be pushed in their wheelchair while traveling the 16 counts in the circle. Students using wheelchairs, crutches, or walkers can easily participate and move forward in the circle for 16 counts while other students are walking. The tempo can be slowed down, or any part of the dance can be eliminated. The goal is to maintain the idea of dancing with a new partner each time the dance is repeated.

Creative Dances

The creative dances described here are examples of dances that the whole class can perform, and which allow students to create movements within the dance structure. Accommodations for students with disabilities are included. Additional dance ideas are included in the article *Strategies for Teaching Dancers of All Abilities* by Cone and Cone (2011).

Greet and Meet Dance

This is appropriate for a beginning activity in inclusive and self-contained classes. The students move in toward the center of the circle and out of the circle many times to establish the basic movement pattern for the dance. Different elements of dance are applied in creating movement variations.

Organization

This dance uses a single circle formation with the students facing toward the center of the circle. Students use plastic poly spots or a tape mark to designate their place in the circle.

Dance Description

The music starts and the students clap, bounce in place, step in place, or wave a hand to the beat. Then on your signal, everyone moves forward toward the center of the circle. A hoop can be placed in the center to provide a visual cue for the center of the circle. When they arrive at the center, the students can wave to each other or clap their hands. Then everyone is signaled to move back to their place in the circle. They repeat moving forward and backward several times to establish a movement pattern. Next, you or the students can suggest movements to express that they are greeting someone, such as a high five, a fist bump, or a greeting in another language or sign language. Students using wheelchairs, walkers, or crutches can easily join in this dance and move at an appropriate tempo. Students with visual impairment can hold your elbow or hand or the elbow or hand of a peer or paraeducator. They will need to be told how far they are moving into the circle and how the other students are moving. Depending on their intellectual disability, students can follow others, be prompted with cue words, or hold someone's hand. Students with pervasive developmental disorders and autism spectrum disorder may need to see the whole dance first so they understand what will happen and then either become involved with the rest of the group or dance the same movements outside of the circle. A paraeducator may use cue words such as *move in*, *wave*, and *move back* or use hand over hand where the adult moves the student's hand to show the waving movement. When students are ready, you can suggest a variety of ways to move in and out of the circle and use a variety of directions, pathways, sizes of steps, levels, and tempos. Also, instead of everyone moving in at the same time, you can call for a few students to do the dance. For example, call out categories, such as all boys or all girls, students wearing something blue, or students with birthdays in a certain month. Providing variations can help group members identify themselves as different and as similar to others in the group (Cone and Cone 2011).

Freeze Dance

This dance uses locomotor movements or wheelchair movement and still shapes. It can be used in inclusive and self-contained classes. While the music is playing, the students travel through the space using different directions and tempos. When the music stops, they freeze in a still shape. You or the students can decide on the movements for traveling in the space and on the type of shapes.

Organization
Students move randomly in the space.

Dance Description
Inform the students that when the music is on, they will move in the dance space, and when the music stops, they will freeze in a shape. Call out a locomotor movement and a direction or tempo, such as "Walk forward slowly." If that is too many concepts for learners to comprehend, call out only the locomotor movement and add a demonstration. Then stop the music and tell everyone to freeze. A type of frozen shape is called a round shape, a wide shape, or a low shape, among many others. Support the verbal instructions with a printed sign for each locomotor movement and each type of shape. Continue the move-and-freeze pattern several times, and then you can add moving with a partner or freezing connected to another student. Students who are deaf or hard of hearing can watch the other students, and you can use a visual stop signal to indicate that the music has stopped. Students who are blind or who have a visual impairment can hear the music and move in the space while the other students watch to make sure they are not bumping into anyone. This dance is also appropriate for students using manual or power wheelchairs, walkers, or crutches. They can use all or parts of the body to make the shapes. Use the paraeducator or peer helper with students when needed to reinforce the directions and cue words.

Shape Get-Together

This group dance requires students to observe other students demonstrating a shape and then reproduce the shapes with their own bodies. All the shapes that each student demonstrates are added together, one at a time, into one dance.

Organization

Students are organized into groups of three to five and form a circle.

Dance Description

Each student in the group is given a number starting from 1 to as many students as are in the group. Each student creates a shape such as big, twisted, round, or any other type. They practice holding the shape for 4 slow beats. The number of beats can vary. The student with the first number demonstrates their shape to the group and, in unison, the group members repeat the shape. Next, the second person in the group demonstrates their shape and, in unison, the group members repeat the action. Then the group repeats the first shape followed by the second shape. The third person then demonstrates their shape and, in unison, the group repeats the shape. Now, the group performs the shapes beginning with the first, then the second, and then the third. This pattern of demonstrating, repeating, and adding the shape to the sequence is repeated until everyone in the group has contributed a shape to the dance sequence. The goal is to remember the sequence, perform in unison, and maintain holding still for 4 beats for each shape. To accommodate students with intellectual disabilities, you or a peer or paraeducator can offer an idea for a shape and use words to describe the shape to support the action with language acquisition. Students who have a visual impairment can feel the body of the person making the shape. This is referred to as body brailing. Using descriptive words also helps to support identifying the shape.

Scarf or Streamer Dance

Students use scarves or streamers to form mirroring and shadowing relationships. In the mirroring relationship, the leader creates various nonlocomotor movements, and in the shadow relationship, the leader uses locomotor movements and still shapes. Students take turns as leaders.

Organization and Equipment Needed

Use a random formation in the space. Students are organized into pairs or into groups of three. Each student has a scarf or a streamer. The streamers can be paper or plastic. The length is determined by each student's size and range of motion. Streamers range from 1 to 3 feet (.3-1 m).

Dance Description

Each student holds a scarf or a streamer. One partner is the leader and the other is the follower. The leader can choose how they want to slowly move the scarf or streamer, and the follower observes and reproduces the movement at the same time as the leader. The movement needs to be slow to help students with processing and reproducing the observed movements. This dance occurs in a stationary space using primarily nonlocomotor movements. The partners or students in the group take turns being a leader and a follower. Music with a slow tempo will support the slow body movements. The students then change from a mirror relationship to a shadow relationship. One student is the leader and the other is the follower. The leader uses locomotor movements to travel in the space while the follower does the same movements. Students take turns as the leader. The leader can also stop and freeze in a shape and then continue moving in the space. To adapt the dance for students with a visual impairment, have a peer or paraeducator use cue words to describe the leader's movements. When they are the leader for the shadow dance, they can hold the elbow of a peer or paraeducator as they move through the space.

Chapter 7 Including All Children in Dance **107**

Going for a Drive Dance

This dance expresses the actions that drivers use. Students suggest actions such as putting on a seat belt, steering, honking the horn, or pressing the accelerator. An action represents each word or phrase. The actions are repeated several times to form a movement pattern. Students can perform while seated or they can use locomotor movements.

Organization and Equipment Needed

Use random formations. You will need large chart paper, a poster, or a whiteboard; markers; and pictures of a variety of cars.

Dance Description

Ask the students the following question: "What are some actions a driver uses when driving a car?" Write the students' responses on a poster, chart paper, or whiteboard. You can ask the students to spell the words or write the words. Next, each word is transformed into an action. For example, to create a movement to express steering, ask the students, "How do a driver's hands and arms move when steering the car?" Students usually pretend to grip a steering wheel and move their hands and arms up and down. To transform this action into a dance, ask the students to do the steering movement slowly and then quickly and then slowly again, developing a pattern based on the dance element of tempo. Students practice the movements and can add upper-body leans to the right and left. Next, select a second word and use the same process: Demonstrate how the body moves to represent the word, repeat the movements several times, add an element of dance, and practice the movement pattern several times. This continues until all the suggested words are transformed into dance movements. Once the students have practiced the movements, you or a student can point to a word or call out a word in any order, and the students respond by performing the movements associated with the word. The caller can determine the duration of the movement before calling out another word.

Bandanna Dance

All students are connected by holding bandannas or scarves. They move in circular, spiral, and curvy pathways as one line of students. You can lead the dance, and the students can lead as they move throughout the space.

Organization and Equipment Needed

Students begin in a single circle, then change to a spiral formation, and then to a curvy line formation. Each student has a bandanna held in or attached to the right hand. If attaching the bandanna to a wheelchair or walker, tie several bandannas together to make one longer bandanna to allow for more space between the students as they move. Always check with the administrator to ensure that tying the bandanna to a student's mobility device is appropriate and safe.

Dance Description

Students begin in a single circle facing toward the center. Each student holds a scarf with the right hand and then holds the scarf of the student next to them with the left hand. Now everyone is connected in one circle by holding the scarves. The first movement is to lift the scarves up and down three or four times using a slow tempo. Next, the right hand rises up, and while the right hand lowers, the left hand raises up. They repeat this three or four times slowly. Students move forward toward the center of the circle and back to their original places. This is repeated two times. Next you, who are part of the circle, have the student on your right let go of the scarf while everyone else continues to be connected. You, now a leader, move slowly forward inside the circle while the students follow. As you move forward on a spiral pathway, the circle forms a spiral formation. When you arrive at the center of the circle, turn to your right and reverse the spiral pathway. As students follow, they will pass by other students. When the spiral unwinds, lead the students around the space in curvy pathways. The dance ends with you forming a circle of students. The beginning movements, raising and lowering the scarves and moving in and out of the circle, are repeated as the final movements in the dance. Using the scarves provides more space in between students and makes it easier for them to follow the pathway. Also, students who do not like to hold hands can hold the scarves instead. For more space, you can tie two or more scarves together. A variation for this dance is to organize students into groups of five or six and have them form a line instead of a circle. One student at the end of the line is designated as the leader; they move slowly in the space choosing where they want to go while the other students, all connected by bandannas, follow. Each student is provided an opportunity to be a leader.

Olympic Sport Dance

Students observe pictures of athletes participating in Olympic sports and then make their bodies into the same shapes as the athletes in the pictures. Three pictures and a variety of locomotor movements are combined to form a five-part dance.

Organization and Equipment Needed

Students use a random formation. Have three laminated photos of athletes in action shapes that represent sports in the Winter or Summer Olympics or Paralympics. You'll also need poster or chart paper and three signs, each with the number 1, 2, or 3.

Dance Description

Adhere the three sport photos to a wall, poster, or chart. Above each picture is one of the number signs to show which picture is first, second, and third. First, the students look at photo 1 and make their bodies into the same shape as the athlete in the photo. They hold the shape for 8 counts. Next, they look at photo 2 and make their bodies into that shape and hold it still for 8 counts. Then they do the same for photo 3. Practice each shape in the three photos several times. Then, in between each still pose, students perform a locomotor movement or move in their wheelchairs for 16 counts. They can choose the pathway, the type of locomotor movement, and the direction. Cue the dance as follows: "Picture 1, hold still 1, 2, 3, 4, 5, 6, 7, 8 and move in the space (count for 16 counts). Picture 2, hold still 1, 2, 3, 4, 5, 6, 7, 8 and move in the space (count for 16 counts). Picture 3, hold still 1, 2, 3, 4, 5, 6, 7, 8."

Olympic sport dance sequence is as follows: photo 1 shape + locomotor movement + photo 2 shape + locomotor movement + photo 3 shape. After repeating the dance several times with your cues, the students can perform the dance on their own time. You can make several variations to this dance. Ask students to change the order of the photos and try a new dance using the same photos in the new order. Another variation is to replace one of the photos with a photo of an athlete in a different sport. Finally, you can add or subtract the number of photos used in the dance.

SUMMARY

Students with disabilities have the right to learn, create, perform, observe, and respond to their own dances and to the dances of others. You are responsible for developing an inclusive learning space where every student is respected for their distinct abilities. That means involving learners with disabilities in all the dancing and making accommodations for meaningful participation when needed. Peers are eager to offer ideas for inclusion and willing to assist when possible. In this way, everyone benefits by learning about acceptance and multiple ways to create and perform a dance. The joy of dancing to music and sharing the dances with friends is the result of a dance program founded on a philosophy that acknowledges the gifts that every student has. When students—all students—dance, they learn that a movement, no matter how small, can express powerful ideas, feelings, and ways of knowing the world.

Questions for Reflection

1. What benefits do students with disabilities gain as a result of participating in dance?
2. Consider an accommodation for a social dance. Is the accommodation safe for everyone, and does it fully include the student with disabilities?
3. Think of a topic for a creative dance lesson, such as the water cycle or animal actions. How can you use a visual schedule to support the sequence of activities in the lesson?
4. What are strategies you can use to help the paraeducator or peer helper be effective when assisting a student with a disability?
5. Where can you locate information about a student's disability? What resources are available?
6. How can you include the student's individualized education program (IEP) goals into your dance lesson?

PART II

Learning Experiences

Part II presents 55 exciting dance learning experiences. These ready-to-use experiences are presented in a style that depicts what the experience will be like when a class of students is actively learning. The descriptions provide you with the language for presenting the learning experience initially and then shaping the content to your own style of teaching. Bracketed notes guide you in the process. The learning experiences included focus on creative dance, social and popular dances, and folk and cultural dances. However, these are just a small sample of the possible types of dances available, and we suggest you use other resources to support and present a comprehensive dance program.

In this book, the term *learning experience* is used to describe a lesson progression, beginning with an introduction and ending with culminating dance ideas in the closure, which focuses on a set of learning outcomes. Depending on the amount of time students spend in dance sessions, the learning experience may be presented in one or more sessions.

In part II, you will find four chapters. The first two chapters, 8 and 9, focus on creative dance experiences for children. Chapter 8 contains 12 learning experiences that are appropriate for children in kindergarten through second grade. The content and flow of the learning experience are interesting to and developmentally appropriate for young children. The 11 learning experiences in chapter 9 focus on students in third through eighth grades who are able to create and learn dances more independently than younger children. Ideas from either chapter, however, can be adapted for all grade levels. For many years, these learning experiences were part of the physical education and dance program at the Brunswick Acres Elementary School and have also been taught in the Teaching Concepts of Dance in Physical Education course at Rowan University. Children as well as college students find the learning experiences enjoyable yet challenging. When a dance unit is announced, the students welcome the opportunity to express themselves through dance and experience the joy of dancing with others.

New to this edition of the book are chapters 10 and 11, focusing on social and cultural dances. The 21 learning experiences in chapter 10 focus on popular, fitness, and social dances that can be taught and adapted for all age and experience levels. Chapter 11 contains 11 learning experiences and presents a small sample of folk and cultural dances to represent a variety of cultural backgrounds. These dances should be presented as authentically as possible to honor each culture represented, but modifications for special circumstances or ability levels are included in many of the experiences.

The learning experiences in part II are organized to help you gain access to the information to make a teaching selection. Each learning experience is formatted as follows:

1. **Title** is the name of the learning experience.

2. **Grades** (chapters 10 and 11) suggest the appropriate age group to teach each choreographed learning experience.

3. **Outcomes** explain what students will gain as a result of participating in the learning experience.

4. **Organization** describes how the students are arranged during the learning experience and specifies whether they will participate individually, in partners, or in small groups.

5. **Equipment needed** is a list of the kinds and amounts of equipment needed for presenting this learning experience to students, including music suggestions.

6. **Introduction and warm-up, descriptions of movements, dance sequence, culminating dance, and closure** describe the specific sections of the total learning experience.

7. **Look for** contains key points to keep in mind when informally observing students' progress in the learning experience. These points are related to the outcomes of the learning experience.

8. **How can I change this?** provides ideas for extending the lesson or presenting a variation.

9. **Assessment suggestions** (chapters 8 and 9) are ideas for developing assessment instruments for student self-assessment, teacher assessment of students' learning, and peer assessment in the psychomotor, cognitive, and affective domains.

10. **Interdisciplinary connections** (chapters 8 and 9) are suggestions for linking the dance experience with content in other subject areas.

Explore, experiment with, and enjoy using these learning experiences. They are for you and your students to share as you all discover the excitement of creating, performing, and responding to dance. Our hope is that, because of your willingness to teach dance, more students will have the opportunity to learn about this meaningful form of expression. The skills and knowledge they gain will last a lifetime.

Chapter 8

Learning Experiences for Kindergarten, First Grade, and Second Grade

Young children delight in dances that use vivid imagery, stories, animals, and familiar characters. Several of the dance experiences in this chapter provide opportunities for children to express their ideas about circus characters, animals, and real or imaginary experiences. As the teacher, you play an important role in planning tasks that are appropriate to the physical, cognitive, emotional, and social needs of a particular age group. In these creative dance experiences, you guide children in creating and expanding their movements within the planned structure of a culminating dance. To facilitate your selection of learning experiences, we have summarized each learning experience in table 8.1.

You will find that each learning experience is outlined in 12 sections that identify outcomes and assessments, equipment and organization, and a detailed description of how to implement the introduction, warm-up, development, culminating dance, and closure. Additional ideas for varying the learning experience and connecting to other subject areas are included. The description of each learning experience follows this format:

- Title
- Outcomes
- Organization
- Equipment needed (including suggested music)
- Introduction and warm-up
- Development
- Culminating dance
- Closure
- Look for
- How can I change this?
- Assessment suggestions
- Interdisciplinary connections

The instructions for each dance learning experience are similar to the dialogue you would use when talking with your students. Any text in brackets indicates suggested instructions that you might use.

113

Table 8.1 Index of Learning Experiences for Kindergarten, First Grade, and Second Grade

Name of dance learning experience	Description of dance learning experience
Neighborhood friendship streamer dance	Children use colorful streamers in dancing a story about celebrating friendship in a community.
Floating clouds and rain showers	Children explore and express the shapes and movements of clouds in a dance depicting how individual clouds connect and form a huge rain cloud.
Run, hop, jump, skip	A poetic text serves as the accompaniment to four dances that express the words that form a rhythm through rhyme.
The playground	Children re-create the activities of playing on a slide, the swings, and a seesaw through moving on different levels and in different directions.
Ocean waves and swimmers	The dancing space is transformed into an ocean and beach in this dance, which uses the level changes of the waves and actions of swimmers in creating a dance about a day at the beach.
Spaghetti dance	Are you ready for a bowl of spaghetti? This experience, which focuses on creating straight and curved shapes and pathways while varying levels and tempo, concludes with a dance about the adventure of a box of spaghetti.
Balloon dance	Inflating, deflating, floating, and popping are the actions explored in a learning experience that uses the image of a balloon in a dance about small and big shapes and movements.
Percussion instrument dance	Light and strong forces are the focus of this dance experience that uses the sounds of a drum, a triangle, and maracas in creating three dances that express the quality of the sounds.
The hungry cat	In this learning experience, children dance the slow and fast movements of a cat who wakes up, chases and then captures a mouse, and goes back to sleep.
Circus dance	Welcome to the circus! A suite of dances portrays the actions of four circus acts: the galloping horses, the tightrope walkers, the lions and tigers, and the funny clowns.
Connect the spots	Children create shapes and locomotor movements as they map out dancing spots in the space. This dance emphasizes sequence memory, body coordination, and balance.
Frog dance	Did you ever wonder what life was like for a frog that lived one day as a small frog and the next day as a big frog? This dance explores how range is used in changing movements from small to big.

Neighborhood Friendship Streamer Dance

Outcomes

As a result of participating in this learning experience, children will be able to do the following:

1. Create and perform locomotor and nonlocomotor movements that use circular pathways on the floor and in the air (cognitive and psychomotor).
2. Create and perform four turning movements (cognitive and psychomotor).
3. Perform circular pathways using a streamer (psychomotor).
4. Demonstrate understanding of how a community celebrates friendship through dance (cognitive).
5. Collaborate as a group to dance together (affective).
6. Perform the complete dance with and without teacher prompts (psychomotor and cognitive).

Organization

Children begin the lesson by exploring movements individually; then they dance with a small group; finally, all the groups dance together.

Equipment Needed

- Paper or plastic streamers (1 meter long) equally divided into four colors—blue, green, yellow, and red—with enough streamers for each child to have one
- Four medium to tall cones to mark the corners of the space—one each of red, blue, green, and yellow
- Suggested music: medium-tempo music for accompaniment that supports a skipping rhythm

Introduction and Warm-Up

Today, we are going to do a friendship dance. The dance uses a lot of circles. You will find ways to travel in the space in a circle, turn in a circle, and use a streamer to make circles in the air. The streamer will be your dancing partner. After I give you a streamer, find a personal space and begin to draw circles in the air.

Find all the places around your body that you can draw a circle with the streamer. Can you draw a circle over your head, on the side of your body, around your waist, in front of you, and in back of your body? Try another way.

Draw the largest circle you can. Reach up high, far out to the side, and down to the floor. Make sure you draw circles with each hand. Can you draw a big circle very slowly? Now, a small circle as fast as you can?

Next, travel in a circle by skipping, galloping, or sliding sideways while making circles with your streamer. Choose one of the ways to travel you didn't select the first time, and make a circle with your streamer in a different way. Now, move the same way you just did, but this time, circle the streamer in another way.

Development

Now, you are going to make circles using your streamer by learning four ways to turn. In your personal space, make a circle with your body by turning on one foot. How can you use your streamer as you do this turn? Next, try a jump turn. This turn can go all the way around or just part of the way. Be sure to land on your feet, and bend your knees as you come down. Now, find a way to turn using a wide stretched shape. On the fourth turn, do it as slowly as you can. Show me how you change levels while you slowly turn. [Children practice each turn several times.]

Next, you are going to practice the four different turns, but now you will add a skip before your turn. Here is the pattern: skip, skip, skip, skip, and turn around. Try this pattern using each turn. [Gallops can be used in place of skips, and you can designate an order for practicing each turn instead of having the children choose the order.]

In the next movement, I want you to toss the streamer high above your head, let it go (making sure not to hit anyone), and watch it fall to the floor. What is the shape of the streamer as it lies on the floor? Is the streamer twisted, folded, straight, or curled?

Find a way to make your body into the same shape as the streamer. Toss your streamer into the air again, let it fall, and see what shape it makes on the floor now. Try out this new shape with your body. Try tossing and making shapes a few more times.

Culminating Dance

Now, we're going to combine all the ideas we explored with the streamer into a dance. This is a dance about celebrating friendship in a neighborhood. In this neighborhood, there are four streets. All the children with blue streamers will live on Blue Street in one corner. Children with red streamers will live on Red Street in another corner, yellow streamers on Yellow Street in the third corner, and green streamers on Green Street in the fourth corner of the room (see figure 8.1).

Each street group will take turns skipping to the middle of the room, doing a turn, and skipping back to their corner. Red Street group, you will do a one-foot turn, the Blue Street group will do a slow turn moving high and low, the Green Street group will do a jump turn, and the Yellow Street group will do a turn in a wide stretched shape. [Provide time for each group to practice moving together toward the center of the room while skipping and turning.]

Now, I will tell the story about the neighborhood friendship dance as you dance each part. Everyone decided to have a neighborhood friendship dance that lasted for three days. On the first day of the neighborhood dance, the people living on Red Street skipped to the middle of the neighborhood to show everyone their one-foot turn, and then they skipped back home. Now, Red Street dancers, show us your skipping and turning. Then, the children living on Blue Street wanted to show the rest of the neighborhood their slow turn, so they skipped to the middle of the neighborhood, did their slow turn, and skipped back home. Okay, Blue Street, we are ready for you. Next, from the third corner, the children on Green Street skipped to the middle of the neighborhood to show their jumping turn and skipped back home. Okay, ready, Green Street dancers? It's your turn. And the Yellow Street dancers said, "Don't forget us! We want to show our wide stretched turn to the neighborhood." So the Yellow Street dancers skipped to the middle, did a big stretched turn, and skipped back home. It's your turn, Yellow Street dancers.

On the second day of the dance, the children on Red Street looked far across the neighborhood to the children on Blue Street and wondered what it would be like to live over there. At the same time, the children on Blue Street looked across at the children on Red Street and also wondered what it would be like to live on Red Street. Both groups decided to go and visit the other street. The Red and Blue groups

Figure 8.1 Children with streamers begin the dance in four corners in the room.

slid sideways, leading with their right side, across the middle of the neighborhood to the opposite street, waving to each other with their streamers as they passed by. [Children slide to the opposite corner, passing the other group on the way.] Then the children on Green Street looked at the children on Yellow Street and wondered what it would be like to live on Yellow Street. And, at the same time, the children living on Yellow Street had the same feelings. So both groups slid sideways across the space to the opposite corners, waving their streamers as they passed by the other group. [Children slide to the opposite corner.] Next, the Red Street children became lonely for their street and wanted to go home, and the Blue Street children felt the same way. So both groups slid sideways back to their own corners, waving to each other as they passed by. [Children return to their original corners.] Then the children from Green Street and Yellow Street wanted to go back home. So they slid sideways back across the neighborhood to their own corners, waving to each other as they passed by. [Children return to their original corners.]

On the third day of the party, the Red Street group decided to have their own party and invite the whole neighborhood. [Assign two children to be the leaders for the Red Street group.] Now, Red Street group, skip over to the Green Street group, stop, wave to them, and say, "Hey, come with us." [Red Street group skips to the Green Street group.] Next, everyone in the Red and Green groups, skip over to the children on Blue Street, stop, wave to them, and say, "Hey, come with us." [Red and Green skip over to Blue, and Blue joins in to make one large group.] And, finally, everyone skip over to the children on Yellow Street, stop, wave to them, and say, "Hey, come with us." [The yellow group joins the others.] Now everyone skip in a big circle around the room, waving your streamers in the air.

Next, the Red Street group leaders stop, face each other, and hold the ends of each other's streamers to make a doorway into the party. Now, each child take turns walking under the doorway and into the party. At the party, everyone is turning and circling their streamers. You can dance by yourself or dance with another person who has a different color streamer. Okay, begin. I see some children turning slowly, some turning very fast, and some children holding hands and skipping. [Children improvise for 1 or 2 minutes.] Now, everyone stop—the party is over. The dance ends with everyone tossing a streamer into the air and making the same shape like we did earlier in the lesson. Ready? Toss. Let the streamer fall to the floor, and now you slowly fall to the floor and make your body into the same shape as the streamer. [You can signal the end of the party, or a child can create a signal that everyone can follow.] Nice job! Let's try the whole dance again. This time, perform the dance without me telling the story. Express the story through your dancing.

Closure

That was great fun. What part of the dance did you like the best? What did you like about it? [Ask several children to share their comments.] How do you think the dance showed friendship? [More children respond.] Take your streamer home with you tonight and talk with your family about our dance. You can show them your turn and the shapes you made with the streamers.

Look For

- How children were able to coordinate the skip-and-turn sequence and maintain good balance. Some children may skip too fast and will not be able to change from the skip to the turn without falling.
- Children who need extra help to match their body shapes to the shape of the streamer. Some children will surprise you with their unique interpretations, and others will not be able to match the shape of the streamer with their bodies. You can ask these children to reproduce only a part of the streamer shape.
- Children who bump into others when exchanging corners. Ask the children for suggestions on solving the bumping problem.

How Can I Change This?

- Replace skipping with galloping or walking.
- Ask each street group to collaborate and choose a locomotor movement and a pathway to travel to the middle of the neighborhood. They could move while connected, move low to the floor, or use different directions or tempos.

118 Teaching Children Dance

- Allow children to choose the streamer color. This may lead to uneven groups, but having some groups with more children can make the dance interesting.
- In the section of the culminating dance where two children hold hands to make a door, you can have everyone in the red group hold hands with a partner to make several doors for the other three groups to use as entrances to the party. This strategy will also alleviate waiting in line to enter the party.

Assessment Suggestions

- Teacher assessment—cognitive: Ask students to describe verbally what happens on each day of the friendship streamer dance to assess their recall of the dance sequence (outcome 6).
- Teacher assessment—psychomotor: Use a checklist to record (yes or no) whether students can perform locomotor and nonlocomotor movements in a circular pathway and whether students can perform the four turning movements (outcomes 1 and 2).
- Teacher assessment—cognitive: Students can create a vocabulary list of words that describe the shapes of the streamers and their bodies after the toss. They can also make drawings of the shapes (outcome 2).
- Student self-assessment—psychomotor: Students, organized by their street group, demonstrate to each other the ways they made circles with the streamers (outcomes 1 and 3).
- Student self-assessment—affective and cognitive: Students can draw a picture of friends dancing together with the streamers (outcomes 4 and 5).

Interdisciplinary Connections

- Social studies: Use this dance to initiate or conclude a social studies unit on communities or friendship.
- Visual arts: Integrate the dance with visual arts by having the children draw pictures of themselves dancing in circular pathways or doing their turns.

Floating Clouds and Rain Showers

Outcomes

As a result of participating in this learning experience, children will be able to do the following:

1. Create body shapes that represent various cloud shapes (cognitive).
2. Demonstrate slow and light and fast and strong movements (psychomotor).
3. Move in different relationships safely—with a partner, in a small group, and in a large group (psychomotor and cognitive).
4. Use coordination and control when changing shapes and movements (psychomotor).

Organization

Children dance individually and then with a partner. Next, partners join other sets of partners to form small groups. Finally, the whole class joins together in one formation.

Equipment Needed

- Paper and crayons for drawing
- Whiteboard or chart paper
- Suggested music: slow and fast music for accompaniment, or use a percussion instrument

Introduction and Warm-Up

Today, we are going to do a dance called floating clouds and rain showers. This dance is about the shapes and movements of clouds. How can you describe the cloud shapes you have seen? Sophia said they are *round*; Caden said *long*. I also heard *puffy, big, soft, oval,* and *straight*. [Write these shape words on chart paper or a whiteboard.] How do clouds move across the sky? I hear *fast, slow, floating, twirling*. Yes, sometimes they are still or they move up and down. [Write movement words on chart paper or a whiteboard.] Now, we are going to use the cloud shapes and the ways clouds move to create a dance. Find a personal space in the room for our warm-up.

Begin your warm-up following me. I will use slow movements while we are standing in our spaces and then faster movements as we travel in the space. [Slowly move various body parts, bending and stretching in different directions. Then, ask the children to walk around the room, followed by galloping, and finally running.]

Development

The cloud-shape words that you described in the beginning of class are on the whiteboard or chart paper. Standing in your personal space, make your body into one of those shapes. Try another one, and now another. Let's try making a round cloud. Can you make the round shape with only your arms? Try making a wide cloud shape, now a long straight shape, and now a small shape. Can you make a cloud shape that uses another body part touching the floor, other than your feet? Meredith has made a long shape on the side of her body, and Tamika is in a wide stretched shape supported by her hands and feet. Try another cloud shape and one more cloud shape.

Choose three cloud shapes, and then decide which one you will do first, second, and third. Let's practice changing from the first shape to the second shape and then to the third shape. Ready! Slowly make your first shape, quickly get into your second shape, and slowly make your third shape. Try the three cloud shapes again using the slow, fast, slow tempos. This time, try a different tempo sequence for your cloud shapes such as fast, fast, slow or fast, slow, slow. Practice this cloud shape dance a couple of times. [Children practice their cloud shapes.]

Choose a cloud shape and find a way to make it travel around the general space slowly; now quickly. Choose another cloud shape and decide the speed it will travel. I see round clouds walking slowly, wide clouds sliding sideways, and fast and long straight clouds rolling on the floor.

Feel like your cloud is floating across the sky, changing shapes and tempo as it moves. Be careful to move around the other clouds. [Children practice their cloud movements. Play music or a percussion instrument while the children practice.]

Does anyone want to show us your cloud dance? Let's watch and see what shapes the dancers are making and if they change the tempo. [Three or four children demonstrate, and you ask observing children to comment on what they see.]

Now, I will assign you a cloud partner, and I want the two of you to find different ways you can connect your cloud shapes to each other and float across the sky. [Organize the children into partners and provide time for exploration.] What are the body parts you can use to connect to another cloud? I see these two children are using their hands; others are using their feet. I see elbows connected to shoulders, hands connected to a back, and heads connected.

Next, find a way you and your partner can combine your two cloud shapes and make a new cloud shape. Try making three different cloud shapes. Remember to stay connected. What other cloud shapes can you make connected together?

Now, find a way to move your new cloud across the sky. Decide if one person is going to lead or if you are going to take turns as leaders. Can you continue to stay connected as you travel?

Find another cloud and connect together into a larger cloud. What are the body parts you can use to connect to each other? Can you find a way for this cloud to travel across the space? Who will be the leader? What is the shape of your large cloud? When you have a large cloud, move slowly so everyone can move together and stay connected. Let me see how you move slowly in your cloud shape and stay connected. [When children move as connected clouds, you want them to enjoy the challenge of moving with another person and remaining safe. Take this opportunity to discuss cooperation in decision-making.

Make sure the children agree about how and where they are going to move before they begin. Remind them to move slowly.]

Now, all the small groups of clouds will join together into one really, really big cloud. Before we move, we need to talk about what shape the large cloud will be, how we will be connected to each other, and how the cloud will move. What shape should we use for the large cloud? Carmen suggests a long straight cloud. How will we be connected to each other? Joe suggests holding hands. How will the cloud move? Constantine says that walking will work best. Let's all join hands in a long line with Carmen as the leader and Joe at the end of the line. [Children assemble.] Carmen, begin to lead the cloud around the room as everyone walks slowly. Bring the cloud to the middle of the room to form a circle, and now close the cloud shape by holding Joe's hand. Now, let go of your hands. Let's try it again with a new leader. Can anyone suggest another large-class cloud? [You can try several ideas, with suggestions from the children about the shape and how to move.]

Culminating Dance

Now, we are going to use all the cloud shapes in a dance. The dance will begin with your individual cloud shape and then move into partner or trio cloud shapes. Next, everyone will join together in one giant cloud. Now, each person finds a personal space to begin the cloud dance. Begin to slowly make your body into one of your individual cloud shapes and travel in the space. As you move, find another person and connect. Remember to connect with different body parts. Now, find another cloud; connect and travel together across the sky. Move slowly so everyone can stay connected and travel together safely. Now, all the clouds join together by holding hands in a long line with Noah as the leader and Olivia at the end of the line. I see everyone is moving slowly and holding hands as you follow Noah around the room. Noah, bring the group into a big circle and join hands with Olivia to make a large round cloud. Now, let's try the dance again from the beginning with a new leader.

Closure

To end the lesson, lie on the floor and rest while you think about the cloud dance. Pretend you are watching a movie of the cloud dance. Watch yourself make cloud shapes. What shapes are you using? Now you are connecting to another cloud. What body parts did you use to connect? Next, partner clouds are connecting to other partner clouds, and you are all moving across the sky. Are you moving slowly? And, finally, everyone connects into one giant cloud. What is the shape of the giant cloud?

[The learning experience can conclude at this point, or you can continue to add the next section, the rainstorm.]

The next part of the learning experience begins with everyone standing in a large circle like a big round cloud. In this part of the dance, the cloud is going to fill up with rain and burst open. How can we make this cloud become bigger and bigger? I hear from Sari that we can let go of our hands and move backward, and Brad suggested that we make big stretching shapes. Let's try both ideas. Let go of hands and move backward 4 steps, growing into a big stretched shape (see figure 8.2). Ready! 1, 2, 3, 4. Hold your big shape still. Let's try it again.

Once the cloud is full of rain, it will burst open. What are some other words we can use instead of *burst*? I hear *explode, break open, pop, bust apart.* How can your body move to show a bursting movement? I hear *up, open, stretched, jumping, turning.* What kind of force is needed? Yes, strong. Where will you move in space? Okay, up and forward, up and backward, or up and sideward. Create three different bursting movements. Ready! Burst,

Figure 8.2 The cloud becomes bigger and bigger, filling up with rain.

burst, and burst. Try each burst in a different direction. Burst, burst, and burst. Practice your three bursting movements each in a different direction.

Now, let's combine the cloud filling with rain and then bursting. First, the circle becomes bigger 1, 2, 3, and 4, and now burst, burst, and burst. Let's try that part again: 1, 2, 3, and 4, and burst, burst, and burst. [You can ask several children to demonstrate their bursting movement while the other children observe the different directions of the burst.]

After the cloud bursts open, it begins to rain all over the room. What are some ways we can use movement to express the rain? Jennifer suggests that we run all over the room with big leaps in the air, like the wind is pushing the rain all over. Trevor suggests that the rain falls straight down and we should show the falling rain by using our arms, starting high and moving low several times quickly. You may use either of these suggestions or create your own movement for the rain. Will your movement travel around the space or stay in your personal space? Let me see what choices you have made to show the rain. [Children practice being the rain falling while you observe.]

In the last part of this dance, the rainstorm stops and the last drop falls slowly to the ground. Stop your rain movement and hold your body still. Now slowly, very slowly, fall to the floor. Can you add a turn to your slow falling? Keep your body in control as you fall. What shape will your body be in at the end of the fall? Think about it! Now, combine your rain movement with the stop, and slowly fall to the floor ending in a shape. Ready! Rain, rain, rain, rain, rain, rain, rain, rain, and stop. Now, slowly fall to the floor, ending in a shape. [Children can practice this sequence several times to coordinate the transitions between movements.]

Now, let's put the whole rainstorm dance together. Begin with everyone holding hands in a large circle. Now, let go as the cloud fills up with rain. Step backward, 1, 2, 3, 4, and make a wide big shape and hold it still, 1, 2, 3. Now, burst, burst, and burst; and now, rain, rain, rain, rain, rain, rain, rain, rain, and stop; and slowly fall to the floor and end in a shape. [Note the sequence of movements on a chalkboard, or draw picture symbols to indicate the order of the movements.]

Now, let's combine the cloud dance with the rainstorm dance. Ready! Find your personal space to begin your individual cloud. Slowly make your body into the shape of a cloud and begin to travel in the space. Find another cloud and join together. Now, find another cloud and join together to form a bigger cloud. Everyone join in one large, long cloud with Carmen as the leader and Joe at the end. Carmen, lead the cloud around the room and come to the middle of the room to form a circle by taking Joe's hand. Let go of your hands as the cloud fills with rain. Step backward and make a wide stretched shape. Now, burst, burst, and burst; and rain, rain, rain, rain, rain, rain, rain, and rain; and stop; and slowly fall to the floor and end in a shape.

Closure

Ask the children, "What are the types of energy you used to express different parts of the rainstorm? What part of the rainstorm did you enjoy dancing? Why did you like that part?"

Look For

- The shapes the children create. Are they able to represent a variety of cloud shapes with their body shapes?
- How children control their movements in the cloud and rainstorm segments. Specifically, can they coordinate the transitions smoothly between each part of the dance?
- How children use directions for the bursts in the rainstorm. Do you see the whole body or body parts moving in a specific direction?

How Can I Change This?

- Children can create smaller clouds that fill up with rain and burst instead of the one large cloud.
- Add creating a rainbow and a shining sun at the end of the rainstorm. Children can make small-group shapes representing the curved line of the rainbow and the shapes of the sun. Ask them for ideas.

Assessment Suggestions

- Teacher assessment—cognitive: Children can draw and label the shapes they used in the cloud dance (outcome 1).
- Student self-assessment—cognitive: Partners can write a list of body parts they used to connect to each other in the cloud dance (outcome 3).
- Student self-assessment—psychomotor: Children use a rating scale to assess their ability to move slowly as a cloud or move strongly in the rainstorm. Rubric includes the following three levels: I was in control for all movements, I was in control for some of the movements, or I did not control any movements (outcomes 2 and 3).
- Teacher assessment—psychomotor: Record observations to assess whether children can burst in three different directions using control by landing on their feet (outcome 4).

Interdisciplinary Connections

- Visual arts: Connect to visual arts by having children observe and draw cloud shapes on a large piece of paper.
- Language arts (literature): Integrate children's literature by using the book *Cloud Dance* (Locker 2003) or *Little Cloud* (Carle 1996) as a guide for making cloud shapes and developing a dance to accompany the story.
- Language arts (literature): Integrate children's literature by using the book *I Can Make a Water Dance* (Ensanian 2021). The text and illustrations will stimulate ideas for creating dance movements.
- Science: Use this dance to reinforce science concepts about the water cycle, cloud formations, or types of weather.

Run, Hop, Jump, Skip

Outcomes

As a result of participating in this learning experience, children will be able to do the following:

1. Perform four locomotor movements: run, hop, jump, and skip (psychomotor).
2. Identify how the run, hop, jump, and skip movements are different or similar (cognitive).
3. Perform a sequence of movements (psychomotor).

Organization

Children will move individually in their personal space for the run dance, the hop dance, and the skip dance. The jump dance begins individually and ends in a small group.

Equipment Needed

- Whiteboard or chart paper listing the four locomotor words and the rhyming words (see figure 8.3).
- Suggested music: Silence is best to focus on the rhyming words and poems. If music is wanted, use soft instrumental music with an upbeat tempo to mimic the feeling of the run, hop, jump, and skip words.

Introduction and Warm-Up

Today, we are going to dance to words that rhyme with run, hop, jump, and skip. [Words are written on the chart paper or whiteboard.] Can you suggest words that rhyme with *run, hop, jump,* and *skip*? [Write children's suggestions.] We will use all these words in our warm-up and then select a few words for the dance.

In your personal space, begin to jog in place as we say the words you listed under *run. Run, bun, pun, fun, nun, sun,* and *stun.* Now, hop on your right foot as we say the words listed under *hop.* Now, repeat the words while you hop on your left foot. *Hop, pop, mop, bop, cop, drop, flop, clop, lop, chop, top, plop, stop,* and *prop.* Next, jump in place while you say the words listed under *jump. Bump, clump, stump, rump, dump, frump, grump, hump, lump, mump, pump,* and *plump.* The last movement in the warm-up is to skip while saying the words listed under *skip. Blip, clip, sip, dip, flip, drip, grip, slip, lip, nip,* and *rip.*

Figure 8.3 Rhyming words listed on a whiteboard.

Development

I have selected a few words from the list to use in the warm-up for the dance. I am going to read the first poem that uses the words *run, fun,* and *sun,* and then we will create different ways to move to each word. [Read the run poem.]

> Let's all begin to run
> And run, and run, and run.
> Everyone stop,
> And have some fun
> Some fun, some fun, some fun
> In the sun, in the sun, in the sun.

First, let's find different ways to run. What are some other ways to run? Let's try Jessica's suggestion to run with tiny steps. Can we think of any other ways to run? Miguel is running with his arms stretched out to the side. [Children try the suggestion.] Now, try your own idea for running. Now, try another idea. [This would be a good time for children to rest and share their running explorations either with the whole class or with a partner.] Think about choosing your favorite way to run for this dance. We will use it in a few minutes.

For the word *fun,* we will create movements that show us doing something fun, like playing ball, jumping rope, petting a dog, roller skating, or playing catch. Think about some other things you do for fun. How can you express them through a movement? Show me now. Exaggerate your movements; make them very big. Choose one you would like to use in this dance. The last rhyming word is *sun.* Create a shape with your arms that is round like the sun. Move your arms from right to left, beginning low on the right side of your body; stretch your round arms high over your head; and end low on the left side of your body. Do you know what this arm movement is like? This movement shows the movement of the sun rising in the morning, moving across the sky, and setting low at night. Try this movement again, starting slowly on the right, reaching up high, and going low to the left. Keep the movement smooth and slow.

This time, as I read the poem, move using the run movement you chose, then the fun movement you selected, and then we will all do the sun movement together. Ready! Do your run movement. "Let's all begin to run, and run, and run, and run." Now, use the fun movement. "Everyone stop and have some fun, some fun, some fun, some fun." What are your fun movements? Everyone does the sun movement all together. "In the sun, in the sun, in the sun." Try it again, but I'm not going to tell you when to do things. [Read the poem again while the children perform their dance.]

Our next dance uses words that rhyme with *hop*. I will read the poem, and you listen carefully for the words that rhyme with *hop*.

One day we all went out for a hop

With our hands placed on our top.

Then someone came by and yelled "Stop!"

We then did a pop and a drop.

What were the words that rhymed with *hop*? Yes, *drop*, *stop*, *top*, and *pop*. Good listening!

Let's begin with the word *hop*. What are the directions you can use for your hop? I see some children hopping forward, some backward, and others sideward. When you hop, remember that one foot is doing the hopping and the other foot is up off the floor. While you are hopping, can you place the leg that is off the floor in front of your body? What about stretched in back of your body? Out to the side? Give each leg a turn to hop.

The next word is *top*. Create different shapes with your hands when they are on top of your head. Pretend your hands are like a hat on top of your head. I see some pointed hats, round hats, flat hats, hats that look like horns, and some that look like a crown. Do you think you can hop with your hands on your top? Choose a hat shape and a way to hop, and give it a try.

The third word is *stop*. Create a still shape. Make a round shape, a twisted shape, a stretched shape, and a shape with many angles in the body. Each time I clap my hands, I want you to make a different still shape and freeze. Ready! [Clap 6 to 8 times.] Remember your still shapes; we will use them when we dance to the poem.

The fourth word is *pop*. We are going to explore ways to pop up in the air. It's like a jump. Make sure you land on your feet with your knees bent. Can you pop in the air and make a stretched shape? Can you take off on two feet and land on one foot? Can you add a turn to your pop? Try a pop where you jump high into the air and a pop that does not go very high.

The last rhyming word is *drop*. I want you to be safe and drop slowly as if you are melting to the floor. Show me how you can slowly lower your body to the floor very carefully. Use your hands to help you as you go lower and lower. Can you add a turn as you drop? Let's practice combining the pop and drop. Ready and pop! And now drop very slowly. I see you can change from a strong, fast movement to a light, slow movement.

Now, I will read the whole poem, and as I say the words, I want you to dance the movements you created. Here's the poem: "One day we all went out for a hop with our hands placed on our top." [Children hop with hands on top of their heads in a hat shape.] "Someone came by and yelled 'Stop!'" [Children freeze in a shape.] "We then did a pop and a drop." [Children jump into the air for the pop, and then slowly drop to the floor.] Try the dance again as I read the poem. [Repeat the poem again.]

Our next dance uses words that rhyme with *jump*. Here's the poem:

We all went out to jump

And jump and jump and jump.

We jumped so close together

We all started to gently bump

And bump and bump and bump

And slowly fell into a clump.

What words rhymed with *jump*? Good, Alyssa, one is *clump*. Yes, Min-Su, another one is *bump*. The first word we will use is *jump*. When I say go, I want you to find a space and try different ways to jump in place. Go! Can you jump so your feet move together and apart? What are the shapes you can make with your arms as you are jumping? Try jumping forward in a zigzag pathway. Find a way to take small jumps and then large jumps, first moving forward, then backward, and finally sideward. As I read the first part of the poem, choose your favorite way to jump. [Read the first two lines of the poem while the children jump.]

The next word is *bump*. We are going to use different body parts to lightly bump against another person. As you walk around the room and come close to another person, lightly bump them with your arm. I want

Curtis and Tamika to demonstrate a light bump with their arms. [Children demonstrate.] They are using a soft touch for the bump. Now, everyone try the soft bump with your classmates. Try bumping with another body part, like maybe your foot, knee, elbow, hand, shoulder, hip, back, or finger. The bumping will be a big change of force from the jumping. Let's combine the jumping with the bumping. Make sure you have a place in the room where you have lots of space around you. I will read the poem, and I want to see how you change from the strong force used in the jumping to the light force used for the bumping. Get ready to move! [Read the first five lines of the poem while the children jump and bump.]

The last word in this poem is *clump*. What is a clump? Ryan says it is a lot of things bunched up together. We are going to be a clump of children at the end of the poem. To make the clump, we will slowly fall to the floor and end in a round shape. In your own space, try slowly falling to the floor in a round shape. Now, I want two, three, or four people to get together in a group and together, using a slow tempo, fall to the floor. Can all of you stay together in a small space and fall slowly at the same time? Try it again.

Now, I will read the whole poem. I want you to end the dance in the clump with the same people you were just with. Start the dance far apart from each other and move toward each other on the jumps, then gently bump the people in your group, and then slowly fall into a clump. [Read the whole poem as the children dance.] Nice job jumping, bumping, and clumping!

This last dance rhymes three words with the word *skip*. Listen to the poem for the words that sound like skip.

We all began to skip

And skip and skip and skip.

Then tried to do a flip

A flip, a flip, a flip.

Instead we began to trip

And fell upon our hip.

Begin the dance with exploring pathways for skipping. First try skipping in a straight path. Now, try a curved pathway. Can you skip backward on the straight or curved pathway? Try different ways to move, or make shapes with your arms as you skip. I will assign you a partner, and I want you to show each other your favorite pathway to use in the skip. Tell your partner what kind of pathway you observed while they skipped. Now, I will read the first two lines of the poem, and you can skip using your pathway or the pathway your partner used. [Read the first two lines as the children skip.]

The second rhyming word in the poem is *flip*. We are not going to really do a flip. That would be too dangerous; but we are going to create a turn that changes levels. Find a way to turn on one foot or two feet so your turn starts on a high level, changes to a low level, and ends on a high level. [Children practice turning while you cue the movements.] Ready! Turn high, low, and high. Try another turn using high, low, high levels. As I read the third and fourth lines of the poem, try your flip turns that change levels. [Read the poem.]

The third word is *trip*. We are going to slowly fall to the floor using your hands to help you lower your body to the floor. Can you add a turn to your slow fall? [Children practice slowly falling to the floor.]

The last word in the poem is *hip*. Point to your hips. Can you lie down with your right hip touching the floor? Now, try your left hip. Find another way to lie down with your hips touching the floor. Try one more way. Now, let's combine slowly falling to the floor and ending the fall in one of the ways you created to lie on your hips. Ready? Slowly fall and have your hips on the floor. Now, as I read the last two lines of the poem, do the falling movements ending on your hips. [Read the last two lines of the poem.]

This time, as I read the whole poem, perform the movements you created to represent the words *skip*, *flip*, *trip*, and *hip*. Let's review all the movements first. Here's the first line: "We all began to skip, and skip and skip and skip." Show me the pathway you chose for your skip. "Then we tried to do a flip, a flip, a flip, a flip." Now, do your high, low, high turn. "Instead we began to trip." Slowly fall to the floor. "And fell upon our hip." End in a shape with your hip touching the floor. I will read the poem again. I want you to dance the movements you created as you hear the rhyming words, but I'm not going to tell you what to do. Ready? [Repeat the poem.]

Culminating Dance

Each of these poems can be performed individually as a culminating dance, or you can combine two, three, or all four poems to form a longer sequence as the culminating dance.

Closure

Ask the children, "What was your favorite poem? Raise your hand when I call out the one you liked the best. The run poem. The hop poem. The jump poem. The skip poem. Does anyone have another movement that we could use to create a poem dance?"

Look For

- Children who are not ready to perform the skip. You can substitute a gallop or present the dance when everyone has learned how to skip.
- Children who tire easily when performing many repetitions of locomotor movements that require strength and balance. Provide more opportunities to rest.
- Changes in the children's use of force in all four dances. All dances begin with strong force and end using light force.

How Can I Change This?

- Children can choose their favorite poem (run, hop, jump, and skip) and perform the dance while other children accompany the dancing by playing percussion instruments.
- Use other locomotor or nonlocomotor movements as the inspiration for rhyming words and creating movements.

Assessment Suggestions

- Peer assessment—psychomotor and cognitive: Students organized into partners or small groups select two of the poems, practice the movements, and perform the poems for another set of partners or another group. The observing students identify the selected movements (outcomes 1 and 2).
- Teacher assessment—psychomotor: Use a checklist to note how well each child performs the locomotor movements in the poem dances. Also, use the checklist format to assess how well children can change from one movement to another in the dance sequence (outcomes 1 and 3).

Interdisciplinary Connections

- Language arts (vocabulary): Ask the classroom teacher about vocabulary words children are learning that could be used for rhyming dances.
- Language arts (writing): Children can write poems using action verbs and then create movements to express the words.
- Language arts (reading and writing): This dance supports language arts content focused on rhyming.
- Language arts (reading): Add children's books that use locomotor movements as content, such as *Stomp, Wiggle, Clap, and Tap: My First Book of Dance* (Burk 2021), *Never EVER Dance with a Dracula: A Funny Rhyming, Read Aloud Picture Book* (Wallace and Nhin 2021), or *In the Small, Small Pond* (Fleming 1993).

Chapter 8 Learning Experiences for Kindergarten, First Grade, and Second Grade **127**

The Playground

Outcomes

As a result of participating in this learning experience, children will be able to do the following:

1. Perform the three swinging arm movements to represent the playground swings (psychomotor).
2. Coordinate changing levels with a partner to represent the seesaw (psychomotor and affective).
3. Remember and demonstrate the movement sequence for the slide (psychomotor and cognitive).

Organization

Children move individually, in partners, and with a large group as they visit the various imaginary playground spaces.

Equipment Needed

- Signs indicating the playground spaces
- Tape
- Suggested music: lively music for accompaniment

Introduction and Warm-Up

Today, we are going to create a dance about the playground. Pretend this room is a playground. What are the ways you play at the playground? I hear sliding down the slide, going on the seesaw, swinging on the swings, playing on the climbing bars (monkey bars). Let's choose three areas to visit on the playground today: the slide, the swings, and the seesaw. I have a sign for each of these areas, and I will place the signs on the walls. The slide will be at this end of the room [place sign on wall], the seesaw will be in this corner [place sign], and the swings will be in the middle of the room around the center circle [place sign on the floor].

For our warm-up, we are going to find ways to travel to the playground. Let's pretend we are walking to the playground. Try walking fast in a curvy pathway; now walk backward slowly. Can you pretend to be riding a bicycle, steering to the right and to the left? Next, let's warm up our arms by swinging them forward and backward, now side to side. Start with small swings and make them bigger and bigger and as big as you can, then smaller and smaller and as small as you can.

Development

Now that we have arrived at the playground, let's go on the slide first. Everyone begin on one end of the room. Pretend the space in front of you is a giant slide. Let's start by using our arms and legs to climb up the ladder using 8 counts. Begin low and reach higher on each count: 1, 2, 3, 4, 5, 6, 7, 8. [Demonstrate while counting to 8.] Now, let's try climbing to the 8 counts all together. Begin in a squat position low to the floor and climb a little higher on each count. [Children practice the imaginary climb while counting to 8.] Now, let's pretend to slide down the slide. Lower your body to the floor, and find a way to move forward as if you were going down a slide. I see some children on the front of their bodies pulling themselves with their hands along the floor, others are sitting and using their arms and legs to push and pull, and others are moving forward by walking on their hands and feet. When you arrive at the other end of the room, go back to where you started. Climb up the ladder for 8 counts, and try another way to move down the slide. Can you travel sideward down the slide?

Next, let's go to the swings. In this dance, we all move in unison. That means we all do the same movement at the same time. I want everyone to join together and make a circle. Now, swing your arms forward and backward, forward and backward, using 4 counts. Let's try it all together: forward, backward, forward, backward, or 1, 2, 3, 4. [Lead the unison practice with the children.] Now, place one foot forward. Rock forward toward the front foot and then rock backward, shifting the weight to the back foot. Add the arms we just practiced to the rocking feet. All together, swing forward, backward, forward, backward. [Lead the unison practice.]

Let's add a second part to this dance. This time make a giant arm swing forward, walk forward 4 big steps, and stretch up on the fourth step. [Demonstrate the walk and stretch.] Ready, all together with me. Swing your arms forward and step, step, step, step, and stretch (see figure 8.4). What happens to the circle when we do this at the same time? Yes, it gets smaller. Now, swing the arms backward and take 4 steps back. Let's try the swing and walk several times. Ready? Swing forward 1, 2, 3, and 4; swing backward 1, 2, 3, and 4. [You and the children practice the swinging forward and backward in unison several times.]

Let's combine the first and second parts of the swing dance. Remember, 4 swings with the arms (4 counts), 4 swings with rocking feet (4 counts), swing walking forward (4 counts), and swing walking backward (4 counts). The whole dance is 16 counts long. Let's try it all together three times.

Now, let's move over to the seesaw. I will assign you a partner or make groups of three. Can someone tell us how seesaws move? Marcos suggests that when one side is up the other side

Figure 8.4 Swing dance part of the playground dance.

is down, and they keep changing. Face your partners and find a way for one person to start low and the other start high, and then change at the same time. Can you hold hands and do the seesaw movement? Can you connect with another body part? Find a way to do the up-and-down seesaw movement while sitting on the floor. You and your partner create three different ways to move in opposition to show the seesaw movement. Practice each of the ways three times. Show me how you can change smoothly from the first way to the second and then to the third.

Culminating Dance

Now, we are going to combine the three short dances into one big dance. The first time we do the dance, we will all go to the same place in the same order. The second time you perform the dance, you can choose the order for your dance. Ready! Let's all travel to the playground by riding our bikes. Here we go. [Children can follow you or choose their own pathway and meet at the slides.] Well, here we are at the playground. Let's all go on the slide first. Ready to climb? Start low: 1, 2, 3, 4, 5, 6, 7, 8, and slide down forward or backward. Go back to the other side of the room and try the counting and climbing again, and this time, choose another way to slide.

Now, let's go over to the swings. Make a big circle. Everyone ready? Let's do this dance together. Arm swings, 1, 2, 3, 4; rocking swings, 1, 2, 3, 4; swing walk forward, 1, 2, 3, 4; swing walk backward, 1, 2, 3, 4.

Now, let's go to the third area, the seesaw. Find your partner and do the seesaw movement, either standing high and low or sitting high and low. Count to 12, and then meet me near the chalkboard.

You can now do the dance by yourselves while I play the music. This time, you choose what area of the playground you are going to play in first, second, and third. Perform the movements we practiced at each area. Start when the music begins, and meet me by the chalkboard when you are finished. [Start the music.] I see Danielle is on the slide—I can hear her counting to 8 as she climbs—and Hector is on the swings moving forward and backward, and Theresa and Steve are at the seesaw moving opposite each other going high and low.

Closure

Everyone show me your favorite movement of the dance. Next, show me the movement that was the hardest for you to perform. Can you think of another piece of playground equipment we could add to this dance? How would you create a dance about that piece?

Look For

- How children perform the skills based on their motor development and fitness level. Can children alternate hands and feet as they represent climbing? Do children demonstrate adequate strength to travel low to the floor as needed in the playground slide? On the seesaw, are the children able to coordinate their muscles to move up and down with even rhythm?
- Children who may need help to make a decision about which playground area to play in during the second part of the culminating dance. These children may need to follow other children.

How Can I Change This?

- Children can make shapes with their bodies either individually or with others that represent the shape of the swings, the slide, and the seesaw.
- Children can draw pictures of the areas of the playground and place them under the signs.
- Children can suggest other pieces of playground equipment for the dance.
- Take time before children try the second part of the culminating dance to have them plan the order, and write or draw pictures of which playground area they will go to first, second, and third.

Assessment Suggestions

- Teacher assessment—psychomotor: Use a rating scale to record how well students can complete the swinging arm sequence. The rating scale uses the following rubric: A = student accurately completes all three parts, B = student accurately completes two of the three parts, C = student completes one of the three parts. Note the uncompleted parts (outcome 1).
- Student self-assessment—psychomotor and affective: Assess using a verbal response to these questions: Can you and your partner perform the seesaw dance with one person up while the other is down and be able to switch? How did you work together to perform the seesaw movements (outcome 2)?
- Teacher assessment—psychomotor and cognitive: Use a checklist to record whether students remember and perform the sequence of climbing up and moving down the slide. The checklist uses the following rubric: yes = student can remember and perform both parts, no = student remembers and performs only one part (outcome 3).

Interdisciplinary Connections

- Math: The dance sequences reinforce math concepts of counting and patterns.
- Social studies and math: Children can use mapping skills to draw a playground map, arranging the playground equipment in different spaces to correspond to the dance or create a new playground map.

Ocean Waves and Swimmers

Outcomes

As a result of participating in this learning experience, children will be able to do the following:

1. Coordinate arm and leg movements to express the swimmer's movements (psychomotor).
2. Remember the three movements used to represent the ocean part of the dance (psychomotor and cognitive).
3. Describe whether they prefer the role of the ocean or the swimmer in the dance (affective).

Organization

Children explore movements individually using levels, pathways, and directions, and in two large groups they perform the culminating dance.

Equipment Needed

- Pictures or video of waves or swimmers
- Drum or other percussion instruments
- Suggested music: music with the sound of ocean waves

Introduction and Warm-Up

Today, we are going to the beach. Did you bring your swimsuit and towel? The ocean will be in this half of the room, and the beach will be in the other half (see figure 8.5). In this dance, we will move high and low and use different pathways and directions. Has anyone been to the beach? Can you describe how the waves move? Now, let's do our warm-up so we are ready for a day of fun at the beach.

Begin the warm-up by walking in the space. Let's pretend we are walking to the beach. I will play the drum with an even, steady beat. As you walk, match the tempo of the drumbeat with each step. Swing your arms as you walk. Can you walk and change levels, reaching up high and bending down low? Now, change the walk to a skip or a gallop as I change the drumbeat. Keep swinging your arms.

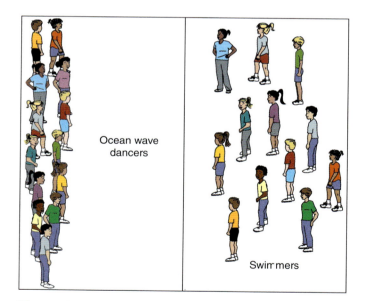

Figure 8.5 Beginning places for the ocean waves and swimmers.

Development

In your personal space, let's first create some movements about the ocean waves. Using your hands and arms, show me how an ocean wave moves. I can see that your hands and arms are moving up and down. Make the up movement bigger and higher, and reach the down movement low to the floor. Try both arms at the same time. Now, add your whole body when you reach up high with your arms, and then bend your whole body as you reach down low with your arms. Let your head follow the up-and-down movement too. Add these 4 up counts and 4 down counts to the movement as I play the drum. Take all 4 counts to move up and all 4 counts to move down. Up-up-up-up and down-down-down-down, and up-up-up-up and down-down-down-down.

Chapter 8 Learning Experiences for Kindergarten, First Grade, and Second Grade 131

This time, find a way to walk forward in the space and move your body high and low. Add the counts up-up-up-up and down-down-down-down. Remember these walks; we will use them later in the dance to represent the movement of the ocean waves.

Now, let's create movements that feel like the splashes of the ocean waves as they hit the beach. Keeping your body low to the floor, how can you use your arms and legs to show the movement of a splash? Where do your arms and legs move in the space? What kind of force will you choose? Can you splash in different directions?

What happens to the wave after it hits the beach and splashes? Yes, it rolls back into the ocean. Show me how you can roll your body sideways as if you are a wave going back into the ocean. Add some of your splashing movements as you roll.

Now, let's combine the three different ways the wave can move. First, in your self-space, do the rising up-and-down movement of the waves. Ready! Up-up-up-up and down-down-down-down. Do it again. Now, add walking forward, up-up-up-up and down-down-down-down, and end down on the floor. Let's repeat this from the beginning: in place, up-up-up-up and down-down-down-down, and, again in place, up-up-up-up and down-down-down-down; now walking forward, up-up-up-up and down-down-down-down, and end on the floor.

Now, add the splashing movements in your self-space on the floor. Ready! Splashing, and splashing, and splashing, and splashing. You really have to use lots of force in your arms and legs. Now, splash in different directions.

The third wave movement is rolling back to the ocean with little splashes of your arms and legs. Ready! Roll, and roll, and roll, and roll, and add splashes each time you roll onto your back.

Remember the three movements of the ocean. We will use them later in our dance. Now, let's create movements for the swimmers. What are the ways your arms move when you are swimming? I see arms moving forward, backward, sideward. Try a movement in which you alternate your arms. Try another way to move your arms so they move together, then apart, and together and apart. Now, add walking to your swimming arm movements. Use forward, backward, and sideward directions in the walking and in the arm movements. Swim all over the room using curvy pathways, as if you are swimming in all parts of the ocean.

I will divide the class into two groups. One group will be the ocean waves, and the other group will be the swimmers. Each child will have a chance to dance as the waves and swimmers today. The swimmers and waves will begin the dance on opposite sides of the room.

Culminating Dance

[At this point you tell the story, and the children listen without dancing.] This is a story about the ocean waves and the swimmers. Listen to the whole story first before we begin the dance. First, the swimmers put on their swimsuits; grab their towels; and walk, skip, or gallop to the beach. They move on the beach side of the room. Next, they find a spot on the beach and pretend to place the towels down by using a swinging arm movement. They lie down on the towel to feel the sun. Think about what shape you will use when you lie down on the towel. It is a very hot day, and the swimmers decide to go for a swim. They stand up on their towels and look toward the ocean. While the swimmers are standing and watching, the ocean waves begin to rise up and down and then move forward and splash. The swimmers walk in between the splashing waves, using their swimming arm movements. Some swimmers are swimming backward, some are swimming forward, and others are swimming sideward. Everyone is using different arm movements for the swimming. Some swimmers may be surfing. Then, the swimmers walk back to the beach for a rest and sit down on their towels, and the ocean waves roll back into the ocean. The ocean waves splash a little as they roll back. This is the end of the dance. Then the ocean waves and the swimmers change places.

Let's begin the dance. This time when I tell the story, you will dance. [Assign each group, and the children go to the designated space. Children are assigned roles, and you tell the story again as the children move. This process helps the children remember the sequence of movements and clarifies how the ocean waves and swimmers interact with one another.] Ready, swimmers move first. [Relate the swimmers' part of the story.] Now, the ocean waves begin to move. Remember to count, up-up-up-up and down-down-down-down and up-up-up-up and down-down-down-down. Now, walk forward up-up-up-up and down-down-down-down, and move to the floor for the splash. Be sure to have a big space around your body, so the swimmers will be able to move around you. Now, the swimmers move around and between the ocean waves. Swimmers return to their towels, and the ocean waves roll back into the ocean. [Cue children for the movement when needed.] Now, switch roles. Can you do the dance by yourself without me telling you the story? Try it to the sounds of the ocean waves.

Closure

Ask the children the following: "If you liked to dance the part of the ocean waves, show me one of the three ocean movements. If you liked to dance the part of the swimmers, show me how you used your arms while swimming."

Look For

- Children to exaggerate stretching up and bending low for the ocean waves. Are they doing the ocean movement with a big change of level?
- How well children can coordinate up-and-down wave movements and counts. Can they move using all 4 counts to stretch up and all 4 counts to move down?
- The ability of the swimmers to keep the arm movements continuous as they walk between the spaces of the splashing waves. Can the swimmers use different directions?
- How well children can use personal space when they perform the splashing waves. Discuss with children why this safety concern is important.

How Can I Change This?

- You can elaborate on the story by adding playing in the sand before children go in for a swim. You could have swimmers lie on beach towels on the front, side, and back of their bodies, and have the swimmers dry off different body parts after the swim.
- Use real towels or towel-size pieces of plastic for the swimmers' props. The ocean wave dancers can hold blue streamers as props and move them up and down to emphasize the ocean waves.
- Children can perform the ocean waves by dancing in partners and moving in unison. Also assign partners so that the swimmers can move together.
- You can give children the choice of performing the dance sequence without your cues. Discuss with the children how they will know when to initiate the different parts of the sequence.
- You can emphasize the concept of unison movement with the waves in the up-and-down wave movements. Talk about what unison means and how children will be able to use it in
- the dance.
- Add ocean fish, crustaceans, and birds as characters living in the ocean (e.g., pelicans, dolphins, crabs, seagulls, lobsters, clams).

Assessment Suggestions

- Student self-assessment—affective: The children draw a picture of themselves performing the dance they preferred (either the swimmers or the ocean waves). They can label the picture or write a sentence about what is happening in the picture (outcome 3).
- Teacher assessment—psychomotor and cognitive: Observe how many students remember all three parts of the ocean dance. Based on the observation, you can review the sequence and add additional practice (outcome 2).
- Teacher assessment—psychomotor: Observe the swimmers' movements as they move around and between the ocean waves to see if the children can continue to move their arms in a swimming motion as they walk (outcome 1).

Interdisciplinary Connections

- Science: Connect this dance to science concepts focused on water forms or ocean study.
- Music: Connect to music when songs and music compositions about the beach or ocean are added as accompaniment to the dance.
- Language arts (literature): Introduce the dance using poetry or stories focused on ocean life or experiences at the beach. Examples of books include *The Crab Dance* (Taylor and Fritz 2021) or *Pete the Cat: Pete at the Beach* (Dean 2013).

Spaghetti Dance

Outcomes

As a result of participating in this learning experience, children will be able to do the following:

1. Move their arms, legs, and whole bodies to create straight and curved shapes (psychomotor).
2. Travel in space using straight and curved shapes and pathways (psychomotor).
3. Change from a straight shape to a curved shape (psychomotor).
4. Reflect on their dance performances and describe the improvements they made from the first performance to the second (cognitive).
5. Identify their body shape as straight or curved (cognitive).

Organization

Children move individually in their personal space for the introduction and development sections of the experience. In the culminating dance, children begin in small groups and then dance as part of a large group.

Equipment Needed

- Drum or wood block
- Suggested music: music with a steady beat

Introduction and Warm-Up

Today, we are going to dance about straight and curved lines. Look at your clothes. Does anyone have any straight and curved lines on their clothes? I see Becka has straight lines on her shirt, and Michael is showing us the straight lines on his pants. Sydney has found lots of curvy lines on her shirt, and Tinesha is pointing to her belt that makes a curved line around her waist.

For our warm-up, let's go on a trip around the room and find all the straight lines. As you walk around the room, I want you to look for straight lines on the ceiling, the walls, the floor, and the objects in the space. When you see a straight line, stop and make your body into a straight shape. I see Kelly has made a straight shape lying next to a line on the floor. Fernando is standing in a straight shape near the door. Now, go to another place, and find more straight lines.

Try making curved lines where you see a curve in the room. Lana has found the round clock and is making a round curved shape on the floor, and Mario is standing with his back curved to the side next to a chair with a curved back. Go and find other places to make curved shapes.

Development

Now, you are going to make straight shapes with your arms, legs, and then your whole body. Stand in your personal space. Make a straight shape with your arm. Find another way to make a straight shape with your arm, now with both arms. Each time I beat the drum, make your arms into a different straight shape. [Beat the drum 8 times.] Try making straight shapes with your legs on each of the 8 drumbeats. Now, make your whole body straight. Use your legs, your arms, and your back. Make a straight shape on each drumbeat. [Beat the drum 8 times.]

This time I want you to make a curved shape with your arms. Use all 4 drumbeats to make the curve. [Play 4 beats on the drum as the children slowly make the arm shape.] Now, make a different curved arm shape and another and one more different curved shapes. Now, use the whole body to make a curved shape. Make the shapes at different levels—some high, some medium, and some low to the floor. Ready, and begin. Make a whole-body curved shape, now another, and another, and one more curved shape. [Play 4 beats on the drum each time as the children slowly make the whole-body shape.]

Now, I am going to ask you to change your body from a straight shape to a curved shape using this sequence: Make 4 straight shapes with a body part or the whole body and then one curved shape. The first 4 drumbeats are for the 4 straight shapes, and the second 4 drumbeats are for the one slow, curved shape. The straight shapes will be quick and sharp, and the curved shape will be slow and smooth. Ready? Straight-straight-straight-straight and curved. Let's repeat it again using different shapes at different levels.

Now, we will explore moving our shapes on straight and curved pathways. This time I want you to find a way to keep most of your body parts straight and walk using a straight pathway. Can you keep your straight shape and change the direction to backward? Try another straight shape and travel sideward. Can you find another way to travel that is different from walking? Remember to use straight pathways.

Let's create different ways to travel in a curved shape on a curved pathway. Can you travel forward, backward, and sideward? Now, try making many different curved shapes as you travel, sometimes reaching high in your curved shape and sometimes letting the curved shape take you low. Keep your body moving into various curved shapes. Change the speed and run and jump into the air as you make curved shapes with your body. See if you can keep your body curved as you jump into the air. This movement looks like someone tossed a rope into the air.

Culminating Dance

We are going to use all the movements you created in a dance about spaghetti. First, let me tell you what happens to the spaghetti in this dance. The dance begins with the spaghetti in a box. This is straight spaghetti. The box is opened, and the spaghetti jumps out and travels from the box to a big round pot of boiling water in the middle of the kitchen. The spaghetti jumps into the water and begins to cook. It changes from a straight shape to a curved shape and travels in curved shapes through the pot of water. Then, slowly, a big bubble appears in the center of the pot. It becomes bigger and bigger, pushing the spaghetti pieces to the edges of the pot until they jump out of the pot and fly all over the kitchen. The spaghetti gets stuck to the wall in a curved shape and then slowly falls from the wall back to the middle of the kitchen and onto the dinner plate.

In this dance, you will be the straight and curved spaghetti. The dance begins with four boxes of spaghetti, one in each corner of the room (see figure 8.6). I will assign you a box of spaghetti for the beginning of the dance. When you get to the corner, organize the group into a line. Everyone is standing in a straight shape. On my signal, the first piece of spaghetti from each box travels from the box to the giant pot of water—the taped or painted circle in the middle of the room—keeping its body in a straight shape moving on a straight pathway. As soon as the first person begins, the next person can start, until everyone is standing around the circle.

Next, the spaghetti will take a small jump into the pot when I hit the drum. Ready, and jump! Very slowly begin to change your straight shape into a curved shape beginning with your feet; then your legs; waist; back; arms; and, finally, your head. Travel slowly in the circle, moving in between each other without touching. Keep changing into many different curved shapes. Use high and low levels as if you are swimming all through the pot of water. I see Krista is really curving her back in various ways as she cooks in the water. Theo is moving high and low as he changes curved shapes.

Now, just listen as I explain how we will add the part where the giant bubble appears. I will be a slow bubble that begins to grow in the middle of the pot. I will start low in a curved shape in the middle of the pot, then begin to make my shape bigger and bigger until I am stretched out in a wide shape. [Demonstrate how you will perform the bubble movements.] The spaghetti will begin to move to the edges of

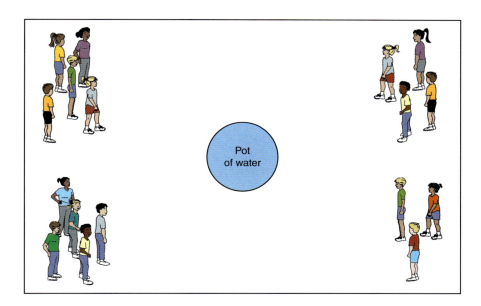

Figure 8.6 Children begin the dance pretending they are uncooked spaghetti standing in four boxes.

the pot until I wave my arms at you as if I am pushing you out of the pot. When you get to the edge, jump out. When everyone is out, the bubble spins around and the spaghetti runs and jumps as it flies around the kitchen. Everyone needs to run and jump in one direction around the circle. Remember to keep your curved shapes as you move around. Ready? Let's try the bubble. I want you to keep cooking as the bubble begins to grow. I am beginning to grow bigger and bigger, and now I stretch out into a wide shape. Begin to move to the edges of the pot, and as I wave my arms, jump out. First, these pieces of spaghetti jump out, now these pieces, and these pieces over here. Oh, I cannot forget these pieces! Now everyone is out, and I begin to spin around. You begin to run and jump in curved shapes.

Now, the spaghetti becomes stuck to the wall. On the drumbeat, I want you to find a place to stick to the wall in a curved shape. What body part will you use to connect to the wall? Great, look at Andrew. He is standing on one foot in a curved shape and his arm is stuck to the wall. Find another way to stick to the wall and keep your curved shape. Now, very, very slowly find a way to keep your curved shape and travel from the wall to the center of the room, where the pot of water has now become the dinner plate. Slowly fall to the floor onto the plate and end in a curved shape. And that is how the dance ends. [You can repeat this section for additional practice.]

Let's go back to the beginning of the dance and try all the parts together. [Conduct a review by asking the following questions.] Who can tell me how the dance begins? What shape are you in? What happens next? When does the spaghetti change from a straight to a curved shape? How can you move in the pot of water and not bump into your friends? What happens to the spaghetti when the bubble appears? What movements do you use when you are flying around the kitchen? When you hear the drum, what happens? What shapes are you in? How will you move from the wall to the plate? What shape will you be in for the end of the dance? This dance starts slowly, becomes a little faster, then very fast, stops, and ends slowly. Any questions? Ready?

Let's try it from the beginning. The first time I will tell the story as you move, and the next time you can do the dance without my directions. [Children dance the story while you provide needed cues.]

Closure

Ask the children to identify which parts of the dance use light force, strong force, large movements, small movements, slow tempo, and fast tempo. Ask children to talk to another child about their favorite part of the dance. This partner discussion is referred to as pair-share.

Look For

- The many ways children create curved and straight shapes.
- How children move between one another when they are cooking in the pot of water. Can they do it without bumping into others?
- The transition from a straight shape to curved shapes. Does this change occur gradually or all at once?

How Can I Change This?

- Use two or three pots of water in the culminating dance, and the children can choose which one they want to use for their dance. You can also use two or three plates at the end of the dance.
- Repeat the section of the culminating dance where the spaghetti flies around the kitchen and sticks to the wall several times, instead of only once, so the children can find different places to stick to the wall.
- Children can travel to the pot of water connected. They can also stick to each other instead of the wall and then travel connected from the wall to the plate.
- Three or four children can dance the part of the bubble instead of you.
- Introduce the dance by reading the poem "Spaghetti" by Shel Silverstein (1974).
- Bring in a box of uncooked spaghetti and a pot of cooked spaghetti to use when you are telling the story.

Assessment Suggestions

- Student self-assessment—psychomotor and cognitive: Record a video of the class performing the dance, then show the video to the children and ask them to observe and describe how they each performed the straight and curved shapes (outcomes 1, 2, 3, and 5).
- Teacher assessment—psychomotor: Observe whether children can change from a straight to a curved shape as they jump into the pot of water and begin to cook. Record the observation on a checklist (outcome 3).
- Student self-assessment—cognitive: The children recall their performance and choose a part they would like to improve and then perform the dance again and talk about what changes they made and how those changes improved their performance (outcome 4).
- Student self-assessment—cognitive: Children draw themselves in a straight or curved shape that they used in the dance and label the drawing (outcome 5).

Interdisciplinary Connections

- Language arts (literature): Introduce the dance using the humorous poem "Spaghetti" (Silverstein 1974).
- Visual arts: Connect to visual arts concepts on how straight and curved lines appear in paintings and sculptures.
- Social studies: Include social studies concepts that discuss how noodles are part of the cuisine in a variety of cultures.
- Language arts (reading): Read from the book *ABC Pasta: An Entertaining Alphabet* (Medina Rosas 2017) or *Oodles and Oodles of Noodley Noodles* (Grant 2021) as an introduction to the dance.

Chapter 8 Learning Experiences for Kindergarten, First Grade, and Second Grade **137**

Balloon Dance

Outcomes

As a result of participating in this learning experience, children will be able to do the following:

1. Identify how they used their bodies to change their movements from small to big and big to small (cognitive).
2. Collaborate with others in a group to create and practice a dance (affective).
3. Perform the balloon dance in unison and demonstrate a slow change in movements from small to big (psychomotor).

Organization

Children dance individually, with a partner, and in small groups.

Equipment Needed

- Balloon
- Drum
- Suggested music: slow music for accompaniment

Introduction and Warm-Up

Today, we are going to dance using small movements that become bigger and bigger. What are some things that start small and become bigger? Our warm-up includes movements that are small and big. Find a personal space and make small movements with your fingers that open and close. Now, make the movement bigger by opening and closing your whole hand several times. Now, the open-and-close movement is bigger and uses your arms. Try the open-and-close movement jumping with your feet apart and then together. First, start with a few small jumps; then make your jumps wider and wider. The last part of the warm-up uses running, skipping, or galloping. Choose one of these three ways to travel in the space. Take 10 small steps, 10 medium-sized steps, and 10 giant steps. Now, do those 30 steps again. [Instruct the children to repeat the warm-up movements several times.]

Development

Sit on the floor and make a small round shape using your whole body. Great! I see that you have rounded your back, legs, arms, and head to make the shape. I am going to beat on the drum 8 times. On each count, make your shape bigger: 1, 2, 3, 4, 5, 6, 7, 8. [Play the drum and count aloud as the children move.] Now, go back to your small round shape in 4 counts, becoming smaller and smaller: 1, 2, 3, 4. Let's try making the round shape big and small again. Ready to become bigger on each count? Now, make a different small shape. Choose a high, medium, or low level as you get smaller. As I play the drum, make your shape grow bigger in 8 counts and then smaller in 4 counts. Ready! Big 1, 2, 3, 4, 5, 6, 7, 8, and small 1, 2, 3, 4. This time, make your shape grow big in 4 counts and smaller in 2 counts. This will feel faster. Ready! Big 1, 2, 3, 4, and small 1, 2. Can you suggest a number of counts for becoming bigger and smaller? Sanam says to use 3 counts to get bigger and 13 counts to get smaller. Let's try it. I will beat the counts on the drum.

We are now going to explore small and big movements with one or more partners. You will face your partners and mirror each other's movements. One partner is the first leader, and then the others will take a turn as the leader. Brian and I will demonstrate. I will be the first leader, and Brian will mirror my movements. As the first partner, I will create movements that start low and small and become big and high. Be sure to go slowly so your partner can follow. [Demonstrate with a child.] Then, the next partner will create movements that start big and high and change to small and low. I will tell you when to switch partners. [Use slow music to accompany this exploration.] I will assign you a partner, and you can choose who will go first. Then begin when the music starts, and change leaders when the music stops.

Now, I will organize you into groups of four or five children and you will stand in a circle. I want you to work together to find a way to make your circle become bigger and smaller. See if you can all move at the same time, as you did when you were mirroring your partner. Select a leader in the group who will tell the group when to begin moving and when to stop. Make sure you listen to everyone's ideas, then try the ideas out, and choose how your circle will move from small to big and back to small. After each group has practiced, we will share our dance with another group.

Culminating Dance

For this next part, you'll stay in your small groups. You are going to create a dance about a balloon that inflates and deflates and, when it is fully inflated, all the air fizzles out. Your dance will be like this balloon I am going to blow up. [Blow up a balloon using the following sequence.] First, I blow just a little air into the balloon and then let the air out while holding onto the balloon. The second time, I blow more air into the balloon so it is bigger and then let all the air out. Then, I blow the balloon up a third time so it is bigger than the first two times and, again, let the air out. Then, the fourth time I inflate the balloon to its fullest and let it go so it flies around as the air comes out. Watch to see how it flies around in the air. How does it move? Show me with your hand. [Let go of the fully inflated balloon.]

Use this sequence for your group dance. Your group will need to decide what movements you are going to use to show the balloon inflating and deflating four times, with the balloon becoming bigger each time before the air goes out. Then, choose what movements you will use to show the balloon flying around as the air comes out. How will the balloon land on the floor? Listen to each person's ideas for the dance, try them out, and choose the movements for the group. One person will need to be the leader to tell the group when to inflate and deflate and when to let all the air out and fall to the floor. I will come by each group to see if you need any help. Practice your sequence several times to make sure everyone is moving together. Can you add any voice accompaniment to your dance? When you are ready, we will stop and show the dances to the other groups. [Visit all the groups as they create their dances.]

Each group will share their balloon dance with the class. Before you perform, tell the class how your group chose the movements for the dance. The observers need to look for the pathway of the fizzle movement.

Closure

I want your group to sit together and talk about how you worked together to create the dance. Each person needs to say something about the dance. Then, make up a name for your balloon dance. [Children spend a few minutes talking, and then they are asked to share some of the comments and tell the rest of the class the name of their dance.]

Look For

- How children perform the mirroring activity. Are the movements too fast to follow, or are the children moving slowly?
- How well the children use unison movements in the small group as they find a way to move from small to big. Can they all make their movements grow bigger at the same time?
- How well the groups work together sharing ideas.

How Can I Change This?

- The dance can be taught as a full-class experience with everyone as part of one balloon circle. Working as a single large group may be more appropriate for young children.
- The children can add a floating part to the dance after the balloon is fully inflated and before the air fizzles out. They can move slowly up and down like they are floating in the air.
- The dance can end with the balloon popping instead of the air fizzling out.

Assessment Suggestions

- Teacher assessment—affective: During the time when students are creating their dances, observe how each group collaborates. Does each person have an opportunity to voice ideas? Does the group try different ideas and then choose one or more for the dance? Are they using the time to practice the dance moving in unison (outcome 2)?

- Teacher assessment—cognitive: As the groups are involved in the closure discussion, visit each group and ask this question: How did you change your movements to show that the balloon was getting bigger each time it inflated (outcome 1)?

- Teacher assessment—psychomotor: Assess the students' ability to move in unison as a group and slowly show how the body shapes change from small to big (see figure 8.7) (outcome 3).

Interdisciplinary Connections

- Language arts (poetry): Introduce the dance by reading aloud the poems "Eight Balloons" (Silverstein 1981) , *The Lost (and Found) Balloon* (Jenkins 2013), or from the book *National Geographic Book of Nature Poetry: More Than 200 Poems With Photographs That Float, Zoom, and Bloom* (Lewis 2015).

- Science: Connect to science concepts on air currents, flight, or force.

- Social studies: Include a discussion on how people use balloons to celebrate events to connect with social studies concepts on celebrations and traditions.

Figure 8.7 Assessment Instrument for Balloon Dance

Groups for balloon dance	Rubric: Excellent Criteria: All students performed the dance in unison, and the movements clearly demonstrated a slow change in tempo from small to big	Rubric: Good Criteria: Only two or three students were in unison and the change from small to big demonstrated different tempos
Group A: John, Sasha, Steph, Arthur	X	
Group B: Chelsea, Nijah, Joe, Carly		X Joe jumped too fast. Carly did not move at all.
Group C: Aiden, Mora, Mason, Meaghan	X	
Group D: Alexa, Jermaine, Emma, Rob	X	

Percussion Instrument Dance

Outcomes

As a result of participating in this learning experience, children will be able to do the following:

1. Match the quality and tempo of their movements to the sound of a drum, a triangle, and a set of maracas (psychomotor and cognitive).
2. Move using contrasting light and strong forces and fast and slow tempos (psychomotor).
3. Balance while moving and while holding still shapes (psychomotor).

Organization

Children begin the lesson moving individually and then divide into three groups for the culminating dance. The room is set up with each instrument in a different space (see figure 8.8).

Equipment Needed

- Drum
- Triangle
- Set of maracas
- Suggested music: live musical instruments placed around room; for demonstration purposes, recorded percussion music featuring a drum, triangle, or maracas can be played during the introduction

Drum

Triangle

Maracas

Figure 8.8 Instruments are placed in three spaces in the room.

Introduction and Warm-Up

Today, we are going to create movements to the sound of a drum, a triangle, and the maracas. I will show you the instruments and then demonstrate the different sounds each one can make. [Play each instrument to demonstrate the sounds it makes. First, a light drumbeat is played 8 times and then a strong drumbeat is played 8 times. Next, the triangle is tapped once, and then after the sound ends, it is tapped again. Next, the triangle is played lightly and rapidly. Finally, the maracas are shaken slowly and lightly and then strongly and rapidly.]

We will use each instrument in our warm-up. First, we are going to begin with the sound of the drum. As I play slowly and lightly, lie on the floor and slowly stretch your arms and legs as if you are just waking up. Now, sit and stretch, and then slowly rise to standing and continue to stretch. Let's repeat the stretching with the drum. Now, I am going to play the drum strongly and quickly, and I want you to reach in different directions on each beat. Next, we'll do the triangle. On each tap of the triangle, take one giant slow step forward. [Tap the triangle 8 times.] This time go backward as I tap the triangle. As I shake the maracas, I want you to take small running steps in the space. When you hear the maracas stop, freeze in a shape. [Play and stop the maracas several times.]

Development

Everyone move to the space where the drum is placed. We will begin to explore movement using the light and strong beats of the drum. Begin standing in a frozen shape. When I play the drum lightly, you will find a way to do small light leaps, hops, or jumps in different directions and stop when the drum stops. [Play the 8 light beats in a medium tempo, and the children explore light leaps, hops, and jumps.] Let's try this a few more times. Can you change your movement and the direction?

Next, I will play 8 strong drumbeats, and on each beat, I want you to take a big strong leap, hop, or jump and then freeze in a shape. [Give the ready cue and then play the 8 strong beats at a medium tempo.] Let's try this again. This time mix up the leaps, hops, and jumps while you move to the 8 beats. Remember to make the frozen shapes when you land. [Play the 8 strong beats.] Let's try this again.

Now, I will play 8 light drumbeats, then 8 strong drumbeats. Take small light leaps, hops, or jumps, then big strong leaps, hops, or jumps, adding the frozen shapes. [Play 8 light beats then 8 strong beats.] Now, let's try this with 6 light beats and 6 strong beats. Now, move using 4 light beats and 4 strong beats. Finally, move with only 2 light beats and then 2 strong beats. This is the drum dance. Let's put it all together, first using 8 light and strong, then 6, then 4, and then 2. Can you do it? [Play the drum while the children perform.]

Now, everyone walk over to the triangle. Listen to how long the sound lasts after each tap. Sit on the floor, move your arms slowly, and keep them moving until you can no longer hear the triangle after the first tap. [Tap the triangle.] Let's try again. Now, stand up and take one step each time you hear me tap the triangle. [Make 4 taps.] Step-step-step-step. Try taking the steps backward or sideward this time. [Tap the triangle.] Step-step-step-step. This time, combine the steps and the slow arm movement for 4 beats. [Tap the triangle.] Now, as I play the triangle faster, find a way to turn your body around quickly; you can choose any level. [Tap the triangle quickly 8 times.] Try a different turn. [Quickly tap the triangle 8 times.] Now, combine the 4 slow steps using the arms with the 8 fast taps for turning. [Play 4 slow taps, then 8 quick taps.] Let's repeat this triangle dance again. Remember to take 4 slow steps and then do your quick turns.

Let's move to the third space where we will dance to a set of two maracas. Listen to how the sound changes when I shake them lightly and then strongly. I will start with a light shake as I move the maracas just a little. [Play the maracas to demonstrate the different sounds.] Begin a small shaking movement in your fingertips as I shake the maracas lightly. Keep the movement small and light. Now, let the shaking go to your hands, forearms, elbows, and all the way up your arms to the shoulders. Now, try the shaking beginning with your toes, then your whole foot, your leg, and then up to your hips. Is there another body part where you can begin shaking and then let it move to other parts of your body? I see Cole and Jenny have chosen their heads, others are beginning the shaking in their bellies, and Carmen chose to start in her shoulder. This time, listen as I change the sound from light to strong, and show that change of force in the shaking of your arm. Begin the shaking small and light, and let it become strong and big as the maracas become louder. [Shake maracas.] Try light-to-strong shaking in your legs, starting with your toes and going all the way up to your hips. Now, begin shaking your whole body, going from light and small to strong and big. Try this lying on the floor, then sitting, and now standing. Each time I play the maracas from light to strong, start the shaking with a different body part. Also, choose if you will be lying down, sitting, or standing. [Shake the maracas for about 10 to 15 seconds.] Find a way to travel with the shaking movement, beginning with light and small movements and increasing the movements to strong and big. Can you take the strong shaking up off the floor into a jump? [Shake maracas for 10 to 15 seconds.]

Now, let's combine the light and strong shaking into a dance. Ready? [Children move as you tell the story.] The children are sleeping on the floor. They wake up slowly by shaking lightly. Then they stand up and continue to lightly shake. The shaking begins in one body part, and then more body parts begin to shake, until the whole body is shaking. The children go out to play. The shaking grows stronger, and the children shake with big and strong movements as they travel in the space. The shaking suddenly stops, and the children freeze in a shape. The children resume the shaking as they return home and slowly fall to the floor and go back to sleep.

Culminating Dance

Now, when you perform the three dances, you may choose which one you want to dance to first, second, and third. Think about your order for the dances. Now, everyone who wants to dance first to the drum, go over to the drum space. Those who are dancing to the triangle first, go to the triangle place. And those who are dancing first to the maracas, go to where the maracas are placed. Only one group will dance at a time while the other two groups sit and observe.

I will play the drum first. Ready, drum dancers? Remember to make clear changes between the light and strong movements as I play the light and strong drumbeats. [Play the sequence of beats while the children dance.]

Now, I will play for the triangle dancers. Who can tell us what type of dance goes with the triangle? Juwon explains, "You take four slow steps on each tap, then fast turns on the fast taps." Okay, ready, everyone? Let's try it all together. [Play the triangle sequence while the children dance.]

The third dance is the maracas. Here, the dancers perform a story about waking up, going out to play, and then going back to sleep—all through shaking movements. Observing children, watch how the shaking starts small and light and becomes bigger and stronger. I will tell the story as I play the maracas. The dancers begin to wake up by lightly shaking. Now, they stand up and begin the light shaking in one body part, and now more body parts begin to lightly shake. Next, they go out to play as the shaking becomes bigger and stronger. They begin to travel in the space shaking and shaking, sometimes jumping into the air. The maracas suddenly stop, the dancers freeze, and then they lose their strong shaking energy and lightly shake all the way home and go back to sleep.

Now, I want everyone to point to the next instrument you want to dance to and walk to that place. [Remind the children to walk as they change from one instrument area to another. Excited children will tend to begin running to an area.] I will play the instruments in the same way, beginning with the drum dance, and then the triangle dance, and ending with the maraca dance. When you are not dancing, I want you to notice how your classmates are showing light and strong force as they dance. [Children perform their second dance and then move to the third instrument to perform their third dance.]

Closure

I will assign partners, and I want you to tell each other the order of your dances and your favorite dance. [Children spend a few minutes sharing their experiences with each other.] Now, I would like to hear about your favorite dance. [Ask a few children to talk about their favorite dance.]

Look For

- How children perform strong and light movements. Are they able to clearly demonstrate the difference in the force?
- What dances the children choose first, second, and third. You may want to discuss with them why they chose a certain order. Which dances did they like to perform, or which one did they least prefer?

How Can I Change This?

- Play different instruments.
- Use more or fewer instruments.
- Add a specific rhythm to each instrument instead of playing the regular beats.
- The children can develop their own stories to accompany the instruments for their dances.
- Ask the children to play the instruments.

Assessment Suggestions

- Student self-assessment—cognitive: Students draw a picture of the instruments or themselves dancing to one of the instruments and add words to describe how they moved their body (outcome 1).
- Peer assessment—psychomotor: Students organized in partners as observers and performers. One partner assigned as the performer dances the movements connected with the instrument while the other partner observes. After the performance, the observer tells the performer if their movements corresponded to the instrument. Partners reverse roles (outcome 1).
- Teacher assessment—psychomotor: Record anecdotal notes about children who demonstrate difficulty with balance in the slow movements and frozen shapes. For example, Shanida was unable to hold the frozen shapes still, and she lost her balance three times (outcome 3).
- Teacher assessment—psychomotor: Use a checklist to note whether the children can demonstrate strong and light and fast and slow movements. At the end of the learning experience, ask four students at a time to perform a strong movement, then a light movement, then a fast movement, and then a slow movement. This procedure continues until all children in the class have had an opportunity to perform (outcome 2).

Interdisciplinary Connections

- Music: Connect to music concepts focused on types of percussion instruments, timbre, and tempo.
- Language arts (writing): Children write stories inspired by the dance sequences, or write stories and then express them through dance and percussion instruments.

The Hungry Cat

Outcomes

As a result of participating in this learning experience, children will be able to do the following:

1. Perform movements using fast and slow tempos (psychomotor).
2. Move a body part in isolation (psychomotor).
3. Remember the dance sequence and perform a dance without teacher cues (psychomotor and cognitive).

Organization

Children will dance individually throughout the entire learning experience.

Equipment Needed

- Percussion instruments—a drum and a triangle
- Suggested music: live musical instruments or recorded music with variations in tempo (fast and slow)

Introduction and Warm-Up

In this dance learning experience, we are going to find different ways to move fast and slow. We will then do a dance about a hungry cat who moves fast and slow. We'll start with a warm-up using slow and fast movements.

When I say go, find a personal space and run in place as fast as you can. Go! Now, run in place as slowly as you can. Now, find a different way to travel through general space as fast as you can. Find another way. What are some of the ways you traveled fast? [Children share their answers with the class.] Now, move through space as slowly as you can, taking a long time for each step. Find another slow way to move. How slow can you go? Can someone show the class how slowly they can travel in the space? [Select several children to demonstrate moving slowly.]

Think of some things that you do to get ready for school in the morning. [Children answer with morning routines such as brushing teeth, getting dressed, eating cereal.] We are going to pretend to do some of these fast and then slow. Ready? Let's all do the movement of brushing our teeth as fast as we can, now as slowly as we can. Now, try slowly putting on your clothes; now, get dressed as fast as you can. The third movement is about eating a bowl of cereal very slowly. Shake the cereal into the bowl slowly, pour the milk slowly, take your spoon and scoop up the cereal slowly, and put it in your mouth slowly. Now, eat the cereal as fast as you can. Feel the difference in your muscles when you move fast and slow. Can someone tell us what that feels like?

Development

Today, I am going to play a triangle for all of our slow movements. Listen to how long the sound lasts after I hit the triangle. Now, begin to move your arms when I hit the triangle and continue to keep them moving until you do not hear the triangle. [Tap the triangle once.] Keep your movement smooth and slow. Feel your arm moving for a long time. Can you keep the movement going? Now, try this with another body part. I want to see if you can listen to the sound and move one body part slowly until the sound of the triangle stops. I see that some of you are moving your arms forward and backward, some are moving their arms together and apart, and some are moving one arm and then the other. Some children are moving their shoulders, their legs, and their whole bodies. Notice how each movement takes a long time when you move slowly.

I will play fast drumbeats to accompany the fast movement. See if you can move your arms as fast as you can until you hear the drum stop. [Play fast drumbeats for a few seconds.] Try moving your arms high and low, forward and backward, together and apart. [Again, play fast drumbeats for a few seconds.] This time, point with your arm to a different corner of the room as fast as you can on each of the 4 drumbeats. [Play 4 drumbeats as the children point.] Try pointing with the other arm. [Again, play 4 drumbeats as the children point.] We will use this movement in our cat dance.

This time, run as fast as you can and stop when you no longer hear the drum. [Play fast drumbeats for 10 seconds.] This time, add a leap or jump to the run as I play the fast drumbeats. [Play fast drumbeats for 10 seconds.] Try this again, and make sure you land on your feet with your knees bent at the end of the jump or leap. [Play fast drumbeats for 10 seconds. Children practice this movement several times.]

Culminating Dance

Now, it is time for the hungry cat dance. Everyone find a personal space and lie on the floor. We are going to practice each part of the dance first and then put them all together. In the first part, the cat is sleeping. What are the different shapes a cat uses for sleeping? Yes, curved, perhaps stretched. Find another sleeping cat shape and another. I see many of you in round curled shapes, some of you are on your backs, others are sleeping on their sides (see figure 8.9). Change slowly from one sleeping shape to another each time you hear the triangle sound. I will tap the triangle four times. Ready? [Make four taps on the triangle.] Make your first sleeping shape, now slowly change to your second shape, now take a third shape, and finish by moving slowly into the fourth and last shape. That was great! You used four different sleeping shapes and moved very slowly into each shape.

Next, still lying on the floor, the cat begins to wake up and stretch slowly. On each tap of the triangle, I will tell you a body part to stretch. [Make one tap on the triangle.] The cat stretches one arm, reaching high with its paw. [Make a second tap on the triangle.] Now, the other arm stretches high. [Make a third tap on the triangle.] Now, the cat stretches one leg up high, reaching with its foot. [Make a fourth tap on the triangle.] Then the cat stretches up the other leg. The cat sits up and slowly moves its head, then its back, and then its shoulders. [Make three taps on the triangle: one each for the head, back, and shoulders.] The cat stands up slowly onto two feet. Make sure you take your time as you stretch each part of your body as you wake up. This is the beginning of the dance. All the movements are smooth and slow. Let's practice this part again.

Now, in the second part, we will change to make fast sudden movements on each drumbeat. The cat will move fast when it suddenly sees and points to a mouse. Move your arm quickly to point to a corner of the room. The cat sees a mouse over there! Now, the mouse has moved to another corner; point to that one. Oh, no, the mouse moved to another corner! Point to it! And now point to the last corner as the mouse

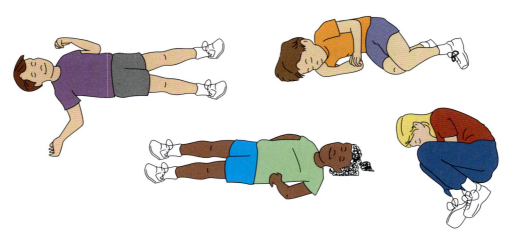

Figure 8.9 In the beginning of the hungry cat dance, the cats are sleeping.

moves one last time. Make your pointing movements strong and fast. I will beat the drum once for each pointing movement. Ready? Point, point, point, point. [Beat the drum.]

In the third part, the cat chases the mouse around the room. I will beat the drum very fast, and you will run, adding leaps and jumps. Ready? [Beat the drum fast for about 10 seconds while the children run after the imaginary mouse.]

In the next part, the cat catches the mouse by taking one big jump. The cat slowly bends forward to pick up the mouse by the tail, opens its mouth, and drops the mouse in. Now, the cat is so tired after chasing and eating the mouse that it slowly moves back to the place where it was sleeping. I will play one loud drumbeat to cue the jump. [Play one loud drumbeat.] Then, I will play the triangle to accompany the slow movements as you pretend to pick up the mouse, eat it, and go back to sleep. Let's try this part of the cat story. Begin with a jump and bend down slowly to pick up the mouse; pretend to drop it in your mouth, and add a stretch and yawn to show you are tired before you slowly go back to sleep. [Play the drum and triangle as the children dance the sequence of movements.] Let's try this part again.

Now, let's put all the story parts together into one big dance. I will play the instruments while I tell the story. Then, the second time you will do the dance by yourself. [Play the instruments and tell the story while the children dance.] Now, I will play the instruments and not tell you the story. You can dance the story because you have practiced it now a few times. Before we begin, can someone describe the dance? [One or more children describe all or part of the dance.] Be clear about making the slow movements slow and the fast movements fast. Feel the difference in tempo as you dance.

Closure

Can anyone suggest any new parts we could add to this cat dance? Are there any parts we should take out of the dance?

Look For

- How well children can change from fast to slow movements. Is the difference clear?
- How effectively children can move in the space without bumping into each other during the mouse chase.

How Can I Change This?

- During the development section, you can divide the room into two zones: the fast zone where the children can perform the fast movements, and the slow zone where the slow movements are performed.
- Develop short movement sequences that combine fast and slow movements. For example, children choose a movement and perform it using this sequence: slow-fast-slow or fast-slow-fast. Try different combinations with nonlocomotor and locomotor movements.
- Children are organized into partners. One partner does a fast or slow movement, and the other partner responds doing the same movement in the opposite tempo. For example, partner 1 touches the head with the hands, turns around, and makes a stretched shape using a fast tempo. Partner 2 responds by doing the same three movements using a slow tempo.

Assessment Suggestions

- Peer assessment—psychomotor: Students are organized into partners. One partner calls out a nonlocomotor movement and chooses a fast or slow tempo, and the other partner performs the movements. For example, "Wiggle your whole body fast," or "Twist slow." Students take turns. Repeat this activity using locomotor movements (outcome 1).
- Teacher assessment—psychomotor: Use a checklist to observe whether children can isolate body parts in the part of the dance where the cat wakes up. You can assess this part of the dance while the children are dancing (outcome 2).

- Teacher assessment—psychomotor and cognitive: Record a video of half of the class performing the dance without teacher cues, and then record the other half. Later, review the video to assess whether the children remember the sequence and can clearly demonstrate the fast and slow movements (outcome 3).

Interdisciplinary Connections

- Language arts (reading): Introduce the cat dance by reading stories or poems about cat adventures. Examples of books include *Cat & Cat Adventures: The Quest for Snacks* (Yi 2021), *Fuddles* (Vischer 2011), and *Adventure Cat! And More True Stories of Amazing Cats* (Weidner Zoehfeld 2019).
- Science: Integrate this dance with science concepts focused on animal life.
- Visual arts: Add visual arts and music by creating cat and mouse masks and using music with an emphasis on slow and fast tempos.

Circus Dance

Outcomes

As a result of participating in this learning experience, children will be able to do the following:

1. Identify and perform locomotor and nonlocomotor movements at different levels that relate to the circus animals and performers (cognitive and psychomotor).
2. Perform one of the four circus dances (psychomotor).
3. Balance while traveling and holding still shapes (psychomotor).
4. Choose a favorite character or animal that they performed in the circus dance (affective).

Organization

This learning experience includes four dances: the galloping horses, the tightrope walkers, the lions and tigers, and the funny clowns. Three of the dances require children to dance individually, and one dance, the funny clowns, uses partners or small groups.

Equipment Needed

- A stick with multiple streamers taped to the end to be used by the circus leader
- Three hoops for the lions and tigers
- Painted, chalked, or taped lines on the floor for the tightrope walkers
- Whiteboard or poster to write the order of the circus dances
- Suggested music: circus-type music or lively music

Introduction and Warm-Up

Has anyone been to the circus? What did you see? [Children share their experiences.] Today, we are going to turn our room into a circus with galloping horses, tightrope walkers, lions and tigers, and funny clowns. You are going to be the circus performers, and I will be the circus ringleader. [You can share books or pictures about the circus.]

For our warm-up today, we will practice moving high and low, forward, backward, and sideward. I will organize you into groups of four or five, and each person in the group will have a number from 1 to 4 or 5. Then, when I play the music, person 1 will step into the center of the circle and create a movement that moves high and low. You can use your whole body or only one body part. Everyone in the group follows the leader and does the same movement. Then, I will say "change," and person 2 will do a different high and low movement and everyone will follow. Everyone will have a turn to create a movement. [Play the music and call "change" after 15 seconds until everyone has had a turn as the leader.] The second part of the warm-up is just like the first except your movements will be forward and backward or side to side. Let's begin this time with person 5 and end with person 1. [Play the music and call "change" after 15 seconds until everyone has had a turn as the leader.]

Development

This learning experience is composed of four short dances about the circus. The first dance is about the galloping horses. Let's explore different ways to gallop. First, make a shape with your hands and arms that are like two front hooves. Your hands can be close together, wide apart, or one high and one low. Keep the hand and arm shape as you gallop forward. Can you gallop in a large circle pathway? Now try a small circle. Can you pretend you are a horse leaping into the air as you gallop? Can two or three horses gallop in the space with one horse as the leader? Now, change leaders and the pathway. [Play the music while the children practice.]

Next are the tightrope walkers. For this circus act, you will use the lines on the floor as the tightropes. Find a line and begin to walk forward. Can you change your level to low and high as you walk? How about walking backward? Can you walk and turn or hop or jump and stay on the line? Find a way to balance on one foot. Be still and count to 5. Can you find another way to make a still, balanced shape? How about another balanced shape? Now, you will choose three tricks for your tightrope act. You will need a locomotor movement, a still balance, and a turn. You can change levels and directions, but keep the movements slow. Now, practice your tightrope act. [Play the music while the children practice. Also, you can write the three components of the tightrope act on the chalkboard or on chart paper.]

Our next circus performers are the lions and tigers. In this circus act, the lions and tigers will stay low to the floor and walk on their hands and feet, stretch up as they let out a loud roar, jump through a hoop, and roll on the floor. Let's practice walking on hands and feet. Show me how you can walk on your hands and feet using small steps, and now big steps. [Children may need a brief rest due to the strength involved in using the arms to support the body weight.] Now, let's practice the lion and tiger roar. Kneel down and sit back on your heels with your hands touching the floor. This is the waiting shape. [You are holding a stick with streamers attached, and when you raise the stick, the children stretch up and use their voices to make a loud roaring sound.] When I raise the stick, this is the signal for the lions and tigers to stretch their front paws and let out a loud roar. When I move the stick down, the lions and tigers stop the roar and return to the waiting shape. Let's try this a couple of times. How high can you stretch your arms, and how loud can you roar? [Move the stick up and down a few times and the children follow the signal.] In the next trick, the lions and tigers jump through the hoop and roll on the floor while reaching with their paws. [You or several children can hold hoops vertically as the children jump through the hoop and then do a sideward roll, similar to a log roll. The hoops can be held at different places in the space. Also, play the music while the children practice.]

The final act of the circus is the funny juggling clowns. You are going to pretend that you are juggling. Let's create many ways to juggle. [A light juggling scarf can be added as a prop.] First, put a big smile on your face and move your arms and hands to show a juggling movement. Can you juggle while walking forward or backward? Try juggling lying on your back, kneeling, sitting, and standing on one foot. What other ways can you juggle? Turn and face another person and pretend you are juggling together. Can you move high and low at the same time or opposite each other? Can you move apart and then together while you juggle? Select three juggling ideas, choose the order, and practice the first idea, the second, and the third without stopping. [Play the music while the children practice.]

Culminating Dance

Welcome to the circus! Now, we will combine the four dances into one dance. The first time we perform the dance, everyone will do all the dances in the order we learned them. The second time, you may choose which dances you would like to perform. When you are not performing, you will be the audience. On the whiteboard, I have drawn a picture of each circus act in the order we will perform them (see figure 8.10).

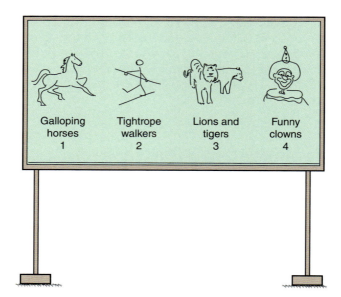

Figure 8.10 Children can refer to the drawings on the whiteboard or poster to see the order of the circus acts.

The galloping horses will start. I want everyone to make one line. When I introduce the galloping horses, you will gallop in a large circle. Then, listen for my instructions to show your horse tricks. Here we go! And now for the talented galloping horses! [Use the stick with streamers to direct the first child in line to lead the gallop. This is also a good time to play the music.] Watch them as they gallop together in a big circle. Now, for their first trick, horses take small gallops in their own small circle. Can you gallop in the other direction? Next, gallop and jump or leap into the air. Horses stop, turn in place, and take a bow.

In our next circus act, I ask you to look high above the crowd to see the amazing tightrope walkers. [Ask everyone to take a starting place on a line.] The tightrope walkers will do three tricks today: traveling forward and backward, a still balance, and a turn. Here they go. [Play the music while the children perform their movements.] Everyone is staying on the line—great balance and control! What a great group of performers. Amazing! Tightrope walkers, take a bow.

The third circus act introduces the fabulous lions and tigers. I want everyone to sit side by side, on a line, facing me. When I introduce the lions and tigers, I want you to walk forward on your hands and feet taking 10 steps and then kneel down in the waiting shape. We will do the roaring stretch three times, jump through the hoops, and roll back to the line where you started. [Assign three children to hold the hoops. One-third of the performers are assigned to each hoop.] And now for the fabulous lions and tigers—here they come! Don't be afraid—they are friendly. Now, watch them roar when I lift my stick. And roar! [Lift the stick up and down three times.] Now, watch how skillfully they jump through the hoops and roll. Will my assistants please hold the hoops? [The children make three lines and jump through their assigned hoop. The jumping may be repeated several times.] Okay, lions and tigers, take a bow.

Our final circus act is the funny juggling clowns. They will perform their many juggling tricks. [Children stand around the perimeter of the room and begin their imaginary juggling when the music starts.] Some are juggling low to the floor, some are moving backward, and some are juggling with other clowns. Wow! Look at all the super juggling! That was great! Now, take a bow.

This time, I will introduce the circus act, and you may choose to perform or be in the audience.

Closure

Each child shows one movement from any one of the dances, and the rest of the group will guess which circus act the movement represents.

Look For

- Ways to encourage leadership in the dances by assigning children a specific role, or asking children to take responsibility for leading a small group or the whole class.
- Children who may need help structuring their sequences in the tightrope and clown dances. They can write or draw the sequence to help them organize and remember their dance.

How Can I Change This?

- Use different circus acts such as the balancing elephants, swinging trapeze performers, dancing bears, jumping and turning seals, or galloping equestrians.
- Children can work in small groups to create their own galloping-horse dance using circle pathways moving right and left and forward and backward.
- Tightrope walkers can perform in partners using a leading-and-following relationship.
- Lions and tigers can create different ways to jump through the hoops using different directions or shapes.
- The juggling clowns can create funny bows at the end of their act.
- Props and costumes can be added, such as scarves and streamers.
- Use a different piece of music for each circus act. Use popular music, or look for music that traditionally accompanies a circus.
- The culminating dance can include a circus parade with the children choosing a character for the parade.

Assessment Suggestions

- Student self-assessment—affective: Students draw a picture of their favorite part of the circus. They can include a movement they performed or draw the circus character (outcome 4).
- Teacher assessment—psychomotor: Complete a checklist that records whether students can perform the locomotor and nonlocomotor movements in the correct order representing the animals or performers in one of the four circus dances (outcomes 1 and 2).
- Teacher assessment—cognitive: Students write a list of the locomotor movements they used in each of the dances. Review the list to note students' accuracy in identifying locomotor movements (outcome 1).
- Peer assessment—psychomotor: Students are organized into groups of three or four and show each other the different balances they performed in the tightrope walkers' dance. Peers comment on how well the performers held their shape still (outcome 3).

Interdisciplinary Connections

- Language arts (literature): Connect to children's literature using the illustrations in *Circus Girl* (Pernice 2014), *The Bear's Surprise* (Chaud 2015), or *The Man Who Walked Between the Towers* (Gerstein 2007).
- Social studies or science: Integrate the circus dance with a unit in social studies or science focused on animal characteristics or how people interact with animals.
- Language arts (writing): Use the dance to initiate writing stories about the circus acts.
- Language arts (vocabulary): Create vocabulary lists based on words connected to the dance, such as *tightrope walkers, galloping, lions, tigers, rolling, balance, hooves, clowns, juggling,* or *roar.*

150 Teaching Children Dance

Connect the Spots

Outcomes

As a result of participating in this learning experience, children will be able to do the following:

1. Perform locomotor movements, such as run, jog, skip, slide, hop, jump, gallop, and walk (psychomotor).
2. Practice making twisted, straight, curved, or round shapes with their body and holding the shape still for 8 counts (psychomotor).
3. Create and perform a dance using twisted, straight, curved, or round shapes and locomotor movements (cognitive and psychomotor).

Organization

Children dance individually with the whole class.

Equipment Needed

- A whiteboard or chart paper listing locomotor movements and shapes
- Plastic poly spots
- Suggested music: instrumental versions of children's popular songs; folk or square dance music with a lively tempo; any freeze dance song with recorded pauses in the music

Introduction and Warm-Up

Today's lesson is focused on creating a dance that uses locomotor movements and still (also called frozen) shapes. The warm-up is a review of locomotor movements and shapes. It is called *move and freeze*. When the music is on, you will move using a locomotor movement. When the music is paused, you will freeze in a shape. First, I will call out a locomotor movement, and you will move using that movement. When the music is paused, I will call out a type of shape, and you will freeze your body in that shape. [The following is a list of locomotor movements and shapes to call out. The music can be played for 10 to 15 seconds and the shapes held still for 5 to 10 seconds.]

Walk slowly taking giant steps (twisted shape).

Skip and swing your arms (tall stretched shape).

Jog at a medium speed (low round shape).

Gallop alternating right and left feet (wide shape).

Slide sideways to the right (curved shape).

Hop on the right foot 4 times then the left foot 4 times and repeat the pattern (twisted shape with stretched arms).

Run forward using small steps (big shape on one foot).

Slide sideways to the left (stretched shape from the waist down and a twisted shape from the waist up).

Walk backward taking giant steps (low twisted shape).

Ask children to suggest a locomotor movement and a shape. This can be repeated two or three times.

Development

Next, you will choose three plastic poly spots, and you will use them to mark spots in the space for your connect-the-spots dance (see figure 8.11). The first spot is like first base, and on this spot, you will freeze in a twisted shape for 8 counts. Go to your first spot, place the poly spot on the floor, freeze in a twisted shape, and let's all count to 8. [Set a medium tempo for the 8 counts, and ask the children to count out loud at the same tempo.] Next, point to another spot in the space; this is like second base. On this spot, you will freeze in a low round shape for 8 counts. Now, go to that spot, freeze in a low round shape, and let's all count to 8. Finally, choose a third spot that is far away from the other two spots, and on this poly spot freeze in a stretched shape that is tall or wide. Move to that spot, freeze in a stretched shape, and let's all count to 8. Let's review the three spots. Move to your first spot, freeze in a twisted shape, and count out loud for 8 counts. Now, move to your second spot, freeze in a low round shape, and count out loud for 8 counts. Now, move to your third spot, freeze in a stretched shape, and count out loud for 8 counts. Now, practice by yourself moving to each spot, freezing in your shape, and counting to 8. [Observe to see if the children are freezing in the shapes and counting to 8.]

Now, it is time to create a dance called connect the spots. You will choose a locomotor movement that will take you from one spot to another. For example, you can begin on spot 1, skip to spot 2 and make your shape, then skip to spot 3 and freeze in your third shape. Or, you can use two different locomotor movements—one movement to go from spot 1 to spot 2 and a different movement to go from spot 2 to spot 3. Let's do the dance together. Everyone go to spot 1, make your twisted shape, and let's count to 8. Now, show me how you are going to move to spot 2. Freeze in your low round shape and let's count to 8. Now, show me how you are going to move to spot 3. Freeze in your stretched shape and let's count to 8. Everyone practice the dance again. Begin on spot 1 in your twisted shape and count out loud to 8. Now, do your locomotor movement to spot 2. Freeze in the low round shape and count to 8. Now, use another locomotor movement to travel to the third spot and show me how still you can be in the stretched shape while you count to 8. Now, go back to the beginning and do the whole dance by yourself. Remember your shapes and locomotor movements. [Observe whether the children can hold the shapes and use locomotor movements to travel to the spots; also listen for the counting.]

Culminating Dance

[As a way to provide imagery and meaning to the shapes and movement, ask the children to think about an animal that will be dancing their connect-the-spots dance.] Think of an animal you would like to be while performing your connect-the-spots dance. The dance will tell the story about the animal. On spot 1, the animal is sleeping in a twisted shape, then it wakes up and goes out to play while moving to spot 2. Let's try this first part of the story. Show me your sleeping animal on spot 1. Is it in a twisted shape? Now, wake up and move using a locomotor movement to spot 2. [Observe the children's actions; you can choose to

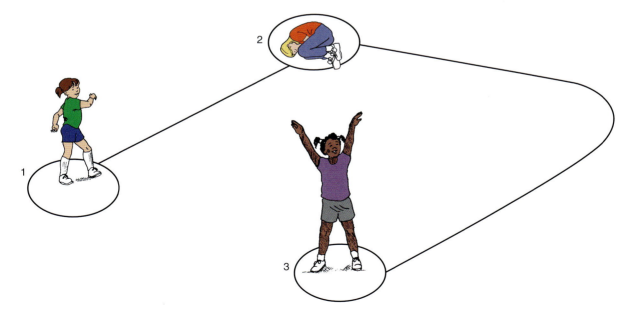

Figure 8.11 Children use poly spots to mark spots in the general space for their connect-the-spots dance.

repeat this first part of the story if needed.] On spot 2 your animal is frozen in a low round shape to show they are looking for food on the ground. Can you stay still and just move your fingers? Next, the animal goes out to play while it moves to spot 3. Show me how you move to spot 3 and freeze in a stretched shape. In this shape, the animal is showing how happy they are. This is the end of the dance and the story. Let's try it again from the beginning. Ready? On spot 1, your animal is still and sleeping. Quietly count to 8. Wake up and move to spot 2. Freeze and nibble on some delicious food. Quietly count to 8. Okay, time to go out to play and move to spot 3. Freeze in your stretched happy shape. Quietly count to 8. Try the whole dance by yourself. Remember your shapes and counting to 8. [The children all perform their individual dances at the same time while you observe.]

Closure

There are a couple ways to bring closure to the learning experience. One way is to add music to the dance. You can use children's popular songs or use folk or square dance music that has a lively tempo. A second way is to ask half of the class to be the audience and watch while the other half of the class performs their dances. Before the children perform, they can tell the audience the type of animal they have selected for their dance. Then switch groups to allow each child to be an audience member and a performer.

Look For

- Children who are having difficulty holding the shapes still for 8 counts. You can stand next to the child while they make the still shapes and count with them, or ask them to move with a peer buddy who can help with the counting.

- A child who may need help remembering where their three spots are located. You can mark their poly spots with a number to identify the dance order.

How Can I Change This?

- The next step is to add a pathway to the locomotor movements. What are different pathways you can move along? Chantelle says straight or curvy, and Gina suggested a circle pathway or a zigzag. Any others? Bella came up with pathways with lots of angles or a pathway that looks like someone scribbled on the page. These are all great ideas. Let's try them with the locomotor movements. [The following are tasks you can use to combine locomotor movements and pathways.]

  Run forward on a curvy pathway, and on my signal, stop and freeze in a low round shape.

  Skip on a straight pathway, and when you come close to the wall, turn and move on another straight pathway. Stop and freeze in a wide stretched shape.

  Gallop on a spiral pathway that begins in a big circle and becomes smaller and smaller. When the pathway becomes very small, reverse the spiral, moving from a small circle back to the big circle. Stop and freeze in a twisted shape using one hand and one foot to support your body.

  Slide using a zigzag pathway using two slides before you change the angle.

  Now, choose a locomotor movement, and each time you hear the drum sound, move on a different pathway. Ready, go! [Allow the children to move for 5 to 10 seconds and then complete on a beat of a handheld drum. This task is repeated several times to allow children to practice moving on different pathways.]

Assessment Suggestion

- Teacher assessment—psychomotor and cognitive: Use a rating scale and recording sheet, and note whether the child can remain still in the correct shape for a count of 8. While students are practicing or performing, observe the accuracy of the shape and their ability to hold the shape still. You can select a spot to focus on for the observation. This strategy will work with a class with many students all moving at the same time (outcomes 2 and 3).

  Record ++ if the child has made the correct shape on the corresponding spot and can hold it for

8 counts.

Record +S if the child has made the correct shape on the corresponding spot but cannot hold still for the 8 counts.

Record +C if the child is not using the correct shape on the corresponding spot but can hold still for the 8 counts.

Record O if the child is not using the correct shape on the corresponding spot and cannot hold still for the 8 counts.

- Peer assessment—cognitive and psychomotor: Ask one partner to be an observer and one partner to be the performer. After the performer completes the dance, the observer tells the partner what locomotor movements they observed. Then the partners switch roles (outcomes 1 and 3).

Interdisciplinary Connections

- Language arts (writing or storytelling): The children can develop their own story to illustrate the shapes and locomotor movements.
- Math: Children can count how many steps they are using to travel from one spot to another or use standard or nonstandard measurements to measure the space from one spot to another.
- Visual arts: Children can draw a map of the spots in the space and include a drawing of how their bodies appear in the shapes.

Frog Dance

Outcomes

As a result of participating in this learning experience, children will be able to do the following:

1. Demonstrate locomotor and nonlocomotor movements that are big and small (psychomotor).
2. Remember and perform the sequence of actions used in dancing the story of the frog dance (cognitive and psychomotor).
3. Choose their favorite part of the frog story to dance (affective).

Organization

Children dance individually among others in the class.

Equipment Needed

- Pictures of frogs
- The following list of words on a single sign or multiple signs in the following order (see figure 8.12).
    Sleep
    Wake up and look around
    Stretch
    Wave
    Jump
    Eat bugs
    Jump
    Sleep
- Suggested music: music of sounds of a tropical forest or frog vocal sounds

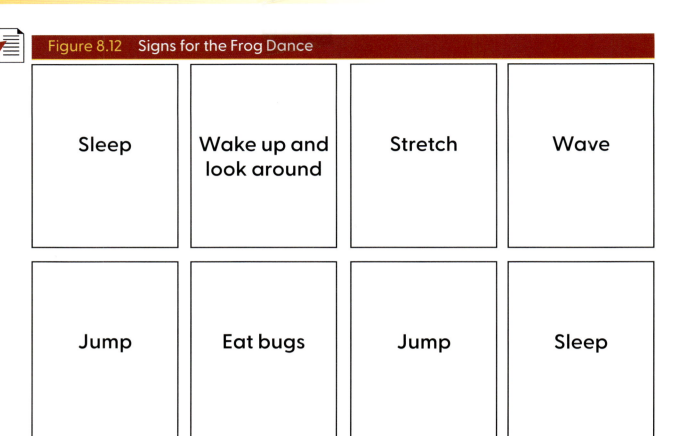

Figure 8.12 Signs for the Frog Dance

Introduction and Warm-Up

Today, we are going to do a dance about the day in the life of a frog. I have placed some pictures of frogs on the wall. Can someone describe one of the frogs? Yes, Mei says that one is small and has red spots. [Ask several other children to share their descriptions.] Next, we need to warm up our frog bodies before we dance. Let's start by walking in the space. Find a way to take very small steps as you walk forward, and now backward. Change your steps to giant steps. How big can you step? Show me how you can do the smallest stretch and bend movement with your body reaching up and down. Now, what does that movement look like when you make it as big as you can? Who can tell me a movement they did this morning on their way to school? Yes, Dre says he was swinging his backpack while waiting for the school bus. Great! Everyone, show me a small swinging movement with your arms. Now, make it a little bigger, now bigger, and now as big as you can. Okay, I think we are warmed up. Let's find out what happens in the frog dance.

Development

While I tell the story, you can create your frog movements to go along with the story. I have posted the actions the frog will do in the story on the wall. Let's read them: sleep, wake up and look around, stretch, wave, jump, eat bugs, jump, sleep. [Point to each word.] First, each person find a personal space and lie on the floor. Now, I will begin the story. Once upon a time, there was a very small pond filled with very small frogs who were all sleeping on very small lily pads. [Children make a small shape curled up on the floor.] One morning, the little frogs woke up and looked around with their small heads. The frogs could only make little movements looking up and down and side to side. [Children sit on the floor and look up and down, right and left.] Then the frogs began to stretch, but they could only do small stretches using their arms, legs, and back. [Children stretch arms, legs, and back, reaching up and down.] The small frogs stood up on the little lily pads and made a tiny wave to each other. [Children wave to each other using small waving movements.] Next, the little frogs decided to go out and find something to eat. So, they did small jumps all over the pond. Some were jumping forward, some backward, and some sideward. [Children perform many small jumps in the space in different directions.] Then the frogs stopped and began to quickly grab tiny bugs to eat. They found bugs high over their heads, behind them, out to the side, and low to the ground. [Children pretend to quickly grab bugs out of the air and place them in their mouth to eat.] Now the little frogs were very full from eating all those bugs, so they did small jumps back to their little lily pads and slowly went back to sleep. [Children jump back to the spot where they began the dance and curl up in a small shape on the floor as if they are sleeping.]

That night, something strange happened to the little frogs. They grew bigger and bigger and bigger. [Children stretch out, changing from a small shape on the floor to a large stretched shape.] That morning, when the frogs woke up, they were very surprised to see how big they had become during the night. They sat up in a big stretched shape and looked around the pond that was also very big. They could look up and down and side to side using big head movements. [Children sit in a wide stretched shape with arms stretched out and move their heads up and down and side to side using big movements.] Then the frogs began to stretch, and because they were so big, they did big stretches using their arms, legs, and back. [Children perform big stretch movements with their arms, legs, and back.] The big frogs stood up on the huge lily pads and did a huge wave to each other. [Children wave to each other using big, exaggerated waving movements.] Next, the big frogs decided to go out and find something to eat. So, they did huge jumps all over the pond. Some were jumping forward, some backward, and some sideward. [Children perform many big jumps in the space.] Then the frogs stopped and began to quickly grab huge bugs to eat. They found bugs high over their heads, behind them, out to the side, low to the ground. [Children pretend to grab bugs out of the air using two hands and place them in their mouths to eat.] Now the big frogs were so full from eating all those bugs that they did big jumps back to their huge lily pads and went back to sleep. [Children jump back to the spot where they began the dance and lie down in a large stretched shape on the floor as if they are sleeping.]

That night, something strange happened to the big frogs. They began to shrink and became smaller and smaller and smaller. And for the rest of their lives, the frogs spent one day as a small frog and the next day as a big frog and then again as a small frog, and so on and so on and so on. The end.

Culminating Dance

This time, you can choose which part of the frog dance you would like to do. The small frog dance is first, and then the big frog dance is second. Those of you who want to do the little frog dance will find a place to start. This time I will not tell the story; you need to remember all the parts by yourself. Those of you who are waiting to dance the big frog story can be the audience for the little frog dance, and then the little frog dancers will be the audience for the big frog dancers. When I put the music on, the little frogs can begin.

Closure

Ask, "Can someone who danced the part of the little frog tell me why you chose that part? Now can someone who danced the part of the big frog tell me why you chose to dance that part?"

Look For

- Children who need a reminder to take off and land on two feet to perform a jump correctly and safely.
- How well children move between each other while jumping in the pond and without bumping into each other.
- How well the children use light energy in the small movements and how they can isolate moving the small body parts such as hands, head, and feet.

How Can I Change This?

- Add other events into the day in the life of the frog, such as swimming or lying on a rock and feeling the warm sun.
- Change the story to the life of another animal, bird, or sea creature.
- Ask children to dance with a partner like twin frogs moving in unison.

Assessment Suggestions

- Teacher assessment—psychomotor: Observe to see whether students can perform the same movement sequence using small and then big movements. Do you observe students demonstrating a clear difference in the big and small sizes of the movement (outcome 1)?
- Teacher assessment—cognitive and psychomotor: Observe during the culminating dance to see how many children can remember and perform all the parts of the dance (outcome 2).
- Student self-assessment—affective: Students identify and perform their preference to dance as the small frog or the big frog during the culminating dance. At the end of the performance, students share their reasons for why they preferred to dance as the small or the big frog (outcome 3).

Interdisciplinary Connections

- Language arts (reading): Read a story about frogs at the beginning of the learning experience, such as *Frogs Sing Songs* (Winer and Oliver 2003), *Leaps and Bounce* (Hood 2016), or *Fanatical About Frogs* (Davey 2019).
- Language arts (writing and reading): Children can write and read their own frog stories and then create a dance to reflect the actions in the story.
- Math: Children can count the number of jumps they did or number of bugs they eat.
- Theater arts: Children create costumes with scarves, paper streamers, or construction paper.

CHAPTER 9

Learning Experiences for Third Through Eighth Grades

Students in third through eighth grades have experienced the basic locomotor and nonlocomotor movements and can use these movements to create dances as individuals, in partners, or in small groups. They can recall sequences of movements, move in unison to counted phrases of movements, and organize movements when composing a dance. You can conduct discussions regarding the historical, social, and cultural contexts of the dance content and ask students to assess themselves and their peers. Although you may find some students in this age group are reluctant to dance, the learning experiences in this chapter offer nonthreatening ways to engage in dance using familiar movements. To facilitate your selection of learning experiences, we have summarized each learning experience in table 9.1.

You will find that each learning experience is outlined in 12 sections that identify outcomes and assessments, equipment and music, and organization, and a detailed description of how to implement the introduction, warm-up, development, culminating dance, and closure. Additional ideas for varying the learning experience and connecting to other subject areas are also included. New for this edition of the book is the addition of modifications for middle grades in the *How Can I Change This?* section. Middle school students (6th to 8th) are often similar to this upper level of elementary school students in their skill and experience level but may need or want a little more challenge within the lesson. The description of each learning experience follows this format:

- Title
- Outcomes
- Organization
- Equipment needed (including suggested music)
- Introduction and warm-up
- Development
- Culminating dance
- Closure
- Look for
- How can I change this?
- Assessment suggestions
- Interdisciplinary connections

The instructions for each dance learning experience are similar to the dialogue you would use when talking with your students. Any text in brackets indicates suggested instructions that you might use.

157

Table 9.1 Index of Learning Experiences for Third Through Eighth Grades

Name of dance learning experience	Description of dance learning experience
Dancing homework machine	A learning experience that begins with students individually exploring the concept of repetition and concludes with a collaborative effort using repetitive movements to create parts of a moving homework machine.
Creative square dance	This creative dance experience is a wonderful addition to a traditional unit on square dance. Students have the opportunity to use their knowledge of square dance to create new movements and call their own creative square dance.
Action words	Students explore directions, levels, shapes, ranges, and tempos through creating ways to perform the action words *run, pause, spin,* and *collapse.* The words are then linked together to form a dance. Students also create their own action-word dances using words they select.
Baseball dance	This popular learning experience is a great way to celebrate the opening of baseball season or the World Series. Students create movement variations for pitching, running, batting, and catching, emphasizing tempo, levels, and direction. These movements are then combined into a dance performed in unison using a double-circle formation.
Birthday celebration	Birthday celebrations are part of the traditions of many cultures. This learning experience focuses on expressing the events at a birthday celebration such as traveling to the party, blowing out the candles, unwrapping gifts, playing a game, and traveling back home. The culminating dance is performed in unison in a circle formation and includes all the birthday events.
Partner dance	Learning to collaborate with another person is the focus of this learning experience. Students learn four partner relationships—mirror, shadow, echo, and call and response—and then use the relationships to choreograph a dance using the ABA choreographic structure.
Three sport dances	The sport dance is a great learning experience to introduce to students who may be reluctant to dance. The sport dance uses sport actions familiar to the students and explores ways to perform the actions using time, range, and levels. Three ways to create sport dances are included. Each way can be taught as a single session, or the three ways can be combined to form a complete creative dance unit.
Dance maps	Students create shapes and pathways that result in drawn maps of their dance. Initially, students create an individual map and then collaborate with a small group to combine their dances into one dance. This learning experience offers a step-by-step process for creating the dances and requires the students to work independently with the teacher in the role of facilitator.
Create your own hip-hop dance	Students demonstrate and teach their own hip-hop movements to the class. Next, they collaborate in a small group to create a new hip-hop dance using the movements they learned.
Funky shape museum	This dance experience uses locomotor movements and still shapes to create individual and group dances. Students dance the roles of the funky shapes and the visitors to the museum.
Stick figures come alive	Stick-figure drawings are the inspiration for students to create partner and small-group dances.

Dancing Homework Machine

Outcomes

As a result of participating in this learning experience, students will be able to do the following:

1. Create repetitive movements using the whole body and isolated body parts (cognitive).
2. Perform repetitive movements that vary in level, direction, tempo, range, and amount of force (psychomotor).
3. Create repetitive movements that represent the parts of the homework machine (cognitive).
4. Collaborate with a small group to create a machine part using repetitive movements (affective).

Organization

Students move individually, in partners, and then in small groups.

Equipment Needed

- Whiteboard or chart paper
- Signs attached to cones naming parts of the machine: in slot, smoother, computer, checker, out slot, homework
- Suggested music: music with a steady beat; drum or wood block

Introduction and Warm-Up

Today, we are going to create movements that are repeated exactly the same way over and over. These are called *repetitive* movements. We will use these movements to create a dance about a machine that does your homework. Now, let's warm up.

In your personal space, move your arms up and down exactly the same way each time as I play the drum. [Students move their arms on each beat of the drum.] Now, take a step forward on each drumbeat. Make each step exactly the same. Now, move backward. As I play the drum at different tempos, see if you can take one step on each beat. [Alternate the drumbeat between fast and slow tempos.] Change the direction of your steps as you move fast and slow.

Now, I will play a steady beat on the drum. I want you to use your head to create a repetitive movement at the same tempo as the drum. Now, try a repetitive movement with your shoulders, now one arm, now alternating arms, and now the legs.

Choose a body part that can repeat the same movement as I play the drum faster and then slower. Make the movement faster as you hear the drum played faster and then slower as the drum is played slower.

This time, choose two different body parts and alternate them as you do a repetitive movement to the drumbeat. For example, if you choose head and arms, move your head up and down for 8 beats, then move your arms apart and together for 8 beats, then repeat the head movement, and then the arm movement. [Students choose body parts and practice to the drumbeat.]

Create a repetitive movement that uses your whole body and changes levels. Travel forward while changing levels.

Development

I will assign partners, and then you will create a repetitive sequence of movements that you can perform in unison. Your sequence should have three different movements. Each movement uses 8 counts before you change to the next movement. Agree on a tempo and practice staying together. [Students explore, select, and practice their sequence of movements.] Now, you and your partner will perform your sequence for another set of partners, who are the observers. Then you will switch places. The observers will be looking to see how well you can perform in unison. After the performance, the observers will tell the performers if they moved in unison while doing three different movements for 8 counts each. [You can call on two sets of partners to model the performance and observation task.]

Today, we are going to build a human homework machine using repetitive movements. I have listed the five parts for our homework machine on the whiteboard: the in slot, which pulls the homework into the machine; the smoother, which smooths out the homework after it comes out crumpled from your backpack; the computer, which does the homework; the checker, which makes sure the homework is correct; and the out slot, which pushes the homework out of the machine. We will also need some human homework to travel through all the parts of the machine. First, everyone will create a repetitive movement for each part of the machine. I will play the drum to provide a tempo to accompany your movements.

Let's begin with the in slot. Create a movement that repeats a reaching and pulling movement to pull the homework into the machine. Begin small and make the movement bigger and bigger. You may need to take a few steps forward and backward as you reach and pull. [Play a medium-tempo steady beat as students practice a pulling and reaching repetitive movement.] Can someone share an in-slot movement? Let's observe how the movement repeats over and over again. [Several students share their movements.]

The next machine part is the smoother. Show me a movement that demonstrates how you would smooth out the crumpled homework. Choose a level for the movement—high, medium, or low. Make sure you can keep repeating the movement. What body parts can you use to smooth the homework? [Play a medium-tempo steady beat as students practice a smoothing repetitive movement.] Let's share your ideas like we did for the in slot.

The next machine part is the computer. What kind of movements can you create that would show the inside of a working computer? Make this movement very big, using your whole body; exaggerate the size of the movement. Keep repeating the movement over and over again. Again, let's share ideas.

Next is the checker, which is going to make sure the homework is done well. Create two different movements for the checker. Can you alternate the movements every 8 beats of the drum? I will play a steady beat while you create your movement and practice. [Students share their ideas, either with the whole class or with another student.]

The last machine part is the out slot. Create a movement that pushes the homework out of the machine. Try this move using light force. Now, try the same movement using strong force. How does the change of force change the way the movement feels? Can you use different body parts to push? Let's share again.

Now, we need to work on making the homework that travels through the machine. What are some ways you think the homework will move? [Students offer locomotor movements.] Let's all try Sarina's suggestion to skip. Can you change levels as you skip? Now, let's try Jamal's idea to walk in a curvy pathway. Can you start low and become higher as you walk and then go lower again? [You can ask for additional responses and use the elements of space, time, and force to create variations.]

Culminating Dance

Now, you are going to work with others in a small group and put together the movements you created for each machine part. Each group will be a different part of the homework machine. I have placed cones around the space with a sign marking the area for each machine part (see figure 9.1). The first time we do the dance, I will choose the machine part or homework for you; the second time, you can choose the part you would like to dance. [Assign students to a machine part, and ask them to work together to create a repetitive movement that represents their part of the homework machine. Next, assign a few students to be the human homework.] While the groups are creating and practicing their machine movements, the students who are the human homework should practice using locomotor movements in different ways to travel through the machine parts.

Now, each group will share what they have created and practiced. [Have each machine-part group demonstrate while the remaining students observe.] Now, let's start up the machine and all dance together. The machine parts begin in a still shape. [Play the music and direct the students when to begin moving.] First, one piece of homework begins to travel to the in slot. Now, the in slot begins and keeps working as each piece of homework passes through. Next, the second piece of homework begins as the first piece travels to the smoother. Next, the smoother begins. Each part of the machine begins to move as the first piece of homework travels by; the parts keep moving while the other pieces of homework move by. Now, the computer starts to move, then the checker, and then the out slot—all perform their repetitive movement. Keep going! I want the homework to show us different ways you would move as you pass each machine part. As the homework approaches the smoother, show me what shape you would be in before you are smoothed out. Start curved, and then stretch out as you pass through the smoother. When all the homework has gone through the machine once, stop. Let's try that again.

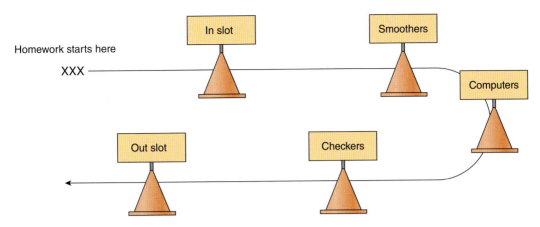

Figure 9.1 Space plan for the dancing homework machine.

Now, I am going to add a story to the homework machine. Listen to the sequence first, and then we'll do it. The machine starts up slowly beginning with the in slot, then the smoother, the computer, the checker, and the out slot. As the machine is moving slowly, homework begins to travel through the machine parts. After all the homework passes through the first time, the machine picks up speed, and the homework travels through again, this time a little faster. There is a lot of homework that needs to get done. So, the machine begins to move faster and faster until it explodes and breaks apart! The machine parts travel through the space in individual pieces, stopping in different places to perform the movement they did when the machine was all together. The homework calls the machine parts back together, and the machine parts slowly reassemble in their original places. The homework travels through the machine once more, and the machine slows down and comes to a complete stop. The parts freeze in a shape.

Let's try the story with our machine. I will tell you the story again as you dance. This time you can choose which machine part you would like to be. Some groups may have a lot of people who need to work together. We will get organized, create the machine part, practice, and then dance the story.

Closure

This activity makes you think about how a machine works, doesn't it? All the parts have to work together. What are other times when you need to work together with others? Let's talk about repetition in movement and how we use it in our daily lives. When do we need to use repetitive movement to accomplish a task? What machines have been invented to replace human movement?

Look For

- How well students can perform repetitive movement in an isolated body part and alternating body parts.
- How well students can coordinate a change in the tempo of their movements.
- Groups that need help to collaborate, share ideas, and practice together.
- The variety of locomotor movements performed by the homework dancers as they travel through the machine.

How Can I Change This?

- The dance can be repeated several times with students choosing to dance a different part each time.
- Small groups of students can design smaller homework machines instead of designating the whole class as one large machine.
- Students create their own stories about what happens to the machine in the dance.
- Students create their own list of machine parts and then create repetitive movements that express each part.

- Students can add props, costumes, and vocal sounds or percussion instruments to accompany the dance.
- Students create a dance about another type of machine.
- For middle school students:
  - Students can research a specific type of machine and create a dance based off the research using abstraction to guide creation of movement.
  - Advanced students can research a machine and write a creative story about the machine's life or work. From this fictional story, students can create a dance to go along with it.

Assessment Suggestions

- Student self-assessment—cognitive: The students write in their physical education or dance journals about how to perform the movements in their favorite part of the machine. They name the machine part and describe how they used one or more elements of dance (outcome 1).
- Teacher assessment—psychomotor: Complete a rating scale of performance criteria for assessing the partner sequence, and check off the corresponding level of performance for each student (see figure 9.2) (outcome 2).
- Student self-assessment—cognitive and affective: Individually, students complete a recording sheet that reflects how their group's machine part performed. The sheet should include the following information (outcomes 3 and 4).
  - Names of group members
  - Machine part
  - A movement that changes levels
  - A movement that changes direction
  - Description of the group's level of cooperation when creating and performing the machine part
  - Suggested changes for this dance

Interdisciplinary Connections

- Language arts (poetry): Read Shel Silverstein's (1981) poem "Homework Machine" to introduce the dance.
- Language arts and science: Display books or pictures of various types of machines. Talk about how repetition is used in the machine parts.
- Science: Connect to science concepts focused on ways in which force is exerted, such as push, pull, squeeze, swing, twist, and lift.

Figure 9.2 Assessment for Dancing Homework Machine

Students' names	1	2

1 = Student can perform a sequence composed of three different repetitive movements with each performed for 8 counts at the correct tempo.

2 = Student can perform all three movements but not at the correct tempo.

Chapter 9 Learning Experiences for Third Through Eighth Grades 163

Creative Square Dance

Outcomes

As a result of participating in this learning experience, students will be able to do the following:

1. Apply their knowledge of traditional square dance movements and formations to create their own new square dance movements (cognitive).
2. Teach others the movements they created (psychomotor).
3. Create, identify, and perform a square dance movement with a partner (cognitive and psychomotor).
4. Perform a creative square dance called by you or a student (psychomotor).
5. Cooperate as a group to create and perform a creative square dance (affective, cognitive, and psychomotor).
6. Demonstrate respect for individual ideas and take responsibility as a contributing member of a group (affective).

Organization

Students are in a square dance formation in partners. When a class does not have complete sets of eight, you can use fewer students on a side of the square or use a triangle formation.

Equipment Needed

- Whiteboard or chart paper
- Microphone for calling the dance cues
- Suggested music: music that is either chosen by the students and appropriate for use in a school environment or traditional square dance music

Introduction and Warm-Up

Today, we are going to create, teach, and perform a new square dance using movements you create. [This learning experience can be an extension of a unit on traditional square dancing.] First, we need to warm up. Find a personal space. What are some ways you can travel while moving on 8 counts? Lisa suggests running. I want you to run through general space taking one run on each of the 8 counts, and then stop. Ready, run, 1, 2, 3, 4, 5, 6, 7, 8. Try it again. What other ways can you travel? Nick suggests skipping, Yuh-lin says sliding, Evan says walking, and Keisha suggests jumping and hopping. Choose one of the ways to travel that was mentioned, and move using 8 counts and stop. Choose another way to travel. [You can specify the locomotor movements and the number of counts.]

Development

Now, I will organize you into groups of four. Stand in a square or circle formation and practice the following movement phrase that has 32 counts. Slide to your right for 8 counts and then left for 8. Next, take 4 steps forward into the square and 4 steps backward out of the square, and repeat the 4 steps forward and 4 steps backward. The goal is to move in unison by finding a way to begin at the same time and perform the movements at exactly the same time. After you practice a few times, add arm movements while performing the slides and the steps forward and backward. [Before students practice, call on one group to demonstrate the sequence of steps.] How did you decide when to start all together?

Next, I will combine two groups of four to make a group of eight and ask you to choose a leader to signal the group to start and move in unison to the 32 counts of movement. [Students practice working on the same sequence of movement they performed as a group of four.]

Now, I will join all the groups of eight to form one large group performing the movement sequence. [Organize the class and select a student to be the leader who signals for the group to start and count out the sequence to keep everyone moving in unison. Each time the class dances this sequence, a new leader can be selected.] We have been moving in unison using the same movements; now, I will organize you into sets of six or eight, and you will create, teach, and practice your own square dance. [It is helpful if students have had some experience with traditional square dancing to provide a reference for creating a new dance.]

Next, each set of partners will create a movement and a name for the movement in one of the following four categories written on the whiteboard or chart paper.

Honor your home partner and corner partner. [This is a movement that greets and acknowledges the home partner and corner partner, such as a high five, funky bow, or clap pattern.]

Circle right and left. [Students can choose a way to travel, such as running steps, jumping, walking steps, grapevine steps, or a combination of traveling steps they create. They can also add arm movements.]

Turn in place. [Students can create ways to turn by changing levels, supporting themselves on various body parts, and adding movements as they turn, such as wiggling or moving their arms up and down.]

Exchange partners. [This exchange is similar to the do-si-do in traditional square dance. Students can jump, walk, skip, move at different levels, or connect using different body parts as they change places and then return to their original spot.]

[Assign each set of partners a category of movements to create.]

After you have created your category movement, each set of partners will teach their movement to the other students in their group, so everyone knows how to perform all the movements in each category. [Students establish an order to teach and practice the movements.] Also, give your movement a creative name. [Ask one group to demonstrate for the class.]

Please show us your movements to honor your partner and corner. [Students demonstrate.] Now, let's see the circle-right-and-left movement. [Students demonstrate.] Now, the turn-in-place movement. [Students demonstrate.] And the partner-exchange movement. [Students demonstrate.] Next, let's see another group's movements. [Each group of students demonstrates the movements they created.]

Culminating Dance

In the next part of the session, I will call a dance sequence that I have designed using the four categories. [Point to the whiteboard or chart paper where the sequence is written.] When I call the category, your group will perform your movement that you created that corresponds to the category. Ready? Stand in your square formation and number each set of partners. Remember from our square dance lessons how each set of partners has a number like this diagram on the whiteboard (see figure 9.3). Ready, here's the first call:

- Partners honor each other.
- Corner partners honor each other.
- Everyone circles 8 counts to the right.
- Everyone circles 8 counts to the left.
- Face your partner and turn in place.
- Face your corner partner and turn in place.
- Partners 1 and 3, move to the middle and do partner exchange.
- Partners 2 and 4, move to the middle and do partner exchange.
- Partners 1 and 3, move to the middle and do partner exchange.
- Partners 2 and 4, move to the middle and do partner exchange.
- Everyone go to the middle and do the turn in place.
- Everyone go back home and say, "Good-bye."

That is the end of the dance. Now, let's try it to music as I call the dance again.

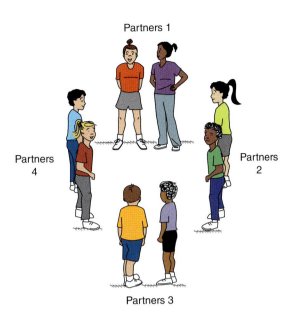

Figure 9.3 Numerical arrangement for square dance partners.

Next, each group will practice their dance using the sequence on the whiteboard; however, this time substitute the names of your movements instead of using the category term. For example, say "happy high five" instead of "honor your partner," or "the tornado twirl" for "turn in place." Select one person in your group to call the dance. They will also dance at the same time. [After students practice, they can share their dances with the class. The caller can use a microphone to call the dance, and another student can take their place in the dance.]

Closure

Did you observe any movements in another group that you thought were creative? Can you describe or show the movement and tell us why you thought so? How did your group show respect for one another?

Look For

- How well students can perform the 32-count sequence in unison. You may need to offer cues to help them start the sequence.
- How partners collaborate to create a movement in the assigned category.
- The strategies that students use to teach their movements to others. Do they use words, do they demonstrate, or do they combine words and demonstrations?
- The process students use to choose leaders. Did they vote? Do they share the leadership? Do they change leaders? Did students volunteer eagerly?

How Can I Change This?

- Suggest other square dance sequences. Look at the sequence of steps from other square dances for ideas.
- Students can design their own sequences.
- Students can write the names of the movements they created and place them in front of their feet so everyone in the square can see the names of the movement.
- Each student in the square can call any of the created movements for the groups to perform. This way, each student has an opportunity to call one of the moves.

- For middle school students:
  - Once students have designed their own sequences, they can take turns teaching their creative square dance to the other students in the class.
  - For advanced students, they could try dancing the sequences in larger groups with more than two sets of partners moving to the middle for the partner exchange to create a more complex sequence of events.
  - Students can create contrasting sequences of movements so that while the partner exchange is happening in the middle, the outside partners are also dancing a sequence simultaneously.

Assessment Suggestions

- Teacher assessment—cognitive and psychomotor: Have an assessment station. While students are practicing their dances, each student or students in partners can record on video their response to a question at a preset assessment station. They will state their name and the response. Examples of questions are as follows: Describe the name of the dance movement you and your partner created, describe how to perform it, and then demonstrate your movement (outcomes 1 and 3).

- Teacher assessment—cognitive: Each student draws a diagram of their dance group, labels the partners by number, and writes the name of the movements they created (outcomes 1 and 5).

- Teacher assessment—affective and psychomotor: The teacher writes anecdotal notes about how well the group collaborated to teach, practice, and perform the movements in their dance (outcomes 2, 5, and 6).

- Student self-assessment—psychomotor: Students complete a rating scale that evaluates their ability to perform a creative square dance. Rubric—awesome criteria: I performed all the steps correctly when called. Rubric—good criteria: I made one or two mistakes and did not do the correct move when called. Rubric—need more time criteria: I could not perform most of the correct steps when called (outcome 4).

Interdisciplinary Connections

- Language arts (literature): Use students' literature focused on square dance as an introduction to square dancing. Use books such as *Square Dance! A Ruckus in the Barn* (West and Capaldi 2012), *Barnyard Dance!* (Boynton 1993), or *Pigs in the Corner: Fun With Math and Dance* (Axelrod and McGinley-Nally 2005).

- Music: Introduce music through showing and talking about the instruments that are used for traditional square dance music.

- Social studies: Discuss the history and cultural contributions of square dance.

- Social studies: Tell students about the Square Dance Legislation Collection (1975 to present) at the American Folklife Center at the Library of Congress. This site documents the history of legislation to designate square dance as a national or state folk dance. Include a discussion on other national symbols that are representative of the United States.

Action Words

Outcomes

As a result of participating in this learning experience, students will be able to do the following:

1. Perform, with control, movement variations using the elements of dance for the action words *run, pause, spin,* and *collapse* (psychomotor).
2. Identify and record the action words selected for their dance. Include the order used in the dance and the number of counts for each action word movement (cognitive).
3. Collaborate as a small group to create and perform a dance using a sequence of selected action words (psychomotor, cognitive, and affective).

Organization

Students dance individually and then are organized into small groups.

Equipment Needed

- Drum
- Whiteboard or large sheet of paper to list action words
- Smaller pieces of paper and pencils for students
- A list of action words for each student (see figure 9.4)
- Suggested music: live drum music or instrumental music with a steady, medium tempo

Figure 9.4 Action Words

Run	Shake	Wiggle	Skate	Wait	Freeze
Jump	Bend	Stretch	Spin	Turn	Pop
Skip	Vibrate	Shiver	Twirl	Burst	Open
Hop	Swing	Reach	Sneak	Close	Slink
Leap	Squirm	Fidget	Shuffle	Prowl	Fling
Walk	Twist	Wring	Roll	Grow	Rise
Step	Bounce	Spring	Pounce	Swell	Shrink
Slide	Fall	Collapse	Squeeze	Explode	Flick
March	Drop	Melt	Dab	Tap	Press
Stamp	Fold	Crumple	Punch	Float	Glide
Crawl	Compress	Contract	Slash	Splatter	Stab
Slither	Inflate	Deflate	Flip	Bump	Push
Gallop	Recede	Advance	Pull	Slam	Kick
Dart	Lift	Dash	Stop	Pause	Pump

Introduction and Warm-Up

Today, we are going to explore four action words using various directions, levels, shapes, tempos, and body parts. The words are *run*, *pause*, *spin*, and *collapse*. We will use these words to create a dance.

The warm-up today is called *quick response*. I will call out a word, and I want you to show me a shape that you think represents the word. Find a personal space, and begin by standing in a straight shape. Ready? Reach, twist, stretch, bend, reach, twist, stretch, bend. Now, let's try jump, swing, squeeze, inflate, jump, swing, squeeze, inflate. Can you suggest other words we could do in our personal space for our warm-up? [Write the words on the whiteboard or large sheet of paper and then call them out.]

Development

The first word we are going to explore is *run*. [Write the word on the board.] Begin running in a forward direction at a medium tempo. Now change the direction to sideways—right then left. [To prevent falling, do not let students run backward.] Change direction after 8 runs in one direction. You can choose to run sideways right, then forward, and then sideways left, or choose another order. Now, change direction after 4 runs. [Play a drumbeat or use music with a clear steady beat.] Now, run using 8 small steps and then 8 large steps. Repeat this running pattern a few times and add different directions.

The next word is *pause*. [Write it on the board next to the word *run*.] What is a pause? Gina says it is a short stop, and your body is still. Can you think of any other words that mean the same as *pause*? Now, I want you to make a different paused shape on each drumbeat. Can you make shapes that are wide? Narrow? Twisted? Curved? Balanced on one foot? Low to the floor? Stretched up high? This time, you will add a pause shape to the run. Begin running when you hear the drum, then pause on the one loud drumbeat. [Play the drumbeats faster for the run and then one loud beat to signal the pause.] Hold your body still. Notice your shape. What is the shape of your arms? Are you leaning in a particular direction? Where are you looking? How are your feet placed on the floor? After the next run, pause in a different shape. [Play the drum.] Is your shape straight? Twisted? Round? Tall? Wide? Stretched? Balanced on one foot? Run again, changing the direction and size of the steps, and pause in a different shape. Keep your body very still. [Play the drum.] Try the run, and pause again. [Again, play the drum.]

The next word to explore is *spin*. [Write the word on the board next to the word *pause*.] Spin while changing to different levels. Can you spin low to the floor? What are the ways you can spin low? What other levels can you use to spin? How high off the floor can you spin? Is there a way to start your spin low to the floor and end on a high level? Can you do the opposite? Now, we will combine run, pause, and spin into a sequence, like a sentence of movements. I will play the drum for the run, the one loud beat for the pause, and fast, light beats for the spin. Each part will be 8 counts. [Play the drum, and call out the words while the students perform the sequence.] Let's repeat this sequence again, making the movements different each time.

The last word is *collapse*. [Write the word on the board next to *spin*.] What happens to your body in a collapse movement? Yes, Kareem, that's it. I see your body carefully falling to the floor; your muscles look loose. Now, everyone raise your arm up high and let it collapse. Try the collapse with both arms at the same time. Now, let your head collapse forward. Now, collapse the top of your body forward from the waist. Stretch your whole body reaching up to the ceiling, and then slowly collapse to the floor. Which direction did you use? Try the collapse forward, backward, and sideways. I am going to watch as you collapse; remember to keep it slow and controlled.

When you perform the four words in this order, you are creating an action word dance. The order is run, pause, spin, and collapse. Let's do this dance all together using the same movements. Which direction will we run and for how many counts? Sue suggests we run forward at a fast speed for 12 counts. What shape and counts will we use for the pause? Aaron suggests a 5-count stretched shape. At what level and counts will we do the spin? Kara suggests we spin at a high level that takes us off the floor for 3 counts. How will we collapse, and how long will it take? Travis suggests the whole body collapses slowly in a forward direction for 10 counts. [Write the counts under the words and review the sequence before the students dance.] Everyone find a place to begin the dance. Ready? [Play the drum or use music to accompany the dance.] Run forward for 12 counts, pause in a stretched shape for 5 counts, spin high off the floor for 3 counts, and slowly collapse forward to the floor while counting to 10. Let's try the dance again. [The students practice the dance.]

Let's try the same dance, but now we will do it in a different order, using the same counts for each word. [Students suggest this sequence: spin, collapse, pause, and run.]

I will assign partners, and you will create your own dance using the four words—run, pause, spin, and collapse. You can change the order of the words and the tempo, direction, level, size, shape, and counts of each movement. Make your decisions, write the word order and number of counts on a piece of paper, and then practice your dance. I will ask one set of partners to share their dance while another pair observes. [Students work together to write and practice their dance.] Now, one set of partners will demonstrate their dance, and when the dance is over, the students watching will tell the dancers the order of the words they observed. Then switch places.

Culminating Dance

In the next part of this learning experience, you will collaborate with a group of three or four people to make your own choice of action words for your dance. I have provided you with a list (see figure 9.4). Choose four words, decide how you will perform the words, and choose how many counts each word will take. Each person selects a word for the dance. Write each word on a separate piece of paper, and rearrange the words until you find an order you like. Try several orders before you make a final choice. Then, practice your dance.

Decide how your group will be organized in the space. Will you use a circle, a line, or a scattered formation? Will the dance be performed in unison, or will different people start and end the dance at different times?

Each group will perform their dance for another group. Then, you will switch. The observers will write down the sequence of action words they observed.

Closure

Ask the students, "What did you like about this learning experience? Can you suggest any changes for the next time? Describe a new way you learned to move."

Look For

- The variety of shapes students create for the pause.
- Spins with control at different levels.
- How carefully students control their bodies on the collapse (safety is important when students use action words such as *fall, melt, deflate, drop,* or *sink*).
- How smoothly students can transition from one movement to another.
- Students who need help choosing action words from the list.
- Strategies that groups use to cooperate as they create their action-word dance.
- How leadership appears while the group is creating and practicing their dance. Does one person assume leadership? Did everyone have an opportunity to contribute to the dance?

How Can I Change This?

- Select a category for the action word dances such as words associated with traveling, sports, animals, food, clothing, or words used in comics.
- Read a story or poem to the students, and select action words from the text.
- Choose more or fewer words for the dance.
- Add descriptive adjectives to the word list.
- Students can create a story that uses the order of the words in their dance. For example, one day, three girls were running to the playground. They paused when they saw a beehive. The bees came out, and the girls began to spin around, waving their arms to get away from the bees. They all got stung in the arm and collapsed to the ground.

- Encourage students to explore many possibilities of how the action words can be performed. Provide a list of the elements of dance to help them make choices of how to vary the action words.
- Students can add percussion instruments or sounds to accompany the movements.
- For middle school students:
  - Once students create a sequence, use the various elements of dance to have them manipulate portions of the dance to make it more complicated. For example, ask students to change the size, tempo, or type of force used to vary the movements in the sequence. Students could dance both the original version and the changed version as one long sequence to show the differences made.
  - Have students create contrasting sequences in which different action words are happening at the same time within a dance.
  - Ask students to create action-word dances as a solo activity, and then randomly put groups of students together and have them find ways to merge their dances into a single sequence, either through teaching each other to create unison or dance different sequences simultaneously to create contrast.

Assessment Suggestions

- Student self-assessment—cognitive: Each student in the group records the selected action words and notes the order of the words for their dance. Next to each word is the number of counts (outcome 2).
- Peer assessment—psychomotor, cognitive, and affective: Students and you compose criteria and a rubric for assessing the dance. The assessment is conducted with one peer group as the observers and another peer group as the performers (see figure 9.5) (outcome 3).
- Teacher assessment—psychomotor: Using a checklist, note how well the students perform each of the four words. The + symbol can denote using balance, coordination, and smooth transitions using control, and the ? symbol can denote a performance where the student loses balance, falls, or uses an inappropriate amount of energy to maintain control (outcome 1).

Interdisciplinary Connections

- Language arts (parts of speech): Integrate language arts concepts about verbs, adverbs, adjectives, and nouns. Include books such as *To Root, to Toot, to Parachute: What Is a Verb?* (Cleary and Prosmitsky 2001) or *Run Like a Rabbit* (Lester 2014).
- Language arts (writing): Use the concept of a sentence in comparison to a dance sequence.
- Language arts (spelling): Ask the students about spelling words they could use for their dances.
- Language arts (writing): Students can use writing and composition skills to write stories that reflect the action-word dances they created.
- Language arts (reading): Students can create dances based on the action words used in novels and poems they are reading in the classroom or at home.

Figure 9.5 Sample Assessment Composed by Teacher and Students

Group name:

Check the box next to the word that describes how the group performed.

✓	Super	The dance had four words. Everyone showed a lot of energy.
✓	Acceptable	The dance had four words, but some of the dancers did not show a lot of energy.
✓	Needs practice	The dance was missing an action word, and not all dancers showed energy.

Baseball Dance

Outcomes

As a result of participating in this learning experience, students will be able to do the following:

1. Perform movement sequences accurately based on baseball skills: running, pitching, batting, and catching (psychomotor).
2. Move in unison with others to the same rhythm (psychomotor).

Organization

Students will learn the dance movements individually and with a partner, and then the whole class forms a double circle for the culminating dance.

Equipment Needed

- Pictures of baseball players using the movements in the dance: pitching, batting, running, and catching
- Suggested music: the song "Take Me Out to the Ball Game"

Introduction and Warm-Up

Today, we are going to celebrate the opening of baseball season across America by learning a new dance that uses baseball movements. I have selected pitching, batting, running, and catching for the dance. Look on the board at the pictures of players using these skills. What do you see? Can someone choose a picture and make their body into the shape in the picture? [Several students are selected to demonstrate the shapes. Ask the students to describe the shape.]

Let's begin the warm-up pretending we are jogging around the bases. Stand on a spot that will be home plate, and now point to a place for first base; now point to second base and third base. When I say go, everyone will take 7 jogs to each of your bases and 1 jump on the base on the count of 8. Ready, go. Jog 1, 2, 3, 4, 5, 6, 7, and jump on 8. Let's repeat. Remember to take one step on each count. Ready, and jog 1, 2, 3, 4, 5, 6, 7, and jump 8! Let's try that again.

The second part of our warm-up is stretching movements you do before a game. Can anyone suggest a stretch? [One student demonstrates, and the other students perform the stretch.] Can anyone else suggest a stretch?

Development

The first baseball movement is the pitch. First, show me how you would pitch a ball to the batter. Try it several times, and think about how your arms move, how your feet move, and how the movement starts and ends. [Students practice pitching overhand.] Now, do the pitch as slowly as possible. Make the movement big, with a feeling of stretching. Practice several times, and hold your shape at the end of the pitch. [Students practice.] Add the following counts to the pitch: 4 slow counts for the windup and 4 slow counts for the follow-through. Ready! Windup, 1, 2, 3, 4, 5, 6, 7, 8. Remember to keep the movement slow and continuous, and lean backward on the windup and forward on the follow-through. Let's try again, and hold your shape still on count 8. Ready? Windup, 1, 2, 3, 4, 5, 6, 7, and hold 8. I can see that you are coordinating your movement with the counts and are moving slowly. We will use this slow pitch in our dance.

Now, let's change our movement to batting. First, bat the way you usually do. Remember how your feet are placed, your knees are bent, your body twists, your hands hold the bat with elbows lifted, and your eyes look at the pitcher. Try a few swings. [Students practice.] You are going to take 3 swings. The first 2 swings take 2 counts each, and on the third swing, you will follow up with a complete one-foot spin for 4 counts. Now, add a stop at the end of your spin, and hold your body still. Ready? Swing, swing, and swing and spin, hold. One more time. Ready? 1, 2, 3, 4, 5, 6, 7, and 8. Let's practice this part again.

The third movement you will need to learn for the dance is running. This part you already know. I want you to repeat the 7 runs and 1 jump from the warm-up. Can someone show us how they performed the runs and jump? Yes, Isabel, it is 7 runs and a jump on the eighth count. Do the runs and a jump four times. The first run begins to the right and the jump pretends to land on first base, then 7 more runs and a second jump on second base, then turn left and do 7 runs and jump on third base, and finally the fourth set of runs and jump on home plate. I want you to practice the runs and jumps in a circle of six to eight students. See if everyone can run and jump on the counts at the same time. Designate a leader to count out loud for the group. See if your group can do the entire sequence of 32 counts with everyone running and jumping at the same time. Remember 16 counts to the right, then 16 counts to the left. [Students practice as you observe and help where needed.]

The fourth movement is catching. We are going to do four catches in a sequence. Show me a catch reaching up high, now a low catch, a catch lunging and reaching to the right at a medium level, and then lunging and reaching to the left at a medium level. Together, let's practice the sequence. Ready? Catch high, catch low, catch right, and catch left. Use 2 counts for each catch. Try it again using the counts 1, 2, 3, 4, 5, 6, 7, and 8. Now, I will assign you a partner. You and your partner will face each other and perform the 8-count catching sequence in unison. Practice several times with your partner.

Now, let's review all the movements in the four sequences. Everyone find a personal space. Ready? Pitching, 1, 2, 3, 4, 5, 6, 7, and hold 8. Now, the batting sequence. Swing, 1, 2, swing, 3, 4, swing and spin, 5, 6, 7, hold 8. Next, 32 counts of running and jumping. Run 7 counts to each base, and jump on 8 four times through. Ready, go. And now, the 8-count catch repeated two times. Catch high, low, right, and left; catch high, low, right, and left.

Culminating Dance

We are going to combine all the movements we practiced today into a dance. The dance will not be exactly like a baseball game; however, parts of the game will be in the dance. The formation for the dance is a double circle (see figure 9.6). I will assign you a place on the inside circle or the outside circle. The dancers standing in the inside circle are the pitchers, and the dancers standing in the outside circle are the batters. You are facing a partner. Let's combine the pitching and batting sequences. First, the pitcher will pitch for 8 counts and hold still while the batters perform the batting swings and a turn sequence. Then, the pitchers go again and hold, and then the batters perform. Alternating sequences with a partner in dance is called call and response. The pitcher's sequence is the call, and the batter's sequence is the response. Pitchers get ready, and batters get in your batting stance. Pitchers, begin the 8-count pitch and hold your follow-through at the end. Ready, pitchers? Pitch, 1, 2, 3, 4, 5, 6, 7, and hold on 8. Batters, now do the batting sequence you practiced. Swing, swing, swing, and spin. Now, the pitchers go again and repeat their pitch. Keep the movement slow, stretched, and continuous as you look the batter in the eye. Batters go again.

Figure 9.6 The dancers are organized into a double circle for the baseball dance.

The next part of the dance uses the 32 counts of running with a jump on the eighth count. Turn to your right, and get ready to run on my signal. Remember, the inner circle will need to take smaller runs and jumps because you have less space to move in, and the outer circle can take a little bigger run and jump because you have more space. Everyone ready! Run, 1, 2, 3, 4, 5, 6, 7, and jump. And, 1, 2, 3, 4, 5, 6, 7, and jump. Turn left 1, 2, 3, 4, 5, 6, 7, and jump. And 1, 2, 3, 4, 5, 6, 7, and jump! Turn and face your partner at the end of the running and jumping. If you are not standing in front of your partner, the inner circle should stay still and the outer circle can take a few more running steps until you meet your partner. Let's try it again and see if you can coordinate your runs and jumps with my counts. [You can play the music and count with the students.]

The third part of the dance uses the catching sequence: catch high, catch low, catch right, and catch left. This sequence is repeated two times by everyone as you face your partner. You and your partner try to move in unison. Practice as I count. Ready? Catch high, 1, 2, catch low, 3, 4, catch right, 5, 6, and catch left, 7, 8. Again, high, low, right, and left.

Next, the pitcher and the batter change places. On the change, they give each other a high five or another type of greeting. If you were the batter, you are now the pitcher; and if you were the pitcher, you are now the batter. [Students switch places and take their new positions.] Let's try the dance again in these new positions. [Students repeat the dance again.] At the end of the second time you complete the dance, you can freeze in a high five with your partner so the dance ends in a still shape, or everyone in their circle can jog to the right and high-five the dancers in the circle with their left hand as they pass by each other. Let's try the dance from the beginning. Return to your original places.

Closure

Conduct a discussion about how baseball is part of the American culture and how it affects people's lives. Explore the concept that dance is a way of recording and representing one's culture. What other events that occur annually as part of our lives could be represented in dance form?

Look For

- A slow and exaggerated pitching movement. Use the image of a slow-motion instant replay.
- How the batters coordinate the three swings and spin. Can they maintain their balance on the spin?
- How well the students can run in a circle in unison and maintain appropriate spacing. When students run in a circle, the circle tends to become smaller, and they may bump into one another.
- Clear changes in level in the catching sequence.

How Can I Change This?

- Any of the movement phrases can be varied. For example, in the pitching phrase, you can have the pitchers do slow pitches the first time and fast pitches the second time.
- Before the students begin the dance, add 16 counts of stretching movements as a game warm-up.
- Ask the students to greet each other using different ways they have seen in athletic events, such as different handshakes or bumping elbows.
- Assign other students to do the counting for different sections of the dance.
- Create a dance using movements from another sport.
- For middle school students:
  - Have students create a dance using movements from sports of American culture or sports of other cultures. Discuss the similarities and differences observed in these types of sports.
  - Have students research a famous baseball player or specific baseball game. Using the information found on this person or event, create a dance from the information.
  - Ask students to brainstorm other action words used in baseball to create movement. Action words could also come from other aspects of a baseball game, including mascots, batboys/batgirls, the fans in the stands, or the umpires.

Assessment Suggestions

- Student self-assessment and teacher assessment–psychomotor: The dance is recorded on a video, and the students observe themselves performing each baseball movement sequence of the dance. They reflect on their performance and write about what part they did well and what part they would like to improve. They perform the dance again and write or talk about how they improved their performance. Also observe the video and the live dancing and note how well the whole class moves in unison to the same rhythm for each baseball movement sequence (outcome 1).
- Peer assessment–psychomotor: One half of the class performs the dance while the other half observes to see how well the whole performing group can perform in unison. The observers raise two hands up if everyone was in unison and one hand up if unison was not observed (outcome 2).

Interdisciplinary Connections

- Language arts (literature): Introduce children's literature by reading books on baseball such as *Baseball Buzz* (Joven 2017), *It's a Numbers Game! Baseball: The Math Behind the Perfect Pitch, the Game-Winning Grand Slam, and So Much More!* (Buckley 2021), or other children's novels or biographies.
- Music: Integrate music through using the song "Take Me Out to the Ball Game," with lyrics by Jack Norworth and music by Albert Von Tilzer, composed in 1908. Use the book *Take Me Out to the Ball Game* (Norworth 2016) as a companion to the music.
- Math: Connect math by adding the number of beats for each movement to complete a total of beats for the entire dance.

Birthday Celebration

Outcomes

As a result of participating in this learning experience, students will be able to do the following:

1. Recall and perform a sequence of dance movements that reflect the events at a birthday party (cognitive and psychomotor).
2. Move in a circle formation in unison, maintaining an even space among dancers (psychomotor).
3. Move using the specific rhythms designated in each section of the dance (psychomotor).
4. Describe the part of the dance they liked to perform and which part they felt they performed best (affective).

Organization

The dance uses a single large-circle formation. For the gift section of the dance, students are assigned partners.

Equipment Needed

- On a whiteboard or a chart paper, a list of events that are related to a birthday celebration, such as traveling to the birthday party, blowing out the candles, unwrapping the gifts, playing a game, and traveling back home
- A piñata if available
- Suggested music: music that has a steady beat

Introduction and Warm-Up

Today, we are going to learn a dance that expresses the events and feelings we experience at a birthday party. Does anyone have a birthday today? This week? This month? Let's celebrate everyone's birthday today. [Ask students about how they celebrate birthdays. Also, before presenting this learning experience, check with students to see if they are able to participate in a dance that celebrates birthdays. Not all cultures or religions celebrate birthdays.]

During the dance, all of you will be running in a circle for 32 counts—16 counts to the right and 16 counts to the left. For the warm-up, practice moving to the 32 counts; however, be sure to run in your own pathway. How shall we travel first? Mike says we should jog. Okay, ready to jog to the right? [Beat the drum for 32 counts.] Jog—1, 2, 3, 4, 5, 6, 7, 8, 9, 10, 11, 12, 13, 14, 15, 16. Turn left and jog—1, 2, 3, 4, 5, 6, 7, 8, 9, 10, 11, 12, 13, 14, 15, 16. What is another way we can travel? Raina says we can skip. Skip for 32 counts. [Ask for several more ways to travel in the warm-up.]

Development

Listed on the board are the birthday party events that we will express in the dance. We will begin traveling to the party. I'd like everyone to organize themselves in a large single circle with a space in between each person. [Students assemble in a large circle.] We are going to travel to the party by riding a bicycle or riding a skateboard. How do you think your hands and arms will move? Kevin says that our hands will hold the bike grips, and we'll twist to show how we steer. Good, good. I also want you to jog lifting your knees up high as if you are pedaling a bike, or jog leaning to the right and left like you are on a skateboard. Turn so your left shoulder is facing in to the middle of the circle. Notice how much space is between you and the person in front of you. Now, take 4 jogging steps forward, keeping the same space between each person. Ready? 1, 2, 3, 4. Stop. Do you have the same amount of space between you and the person in front of you? Now, let's try 8 runs. Ready? 1, 2, 3, 4, 5, 6, 7, 8, stop. Now, look at the space. Is it still the same? Let's try 16 counts. Ready? 1, 2, 3, 4, 5, 6, 7, 8, 9, 10, 11, 12, 13, 14, 15, 16, stop. Now, look at the space. What did you do to keep the same amount of space as you jogged? At the end of our 16 jogs, we are going to turn our bikes and skateboards around and go in the opposite direction just like in the warm-up. Then, your right shoulder will face in to the center of the circle. In your space, show me how you will turn your bike or skateboard around. Will you use a jump turn? A one-foot turn? A two-foot turn? Let's practice adding your turn at the end of the 16 counts. Ready? All together, 1, 2, 3, 4, 5, 6, 7, 8, 9, 10, 11, 12, 13, 14, 15, 16, and turn on 1, 2, 3, 4, 5, 6, 7, 8, 9, 10, 11, 12, 13, 14, 15, 16, and stop. Great, you are all taking one step on each count and keeping a space between each person. Let's try it again. [You can add the music or continue to use the drum.]

The second part of the dance is blowing out the candles. Pretend there is a giant cake in the middle of the circle. Show me how your body moves when you blow out candles on a birthday cake. How does your body move when you inhale? I see you are leaning backward. I want everyone to exaggerate the inhaling movement and lean backward for 4 counts. Stretch and reach up and backward with your arms. Inhale and stretch backward, 1, 2, 3, and 4. Next, move this stretched shape toward the middle of the circle, taking 4 steps, 1, 2, 3, 4. To blow out the candles, lunge forward and make a strong exhaling movement for 4 counts (see figure 9.7). Then, take 4 large steps backward to where you began inhaling. Blowing out the candles uses 16 counts. Let's combine the inhaling movement with walking 4 steps forward, then exhaling, and then walk-

Figure 9.7 Blowing out the candles during the birthday celebration dance.

ing 4 steps backward. Ready? Inhale, lean backward, 1, 2, 3, 4. Walk forward, 1, 2, 3, 4. Lunge and exhale strong, 1, 2, 3, 4. Walk backward, 1, 2, 3, 4. Let's try the sequence again and move in unison.

The next part of the party is when the gifts are unwrapped. You will dance two parts—a gift and a person who unwraps the gifts. First, we will practice the gift part. I want each person to think about a toy for the gift and make your body into a shape that represents the toy. Is your shape low to the floor, at a medium level, or at a high level? Each student will tell the class what toy their shape represents. Let's start with Trent and go around the circle. [Each student shows their shape and identifies the toy.] Remember your shape. Next, we will create movements that express the excitement you feel when you unwrap a gift. First, I will assign partners, and you will take turns dancing the part of the gift and the person who unwraps the gift. [Assign partners by selecting students who are standing next to each other. One partner is identified as *happy*, and the other partner is identified as *birthday*.] The birthday people will be the gifts first, and the happy people will unwrap the gifts first. Birthday people, make your gift shapes. Now, the happy people skip, gallop, or jog in a circle around the gift, using fast arm movements that represent pulling off the ribbon and paper. You have 8 counts. [Students practice the unwrapping movements.] Now, switch parts with your partner so they can practice the unwrapping. Let's practice this section of the dance again.

Now, before we play the party game, let's see if we can combine the first three parts. You travel to the party on your bikes or skateboards, blow out the candles twice, and unwrap the gifts twice. Start in a big circle with your left shoulder facing in to the center of the circle. Remember to keep the same space between each person and perform the movements together to the music. [Turn the music on.] Ready? Begin. [Students practice the first three parts of the dance while you cue the counts.]

The next part of the dance is the party game. Today, we are going to hit a piñata. [Show the class a piñata: a decorated container filled with candies and gifts that is hung and broken open by hitting it with a stick. Explain a brief history of the piñata: there are multiple stories as to where the piñata originated. Some say it began with the Aztecs, while others claim Marco Polo saw it used in China. Both stories involve a hollow vessel that was stuffed with items and meant to be hit or struck in order to break it open and have the contents spill out during a celebration.] Has anyone played this game at a party? In this part of the dance, the happy students take 4 walking steps toward the center of the circle and pretend they are holding a stick performing this sequence: swing, swing, and spin around for 4 counts. [You or a student demonstrates the swing-and-spin sequence.] This movement sequence represents swinging a stick at the piñata. Then, you will open your arms and reach up to catch all the candy for 4 counts and walk backward 4 steps to your place in the circle. Ready? Happy people walk forward, 1, 2, 3, 4, and swing, swing, and spin around, 1, 2, 3, 4, open your arms and catch candy, 1, 2, 3, 4, and walk backward, 1, 2, 3, 4. Now, the birthday people do the same. Now, each group will practice this part of the dance again.

Now, it is time to go home after the party. In this section of the dance, the happy people will go home first. They begin riding their bicycles or their skateboards to the right, weaving in and out of the circle among the birthday people without bumping into them. How would you describe the pathway they are traveling on? Keep jogging until you get back to your place. Next, the birthday people do the same. Let's try this once. [Both groups of students practice this weaving pathway.]

Culminating Dance

Now, let's combine all the sections of the dance we learned into one dance. Can someone tell us what happens first? What is one important thing to remember in the traveling-to-the-party section? What section is second? Can someone show us the sequence of movements for blowing out the candles? What happens in the third part? Can one set of partners demonstrate the gift and the unwrapping? Now, the piñata game. Can someone describe how to do it and then show the movements? Finally, the party is over and the guests travel home. How is this part the same as traveling to the party, and how is it different?

Now, we are ready to put it all together. I will play the music and cue the counts for each section. [Call out the counts as the students dance.] Now, you perform the dance by yourselves. I will ask five students to count out loud so everyone can dance in unison. [Select a different student to count each section while they also dance.]

Closure

Ask students to describe the part of the dance they enjoyed most. Ask students what they learned about dancing in this learning experience.

Look For

- How well students can maintain an even space between each other as they travel in the circle.
- How well students perform the movements in each section of the dance using the appropriate tempo and space.
- Whether students can coordinate the 32-count run with a change of direction after 16 counts.
- How well students can move between each other without bumping into one another.

How Can I Change This?

- Suggest other means of traveling to the party, such as driving a car, taking a subway, using roller skates, using a skateboard, or flying in a plane.
- The whole class can represent the same gift instead of making individual choices.
- Use a different game played at a party.
- Students dance in groups of eight to demonstrate different birthday parties happening in the neighborhood.
- For middle school students:
  - Have students write a story about a birthday party. Either using their own story or swapping with a classmate, have the students turn the story into a dance.
  - Students could research different ways birthdays are celebrated in various cultures or countries. Have them incorporate these rituals into movement sequences.

Assessment Suggestions

- Student self-assessment–cognitive: On one sheet of paper, students can draw and label a series of pictures that describe the correct order of events in the dance (outcome 1).
- Teacher assessment–psychomotor: Use a checklist to note students who demonstrate difficulty with performing movements on the beat and maintaining appropriate space in the dance (outcome 2).
- Peer assessment–psychomotor: Students are organized into observers and performers. Each observer is assigned a performer to assess. While the performers are dancing, the observers note if the dancer is on the music beat during each birthday event. They receive a + if they are on the beat and a $\sqrt{}$ if they are not on the beat (outcome 3).
- Student self-assessment–affective and psychomotor: Students verbally share with another peer which part of the dance they liked performing and during which part of the dance they feel they stayed on the beat (outcomes 3 and 4).

Interdisciplinary Connections

- Social studies: Combine this dance with a social studies unit focused on cultural traditions. A birthday is one cultural tradition that is celebrated in many ways. Incorporate these cultural traditions into the birthday dance.
- Math: Integrate math concepts by adding together the ages of all the students, then use the total number as the number of counts for the dance. Students can divide the total counts and assign a number of counts to each section of the dance. The total counts for the five sections will equal the total age of the students.
- Music or world language: Students can combine the dance with music as they sing "Happy Birthday" during the dance. They can also sing the song in other languages or learn the birthday songs of other cultures.

178 Teaching Children Dance

Partner Dance

Outcomes

As a result of participating in this learning experience, students will be able to do the following:

1. Create, perform, and observe movements that use four partner relationships: mirror, shadow, echo, and call and response (cognitive and psychomotor).
2. Identify the four partner relationships (cognitive).
3. Create and perform a dance with a partner using the ABA choreographic structure (cognitive, psychomotor, and affective).
4. Identify preferences for moving using four partner relationships (affective).

Organization

Students will collaborate with various partners during the learning experience.

Equipment Needed

- Whiteboard or chart paper listing the four partner relationships and their definitions
- Paper and pencils for students to record their choreography
- Suggested music: lively music in fast and slow tempos

Introduction and Warm-Up

Who can tell us what they know about the word *duet*? How is a duet used in music? Any other ideas about duets? In this dance unit, we are going to create duets with a partner. You will have the opportunity to create and perform movements with many partners.

First, we are going to warm up. Sit on the floor in a personal space. Pretend your arms and hands are partners. Can you move your arms so they both do exactly the same movement at the same time? Try using slow motion. Now, increase the tempo faster and faster. Can you move both legs exactly the same way in a leg-dance duet? Can you move your legs far apart and close together? Can they change shape and levels? Now, try moving both your arms and legs in unison. [You can play music that will be used during the lesson.]

In the next part of the warm-up, we will all stand in a circle. One student will volunteer to be the leader in the center of the circle, and everyone will follow. They will move using one of the elements of dance that I call out, and then another person will lead. Ready? Who will be first? Create a slow movement. Next person, do quick and light movements. [Continue to change leaders after 15 seconds and call a way to move, such as one body part, twisting movements, changing frozen shapes, jumping apart and together, low movements, small movements using the hands, bending and stretching, turning, or strong and slow movements.]

Development

This unit will focus on four ways to dance with another person: mirror, shadow, echo, and call and response. These relationships are called partner relationships. You and a partner will create and perform movements for each relationship and choose two of the relationships to compose a dance.

The first one is mirror. In mirroring, you face your partner and move at the same time using the same movement (see figure 9.8). One person is the leader, and one is the follower. If the leader is using the right hand, the person following will use the left hand, like looking in a mirror. The leader moves slowly so it is easy to follow. [Demonstrate mirroring with a student.] I will assign partners, and you decide who will lead first. Begin when I play the slow music, and stop and switch leaders when the music stops. [Play the music for 1 minute, and when the music stops, students switch places.] Now, I will assign you a different partner, and we will try the mirroring again.

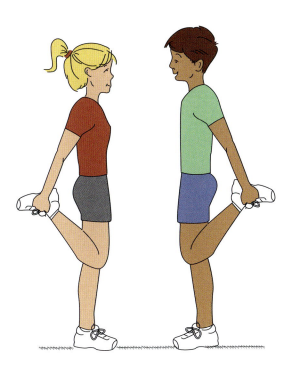

Figure 9.8 Mirroring is performing a movement with your partner as if you are looking in a mirror.

The second relationship is shadow. In the shadowing relationship, the leader moves with their back facing the follower; one partner stands behind the other. The partners do the same movement at the same time. This time, the leader chooses different ways to travel in the space using locomotor movements, stopping occasionally to freeze in a shape. [You and a student demonstrate.] I will assign new partners, and again, you decide who will lead first. When I play the music, you will begin, and when the music stops, switch places. [Play medium-tempo music.] Remember to stop and make a shape. [Students practice.] Now, I will assign you a different partner, and we will try the shadowing again.

The third relationship is echo. Can someone tell us what you know about the word *echo*? What do you think it would look like in movement? [Ask several students to share their responses with the class.] In the echo, one person performs one or two movements and then freezes while the partner observes. After the freeze, the observing partner repeats the same movement. Then the partners switch roles. Partners keep switching the echo-leader role with the echo-follower role. [The students and you discuss what makes the echoing relationship successful and then have students demonstrate.] When you perform the echoing movements, make small and big movements and slow and fast movements. I will assign you a new partner; you decide who will be the first leader. When I play the music, you will begin, and keep switching on your own time. [Play medium-tempo music while the students practice echoing.] Now, I will assign you a different partner, and we will try echoing again.

The fourth relationship is call and response. This relationship is like having a conversation with someone. First, one person briefly expresses a feeling or thought through performing one or two movements and then freezes in a still shape. Next, the other partner responds using a different movement and freezes. It is like having a conversation using movement instead of words. You may say something using small, light, and quick movements or strong, slow, and big movements. What are other types of movements you could use? I would like two students to demonstrate this relationship for the class. [Students demonstrate the call and response using a variety of movements.] The movements can contrast with each other or be similar. Be creative, and try different amounts of force and a variety of ranges of movement, body parts, tempos, and levels. I will assign new partners, and you decide who will start the conversation. When I play the music, you will begin, and when the music stops, freeze. [Play medium-tempo music while the students practice the call and response.] Now, I will assign you a different partner, and we will try the call and response again.

Culminating Dance

You will work together with your partner to create a dance that includes two of the four partner relationships using the ABA choreographic structure. The ABA structure is like a pattern. For example, if you chose call and response and echo for the dance, the sequence in ABA would be call and response, echo, call and response. You and your partner will create the movements and decide on the tempo for each part and the range (size) of the movements. Let me know if you need help. Be prepared to write down the type of relationship you are using and how it follows the ABA structure. After everyone has created and practiced their dance, you will perform your dance for another set of partners who will be the observers. Then, you will become the observers as they perform.

Closure

What part of the dance did you practice the most before the performance? Why did that part need extra practice? I will call the four types of relationships; raise your hand when I mention the one you liked the best. Now, someone share which one they liked and why they liked it.

Look For

- Smooth, slow movements in the mirror relationship. Moving slowly is a challenge for some students.
- How students cooperate and relate to each other positively when they change partners.
- How well students can accurately reproduce the movements their partner is performing in the mirror, shadow, and echo relationships.

How Can I Change This?

- Introduce different partner relationships, such as connected, supported, or meeting and parting.
- Organize students in groups of three or four instead of in partners. One student is the leader and the others follow. Students take turns as leaders.
- Assign different choreographic structures, such as ABC, ABAB, or ABCD.
- For middle school students:
  - Assign the students a theme or mood to the dance, which should be shown in the choreographic structure. For example, if students used a simple AB format, the A section could be "happy" while the B section could be "mad."
  - For advanced students, small groups could combine sections into one larger class dance or organize by similar structures. For example, all partners whose ABA was echo, shadow, echo could dance their sequences simultaneously as one group with formations.
  - Incorporate additional elements of dance to challenge or modify students' choreography, such as the requirement to change tempo, size, or pathway.

Assessment Suggestions

- Teacher assessment—cognitive: Students identify the two relationships they used in their dance and write down the definitions (outcome 3).
- Student self-assessment—affective: Students verbalize, draw, or write the partner relationship they liked the best and the one that was the hardest to perform (outcome 4).
- Peer assessment—cognitive: Peer observers watch the performance of another set of partners and write the partner relationships the performers used as they appeared in the ABA choreographic structure (outcome 2).
- Teacher assessment—psychomotor and cognitive: During the partner performance, use a checklist to record how well each student performs the selected partner relationships (outcomes 1 and 3).

Interdisciplinary Connections

- Science: Integrate the dance with a science lesson focused on the sun and shadows.
- Social studies: Use this dance as a way to illustrate a social studies concept that looks at roles and responsibilities of leaders and followers in a community or partnership.
- Music: Connect the choreographic structure ABA to the ABA music composition form.
- Science: Use the dance as a way to illustrate the science concept of echoing.

Three Sport Dances: Sport Add-On, Sport Web, and Sport Pictures in Action

Outcomes

As a result of participating in this learning experience, students will be able to do the following:

1. Create and perform individual, partner, and group dances using sport actions (affective, cognitive, and psychomotor).
2. Create and perform variations to sport actions using the elements of dance (cognitive and psychomotor).
3. Select and use pictures of sport actions in creating and performing a partner dance (cognitive and psychomotor).
4. Perform the sport add-on dance in unison (psychomotor).
5. Respond to their performance of one of the three sport dances (affective).

Organization

Students dance individually for the sport web dance and as part of a small group for the sport add-on dance and the sport pictures in action dance.

Equipment Needed

- Whiteboard or chart paper
- Sport web dance recording sheets
- Pencils
- Pictures of sport actions (sport pictures can be obtained from magazines, newspapers, the Internet, photographs, or a display of books)
- Suggested music: music with a clear beat

Introduction and Warm-Up

This dance unit uses sport actions and sport pictures as the topic for creating and performing dances. Sports are part of our everyday world. We see sports in person, on the Internet, and on television. We hear sports on the radio. We read about sports in magazines, in books, on the Internet, or in the newspaper. We view sport movies, videos, photographs, or works of art. We wear clothing with sport logos. You may choose a career in sports as a writer, an announcer, an official, or a coach, or you can participate as an athlete.

Can each person share your favorite sport you like to play or watch? [Each student in the class comments on a sport. You can write the sports on the whiteboard or chart paper.] Before we start our dances, we need to warm up all parts of the body. Let's begin with jogging in place, and when I call out one of the sports you mentioned, I want you to freeze in an action shape from that sport. Ready, jog in place and freeze in a tennis shape. [Repeat the sequence of jogging and still shapes several times, calling out different sports on the freeze.]

Development

Students participate in three activities in which they learn three ways to create and perform a sport dance.

Sport Add-On Dance

The first sport dance is the sport add-on dance. I will organize you into groups of five or six, and I want you to stand in a circle. [Give each student in your group a number that follows consecutively around the circle.] Next, each student selects a sport and one action from the sport. Practice performing the action in 4 counts. [Students practice individually while in the group circle.]

I will demonstrate how your group will add the actions together. I'll use this group to demonstrate. The first student demonstrates her action to the group, and in unison the group members repeat the movement. [One student demonstrates, and then everyone in the group repeats the action.] You may need to practice a couple of times to repeat it accurately. Next, the second person in the group demonstrates their action, and in unison the group members repeat the movement. Then, the first movement is repeated followed by the second movement, which is added to the first. [Students demonstrate.] Then, the third person demonstrates their action, and in unison the group repeats the action. Now, the group combines the actions beginning with the first, then the second, and then the third. This pattern of demonstrating, repeating, and adding the movement on to the sequence is repeated until everyone in the group has contributed an action to the sequence. The goal is to remember the sequence, perform in unison as a group, and continue to do each movement in 4 counts. [Direct the demonstration, adding two more actions.] The options for using the 4 beats are as follows: One action is performed four times, once on each beat; one action is performed twice, taking 2 beats for the action; or one action is performed once, taking all 4 beats for the action. [Observe the groups and offer help where needed.]

Now, each group will demonstrate their dance to the class. The other class members will observe the performance. After the performance, I will ask the observers to tell us what they saw. Here are the questions I will ask: Did the group perform in unison? What sport actions did you observe? How did the performers use their 4 beats? [Groups can be paired as performers and observers instead of one group performing for the entire class.]

Next, your group is going to revise your sport dance. Each person will make a change in the size or the level of their action. You will show the change to the group, the group members will try the change, and then the whole group will practice the dance again using the changes.

Next, I will combine all the groups into one large circle. You will maintain the same order you had in your small-group circle. As you become organized, notice that there will be people from the other groups mixed in between your group members. [Organize all the groups into one combined circle.] Point to the members of your group so you can see where they are. Now, all the group dances will be performed at the same time. Freeze in your last shape until all the groups have finished. Ready, begin. [Students perform their dances.] How did it feel to perform your dance while all the groups danced at the same time? Did you notice any of the other group's movements? [You can omit the whole-class dance with all the groups combined into one circle. The sport add-on dance can be completed in a single dance session as a lesson in a unit on creating sport dances.]

Sport Web Dance

The second way to create a dance using sport actions is the sport web dance (Cone and Cone 2002). In this experience, you will create and perform an individual sport dance using your favorite sport. First, we will create a dance together to demonstrate how you will create your individual dance. Let's select a sport, and I will write it in the center of the web (see figure 9.9). [The students and you select a sport, and you write the sport in the center oval of the web drawn on the whiteboard or on a large sheet of paper.] On the lines of the web, I will write the actions performed by someone playing the sport. We selected basketball. Tell me some of the actions used in basketball. [Students respond with passing, shooting, rebounding, dribbling, and guarding.] I will write one action on each line of the web.

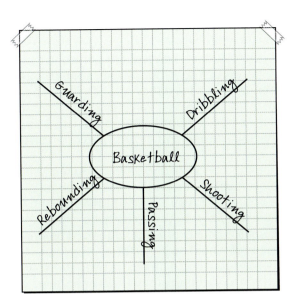

 Figure 9.9 Sport web dance using basketball actions.

Now, make a still shape for each basketball action when I call it out. This is similar to a photograph of a player caught in action. [Call out the actions, and all the students perform the same action at the same time in their own way.] Hold the shape for 8 counts. Ready? Shooting, 1, 2, 3, 4, 5, 6, 7, 8. [Call out the actions of dribbling, guarding, passing, and rebounding, and direct the class to hold each shape for 8 counts.] Now, can someone show us one of your shapes? [One student makes a shape.] Now, look at Mariah's shape. Is the shape high, low, big, small, reaching forward, or leaning backward? What action do you think the shape represents?

Next, we are going to choose three of the basketball actions and create an action shape dance. [The students choose the actions jump shot, rebound, and dribble.] Everyone make one still shape for each action you selected. Freeze in each shape for 8 beats. [Students make the shapes while you count to 8 for each shape.] Next, you are going to connect the three shapes by moving in slow motion from one shape to another. Begin by making the first shape. Hold it for 8 beats, and then slowly move into the second shape. Hold the second shape for 8 beats, and end the dance by moving into the third shape and holding it for 8 beats. [Students practice their dance several times to music.]

Now, you will create your own sport dance using the same process we used for the basketball dance. I will give each of you a sport web sheet. Choose a sport, and write the sport in the center of the web and the actions on the web lines. Then, create a shape for each of the actions. Next, choose three actions for your dance. You can select the number of beats to hold each sport shape. [Students complete the web, practice the actions, choose three actions, and connect the actions with slow motion.] You can travel slowly to another space between the action shapes. [Students practice while you observe and help where needed.]

To finish this web dance, I want everyone with the same sport to perform at the same time. I know you will all have a different dance using the same sport. Can all the football players perform? Now, swimmers. Now, ice hockey players. What other sports have you selected for your dances? [The sport web dance can be a lesson within a unit on creating sport dances or taught as an individual dance lesson.]

Sport Pictures in Action Dance

The third way to create a sport dance is sport pictures in action. I have a box of sport action pictures that I have collected. They are from newspapers and magazines and show one or more players caught in action. I have organized the pictures into a large circle on the floor facing out of the circle. Each student stand behind one of the pictures so you are on the outside of the circle. Look at the picture, and make your body into the same shape as the athlete in the picture. Hold the shape for 8 counts. On my signal to switch, you will move to the picture on your left. Ready? Switch. Now, look at this picture and make the same shape for 8 counts. [Repeat the switch until the students have reproduced 15 to 20 pictures. You can also offer a way to change from one picture to the next, such as move slowly, jump, turn, take small steps, or move quickly. Another arrangement for the pictures instead of the floor circle is to tape the pictures to cones placed randomly in the space. Students begin at one cone and then switch to another.] Now, I will organize you into partners or small groups and you will select one picture for your dance. The dance is composed of three parts. In the beginning of the dance, movements are performed that represent actions that may have occurred before the picture was taken. Use 8 counts for this section. The second part is a frozen shape that represents the player's shape in the picture. Use 8 counts for this section. In the third section of the dance, create your own movements that may have occurred after the picture was taken. Use 8 counts for this section.

When you choose a photo, look at it and talk about what you see. What are the players doing in the picture? What shapes are the players using? Are the players in a high, medium, or low level? In what direction are they facing? What type of energy do you think the players are showing? Can you make your body into the shape of the person in the picture? Practice holding that shape for 8 counts.

The whole dance takes 24 counts: 8 counts of what happened before the picture, 8 counts showing what is in the picture, and 8 counts of what happened after the picture. [Students choose pictures and collaborate to create the dance. Observe and help where needed.] Now that everyone is finished, one group or set of partners will perform for another group or set of partners who will be the observers, and then switch places. Before you begin, hold up the picture. Observers, take a look at the pictures you will see in the dance. [Students perform their dances.]

Culminating Dance

For your final sport dance, you will be in a group of four or five. The group will choose one of the three ways you learned to create a sport dance: sport add-on, sport web, or sport pictures in action. If you have selected the sport add-on dance, each person chooses a sport action. If you have selected the sport web dance, the group decides on a sport and the actions and performs all together. If you have selected sport pictures in action, your group selects one picture and performs the movements together. Give your group a name and then create and practice your dance. When each group is finished, you will perform your dance for another group.

Closure

Ask the students, "Which way of creating a sport dance did you find most interesting? Why? How did you change your sport action to make it different from the way it is performed in a real game?"

Look For

- How students create variations for a sport movement. How did they apply the elements of dance to make a movement variation?
- Students who need help with transforming a sport action or picture into a movement or shape. They may need to see how another student has transformed words and pictures into movement.

How Can I Change This?

- Use categories of sports such as winter sports, Olympic sports, water sports, team sports, or extreme sports.
- The sport web dance can become a partner dance.
- Students can bring in photos of themselves playing sports or use drawings for the sport pictures in action dance.
- Students create a dance that uses a group sport tableau (see Rovegno and Bandhauer 2017) using sport action shapes designed by the students.

- For middle school students:
  - Students can add in props or equipment from the particular sport they are creating a dance about. Advanced students could work to abstract the use of the prop or equipment in their movement choices.
  - Have students research a particular sport, sporting event, or athlete. From the research, have students create a dance using the historical or biographical information.
  - Ask students to incorporate the entire experience of a sport into their dance sequence, such as considering what the fans or referees do during the game. Advanced students could incorporate these into an AB or ABA choreographic form with A representing the movements of the athletes and B representing the movements of the fans or referees.

Assessment Suggestions

- Teacher assessment—psychomotor: Observe each group's sport add-on dance and record the group's ability to move in unison using a checklist (see figure 9.10) (outcome 4).
- Teacher assessment—psychomotor: Observe individual student's performance of the sport web dance and record the student's ability to hold the shapes still and move slowly from one shape to another (figure 9.11) (outcome 1).
- Peer assessment—cognitive: Peer assessment for the sport pictures in action dances. The following questions are presented to the observing group. Their answers can be either spoken or written: What sport did the dancers use for their dance? What types of pathways did the dancers use in their dance? Did the dancers change level or direction during their dance? Can you suggest any variations for the dance (outcomes 2 and 3)?
- Teacher assessment—affective: Use a checklist to note which of the three dances the group chose for their culminating dance (see figure 9.12). Use the letter A for the sport add-on dance, the letter B for the sport web dance, and the letter C for the sport pictures in action dance. The checklist also notes the level of cooperation that you observed as the group selected, created, and practiced their culminating dance. A rubric can be used, such as excellent (E), which means that the group worked well together or independently to practice and perform their dance, or needed help (NH), which means that the group needed the teacher's assistance to organize and practice their dance (outcome 1).
- Student self-assessment—affective: Each student in the group writes a response to the following questions: What dance did your group choose for their culminating sport dance? Why did you make that choice? How did you feel about your performance in the dance as part of the group (outcome 5)?

Figure 9.10 Group Assessment Tool for the Sport Add-On Dance

Group	Excellent: All students remembered the sequence and performed in unison using 4 beats for each sport action.	Very good: Some students (one or two) had trouble moving in unison with the other members of the group.	Needs improvement: Most students in the group were not in unison.
A			
B			
C			
D			

186 Teaching Children Dance

Figure 9.11 Assessment Tool for the Sport Web Dance

Name	Excellent: Student held still in all three shapes and clearly demonstrated slow movements between shapes.	Very good: Student had trouble holding the shapes still or did not move slowly to connect one shape to another.	Needs improvement: Student was unable to hold any of the shapes still and could not move slowly from one shape to another.
Samir	X		
Cara		X *Wiggled in shapes.*	
Star			X *Held balance for 1 count and did not use slow movement.*
Lauren	X		

Figure 9.12 Sample Teacher Checklist for Culminating Dance

Students' names	Group name	Type of sport dance	Cooperation used in creating, practicing, and performing
Sam	**Red Dogs**	**A**	**E**
Bart	Magic Steppers	B	NH
Christos	Super Dancers	C	E
A = sport add-on dance, B = sport web dance, C = sport pictures in action dance, E = excellent, NH = needed help.			

Interdisciplinary Connections

- Language arts (writing): Discuss how using a web for developing the sport dance is similar to using a web for developing ideas when writing.
- Language arts (literature): Use the text and illustrations in literature books and poems based on sports, such as *Soccerverse: Poems About Soccer* (Steinglass 2019) or *My First Book of Basketball: A Rookie Book* (Bugler and Bechtel 2018) for initiating ideas for a sport dance.

Dance Maps

Outcomes

As a result of participating in this learning experience, students will be able to do the following:

1. Create, perform, and record an individual dance using pathways and still shapes as the theme of the dance (cognitive and psychomotor).
2. Collaborate with a small group to create and perform a group dance (affective and psychomotor).
3. Observe a group's dance and identify shapes, locomotor movements, and pathways (cognitive).
4. Choose a music selection to accompany their dance and explain why they chose the selection (cognitive).

Organization

Students will work individually and then as part of a small group.

Equipment Needed

- Four place markers for each student such as rubber spot markers, beanbags, construction-paper shapes, foam cylinders, or hoops
- Whiteboard or chart paper listing the instructions for the map dance
- Paper and crayons for recording dance maps
- Suggested music: three different selections of music (choose from a variety of styles such as classical, jazz, contemporary, new age, cultural, blues, hip-hop, or rock)

Introduction and Warm-Up

This dance experience will focus on making a map of a dance. The map will show the pathways that are straight, curvy, spiral, circular, or zigzag; the different shapes; and locomotor movements that you use in your dance. You will also select music to go with your dance.

First, we are going to do a warm-up focusing on shapes and pathways. Find a personal space, and pretend you have a giant crayon in your hand and you are standing inside a huge cylinder of paper. Begin to draw curved pathways. Reach high, low, out to the side, and over your head. Place the crayon on another body part, perhaps your elbow, nose, knee, or heel, and draw straight pathways vertically, horizontally, and diagonally. Can you place the crayon in the middle of your back and draw zigzag pathways? What other body parts can you use to draw? Each time you hear me call out the word "change," draw with a different body part using a different pathway. Ready, change, change, change, and change. [Pause for a few seconds before calling out the next change of body part.]

Now, step out of your cylinder and pretend you have a giant bucket of paint in front of you. Jump in and out of the paint bucket, and walk in a spiral pathway in the general space. See if you are leaving a painted pathway behind you. Return to the bucket and jump in and out, and then travel in the space using another locomotor movement and a different pathway. Each time you hear me call out the word "change," travel using another locomotor movement on a different pathway. Ready, change, change, change, and change. [Again, pause for a few seconds before calling out the next change of movement and pathway.]

The last part of the warm-up is pretending you are a rubber band. Stretch your body as wide as you can, and hold the shape still while you count to 5. You can make your shape while standing, sitting, kneeling, or lying down. Now, try stretching as high as you can. This time, stretch and hold a shape for a count of 5, and then slowly retract the rubber band and stretch into another shape. Move in and out of your shapes slowly. [You can use a drum to keep an even beat for the counting.]

Development

The step-by-step instructions for completing the map dance are listed on the whiteboard (see figure 9.13). We will create each step and then you will have time to put the dance together. First, you will receive four space markers. These markers will show the places you will make still shapes in your dance. Find a different place on the floor to put down each marker. Now, identify each of your markers as 1, 2, 3, and 4. Stand on marker 1, now go to 2, now 3, and now 4. [You can have students stand on the markers in numerical order a few times to help them establish a sequence for the dance.] This will be the order of the spaces you move to in your dance.

In step 1, you will make a different shape on each of the markers. Shapes can be wide, tall, low to the floor, twisted, curved, straight, or a combination of shapes. Hold still in each shape. You can choose the number of counts. [Provide time for students to create and practice their shapes on each of the markers.] I want you to show the shapes you have created. This half of the class will observe, and this half of the class will demonstrate their shapes. Demonstrators, you will begin on your first marker, hold each shape still for the number of counts you have chosen, and then go to each of the next three markers. Sit down when you have finished. [The students demonstrate, and then the demonstrators and observers switch roles.]

Now, let's go to step 2. Create a pathway between each marker. You can use straight, curved, zigzag, or a combination of pathways. Look at this example on the whiteboard. [Show the students a sample drawing] (See figure 9.14.) Try a couple ideas, and then use a piece of paper to draw your pathways. You can use different-colored crayons for the different pathways. [The students create and practice making the pathways, then they draw the pathways connecting the four markers as shown in the example.]

Figure 9.13 Instructions for the Map Dance

Step 1: Make a different shape on each of the markers.

Step 2: Create a pathway between each marker.

Step 3: Choose a locomotor movement for traveling on each pathway.

Step 4: Combine the shapes and locomotor movements to create your dance.

Step 5: Practice performing your dance.

Next, we have step 3. Choose a way to travel on each pathway. Incorporate a locomotor movement, a level change, and a direction for each part of the pathway. For example, you may walk backward slowly taking big steps on your first pathway, then quickly slide sideways to the third marker, and walk on your hands and feet while turning to the fourth marker. Remember to practice your shape when you arrive at each marker. [You or a student can demonstrate the example. The students work on their traveling movements.] When you finish, next to the pathway on your map, write down how you are traveling.

Last, let's work on step 4. Combine the shapes and locomotor movements to complete your dance. Make your beginning shape on your first marker, then travel on your pathway to your second marker and make your second shape. Next, travel on your second pathway to your third marker and make a shape. And finally, travel on your third pathway to your fourth marker to make your ending shape. Do you want to make any changes to your dance? Work on making the

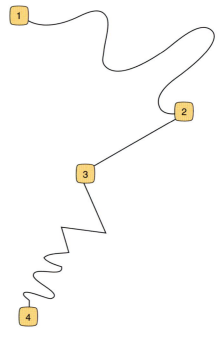

Figure 9.14 Teacher's example of pathways connecting four place markers.

transitions smooth between the shapes and the traveling movements. Now finish with step 5: Practice your whole dance several times. [Provide time for the students to practice and make changes to the dance.] Now, I want everyone to perform their dance all at the same time. Be careful of others who may be moving across one of your pathways. Ready? Start in your first shape. At the end, hold your fourth shape until everyone has finished. [You can complete an informal observation to see if the students have all completed the components of the dance.]

Culminating Dance

In the final dance, three or four students will combine their individual dances into one dance. I will organize you into small groups, and you will all demonstrate your dance to the others in the group. First, explain your map to the group and show them where you have placed your markers. Then, perform your dance. [Each student in the group performs while the others in the group observe.] Now, I would like everyone in each group to perform their dance at the same time. As you dance, make eye contact with each other, and notice when others in your group are in their still shapes and where they are traveling in the space.

Before you perform the dance again, your group will agree on a beginning place in the space to make a connected group shape and decide for how many counts you will hold the shape. Then everyone will agree on one way to travel from the group shape to their first marker. This is now the beginning of your group dance. In the middle part of the dance, everyone performs their individual dance. To end the dance, the group returns to the same place they started using the same way to travel and freezes in the same group shape. [Students collaborate to create a group shape and a way to travel to and from their individual dance.]

The final decision your group needs to take is to select a piece of music to accompany your dance. You will listen to each piece of music, practice your dance to each piece, and then choose the one you want to use. I will play 30 seconds of three different pieces of music. [Play each music selection twice while the students listen.] Now, I will play each piece of music again, and I would like your group to perform their dance while the music is playing. [Students perform their dance three times, once to each piece of music.] Now, after listening and dancing to each selection, your group can make a decision on the music selection.

To conclude this learning experience, each group will perform their dance for the class. Tell us which piece of music you selected, and take your beginning place in the group shape. When the music begins, start your dance. I will stop the music when everyone returns to the group shape to signal the end of your dance. Which group would like to perform first? After each group performs, the observers will complete the group observation form (see figure 9.15). Before you perform, tell us why you chose the music piece for the dance. [Each group performs for the class, and the observers assign a recorder for their group and jointly complete the observation form or each observer completes a form.] Now, on one large piece of paper, each person in the group will draw their dance. Assign a different-colored crayon to represent each person. At the end, all the pathways of each of your dances will overlap one another to form one drawing. Then, clip your individual drawings to the group drawing and give them to me. [You can display the drawings as part of a bulletin board display about dance maps.]

Closure

What part of this learning experience did you enjoy the most? What ideas would you add to this learning experience to make it different? What was the most challenging part of the learning experience?

Look For

- How students use different pathways and locomotor movements. Help students to expand their choices so all movements and shapes are not the same.

- Students who need help drawing the pathways and writing the words.

- Students who may have trouble getting started with the shapes and locomotor movements. Ask guiding questions such as these: What type of shape do you want to start in? What level do you want your shape to be in? What are some ways you like to move? These guiding questions can provide students with ideas yet still allow them to make their own decisions.

How Can I Change This?

- Reduce or increase the number of shapes and pathways.
- Students can work in pairs to create the dance.
- Individuals or groups can create stories to accompany their dance.
- Students can enlarge their paper maps by drawing them on the facility's sidewalk or blacktop with chalk. They can label the movements and draw the markers and then move on the chalk pathways.
- For middle school students:
  - Have students work backward by playing a piece of music and have students draw a dance map based on what they hear in the music. Then have them pick 2-4 spots along the pathway to input shapes.
  - Make the map follow a choreographic structure such as ABA with A being the students following the map from beginning to end and B being the reverse order of the map in which they go from the end to the beginning.
  - Have students focus on other elements of dance in the various locations rather than only shapes. For example, dancers could show a change in size, force, or level.

Assessment Suggestions

- Teacher assessment and student-self assessment—cognitive: Students complete a drawing of the pathways used in their dance and identify the locomotor movements. They may also include a description of each shape and the number of counts (outcome 1).
- Teacher assessment—psychomotor: During the performances, use a checklist to note whether the students have performed the four shapes and three pathways in their individual and group dances (outcomes 1 and 2).
- Peer assessment—cognitive: Students, organized into groups, complete an observation form (see figure 9.15) after observing a performance of another group (outcome 3).
- Student self-assessment—cognitive: Before the group performs their dance, they identify which of the three music selections they chose and explain their reasons for the choice (outcome 4).

Interdisciplinary Connections

- Social studies: Connect with social studies by discussing the purposes of maps. Bring a variety of maps to the dance lessons.
- Math: Use math to estimate and measure the distance between the markers used in the dance.
- Language arts (writing): Create a story that describes an imaginary journey taken along the pathways of the dance.
- Music: Integrate music by talking about and listening to different styles of music that will accompany the dance.

Figure 9.15 Group Observation Form

Names of dancers:

Names of observers:

Write three words that describe the beginning and ending shape of the group.

1.
2.
3.

What was the common locomotor movement the group used in the beginning and the ending of the dance?

List three different pathways you observed the students using in their dance.

1.
2.
3.

Create Your Own Hip-Hop Dance

Outcomes

As a result of participating in this learning experience, students will be able to do the following:

1. Learn and perform four hip-hop movements demonstrated by their peers, learn a link step, and identify their preferences (psychomotor and affective).
2. Create and perform a hip-hop dance using all five movements (the link step and the four peer-taught movements) and include a change in tempo and level (cognitive and psychomotor).
3. Collaborate with their group to practice and perform their hip-hop dance (affective and psychomotor).

Organization

Students warm up individually and then collaborate in groups of four or five to compose, practice, and perform a hip-hop dance.

Equipment Needed

- Student self-assessment forms
- Paper and markers for writing the hip-hop steps
- Composition sequence cards
- Poster
- Whiteboard or chart paper and markers
- Suggested music: appropriate music brought to class by the students

Introduction and Warm-Up

Today, we are going to create a hip-hop dance using movements that you suggest. Remember, you were asked to watch TV or online videos, look in magazines, or ask friends for hip-hop moves that you could bring to class. Today is the day—we are going to use your ideas. Where have you seen hip-hop dancing? What did you think about the movements you saw? Before we begin to list and learn your moves, we need to warm up our bodies. Find a personal space. When I say go, begin to jog in place slowly for 10 seconds. When I call stop, freeze in a straight, round, or twisted shape. Ready? Jog slowly, stop, and freeze. Next, jog at a medium speed for 10 seconds. Ready, go. Stop and freeze in a different shape. This time, you will jog in place at a fast tempo. Ready, go. Stop and freeze in a low shape. The last jog is at a superfast speed. Ready, go. Stop and freeze in a stretched shape. Stay in the stretched shape and bend it slowly forward, then to the right side, and now to the left side. Finally, I want you to practice a link step that will be used in the hip-hop dance. [Demonstrate a side-to-side step and ask the students to mirror.] Stand and face me. As I step to my left with my left foot, you will step to your right with your right foot. Then my right foot will move beside the left, and your left foot will move beside your right. This is called a *side step*. Let's practice moving to the right and left. Here we go. Step together, step together, step together, step together. Great! Now you have step 1, called the link step, ready for your dance.

Development

Now, we will create the movements for the dance. Can someone demonstrate a hip-hop movement? I see Roberto is showing us his step. What is the name of your step? I call it the double cross. [Record the name of the step on the whiteboard or chart paper.] Everyone observe Roberto and follow him as he demonstrates his step. [Students observe and practice the step. In this way, student leadership is used in teaching a step.] This step will be step 2. [Continue to ask for students to demonstrate a step, name it, and teach it to their peers while you write it on the whiteboard or chart paper and give it a number. This continues until there are four student-suggested and student-demonstrated steps.] Now you all know five hip-hop movements that you will use in composing your dance. I will organize you into a group, and you will practice the five movements. [Groups of four or five are organized and students collaborate to remember the dance movements and practice together.] Refer to the list of five movements on the whiteboard or chart paper and practice each one. Also, remember the number next to each movement (see figure 9.16).

I will now give each group a recording form that identifies the order of the hip-hop steps for your dance (see figure 9.17). [Determine a different order for each group. If there are five groups, there are five orders of the hip-hop steps.] On the form, next to the number, write the name of the corresponding hip-hop step. This is your dance order. You can decide how many times to repeat each step before you add the next one. Practice the order with your group. [Students practice the movements in the assigned order of the hip-hop steps while you observe and offer help where needed.] Next, you need to make two changes to your dance. First, one of the movements is performed very slowly and another movement is performed at a low level. [Students decide on which of the five movements will be performed slowly and which one is performed low. They practice their dance with the added changes.] I have one more part to add to your dance. Find a still beginning shape and a still ending shape. Everyone can be in the same shape or you can all be different. This is like the group is posed for a picture in the beginning and at the end. Practice the whole dance with the new beginning and ending. [Students practice making different group shapes and add one to the beginning and to the end of their dance.]

Figure 9.16　Steps and Numbers

1. Link step
2. Double cross
3. Sprinkler
4. Spin jump
5. Body pop

Figure 9.17 Recording Form for Composition Order

Group 1

Step order	Hip-hop step
5	Body pop
3	Sprinkler
2	Double cross
4	Spin jump
1	Link step

Group 2

Step order	Hip-hop step
3	Sprinkler
1	Link step
4	Spin jump
2	Double cross
5	Body pop

Culminating Dance

Each group will now perform their dance for another group. I will organize you into paired groups. One group is the observers and the other group is the performers. Then you will switch. The observers will look for one slow movement and one low movement and give the performing group two thumbs up if they see the slow and low movements or one thumb up if they see only the slow or only the low and no thumbs if the slow and low movements are not seen.

Closure

Students complete a self-assessment of their performance (see figure 9.18) and identify their movement preferences.

Figure 9.18 Student Self-Assessment of Hip-Hop Steps

Name:

Rate how well you can perform the following steps. List the steps in the left column. Complete the two questions at the end of the form.

Step name	I am excellent. This step was easy for me.	I am still working on learning to do this step accurately. I can do some of it well.	I was not able to perform this step today. More practice is needed.
Link step			

What was your favorite step, and why did you like that one?

Suggest a change to one of the steps to make it better.

Look For

- Students who are reluctant to try any of the movements and feel they cannot perform.
- Students who have a background in hip-hop and can be used as student leaders to help others learn.

How Can I Change This?

- Students can add more steps or decrease the number of steps in the dance.
- Show a video of appropriate hip-hop movements as the movements students can choose for their dance.
- Ask students to bring in music that is appropriate for use in a school environment.
- Students can create their own order for the dance movements.
- Students can add solo performances that are variations on the selected movements. For example, to vary the link step, students can add waving their arms overhead or making the body twist on each step.
- Students can add a prop to their dance, such as a playground ball, a hoop, a scarf, or other equipment that is easily manipulated.
- For middle school students:
  - Find a popular hip-hop or party dance and have students abstract the movement to make a new version of the dance. Abstraction could include using the various elements of dance to manipulate the original movements.
  - Have students research a particular style of hip-hop dance, such as breaking, locking, or krumping. Students then focus on creating movements within that particular style. They could add music or props to their dance that fit into the specific style researched. Then group students together by style to create a larger or longer dance using their knowledge.

Assessment Suggestions

- Student self-assessment—affective and psychomotor: At the end of the learning experience, students will complete a self-assessment describing how well they perform each step. They will also identify their favorite and least favorite movement and provide a reason for their choice (see figure 9.18) (outcome 1).
- Peer assessment—cognitive: Students will complete a peer assessment after observing a group's performance and identify whether the performing group's dance used a slow tempo and a low level (outcome 2).
- Teacher assessment—psychomotor and affective: Observe students as they are in the process of organizing and practicing their dance. Use a checklist for recording the observation (see figure 9.19) (outcome 3).

Figure 9.19 Teacher Observation Assessment for Hip-Hop Dance

Group name:

Criteria	Observed	Not observed	Comments
Group included all 5 movements in their dance.			
Group members agreed on which step has a tempo change and which step has a level change.			
Group created a beginning shape and an ending shape.			
Group was focused and practiced their movements.			
Group members encouraged each other.			

Interdisciplinary Connections

- Visual arts: Students can create a poster using graffiti-type letters or pictures to accompany their dance.
- Theater art: Students can create costumes using scarves or their own clothing, such as hats, hooded sweatshirts, gloves, or belts.
- Music and language arts: Students can create a rhyming rap to accompany their dance or use it to introduce the dancers or the dance.
- Math and music: Students can add the counts for each step and then complete a count total for the entire dance.
- Social studies: Students can research information on the origin of hip-hop, breaking, krumping, B-boys, or B-girls.

Funky Shape Museum

Outcomes

As a result of participating in this learning experience, students will be able to do the following:

1. Create and perform a variety of still shapes that use levels, range, direction, and different body parts for support (cognitive and psychomotor).
2. Observe and reproduce a variety of shapes created by their peers (psychomotor).
3. Move between the still sculptures using locomotor movements that travel in slow and fast tempos (psychomotor).

Organization

Students will create and practice the shapes individually and then collaborate with a partner or small group to create group shapes.

Equipment Needed

- Images from museums including various types of sculptures
- Suggested music: music that has a slow tempo and music that has a fast tempo

Introduction and Warm-Up

Today, we are going on a visit to an imaginary funky shape museum. You will all have an opportunity to be a funky shape in the museum and a museum visitor. Has anyone been to a museum and seen still sculptures? Yes, Matt says that he's been to the Philadelphia Museum of Art and saw a metal sculpture that used old car parts. Matt, can you make your body or a part of your body in a shape you saw in the sculpture? [Student demonstrates what he observed. Ask one or two other students to share their observations of a sculpture. Show images from museums if students need ideas.] Now, we are going to do a warm-up called stuck like glue. When I say go, you will skip forward on any pathway. When I say, "Stuck like glue," you will connect to another person. Two or three people can be connected. I will call out the body part that gets stuck together. Ready? Stuck like glue with your elbow. Ready, now skip again on a straight pathway. Stuck like glue with a knee. This time skip backward. Stuck like glue with five toes and one finger. Now, skip on a curvy pathway, swinging your arms as big as you can. Stuck like glue with a shoulder and be in a stretched shape. Skip and add a turn. Stuck like glue with one person in a round shape and another person in a wide shape. Last time, skip and clap your hands. Stuck like glue in a twisted shape and connected by three body parts.

Development

Now, you will create a variety of funky shapes. Each person find a personal space. I will call out a funky shape, and you will have two seconds to quickly make your interpretation of the shape with your body. Stay in your personal space. Ready? Wide shape like a stretched piece of bubble gum. Hold it still. Great. Make a shape like a piece of clothing thrown down on the floor; go. Now, a shape like a pencil with a broken point. [Continue to offer ideas for shapes such as in the following list.]

- A deflated basketball
- A letter in your name
- A giant balloon ready to burst
- A flat pancake
- A piece of gum stuck to a shoe
- A backpack that is heavy on one side
- A giant's sneaker that is untied

Now, I will organize you into groups of four or five. One person will be the funky shape teller and the others will make the shape. Each person takes two turns to tell the group what funky shape to make. [Students are organized, and each person offers an idea for a funky shape for the group to complete.]

Culminating Dance

For our final dance, half of the class will be the statues in the funky shape museum and the other half will be the visitors. [Assign the students as statues and visitors.] First, the statues find a personal space and make a shape that you did when I called out a shape or you did in your group. Hold your shape still. Next, the visitors will use a locomotor movement as they move around and between the shapes. They will stop by a shape, make the same exact shape, hold still for 8 counts, and move to another shape. Chris, show the class what you will do as a visitor. [Student models the visitor's role to clarify the task.] Ready, visitors all skip as you tour the museum. [Observe students as they travel through the statues and make shapes.] Great, now switch roles. The visitors become the statues, and the statues are now the visitors. This time, the visitors will jog at a medium speed. Ready, go. Everyone stop. Switch roles again. This time, the visitors must move using slow motion as they walk through the museum. It is like time is distorted in the museum. This time, the sculptures change slowly to another shape after a visitor has copied them for 8 counts. The sculptures change after each visitor. I will play slow music to help your movements stay slow. [Students perform this new part of the dance, and then you announce to switch roles.]

In the final dance, the visitors will move through the museum as fast as they can, and when they stop by a sculpture, they freeze. This makes the sculpture come alive, and now the sculpture becomes a visitor and the visitor is a sculpture. In this way, the visitors and sculpture will keep changing places. I will play the fast music for this final part of the dance. Ready? Here we go.

Closure

Who can show us a shape they created and tell us what the shape represents? [Ask several students to share their shapes with the class.]

Look For

- When students are in the group and offering ideas for shapes, and they cannot think of what to say and may need a prompt.
- Students who need a reminder to move slowly. Tell them to feel how slowly their muscles can move.
- Students who move fast and are unable to stop quickly without falling or bumping into the sculpture.

How Can I Change This?

- Use a category of shapes for the museum, such as the baseball player museum, the cartoon character museum, the monster museum, or the machine museum.
- Sculptures can add a nonlocomotor movement to part of their body while in their shape.
- Visitors can pretend to take a picture of the sculpture and then make the shape.
- Visitors can move the hand of the sculpture into a different position.
- Add a story to the dance. For example, the visitors fall asleep on the museum floor and the sculptures come alive and dance around the visitors, matching their sleeping shapes. Then when the visitors wake up, the sculptures are back in their original places.
- For middle school students:
  - Visitors can focus on moving shapes rather than just using locomotor movements.
  - Allow students to create a dance, either solo or in groups, in which they demonstrate an AB or ABA form with one section being the visitor and the other being the sculptures.

Assessment Suggestions

- Teacher assessment—cognitive and psychomotor: Use a checklist to assess whether students can create a body shape and hold it still for 8 counts (outcome 1).
- Peer assessment—psychomotor: While the visitor is making the sculpture shape, the sculpture looks to see how accurate the visitor's shape is and says "Okay" if the shape is correct or "Do again" if the shape is not correct (outcome 2).
- Student self-assessment—psychomotor: Students reflect on how well they were able to move slowly and fast using body control. At the end of the learning experience, ask the students to place two thumbs up if they were able to move slowly and quickly without falling down or bumping into another visitor or sculpture. One thumb up if they fell down or bumped into another person or sculpture (outcome 3).

Interdisciplinary Connections

- Visual arts: Talk with the art teacher about books they could suggest on sculpture, and share the books in class.
- Visual arts and language arts: Students can draw or write a description of a shape they
- created.
- Language arts: Students can create a story about what happens to their sculpture when the museum closes at night.

Stick Figures Come Alive

Outcomes

As a result of participating in this learning experience, students will be able to do the following:

1. Reproduce the shape of a drawn stick figure and demonstrate the shape with their bodies (psychomotor).
2. Perform the dance using the sequence outline of selected stick figures and transitions between figures (psychomotor).
3. Collaborate with a partner or small group to select stick figures, organize a dance order, create a formation, and practice and perform a dance (affective, cognitive, and psychomotor).

Organization

Students dance individually and then with a partner or small group.

Equipment Needed

- Stick figures drawn on poster paper, with each figure on a separate poster (see figure 9.20)
- Individual stick figure sheets with 14 figures on one side and a space for students to draw a figure (see figure 9.21)
- A dance outline on the other side of the figure sheet (see figure 9.22)
- Suggested music: instrumental music with a medium tempo and a steady beat

 Figure 9.20 Teacher's stick figures for posters.

 Figure 9.21 Student's stick figure sheet.

Introduction and Warm-Up

Today, you are going to be transformed into a stick figure and create a dance that jumps off the page. For the warm-up, we are going to do the aerobic alphabet. This warm-up uses locomotor movements and letters of the alphabet. Begin to jog in the space. When I call out stop, listen for the letter I call out, and then make that letter with your body. Ready, go. Stop. Make an uppercase letter that has all straight lines. [Students hold the shape still for 5 seconds, and then the go signal is repeated. The following is a list of tasks for the letter shapes.]

- A lowercase letter that is curved.
- A letter lying on the floor.
- A letter in the school's name. Now, find a way to twist the letter.
- A letter that has a straight line and a curved line.
- The first letter of your name. Find a way to make the letter travel in the space.
- Make two different letters with your body at the same time.
- Find a partner and together form one letter.
- Four or five people get together and make a word; each person is a letter. Try it lying on the floor.

Development

In this part of the lesson, I will show you a stick figure drawn on a poster and ask you to make the same shape with your body. Ready, here is the first figure. [Show the drawings listed in figure 9.20 and add the following tasks to each stick figure. Then place the figure poster on the wall.]

- Figure 1. Now, I want you to slowly turn your body while staying in this shape.
- Figure 2. Can you switch the arm shapes? Try it a couple of times and increase your speed.
- Figure 3. Show me how you can slowly bend and stretch your supporting leg. Try the same shape on the other foot.
- Figure 4. See if you can add a twist to this shape. Now, turn over so the front of your body is facing the floor, and add a twist.
- Figure 5. Find a way to make this shape rock forward and backward and then side to side.
- Figure 6. Keep still and move only your head. Now stop, and move only one leg. Now move only one arm.
- Figure 7. Hold the figure for a count of 5, then run and jump and freeze in the figure again. Repeat this a couple of times, each time facing a different wall.
- Figure 8. How would this figure travel in the space? Find another way, and now one more way.

Now, I am going to assign you a partner or a group of three people and give you a sheet (see figure 9.21) that has a variety of figures and an empty space for you to draw your own, if you would like to add another figure. [Assign partners or groups and distribute figure sheets.] Here are the rest of the instructions. First, you and your partner or group will have three minutes to try making as many of the figures as you can. Begin on the top left and continue across the page, like when you read, to complete as many shapes as you can. Hold each shape without moving for a count of 5. [Students practice making the shapes while you circulate and help where needed.] That was great. Now, here is the next part of the instructions. Choose four different stick figures. Under each figure, write the order you would like to perform them. You can choose a horizontal or vertical line as your order or choose at random. Then, practice making each shape. [Students choose shapes and an order and practice.] You are all doing great. I can see how similar the figures are to your body shapes. Now, I will give you the last part of the instructions for you to complete your dance. The first shape is the beginning of your dance, then in super-slow motion transform into the second shape. It is like the first shape melts and re-forms into the second shape. Everyone try this part of the dance. Fantastic! That was really slow and controlled. Now as fast as you can, make the third shape. Ready, go. Practice beginning in shape 1, slowly transforming into shape 2. Then quickly make shape 3. [Students practice while you circulate and comment on body control and accuracy of the body

Chapter 9 Learning Experiences for Third Through Eighth Grades **201**

in reproducing the figure shapes.] Next, make the third shape travel in the space, and then melt it into the floor and grow into the fourth shape. The fourth shape is the end of your dance. You can decide how long to hold each shape and the locomotor movements you want to use to travel in the space. I have listed the dance outline (see figure 9.22) on the back of your figure sheet. [While the students practice, check with students to make sure they have completed the dance outline.]

Culminating Dance

Now, it is time for the performance of stick figures to come alive. I will pair your set of partners or group with two other partners or groups. One group will perform first. They show the four stick figures they selected for their dance to the observers and then perform the dance. Then the second and third partners or groups perform.

Closure

Gather the students and ask if anyone drew their own stick figure and used it in their dance. If so, the students are asked to show the shape. If not, point to the figures on the sheet and students can raise their hands if they used the designated figure in their dance.

Look For

- Students who need help translating the stick-figure drawing into a body shape. They could begin with symmetrical figures and then use asymmetrical figures.
- How well students can use the slow-motion and quick transitions. Before placing this into the dance, the students can practice while in the warm-up.

How Can I Change This?

- Students draw their own stick figures.
- Substitute stick figures for pictures of people in a variety of poses.
- Ask students to take pictures of themselves in various positions using the pictures in place of the stick figures.
- For middle school students:
  - Put students into small groups, and through the use of chance or randomization, give each group 3 to 5 images in a particular order. Tell students they must make a group dance by putting those shapes into a sequence in the order given.
  - After students have created a dance, have them go back to manipulate the poses by changing certain elements of dance. For example, each pose must be a different size, or every other pose must show a change in tempo.
  - Without showing the images used by the dancers to the audience, have audience members try to draw the stick figures they think the performers are dancing. The audience can share their images with the dancers and discuss. From these images, new dances could be created.

Figure 9.22   Dance Outline for Stick Figures Come Alive

1. Hold stick figure 1 for beginning shape.
2. Use slow motion to change into stick figure 2.
3. Use fast motion to change into stick figure 3.
4. Travel in the space using stick figure 3.
5. Stop and melt down out of stick figure 3.
6. Grow slowly into stick figure 4.
7. Hold stick figure 4 for the end shape.

Assessment Suggestions

- Teacher assessment—psychomotor: Observe students' accuracy in reproducing shapes from the posters. If students have difficulty, repeat the poster and offer a demonstration by a student who is accurate (outcome 1).

- Teacher assessment—affective: Observe students collaborating in partners or small groups to complete the dance outline. Check with each group and clarify instructions when needed (outcome 3).

- Student self-assessment—cognitive: Students place a check next to the parts of the dance outline (see figure 9.22) indicating that they have completed the process from selection to performance (outcome 3).

- Peer assessment—psychomotor: Peers observe the performance of their peers and use a deck of cards to show their assessment. The observers share cards from 1 to 10 in a suit, such as hearts, clubs, spades, or diamonds. They watch the performance and observe whether the shapes were held still and the transitions from one shape to another were clear. At the end of the performance, they hold up a card from 1 to 10 to indicate how well they believe the performers completed the dance (outcome 2).

Interdisciplinary Connections

- Visual arts: Ask the art teacher to help students draw a variety of stick figures in different positions.

- Language arts (writing): Students write a descriptive word to correspond to a stick figure's shape.

- Math: Students create stick figures that represent letters and numbers.

Learning Experiences in Popular, Fitness, and Social Dances

Students of all ages enjoy being social and having fun while experiencing dance. Popular, fitness, and social dances emphasize using dance as a way to experience the joy of moving with others and expanding an individual's movement experiences. These types of dances allow people to share, celebrate, and experience life as a community.

Popular, fitness, and social dances are often easy to follow and repetitive in nature so people of all abilities and skill levels can enjoy the experience. Many variations of the same movement or dance might have been created and adapted over time by the many groups of people who dance together. These variations might have been done to change the difficulty level, express regional or cultural differences, or they might happen naturally in the learning process. For students, experiencing popular, fitness, and social dances helps develop and encourage a lifetime love for movement, and dance educators play an important and powerful role in that experience. It is important for dance educators to acquire a wide knowledge of basic dance steps and learn different forms and styles to teach a variety of students. This chapter includes learning experiences based on several popular, fitness, and social dances to add to the knowledge base of the dance educator and create fun, engaging experiences to share with students of all ages.

We begin the chapter with a basic overview of popular, fitness, and social dances to provide a foundation for understanding the origin of these types of dances and their value in the physical education and dance education classrooms. Following the overview, we discuss teaching strategies for choreographed dance. Whether in a physical education or a dance education classroom, with elementary school or secondary school students, there are some strategies and tools that can help make the dance experience enjoyable for both students and teachers. Those who are less familiar with teaching choreographed dances may find these strategies useful in implementing a new dance unit into their curriculum. For the seasoned educator, these strategies may serve as a reminder of best practices when teaching dance to students of all ages. We have also dissected several basic steps found in a majority of popular, fitness, and social dances, including the ones written in this chapter.

OVERVIEW OF POPULAR, FITNESS, AND SOCIAL DANCES

It is impossible to pinpoint the exact time when dance was created or when it became an important part of everyday life. However, evidence from records made by early human ancestors shows that dance practices existed in many forms, including war dances, ritual dances, and entertainment dances (Kassing 2017). Throughout the ages, societies around the world have continued to build their own dance practices using movement to provide meaning for a variety of social events, from weddings to house parties to funerals. Although there are many different styles and rituals for dance around the world, the art of using dance for socializing and maintaining health is universal across cultures. Additionally, there are many health and social benefits associated with all types of dances, regardless of skill or ability level, and dance in the school curriculum can provide a counterbalance to competitive sports or games (Doan, MacDonald, and Chepko 2017).

Popular and Line Dance

Popular dance is a common type of dance presented and taught in physical education and dance education programs, especially at the middle school level. Although sometimes also referred to as *social* dance, we use the term *popular* here to mean connected to pop culture. These dances can include line dances and are often created for a specific song, making it easy for the dance to spread across various groups of people. Introducing these types of dances to students of any age allows you as the dance educator to help build confidence in basic movement skills and help guide students toward a new personal pursuit or recreational outlet. Students and their families are often experts in several popular dances and may perform them at home, at parties, or when hanging out with friends at school. Using popular dance in the physical education and dance education classrooms helps engage students of all backgrounds into other movement activities, making class an enjoyable and social experience while also opening their minds to the historical significance behind these dances.

Fitness Dance

Like other types of dances, fitness dances build on social and community relationships while also adding a focus on developing physical literacy. These dances often require working at a higher intensity with a focus on cardiorespiratory or bone- and muscle-strengthening exercise. The fitness-dance learning experiences in this chapter are simple and repetitive with variations added to modify the movements based on the needs of individuals or the group as a whole. For students in the physical education and dance education classrooms, fitness dance provides a fun and dynamic way to get active and develop lifelong fitness skills. Using music and a variety of movement options, fitness dance allows the educator to move students from begrudgingly doing basic exercises to enjoying and engaging in a dance with exercise as the focus.

Fitness dances are accessible to students of all ages and fitness levels because the choreography can be easily modified to fit the needs of the individual or class. Beginning students might opt for low-intensity movements, such as taking smaller

Fitness dances help all students feel successful while getting a good workout.

steps, decreasing the size of an arm swing, or performing the dance sitting in a chair. Advanced students can participate in the same fitness dance and intensify their workout by adding jumps to a step or making movements larger or with greater force. The inclusive nature of fitness dance helps all students feel successful and accomplished while gaining a good workout.

Fitness dance is unique in that the educator does not need to spend hours learning a specific style or technique for the dance steps. Instead, they just need to discover a type of fitness dance they are comfortable with and share the joy of movement with their students. There are two categories of fitness that dance educators can study and modify to fit their needs and their students' needs. The first is cardio-based fitness dance, in which the focus is on cardiorespiratory exercise with easy-to-follow choreography. Examples include exercise video games like *Just Dance* or aerobic programs like Zumba and Drumming for Fitness. The second category is slow-paced dance fitness. These types of classes focus on other elements of physical and motor fitness, like flexibility, balance, and coordination. They are typically low-impact, moderate intensity, and add mind-body elements to the workouts. Popular programs include yoga, Pilates, and tai chi workouts.

Social Dance

Social dance, also commonly referred to as ballroom or partner dance, is divided into two common categories: Standard and Latin, also known as progressive and spot dances (Wright 2012). Standard, or progressive, ballroom dances typically developed from European-based social dances that were performed as early as the 17th century. Common ballroom dances of this style include the waltz, tango, and foxtrot. They are sometimes referred to as smooth ballroom dances. Latin, also known as spot or rhythm, ballroom dances are influenced by social dances found in Latin and Afro-Caribbean cultures. Common dances of this style include salsa, swing, and cha-cha.

Ballroom dance can be competitive and performed in formal attire, but is also useful for students to learn as part of a dance program. These types of dances can help develop competence and confidence in engaging in partner dances, a skill that can be useful in many stages of a learner's life. Students of all ages can learn about proper touch through closed and open positions of partner dances. They can also learn about the various cultural influences made on the different dances, how to understand and respect the steps and music, and about the attire associated with both types of ballroom dances. Learning social dances provides students a variety of common dance steps they can use in attending social events throughout their lives.

TEACHING STRATEGIES FOR CHOREOGRAPHED DANCE LESSONS

Teaching choreographed dance requires several different skills to happen simultaneously for the experience to not only be accessible for students of all ages but also fun and successful. In this section, we outline a few basic strategies for teaching choreographed dances. These strategies come from our learning and teaching experiences in the classroom and serve as a basic guide, especially for those who may be new or less comfortable with teaching dance to any age group. The strategies will guide you in understanding the music, how to position yourself while teaching dance, and ways to encourage and incorporate partner dances.

Understanding Music

One of the first parts of leading a successful dance class, especially for social or popular dances with prescribed songs, is having a basic understanding of music. No one expects a dance teacher to be an expert musician, but some basic concepts will take teaching dance from awkward to enjoyable.

Teaching dance to a specific song requires the teacher to be familiar with the song. No one should go into teaching dance—especially dance associated with specific music, such as salsa or other social dances—without first having listened to the music. This is especially true for teachers who will introduce and use the music with students.

You will need to know how to count the music for your students so that it matches the choreography. Counting means providing a guide to the rhythm and beat in the music and distinguishing among the various instruments and lyrics if and when possible. Children are often naturally inclined to dance along to the beat of a song, as seen when babies bounce up and down when they hear music. As the instructor, you should be able to clap along to the beat of the song so as to help the students stay on the same timing. In dance, instructors typically count from 1 to 8, unlike musicians who typically count from 1 to 4. This is because music is written in what is called a *measure* or a *bar*. Most commercial or popular music uses a time signature of 4/4, giving each measure a total of 4 beats. Dances use a 2-bar set equaling 8 counts, hence the counting from 1 to 8 when calling out or instructing in a dance. Adding an "and" between each count allows you to add more steps or movements within the beat, such as in counting "1 and 2 and 3 and 4 and."

Counting the beat or pulse of the music guides your steps and timing in a dance. Not only will this help you know when to add movements or go to the next step of the sequence, but it will help you build confidence in your students as they learn dances to music. Staying on the beat allows dancers to pick up steps easier and faster, as the beat typically remains steady from start to finish within a song. As the instructor, you need to listen to the music before instruction to figure out the beat and how to count it for your students. Every song is different, but the more you listen to music, the more you will hear similar patterns develop and be confident in counting out the 8-count pattern.

Counting the pattern also means providing a lead-in for students when you want them to start dancing to a particular part of the song by giving a heads up with a "5-6-7-8" or some other similar cue. For younger children, this could mean using single-syllable words to match the beat, so they understand when they are supposed to start (for example "here-we-go-now"). Older students also appreciate these types of cues, as they may be self-conscious and uncomfortable about dancing around peers. Providing clear starts and stops with the music enables students to feel confident in the steps they are about to perform. The best way to get an understanding of the music needed to assist in teaching dance is to listen to the music and practice the counts. The benefit of knowing music makes dancing easier to teach.

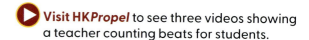 Visit HK*Propel* to see three videos showing a teacher counting beats for students.

Positioning to Teach Choreographed Dance

Where and how a teacher stands in the dance space is an important part of engaging students of all ages in a dance lesson. Although different styles or types of dances may lend themselves to certain positioning in the space, an expert dance teacher is aware of the many spaces that can be used to make dance an enjoyable experience for all students in the classroom.

Positioning oneself at the front of the space in front of a classroom of students is likely a normal and comfortable spot for any educator. In dance, this is no exception, and it can be an important place. When teaching the same dance steps to an entire class, such as learning the 16-step contra dance or the grapevine slide dance explained in this chapter, being at the front of the space with your back to the class gives you the ability to demonstrate the steps clearly to all students at one time. However, expert dance teachers employ some strategies in this scenario to ensure an equal and equitable learning experience for all.

First, as the leader at the front of the room, you may choose to face either away from your students (with your back to the group) or turn to face them. Some dance and physical activity spaces come equipped with mirrors, making it easy for the instructor to have their back to their students while still being able to view students in the mirror. If this is an option, you can use this to your advantage by demonstrating the dance by facing the same direction as your students and using the same sides of the body. However, not every space has a mirror, and even in spaces that do, the mirror should be used sparingly. Students want to engage with you during dance class and not see only your reflection. That means turning to face your students can be highly beneficial. Not only does it give you a chance to see your students, especially in a non-mirrored space, but it also lets you engage with your students socially and with direct eye contact. The trick when facing your students is to make sure that, as the instructor, you know how to mirror your own movements. For example, if you step out to your left, that will be your students' right side, and if calling out directions, you will have to state the opposite of what your own body is doing. This can take some practice but is an important skill to have for those in spaces without dance mirrors.

Other strategies can also include moving around the space so all students have an equal opportunity to see the body movements you are demonstrating. This could be as simple as having students switch lines as they learn a dance, giving every student the chance to be in the front, middle, and back of the space. It could also mean the instructor moves around the space. Although the front and center of the room may be a place of ease and comfort for the instructor, dance is a social activity, especially for popular, fitness, and social dances. Students of all ages want to engage and receive feedback during the process, and an instructor who moves around the space during appropriate times to ensure that all students are learning can make the dance class more fun.

Encouraging and Incorporating Partner Work in Dance

A final strategy for teaching choreographed dance is to find ways to encourage interaction and partner work. These types of dances are meant to build community relationships. Those skills are learned through the environment and from direction by the dance instructor. Engaging in this type of social behavior may not come naturally for some students, and as children get older, their social boundaries and awareness levels change. It is often necessary for the dance instructor to find new ways of engaging students so that working with or touching a partner is an enjoyable, not off-putting, situation.

Social and popular dances are often taught in three basic formations for a group: partner, line, or whole group. Whole-group dance is the typical setup for those who have ever danced at a party or other type of social gathering. All dancers are on the dance floor, possibly facing a variety of directions, and they engage in the same dance sequence without touching or invading one another's space. The other two types, line and partner, involve more connection or contact between dancers. Although these dances can be fun, some students have difficulty with eye contact or touch. The physical or dance education classroom may be one of the few times students have to engage with each other in this way. A dance educator needs to know how to approach these situations so all students feel comfortable and can enjoy learning these dances. We have included some strategies to make the use of partner work and connection easier for students of all ages.

When teaching choreographed dance, find ways to encourage interaction.

Line Dancing and Contra Dancing

Line dancing involves a group of people standing in lines and dancing a choreographed sequence of repeating steps. Dancers are typically facing the same direction and performing the steps in unison. Basic line dances focus most of the movement on the legs and feet, with more advanced dances including upper-body movements of the arms and hands. Line dances are familiar to children of all ages because the dances are choreographed using popular music, such as the macarena, the cupid shuffle, or dances set to a country song like "Cotton-Eyed Joe." Because the steps in line dances are simple and do not involve a partner, line dancing is an easy way to introduce social dancing to a hesitant dancer.

Contra dancing is a variation of line dancing in which the dancers form two parallel lines and perform a sequence of dance moves presented by a caller. Many contra dances involve each dancer progressing up the parallel line to dance with each dancer in the opposite line. Because some contra dances are more traditional and fall into the category of folk dancing, they will be explored further in chapter 11. However, this chapter includes a few popular culture contra dances, as students may enjoy learning these social and popular dance movements without the stress of handholding.

Partner Dancing

A partner dance requires two dancers—a follower and a leader—to work together to perform the steps. Often, this requires the partners to turn toward each other with direct eye contact and some form of handholding or touch. Dance-partner connections should be introduced in a comfortable setting and can be gradually sequenced from face-to-face eye contact to partners touching hands. It is also important to explain to students why handholding contact is important for some social and popular dances, as it allows the leader to guide their partner (the follower). For instructors who wish to lessen the power imbalance that the terms *leader* and *follower* may imply, other kid-friendly paired terms can be used, such as *rocker* and *roller*. Other ways to ease the awkwardness of introducing touch in dance include allowing students to choose their partners and changing partners often so all dancers connect with every dancer at some point during the class. The following strategy is a sequence we have used to introduce partner dance and touch that you can try with your students to ease them into the process.

▶ **Visit HK*Propel*** to see video demonstrations of the side-step touch, forward and backward step touch, high-five connect, two-hand hold, and lead-in for a two-hand hold.

Side-Step Touch

This first sequence has leaders and followers face each other using only eye contact. Have the partners move to the side in 2 counts by stepping the outside foot and touching the inside foot without physically connecting. Partners should mirror each other so they are stepping toward the same wall, introducing the concept of moving in unison with a partner. In figure 10.1 the partners are demonstrating moving in unison. You can practice this side step to music for several counts and then have students switch to a new partner to continue the skill practice.

Forward and Backward Step Touch

Using the same concept as in the first sequence, in this sequence, leaders and followers continue to face each other without physically connecting. However, now students have to mirror each other's steps while moving forward and backward. Leaders step forward with their left foot and tap their right foot next to their left foot, then they

Figure 10.1 Partners move in unison while holding hands.

step backward with their right foot and tap their left foot. Followers should mirror this movement at the same time as the leader, first stepping back with the right foot and tapping the left foot. Then they step forward with the left foot and tap the right foot (see figure 10.2). Again, you can have the students practice these forward and backward movements to the beat of the music, then switch partners to continue the skill practice. It also is beneficial to make sure all students have a chance to practice both the role of leader and of follower.

High-Five Connect

In this third sequence, students remain in face-to-face partnerships, but now they place their hands at chest height in a high-five connection (see figure 10.3a). This allows the partners to practice both the side-step touch as well as the forward and backward step touch while easing into the push-pull collaboration needed in partner dances. If touching hands is uncomfortable for students, you can use equipment such as scarves or bandannas to introduce the leader-follower connection before the hand-to-hand high-five connection (see figure 10.3b). The scarves allow the partners to be connected as one unit without having to touch a partner before that feels comfortable.

Two-Hand Hold

The fourth sequence, which is called the two-hand hold or sometimes the open hold in ballroom or social dances, introduces the typical handholding connection of partner dancing. Leaders place their hands in front of them, shoulder-width apart, bent at 90-degree angles, and with their palms up. Followers, with arms similarly positioned, place their hands palms down on top of the leaders' hands (see figure

Figure 10.2 Partners mirror each other in the forward and backward step touch.

Figure 10.3 Partners practice the high-five connection with hands (*a*) and with scarves (*b*).

10.4). Dancers should continue to use the same push-pull collaboration used during the high-five sequence, keeping their arms engaged so their body moves when dancing. Students can practice the side-step touch and the forward and backward step touch with their partners in this connection, switching partners throughout the skills practice. If your students are older or already comfortable with touch and connection, this two-hand hold can be a starting sequence for teaching social dances.

Partner Hold

If your students master the basic two-hand hold with a partner, they are ready for the more formal partner hold, which is called the closed hold in ballroom dance. This hold is not necessary for teaching partner dances in most classrooms, but if students are comfortable and advanced enough, it can create an exciting way to continue evolving the leader-follower collaboration.

To create this partner hold, have the leader lift their left hand in a high-five motion while the follower places their right hand against the leader's left hand, with their palms touching. The partners' fingers should close around each other's hands. Then the leader places their right hand against the follower's left shoulder blade, keeping the elbow parallel to the floor. The follower places their left hand on the leader's right bicep or shoulder, resting their left arm lightly on top of the leader's right arm. There should be about 6 to 12 inches of space between the partners' torsos (see figure 10.5).

BASIC SOCIAL AND POPULAR DANCE MOVEMENTS

In this section, we introduce the basic dance movements that are found in many social and popular dances. This section intends to provide clarity for each step, as many of these terms will appear in the chapter's learning experiences. The

Figure 10.4 Partners demonstrate the two-hand hold, or open hold.

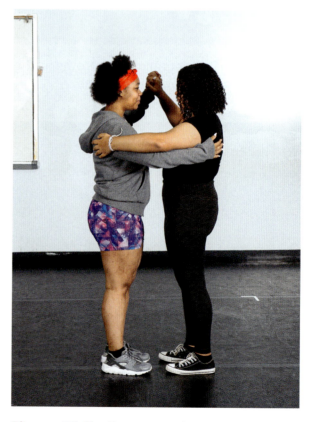

Figure 10.5 Partners demonstrate the partner hold, or closed hold.

outline for each step will include the name of the step, the rhythm of the step, the basic movements of the step, the variations of the step, and the social or popular dances from this chapter in which the step is performed.

 Visit HK*Propel* to see students demonstrating the step touch, grapevine, heel kick, slide, skip, rock step, jump and hop, and pivot turn.

Step Touch

Rhythm: 1-2, 3-4 (one-two, three-four)

Movements: Step out to the side on one foot to bear your weight, then tap or touch the other foot next to the instep of the first foot with little weight-bearing. Repeat on the other side.

Variations: Common variations include changing the rhythm of the step (1-and, 2-and), changing the direction by going forward and backward, or adding movements before the touch happens, such as a slide, drag, or additional steps.

Used in: Rockin' shuffle, Tabata dance

Grapevine

Rhythm: 1-2-3-4, 5-6-7-8 (one-two-three-four, five-six-seven-eight)

Movements: Step out to the right with the right foot. Step the left foot to the right, crossing behind the right foot. Step the right foot out to the right again. Touch or tap the left foot next to the right instep. Repeat to the left: Step out to the left with left foot. Step the right foot to the left, crossing behind the left foot. Step the left foot out again. Touch or tap the right foot next to the left instep.

Variations: The step can be made twice as long if the stepping out and crossing is continued for 4 more counts, crossing in front instead of back the second time (out, cross back, out, cross front, out, cross back, out, touch). Students can also add a 360-degree turn in each direction during the 4-count version. The step can be used to travel forward and backward with the same stepping and touching, but without the feet crossing over each other. Turning to face a new wall can also continue the step to the left and right without taking up more space.

Used in: Grapevine slide dance, hey baby line dance

Heel Kick

Rhythm: 1-2, 3-4 or 1-&, 2-& (one-two, three-four or one-and, two-and)

Movements: Step with weight on the right foot, and extend the heel of the opposite foot out in front of the body, either resting it on the ground or lifting it slightly in the air. Repeat to the other side. For example: Step to the right with the right foot and then kick the left heel forward, either on or off the floor. Step to the left with the left foot. Kick the right heel forward, either on or off the floor.

Variations: Add in a leap when transitioning from side to side. Add in the additional swinging of the leg that kicks by bending in front of or next to the standing leg, adding additional counts to the movement. You can also double the number of kicks or touches by tapping the right heel twice, followed by two taps with the left.

Used in: Honky tonk line dance, disco fever dance

Slide (Gallop)

Rhythm: 1-&-2, 3-&-4 (one-and-two, three-and-four)

Movements: Step out to the right side with your right foot. Bring your left foot in so your feet are touching. Step out again to the right side with your right foot, bearing all the weight on that foot. Then repeat to the other side (step left, together right, step left). During this step, there is often a push off on the first step, causing a small lift into the air as the legs come together, before landing back down on the starting foot.

Variations: Enlarge or remove the lift into the air as you travel from side to side. Change the direction of the movement by traveling forward, backward, or diagonally instead of sideward.

Used in: 5,6,7,8 steps line dance; 16-step line dance

Skip

Rhythm: 1-2, 3-4 or 1-&, 2-& (one-two, three-four or one-and, two-and)

Movements: Step down on the right foot with a slightly bent knee. Hop on the right foot while lifting the left foot off the floor. Then step down on the left foot with a slightly bent knee, and hop on it while lifting the right foot off the floor. Repeat. This can also be called a step-hop action.

Variations: Travel the movement around the space in a forward, backward, or sideward direction. Change the size of the movement by increasing the size of the hop with higher knee lifts and bigger arm swings.

Used in: Baba hou fitness dance

Rock Step (Ball Change)

Rhythm: 1-2, 3-4 or 1-&, 2-& (one-two, three-four or one-and, two-and)

Movements: Step forward with the right foot, placing a significant amount of weight onto the ball of the foot (the area where the toes meet). While stepping forward, the left foot behind you should lift slightly off the floor, and you should feel your upper body rock in this direction. Then place the left foot back down on the ground to shift your weight again. You can also repeat this step by first stepping on your left foot, lifting the right foot slightly, and then placing the right foot back down.

Variations: You can step out in any direction to rock, including forward-backward, right-left, backward-forward, or left-right. There is often a step down to make the weight of the body even on both feet between a ball change to change to another step. For example, you can rock forward on the right foot, step down on the left foot, and then step together with the right foot. You are now back at center to start a new step. While adding in the extra step, you can travel a ball-change step around the space in any direction.

Used in: Salsa, disco fever dance

Jump vs. Hop

Rhythm: 1-2-3-4 or 1-&-2-& (one-two-three-four or one-and-two-and)

Movements: A jump is a lift or flight into the air beginning and ending on both feet. A hop is also a lift or flight into the air, but it begins and ends on only one foot (either the right or the left). Both steps should begin and end with a slight bend in the knee to aid in the takeoff and landing.

Variations: You can switch between hopping and jumping by either putting down one foot or lifting one foot to change from two feet to one foot. Jumps and hops can be done in place or while traveling in any direction. Change the size of the jump or hop by increasing or decreasing the amount of space taken up when taking flight.

Used in: 5,6,7,8 steps line dance; the hit man contra dance

Pivot Turn

Rhythm: 1-2, 3-4 (one-two, three-four)

Movements: A pivot turn is a half-turn that keeps either the balls of the feet or the toes on the ground while the rest of the body turns around those two pivot points. A pivot turn often involves first taking a step forward, followed by the turn. A right pivot turn would therefore be a step forward with the right foot and a half-turn counterclockwise while pivoting on the toes. Then you would take another step forward with the right foot and again toward the left shoulder while keeping both feet on the floor. This will complete 360 degrees of a turn. A pivot turn can also be completed on the left side by stepping forward on the left foot and making a half-turn clockwise, pivoting on the toes.

Variations: Dancers can put a right and left pivot turn together in sequence, which would have them turn back in the direction they started rather than completing the full 360 degrees of a turn. For example, dancers could step forward with the right foot and pivot turn. Then they could step their right foot together back to a neutral stance. From this stance, they could step their left foot forward and pivot turn back to their beginning wall facing and place the left foot back to a neutral stance to complete.

Used in: 16-step contra dance, circle jam fitness dance

One Wall Versus Two Walls Versus Four Walls

Rhythm: Single count or a count and a half (either on the "8," "1," or "and 8" of many dances)

Movements: This terminology describes how many walls one will face throughout the course of a dance. In a one-wall dance, the dancers will face only the front of the space without any changes of facing. In a two-wall dance, the dancers can expect one facing change, often flipping between facing the front and the back of the given space at various points throughout the dance. Four-wall dance means four walls in the space are used, often in a square pattern. Dances will often repeat the steps while facing the next (or new) wall. Changing walls usually happens in either a clockwise or counterclockwise direction, toward the right shoulder or left shoulder, and often both directions do not happen within the same dance.

Variations: The use of one, two, or four walls in a social dance allows for a dance to continue without needing to take up much space. This is a great way to add variation to the created line dances and social dances in the classroom so the movement exercise can remain continuous. Some harder variations may call for flipping front and back and then using the side walls as the new front and back, so the rotation becomes more angular than circular in nature.

Used in: One wall: 5,6,7,8 steps line dance; two wall: 16-step contra dance; four wall: grapevine slide dance; and rock this party line dance

LEARNING EXPERIENCES

This chapter's dance learning experiences are presented in three sections: line and popular dances; fitness dance; and social dance. Each experience outlines outcomes, grade level, suggested music and equipment, and formation, along with a detailed description of how to implement the introduction, warm-up, development of movement sequences, and closure. Additional ideas and suggestions for varying the dance lessons are also included. The description of each dance learning experience follows this format:

- Title
- Grades
- Outcomes
- Organization
- Equipment needed (including suggested music)
- Introduction and warm-up
- Movements
- Sequence of dance steps
- Closure
- Look for
- How can I change this?

Sample rubrics for elementary school and middle school levels that can be adapted for any of these dances are included at the end of the chapter. Although the focus of these types of dances is enjoyment of physical activity and learning lifelong physical literacy, it is important for the educator to take time to assess the progress of students in any learning experience. Using a variety of assessment strategies allows for timely and specific feedback for improvement in these popular, fitness, and social dances. You can also refer to chapter 6 on the importance of assessment in student learning for more specific guidelines regarding the use of rubrics and assessments.

The instructions for each learning experience offer detailed descriptions of the movements and counts in each dance step that are needed to complete the dance. To facilitate your selection of learning experiences, we have summarized each one in table 10.1.

Table 10.1 Index of Learning Experiences in Popular, Fitness, and Social Dances

Name of dance learning experience	Description of dance learning experience
LINE AND POPULAR DANCES	
5,6,7,8 steps line dance (Grades 3 to 8)	This is a 32-count basic line dance using locomotor skills and offering students an opportunity to add new style to each step.
16-step contra dance (Grades 6 to 12)	This versatile learning experience can be performed as a line dance, a contra dance with the same partner, a circle partner dance, or a contra dance with changing partners. It also matches a wide variety of music.
Disco fever dance (Grades 6 to 12)	This line-dance learning experience provides students a taste of dances from the 1970s, inspired by the popular partner hustle from the 1977 movie *Saturday Night Fever*.
Funky cowboy line dance (Grades K to 3)	This 32-count learning experience is designed for kindergarten to third grade but can also be successful with students in grades four to six. The movement terms for the dance—reach, reach, clap, clap, brush, brush—make it an easy dance to teach younger students.
Grapevine slide dance (Grades 3 to 8)	The grapevine slide is an adapted version of the original electric slide that became an international dance craze in the 1970s and '80s. This learning experience provides students the opportunity to learn a basic four-wall, 18-count line dance that remains a popular dance at many social events.
Hey baby line dance (Grades 3 to 8)	This learning experience is a dance for all ages and a fun line dance to use with scarves. You can also adapt the same steps and make it a circle dance with changing partners to many popular songs.
The hit man contra dance (Grades 6 to 12)	This learning experience can be taught as a line dance, a contra line dance with the same partners, or a contra line dance with changing partners after each 32-count sequence. This dance offers students the opportunity to work in teams to create the steps to a new song. The dance also offers many types of songs to dance the steps.
Honky tonk line dance (Grades 4 to 8)	This dance is an adapted version of a popular line dance called the boot scootin' boogie. This learning experience uses four simple movements that can be practiced separately in a warm-up and then blended as a line dance without changing direction. Due to the simplicity of the dance, students have many opportunities to stylize it.
Honky tonk circle dance (Grades 4 to 8)	This learning experience is an extension of the honky tonk line dance. To introduce partner work, bandannas are used instead of holding hands. It also offers opportunities to change to a new partner after every 16 counts of the gallop step in the dance.
Rockin' shuffle (Grades 3 to 12)	This learning experience is similar to the cupid shuffle created by rapper Cupid and was released in 2007. This dance can be performed as a line dance or a four-wall dance and encourages all dancers to move in sync.
Rock this party line dance (Grades K to 5)	This learning experience offers 32 counts of five different dance moves that students can stylize to their comfort levels. The 32 counts are repeated throughout the song, and intensity can be added to each dance move to improve cardiorespiratory health.
FITNESS DANCES	
Baba hou fitness dance (Grades 6 to 12)	This learning experience offers simple and repetitive movements with variations added to challenge the students and increase their intensity. Students learn the components of fitness, the FITT principle, and how to use perceived exertion as a way to measure one's exercise intensity.
T fitness dance (Grades 3 to 12)	Adapted from the famous bunny hop social dance, a physical educator from Wisconsin created this dance using the same steps while allowing students to perform in their own space with a T or + sign pathway on the floor.
Cha-cha plank fitness dance (Grades 6 to 12)	This learning experience is a fun way to have students develop their core strength by incorporating components of fitness and easy-to-follow line dances into one activity.
Circle jam fitness dance (Grades 6 to 12)	This learning experience is designed to be performed in a circle without partners or students holding hands, giving freedom for students to add their own energy but still have the feel of a group performance. Students can add intensity to the steps to increase aerobic fitness.
Tabata dance (Grades 4 to 12)	Tabata is a type of high-intensity interval training (HIIT) that combines aerobic and anaerobic training. Students complete 8 sets of fast-paced exercises, each performed for 20 seconds, interspersed with a brief rest of 10 seconds.

Chapter 10 Learning Experiences in Popular, Fitness, and Social Dances 215

Name of dance learning experience	Description of dance learning experience
SOCIAL DANCES	
Salsa (Grades 6 to 12)	This learning experience is a great way to engage students in partner dances with a fun, upbeat dance performed to popular music. Students learn some of the basic salsa movements, such as hip and body action, turns, and fancy footwork.
Swing (Grades 6 to 12)	This swing dance introduces students to basic swing steps with its quick, partner-based movements that can be danced to any style of music. Adaptations include allowing students to dance individually or with a modified partner handhold.
Cha-cha (Grades 6 to 12)	The cha-cha is a fun, up-beat partner dance that uses a rock step as the base for the dance. Current popular music can be used to engage and encourage students to participate.
Create your own fitness dance (Grades 3 to 12)	This learning experience is designed to help guide a dancer in creating a new fitness dance similar to the ones in this chapter. Instructors can use this lesson to have students, especially those at the secondary level, create their own fitness dances to share. It can also guide the novice dance instructor in how to create their own fitness dance to teach their students.
Create your own popular dance (Grades 3 to 12)	Students are directed to create a new popular dance using creative dance elements, guided by the instructor. Students will have fun and learn collaborative skills while developing new dance movements to perform and teach the rest of their classmates.

Line and Popular Dances

Jumping Steps Line Dance

 Visit HK*Propel* to see students demonstrating the jumping steps line dance.

Grades

3 to 8

Outcomes

As a result of participating in this learning experience, students will be able to do the following:
1. Perform the 32-count basic steps to the dance (psychomotor).
2. Increase intensity with more arm swings and jumps added to steps (psychomotor).
3. Choreograph the 32 dance steps in a different sequence to match a faster-paced song (cognitive).

Organization

Students are arranged in multiple lines facing the front, completing the dance individually.

Equipment Needed

Suggested music:
- "5, 6, 7, 8" by Steps
- "Crazy Little Thing Called Love" by Dwight Yoakam
- "Blue Suede Shoes" by Elvis Presley

Introduction and Warm-Up

Today, we are going to learn a basic line dance, where each of you will dance together while maintaining your individual space. The dance is not difficult, but our goal is to be able to increase the intensity, or amount of movement, as well as the speed as you feel more comfortable. To start, let's practice and warm up by trying out all the steps that will be in the dance before putting them into a sequence. Make sure you are in lines with plenty of space on each side of you to move freely. First, let's try a few jumps together. Remember, that means both feet leave and land on the floor together. [Have students jump on beat with music or hand claps. Students can keep their arms by their sides or be given specific movements to try while jumping.] Now, I want you to try the grapevine step. It is called a grapevine since our feet are weaving like a vine with grapes. Let's start off with a slower rhythm and try to move faster as we speed up the tempo. [Students complete a grapevine to both sides several times.] The next move is a step touch moving forward on the diagonal. Try to clap for each diagonal step touch. We will be traveling forward for 4 step touches (8 counts). [Have the students add a clap with each step touch. To finish the warm-up, combine the grapevine and the diagonal step touches, add 8 marches, and repeat two or three times to increase heart rates.]

Movements

- Jump
- Grapevine
- Diagonal step touch: Step forward on the right foot to the right diagonal, and then touch the left foot next to the right foot. As the right foot steps forward, scoop the arms down by the sides and forward, clapping your hands together when the left foot touches. Repeat on the left by stepping the left foot forward to the left diagonal while scooping the arms down and forward, clapping together when the right foot touches next to the left foot.
- March clap sequence
  - March 1: The right hand slaps the right thigh on the march.
  - March 2: The left hand slaps the left thigh on the march.
  - March 3: Slap the right hip.
  - March 4: Slap the left hip.
  - March 5 and 6: Clap two times.
  - Match 7 and 8: Touch your forehead with your right hand, then lower your right hand down as if you are taking off a hat.
- Walk backward.

Sequence of Dance Steps

- Counts 1 to 4: Jump (If using the original song for this dance, jump when the song says 5, 6, 7, 8) for 4 counts.
- Counts 5 to 12: Grapevine to the right, then grapevine to the left.
- Counts 13 to 20: Do four diagonal step touches.
- Counts 21 to 28: March-clap sequence.
- Counts 29 to 32: Walk backward.
- Repeat the dance sequence.

Closure

- What part of this learning experience was the most difficult or challenging for you and why?
- What would you add to this learning experience to make it different? Let's name some different types of jumps or arm movements we could include (examples include jumping jacks, heel jacks, or specific arm movements while walking backward).

Look For

- How smoothly students can transfer from one movement to another.
- Students coordinating the 5, 6, 7, 8 jumps on the same beat.
- Students coordinating the step touch and clap movements together.

How Can I Change This?

- Have students perform the 32 counts with the 5, 6, 7, 8 music by Steps, and then provide other music options.
- Have students perform the steps to new music but restructure the sequence or add 8 more counts to the sequence to match new music, such as "Crazy Little Thing Called Love" by Dwight Yoakam.
- Perform the dance at a faster pace to "Blue Suede Shoes" by Elvis Presley, but begin the dance with the grapevine.
- Allow students to stylize the dance to add more flair and increase the difficulty level. This could include specific arm or hand movements during the jump, grapevine, or walk backward sequences. Advanced students could also add additional jumps or turns. Students can share their stylized version with a classmate, and they can try the new version together.

16-Step Contra Dance

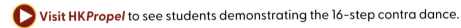

▶ Visit HK*Propel* to see students demonstrating the 16-step contra dance.

Grades

6 to 12

Outcomes

As a result of participating in this learning experience, students will be able to do the following:

1. Perform the dance sequence across from a partner in a contra line (psychomotor).
2. Stomp in unison with a partner for each sequence (psychomotor).
3. Dance the sequence at least two times without the teacher's cues (cognitive and psychomotor).
4. Choreograph the 16 counts of the gallop section while moving toward their partner to demonstrate different types of locomotor movement (cognitive and psychomotor).

Organization

Students work in parallel lines (contra lines), with each student facing a partner.

Equipment Needed

Suggested music:
- "Dance" by Twister Alley
- "Thank God I'm a Country Boy" by John Denver (faster pace 16-step dance)

Introduction and Warm-Up

Today, we are going to work on a fitness dance that incorporates the use of a contra line. A contra line is when there are two parallel lines of dancers facing each other. The tricky part of this dance is performing the movements on the opposite foot from your partner. Let's spread out into our space and learn some of the movements while facing the same direction before we dance across from a partner. [Have all the students face the same way, toward the front of the room, and lead the warm-up.] To begin, we are going to practice tapping our heels forward on the beat of the music. We will start a simple tap of our right heel forward, then step back into place. Then we will tap our left heel forward and step it back into place. Right tap, right step, left tap, left step. Practice that several times. [Repeat sequence, looking for students to remain on beat. You can increase the tempo if students are advanced.] Now, let's add a crossing movement to our tapping. You will tap your right heel forward, then cross it over the left foot to tap your toe, then tap the right heel back out, and then step it down in place. You should be on beat with the music for those 4 counts with a heel tap, toe tap, heel tap, and step down. Let's try that together. [Practice the right side several times.] Remember, we have to be versatile dancers, so we are going to try the same sequence but now starting on the left foot. [Walk through the sequence starting on the left. Once students are comfortable, you can speed it up or practice moving from the right sequence straight into the left sequence.]

Now, I want to make sure we know how to gallop safely in space. We are going to practice galloping forward for 16 counts and turning around to face the back on the last gallop. You will have to do this when you are facing your partner, so we want to make sure we know how to gallop individually first. [Students gallop forward, turning around to face the back wall on the last gallop. If all the students have made the turn, repeat this sequence traveling toward the back wall and then turning to face the front wall on the last gallop. Repeat this several times as needed.] Now that you are experts at tapping your toes, heels, and galloping, we are going to practice the same movements but in our contra lines. [Split the students in two equal groups and have them face a partner while standing in two parallel lines with space between the two lines. Lead the students through the same sequence of heel and toe taps, followed by the galloping sequence.] Notice how as we practice our steps, your right and left sides face opposite your partner. Remember to trust yourself to know how to perform the steps and not watch your partner, or you will be backward. Now that you can dance independently across from your partner, I think we are ready to learn the entire dance.

Movements

- Heel-toe sequence (16 counts):
  - Tap the right heel forward (count 1).
  - Cross the right foot over the left foot, tapping the right toe down into floor (count 2).
  - Tap the right heel forward (count 3).
  - Stomp the right heel next to the left foot (count 4).
  - Tap the left heel forward (count 5).
  - Stomp the left heel next to the right foot (count 6).
  - Tap the right toe back behind (count 7).
  - Stomp the right foot next to the left foot (count 8).
  - Tap the left heel forward (count 9).
  - Stomp the left heel next to the right foot (count 10).
  - Stomp two times with the right foot in place (counts 11-12).
  - Pivot: step forward on the right (count 13), then pivot by turning toward the left shoulder to face the back wall (count 14).
  - Pivot back: step forward on the right (count 15), then pivot by turning toward the left shoulder to face forward (count 16).
- Gallop sequence (16 counts): Take eight gallops forward beginning with the right foot, then switch places with your partner and turn to face your partner on the last gallop.

Chapter 10 Learning Experiences in Popular, Fitness, and Social Dances

Sequence of Dance Steps

- Counts 1 to 16: Heel-toe sequence.
- Counts 17 to 32: Gallop sequence. Repeat the dance sequence until the end of the song.

Closure

- What was your favorite part about dancing in a contra line today?
- Was there anything you found challenging while performing this dance? [Have several students share their experiences and give any solutions they had for overcoming these challenges.]

Look For

- Students who lose the beat but can pull together and stomp the two stomps in unison with their classmates.
- Students counting the 16-count gallop steps to keep them on a beat and turning to face the opposite direction on the last 2 counts of the gallop.
- Students who use the space safely and are able to switch spots or partners at the correct time.

How Can I Change This?

- Partners can switch to a new partner after 4 of the 16-step sequences and use the 16-count gallop portion of the fourth sequence to move to the right in both lines to face a new partner.
- Perform the dance to a variety of songs with slower or faster tempos.
- Provide variation options for other ways of traveling across the lines for the 16-count gallop sequence. Students could use movements such as high knee skips, turns, leaps, meeting partway and then returning to their original spot, or elbow swing with their partner.
- Students work with a partner and develop strategies on how to increase the intensity of each dance movement. More advanced students can teach other students their created strategies.
- Advanced students can reverse the first 16-count sequence by beginning the heel-toe sequence with their left heel out and flipping the right and left sides to create a dance that is twice as long.

Disco Fever Dance

 Visit HK*Propel* to see students demonstrating the disco fever dance.

Grades

6 to 12

Outcomes

As a result of participating in this learning experience, students will be able to do the following:

1. Perform each dance step in general space during the warm-up for 8 counts to the beat of the music (psychomotor).
2. Perform the correct dance movements when the dancing cue word is called out by the teacher (cognitive and psychomotor).
3. Perform the dance sequence to a variety of music tempos (psychomotor).

Organization

Students dance individually in multiple lines facing the same direction, completing this four-wall dance.

Equipment Needed

- Images of dancers from the disco era
- Suggested music:
  - "The Hustle" by Van McCoy and the Soul City Symphony
  - "Night Fever" by the Bee Gees
  - "You Should Be Dancing" by the Bee Gees (faster version)

Introduction and Warm-Up

For today's disco fever dance, we are going to travel back in time to explore some different movements. Can anyone tell me what disco is or when it was created? [Have several students give suggestions.] The disco era became popular in the 1970s. You may have seen popular clothing styles from this time, including bell bottom pants and platform shoes. [Show students the images you gathered.] Some well-known artists who played an important role in the development of disco include the Bee Gees; the Village People; Donna Summer; Gloria Gaynor; and Earth, Wind, and Fire. There were also popular dances such as the hustle and the bump, which were seen in movies of the time like *Saturday Night Fever* and *Thank God It's Friday*. Our disco fever dance is inspired by the hustle, which the band Van McCoy and the Soul City Symphony made popular in 1975. The hustle also appeared in the 1977 movie *Saturday Night Fever*. We are going to spread out into our space to face the same wall to warm up by learning some of the movements before putting them together in a sequence. [Have students spread out and all face the same direction.] To begin, we are going to start by walking on beat. However, I don't want you to do just any walk. I want you to strut. When I say strut, I mean show me your personality or confidence in your walking, but make sure you clap on count 4 so I can see you keep the beat. I am also going to have you walk in different directions for each set. Ready? Here we go now. [Students walk on beat to a medium-tempo song, clapping on count 4. Call out the different directions you want students to travel before they start walking, including forward, backward, right, or left. Repeat this several times.]

Now, we are going to practice a turning grapevine. You still have to clap on count 4 and demonstrate staying on beat. We will start by turning to the right. [Have students slowly demonstrate the right, then the left. As they advance, you can speed up the tempo.] Let's give our feet a little bit of a break and practice some arm movements. I am going to demonstrate two moves, and then I want you to copy them as best as you can. Be sure to watch carefully! [Demonstrate the eggbeater and the seat belt disco move. Give students time to copy you before changing to the next one. Switch back and forth between the two a few times until students can complete the movements.] The tricky part of this dance is that it will keep changing to face different walls, so let's finish our warm-up by practicing some of these steps and take turns facing all four walls together. Be ready to switch when I call it out. [Have students practice the strut, then turn the grapevine, eggbeater, and seat belt disco move as you call them out. Then tell the students to turn to their left to face the next wall. Repeat this warm-up, calling out different movements and changing to face each next wall until they have faced all four walls.]

Movements

- The strut: Walk backward for 4 counts and clap on the fourth count (right, left, right, feet together and clap); walk forward for 4 counts and clap on the fourth count (left, right, left, feet together and clap).

- Turning grapevine: Perform a grapevine while turning 360 degrees to the right and then to the left (right, left, right, clap and left, right, left, clap).

- The eggbeater: Hold the arms at chest height and circle the hands quickly around each other while taking two marching steps in place (2 counts to the right and 2 counts to the left).

- Kick ball change: This dance move consists of three distinct actions—a kick followed by the ball change or step-step. It uses a split-beat count of 1 and 2 and has a syncopated feeling, with the accent of the motion on count 2.
  - Count 1: Kick the right foot forward.
  - Count "and 2": Place the right foot on the floor behind the body and slightly push off the floor with the ball of the right foot ("and"). Then transfer weight to the left foot as you step in place with the left foot ("2").
- The skate: Starting with the feet shoulder-width apart, extend the right arm out to the side of the body with the palm up, and at the same time extend the left arm out to the left side of the body with the palm down, then switch hands and palms up and down a total of four times while leaning into the hips and body of the side that has the palm facing up (lean right, left, right, left).
- The seat belt disco move or the Travolta move (a step influenced by John Travolta's performance in the movie *Saturday Night Fever*): Point up diagonally across the body to the right with the right hand, and then point down diagonally across the body to the left with the right hand. Repeat the up and down pointing two times using 1 count for each point. At the same time, put the left hand on the left hip and swing the hips away from the direction of the pointing hand (perform two points for 4 counts).
- The chicken: Place the hands on both hips and then move elbows forward and backward quickly while taking four marching steps in place or standing for the 4 counts of the chicken arm movements (1 count for each step).
- The hustle step: With the right foot, do a toe touch two times in the front then two times in the back, then one time in the front, then one time in the back, then one time to the right side, and do a quarter turn to the left on the left foot while keeping the right foot up (8 counts; 1 count for each toe touch and 1 count for the quarter turn).

Sequence of Dance Steps

- Variation A
  - Counts 1 to 8: The strut
  - Counts 9 to 16: The turning grapevine
  - Counts 17 to 20: The seat belt disco or the Travolta move
  - Counts 21 to 24: The eggbeater
  - Counts 25 to 32: The hustle step
  - The dance sequence repeats facing a new wall.
- Variation B
  - Counts 1 to 8: The strut
  - Counts 9 to 16: The turning grapevine
  - Counts 17 to 20: The seat belt disco or the Travolta move
  - Counts 21 to 24: The skate
  - Counts 25 to 28: The chicken
  - Counts 29 to 32: The kick ball change (on the second kick ball change, do a quarter turn to the left)
  - The dance sequence repeats facing a new wall.

Closure

- What dance move from the '70s was the most fun to perform, and which one made you feel like you were in a different era?
- Have you seen any of these dance moves in a movie or TV show?
- What would you add to this learning experience to make it different?

- What would the dance look like if we made it a partner dance?
- To finish the lesson, let's have each of you share and teach your stylized dance version to a classmate.

Look For

- Students performing the correct movement when the dancing cue word is called out by the teacher.
- Students turning in the correct direction during the 4-count grapevine 360-degree degree turn to the left.
- Students adding new arm movements to each step to stylize the dance while remaining on the beat.

How Can I Change This?

- Students could be challenged to choreograph their own variations of the dance after they research the disco era.
- Encourage students to stylize the dance to add more flair and increase the difficulty level. This could include arm or hand movements during specific steps, such as the strut, the grapevine, or the hustle.
- Have students perform the dance steps to a faster version of a new song, such as "You Should Be Dancing" by the Bee Gees. In this faster version, the hustle step repeats more often than in the slower version explained previously.
  - Complete steps 1 to 32 as stated above at the new tempo of the song.
  - Perform the dance sequence (8 counts) by repeating it four times without making it a four-wall dance.
  - Combine the dance movements in a different sequence to create a new four-wall dance sequence.

Funky Cowboy Line Dance

 Visit HK*Propel* to see students demonstrating the funky cowboy line dance.

Grades

Kindergarten to 3

Outcomes

As a result of participating in this learning experience, children will be able to do the following:

1. Perform the dance steps in a general space following the teacher's step cues (psychomotor).
2. Perform the correct dance movements when the dancing cue word is called out by the teacher (reach, reach, clap, clap, brush, brush, clap, clap, slide 4 counts, slide 4 counts, funky cowboy, funky chicken, lasso) (cognitive and psychomotor).

Organization

Students are arranged in multiple lines facing the front, and facing the same direction.

Equipment Needed

- Scarves or bandannas (one per student but not required)
- Suggested music:
  - "Funky Cowboy" by Ronnie McDowell
  - "Achy Breaky Heart" by The Countdown Kids
  - "Cotton-Eyed Joe" by Crazy Frog

Introduction and Warm-Up

Has anyone been to a rodeo or a farm or ranch with cattle? Today, we are going to pretend to use the skills needed to round up the cattle and pretend that we are in a competition to show off our cool-looking dancing round-up skills. The cool part is that we will use bandannas, just like real cowboys and cowgirls. So, who is ready to put on their pretend country boots and hats and try a simple and fun line dance? This dance will look similar to other dances we tried, and it has similar dance moves. First, we need to warm up and practice each of the movements. Everyone spread out in your own space and stretch your arms to both sides of your body, making sure you are not near any of your neighbors. We will practice each of the movements without the bandannas, and then when we are well practiced, we will add the bandannas.

We are ready to warm up our bodies with the dance steps. The first movement is called reach, clap, and brush. Reach your right arm forward while holding your arm straight, then reach your left arm forward while holding your left arm straight, then clap your hands twice, then brush your hands on your hips backward and forward two times, and then clap your hands two times again. I will say "reach, reach, clap, clap, brush, brush, clap, clap." Let's try this a few times. [Students practice in their self-space to the teacher's cues.]

Now, we are ready for the next movement, which is called the grapevine. You might remember this dance step from other dances. You weave your legs to the right and to the left for four steps, and then add a clap on the fourth step. [Have students practice the grapevine at a slower pace to your counts, and then at tempo.] If we wanted to increase our heart rates, we could slide with quick steps to the right and to the left and pump our arms instead of doing a grapevine. Let's try to slide to the right and to the left two times in each direction. [Have students practice the 4-count slide right and left on your count.] Are you breathing heavier now because we did a faster movement? That means your aerobic system is working harder, which is a good thing for your body.

Let's have some fun with the next three movements. The first movement is called the funky cowboy. Watch me as I move my knees in and out, and my hands cross back and forth in front of my body. Now, you try it, and have fun with the arm movements; be creative. Let's try the funky cowboy for 4 counts. Ready, go, 1, 2, 3, 4.

The next fun movement is called the funky chicken. On a ranch or a farm, the chickens run and flap their wings fast, so we will pretend to be chickens. [Demonstrate this move for the students.] Watch me first. I will move my knees in and out, just like in the funky cowboy, but now I put my thumbs under my armpits and flap my elbows up and down. Let's try the funky chicken for 4 counts. Ready, go, 1, 2, 3, 4. Now, let's put the funky cowboy and the funky chicken together. Ready, here we go. Do the funky cowboy for 4 counts and the funky chicken for 4 counts. We have one more dance movement to practice, which is called the lasso. Put one arm above your head, and circle it around as if you are trying to round up the cattle on the ranch, and move your body in a small circle in your own space. This is where we will use our bandannas to make the dance creative and show off our skills. Now, we are ready to put all the dance movements together to perform the funky cowboy line dance.

Movements

- Grapevine.
- Funky cowboy: The knees move in and out and the hands cross back and forth in front of the chest.
- Funky chicken: The knees move in and out; put the thumbs under the armpits and flap the elbows up and down.
- Lasso: Turn in a circle while keeping one arm above the head and circling it around, using the bandanna as a lasso.
- Reach, clap, and brush: Reach the right arm forward, then reach the left arm forward, then clap the hands together twice, then brush the hands on the hips backward and forward for 2 counts, and then clap the hands for 2 counts again.

Sequence of Dance Steps

- Counts 1 to 8: Reach, clap, and brush.
- Counts 9 to 12: Grapevine to the right.

- Counts 13 to 16: Grapevine to the left.
- Counts 17 to 20: Do the funky cowboy.
- Counts 21 to 24: Do the funky chicken.
- Counts 25 to 32: Do the lasso.

Closure

You did such a great job working on the ranch and rounding up the cattle! Think about what your favorite part of the dance is and demonstrate it for the person next to you.

Look For

- Students who are clapping at the same time.
- Students who can remember the order of the sequence with and without it being called out by the instructor.

How Can I Change This?

- Make the dance a four-wall dance by having the students turn an extra quarter turn on the lasso to face another wall.
- Allow students to change the 8 counts of the grapevine or modify movements to have more flair.
- A quick step slide or step touch to right and to the left can be used instead of the grapevine if students need to adjust the movement for their ability or skill level.
- Use props such as scarves, bandannas, western hats, and ribbon sticks.
- Have the younger students perform the dance to "Achy Breaky Heart" by The Countdown Kids and complete each dance sequence for double the counts.
- Have students perform as one large group or in two groups with one watching as an audience while the other group performs.
- Try songs that are slower or faster. "Achy Breaky Heart" by The Countdown Kids is a slower version of the dance. "Cotton-Eyed Joe" by Crazy Frog is a faster version and more challenging but lots of fun.

Grapevine Slide Dance

Grades

3 to 8

Outcomes

As a result of participating in this learning experience, students will be able to do the following:

1. Perform two new versions of the grapevine slide dance to a variety of music (psychomotor).
2. Perform a 360-degree turn during the grapevine segment of the dance (psychomotor).
3. Collaborate as a small group of four classmates to create and perform a new version of the grapevine slide dance (psychomotor, cognitive, and affective).

Organization

Students are arranged in multiple lines facing the front and facing the same direction, completing the dance.

Equipment Needed

Suggested music:

- "Electric Boogie" by Marcia Griffiths
- "The Electric Slide" by Grandmaster Slice
- "Another One Bites the Dust" by Queen
- "A Night to Remember" by Shalamar
- "Addicted to Love" by Robert Palmer
- "All Night Long (All Night)" by Lionel Ritchie
- "All She Wants to Do Is Dance" by Don Henley
- "And the Beat Goes On" by The Whispers

Introduction and Warm-Up

[This dance does not need a specific warm-up, but you could practice the grapevine move as a simple warm-up. You could also teach the steps as your warm-up as described below, and then have students perform the dance together with different music.]

Friends, today we are going back in time to learn a very popular dance from the 1970s that's still danced at many celebrations today. Can you name some celebrations? I hear you naming weddings, birthday parties, family celebrations, holiday events—these are great answers! I also see football players showing off their dance skills in the end zone after a touchdown! Where do you like to dance?

Today, I am going to teach you an adapted version of the original electric slide dance that became an international dance craze in the 1970s and '80s. This four-wall, 18-count line dance has been popular at many social events since its release in 1976. The original song is known as the "Electric Boogie" sung by Marcia Griffiths. The choreographer, Ric Silver, created a simple but funky dance based on the song's catchy melody and mid-tempo groove. The music and the original dance allow for the creativity of individuals as dancers to move to the easy beat.

First, let's warm up by practicing each step separately, giving you an opportunity to stylize your movements to your comfort level and to match the tempo of the music. Spread out in our space, and make sure you have room to move. Everyone should be facing the front of the room. We will practice each 8-count movement several times, and then we will blend the steps together. [Have students perform individual movements, and then add music so they feel the tempo.]

The first step is a grapevine, which you are all familiar with. I am going to first have my back to you so you can follow my leg movements to each side for the 8-count grapevine. We will grapevine to the right first. Ready, 5, 6, 7, 8, step to the right, step left foot behind, step right, tap the left foot next to the right foot, and add a clap. Now, let's try the grapevine to the left. Ready, 5, 6, 7, 8, step to the left, step right foot behind, step to the left, tap the right foot next to the left foot, and add a clap.

Let's put the 8-count grapevine together at tempo. Ready, 5, 6, 7, 8, step right, left foot behind, step right, tap together and clap, step to the left, step right foot behind, step left, tap together and clap. Let's practice the grapevine two more times. But this time, I am going to face you so I can see how you are improving. I will be performing the grapevine on the opposite foot, so we will all move in the same direction. [Have students practice on your count.] Now, let's add the music so you can feel the beat. [Add music and practice the grapevine a few times.]

Now, let's try the next dance movement, which is called the backward walk. Step back with the right foot, now the left foot, now the right foot, and now stomp the left foot next to the right foot.

Now, let's put the grapevine and the backward walk together. Everyone face forward, and make sure you have space to move. I will dance facing you and move in the direction you should move. Ready, 5, 6, 7, 8. [Call "grapevine" instead of the numbers 7 and 8.]

[Have students practice connecting the grapevine and the backward walk.]

We have developed a good tempo, and we are ready to add the jump sequence. The jump sequence is a total of 4 counts. Watch me first so you can see when and how the quarter turn is incorporated into the sequence. Jump forward two times for 2 counts, then jump one time with a quarter turn at the same time to the right for 2 counts.

Let's all try it together. Ready, 5, 6, 7, 8. [Call "jump" instead of numbers 7 and 8.] Jump, jump, jump with a quarter turn. Now you are able to start the grapevine by facing a different wall, making this a four-wall dance. Practice the jump sequence four times on your own.

We now know all the movements to the dance and are ready to combine them together. [Have students walk through the entire dance on your counts, then have them form lines and perform the dance to music.]

Movements

- Grapevine
- Gallop
- Backward walk: Step back with right foot, then the left foot, then the right foot, then stomp the left foot next to the right foot.
- Jump sequence: Jump forward two times for 2 counts, then jump one time with a quarter turn at the same time to the right for 2 counts.

Sequence of Dance Steps

- Counts 1 to 4: Grapevine to the right or 4 quick gallops to the right
- Counts 5 to 8: Grapevine to the left or 4 quick gallops to the left
- Counts 9 to 12: Backward walk
- Counts 13 to 16: Jump sequence
- Repeat the grapevine or gallops to the right to start the dance over.
- During the first attempt of the dance to music, try to minimize the cues for the dance to see if students can perform without verbal assistance.
- After completing the dance to one song, students get in groups of four to collaborate and choreograph a new version of the grapevine slide dance. Have the students share their new dance movements with the class.

Closure

Show a classmate next to you how you stylized one of the dance moves. I will play the music, and you each show the movements for eight counts. [Have students demonstrate.] Thank you for being open-minded and trying new dance moves. When you are with your family, show them this dance and see if they know the original version.

Look For

- How well the students can perform the 16-count sequence in unison.
- How well the students can move in dance lines without bumping into each other.
- Whether students can coordinate the 16-count dance sequence with a change of direction on the quarter-jump move.

How Can I Change This?

- While performing the grapevine for counts 1 to 8, the students could perform a 4-count, 360-degree turn in each direction.
- During counts 9 to 12, the students could perform a 360-degree turn moving backward instead of the 4-count walking backward.
- Allow students to stylize the dance to add more flair and increase the difficulty level. Suggestions include adding claps, slaps, or other arm and hand movements during the grapevine, walk, and jump steps.

Chapter 10 Learning Experiences in Popular, Fitness, and Social Dances   227

- While working with a partner, students can perform the dance as a line dance and not a four-wall dance and create at least two movements that can be performed together.
- Students can change the grapevine to a side slide step to the right, stepping together with the left foot, then stepping right, then left again, and then repeating that in the opposite direction.
- Students could compare and contrast the movements of the traditional electric slide dances and the grapevine slide version dance.
- Students could be challenged to choreograph their own variations in the dance.

Hey Baby Line Dance

 Visit HK*Propel* to see students demonstrating the hey baby line dance.

Grades
3 to 8

Outcomes
As a result of participating in this learning experience, students will be able to do the following:
1. Keep scarves in their hands for the entire dance and use appropriately for dance movements (psychomotor and cognitive).
2. Perform the 32-count sequence in unison (psychomotor).

Organization
Students are arranged in multiple lines facing the front, holding a scarf in each hand.

Equipment Needed
- Colorful scarves (two per student)
- Suggested music:
  - "Hey Baby" by Crazy Frog
  - "Hey! Baby!" by Bruce Channel (slower version)

Introduction and Warm-Up
As you have learned from your physical education class, dance is a great aerobic lifetime activity. Dance improves your heart and lung capacity (which is good for overall health), helps you become more coordinated, and helps you develop rhythm. Dance is great for you at any age! When you look back at your younger childhood pictures and videos, I am sure you will see some versions of yourself dancing and singing. Does anyone remember a song you liked to sing and dance to? What about dances to the songs "Hokey Pokey" or "If You're Happy and You Know It?" Does "Baby Shark" ring a bell?

The dance we are going to learn today is one of my favorites. It's easy, upbeat, and fun to sing along to while dancing. The dance is called hey baby. Let's warm up with all the dance movements before we put the entire dance together. Everyone stand in your own space, and make sure there is room between you and a classmate. I am going to stand in front of you and have you follow along with me; that is how easy this dance is. I will not need to call right or left, because you will move your arms in the same direction my arms will be moving. [Face the students and perform the dance so students mirror your movements and directions.] Once we learn all the steps, we will put the entire dance together and add the scarves to give the dance some flair.

228 Teaching Children Dance

Let's begin. First, shake your hands up over your head to the right two times, then shake your hands up over your head to the left two times, then shake your hands down to the right two times, and then shake them down to the left two times. Let's try the shaking movement again at tempo. Ready, 5, 6, 7, 8. [On counts 7 and 8 say, "Shake it up."] Shake to the right, shake to the left, shake down to the right, and then shake down to the left. Let's try it one more time. [Have students practice.]

Now we can add the next movement. Perform the movements with me as I demonstrate. We clap two times, jump forward, say "oooh" and reach our arms forward, then jump backward, say "aaah" and stretch our arms backward, then clap two times. Now combine the shaking and the jumping together.

Ready, 5, 6, 7, 8. [Say "ready shake" for counts 7 and 8.] Shake it right, shake it left, shake it down, shake it down, clap two times, jump forward, say "oooh," jump backward, say "aaah," and clap two more times.

The next moves are two jumping jacks. These jumping jacks are a bit different because you are going to try to cross your legs while you jump and cross your arms overhead too. Ready, jumping jacks, go. See if you can cross your legs on the jump and cross your arms overhead while you are performing your jumping jacks. Practice a few more times.

Now, add a grapevine just like in the other dances we have tried. Grapevine to the right. [You are still facing the students and you grapevine to your left, which is the student's right—this takes some practice on your part. You can put your back to the student, if that makes it easier for you.]

Grapevine to the left. Let's try the grapevine movements again, and pretend you are holding scarves. How will you wave the scarves while performing the grapevine? Be creative.

We are ready to combine the shake, the jumps, the jumping jacks, and the grapevine movements.

Ready, 5, 6, 7, 8, shake up to the right, shake up to the left, shake it down to the right, shake it down to the left, clap two times, jump and say "oooh," jump and say "aaah," clap two times, do 2 jumping jacks, grapevine to the right, and grapevine to the left. Let's try it again at tempo.

The last movement is 4 strong marches in place, with arms pumping to get your heart rate higher. When you march three times say, "Uno, dos, tres, cuatro." These are the numbers one, two, three, and four in Spanish. The song sings the numbers, so we will sing along. Let's try this again. Ready, 5, 6, 7, 8, march—uno, dos, tres, cuatro. Good job pumping your arms too. Try one more time.

Now that you are warmed up and know the basic dance steps, you are ready to learn the dance.

Movements

- Side lunge: Lunge to the right, shake your hands to the right two times, and then to the left.
- Clap.
- Jump sequence: Jump forward one time and reach arms forward, pause one count, jump backward and stretch arms backward, and pause one count.
- Crisscross jumps: Cross your arms overhead with your scarves waving, and as you jump, cross your legs.
- Grapevine.
- March.

Sequence of Dance Steps

The dance starts when the song says, "Hey baby" at the beginning.

- Counts 1 to 4: Side lunge, with hands shaking up.
- Counts 5 to 8: Side lunge, with hands shaking down.
- Counts 9 to 10: Clap two times.
- Counts 11 to 14: Jump sequence.
- Counts 15 to 16: Clap two times.
- Counts 17 to 20: Perform 2 crisscross jumps.
- Counts 21 to 24: Grapevine to the right.
- Counts 25 to 28: Grapevine to the left.

- Counts 29 to 32: March in place and pump your arms with your scarves.
- Have students practice all the steps together while you demonstrate and say the cue words for the dance.
- Have students perform the dance for the entire song. You can give the students two scarves to use during the dance. They should practice clapping and holding the scarf at the same time.
- Once the students have practiced the dance steps, ask them to add different movements during the grapevine section of the dance.

Closure

- Hope you enjoyed this fun, upbeat dance. Raise your hand if you felt like your heart was beating faster and your breathing was a bit heavier. Increased heart rate and breathing heavier are two good signs that you are improving your aerobic health.
- Share your favorite dance move with a classmate.

Look For

- How well students can perform the 32-count sequence in unison.
- When dancing to different songs, how well students can coordinate a change in tempo of their movements.

How Can I Change This?

- Allow students to stylize the dance to add more flair and increase the difficulty level. This could include finding more ways to incorporate the scarves during movements such as the grapevine, marching, or jumping.
- Students can share their stylized version with a classmate, and they can try the new version together.
- Have students create a new version of the hey baby line dance with changes of basic movements, or try the different versions to one of the other suggested songs.
- During the grapevine counts, students can choreograph 4 different movements rather than completing the grapevine step. Examples include forward, backward, or sideward slides; marching and changing arms movements; cartwheels; 360-degree turns; or moving laterally while waving the scarves.

The original dance created by Gregg Montgomery, physical education teacher in New Jersey, was adapted by Susan Flynn, South Carolina.

The Hit Man Contra Dance

Grades

6 to 12

Outcomes

As a result of participating in this learning experience, students will be able to do the following:

1. Perform each of the 32 counts in sequence in a contra-line formation for a minimum of 3 complete sequences (psychomotor).
2. Choreograph their own movements to stylize the boogie walk (psychomotor and cognitive).

Organization

Students are arranged in parallel lines facing a partner.

Equipment Needed

Suggested music:

- "The Hitman (7" Mix)" by AB Logic
- "U Can't Touch This" by MC Hammer
- "T-R-O-U-B-L-E" by Travis Tritt (quick pace)

Introduction and Warm-Up

We have experienced different types of dances thus far. Today, we are going to take a fun, face-paced line dance and convert it into a contra dance where you will be dancing across from a partner. Contra dance is made up of long lines of partners, where dancers progress up and down the line to dance with other partners.

Our warm-up today is going to involve learning the basic steps before we dance the steps to music or in contra lines. Spread out and give yourself plenty of room to move forward and backward. Make sure you are facing the front of the room as we try this dance without a partner. I will have my back to you for this demonstration so it will be easier for you to follow along with me. The first dance sequence is called the heel and hitch steps. Put your right heel forward and tap two times quickly, then lightly toe-tap behind you for 2 counts. Tap forward again for 1 count using the same right foot, then behind for 1 toe tap. The hitch step involves a tap to the right side, then you lift your right leg and bend the leg behind your left leg so that the right leg forms an upside-down L shape. Tap your left hand on your right foot as it hitches behind your left leg in that L shape. Let's try this movement sequence again two more times at a slower pace. Ready, 5, 6, 7, 8. [Call the skill cues as students dance with you. Tap two times forward, tap two times backward, tap one time forward, tap one time backward, tap to the right side, then do the L-shaped hitch step. Increase the pace, continuing to call out the cues.]

Another step in this dance is the grapevine. Let's practice the grapevine to the right and to the left a few times. The gallop is another common dance step used in this dance. Start by facing a partner. We will gallop to the right, then left, then right, then left forward for 8 counts. [Add music to help students with the fast-paced tempos of the dance.]

Now, we will practice the next movement. From the hitch step, your right foot is behind you and ready to be placed on the floor to the right side of your body for a grapevine, going 4 counts to the right and 4 counts to the left. Now, let's put the 2 counts of 8 counts. Ready, 5, 6, 7, 8, tap, tap, forward, backward, to the left side, hitch, grapevine right, and grapevine left. [These are the skill cues for the dance moves.]

Once you have completed the grapevine, you should be back to the original spot where you started this dance. The next movement is the gallop with a half-turn. The total number of gallops is 4, but the sequence is a total of 8 counts. Let's try the gallops together so we practice the gallop half-turn at a slower pace. Gallop with your right foot, gallop with your left foot, make a half-turn on the third gallop with your right foot, and as you pivot, turn backward to the left counterclockwise, then gallop backward on the left foot for the fourth gallop. Move back to your space on the floor, and let's try the gallop sequence again. [Practice with the students until they can perform the gallop sequence with flow.]

It's time to try all three of these 8-count sequences together. [Have the students perform the tap, the hitch for 8 counts, the 8-count grapevine, and the 8-count gallops with the turn.]

It's time to add the last 8 counts before we put the dance to music.

From the backward gallop, jump backward two times (jump, pause, jump, pause, for a total of 4 counts) Next is the boogie walk, where you walk 4 steps forward and alternate pumping arms toward the floor as you walk on each step while walking forward. [Or students can stylize their own hand movements.] When we perform this dance as a contra-partner dance, this sequence is when you meet with your partner. [Practice these 8 counts a few times with your students. Once students feel comfortable with the dance sequences and can perform the movements at tempo, try it with music, then with a partner in contra lines.]

Movements

- Heel and toe taps: Lightly tap the right heel forward for 2 counts, then toe-tap behind you for 2 counts.
- Hitch step: Lift the right leg and bend it behind the left leg so the right leg forms an upside-down L shape. Tap the left hand on the right foot as it hitches in the L shape behind the left leg.
- Gallop with a half-turn: Perform the basic gallop with the right foot and then the left foot, but on the third gallop with the right foot, complete a pivot half-turn while turning backward to the left in a counterclockwise direction to end up facing the space you just moved from, then gallop backward on the left foot one time. The gallop sequence is a total of 8 counts.
- Jump backward sequence: jump, pause, jump, pause.
- Grapevine.
- Boogie walk: Alternate pumping arms toward the floor on each step while walking forward (or students can stylize their own hand movements).

Sequence of Dance Steps

- Counts 1 to 4: Heel and toe taps
- Counts 5 to 8:
    - (5) Tap right heel forward.
    - (6) Tap right toe backward.
    - (7) Tap the right toe out to the right side.
    - (8) Hitch step.
- Counts 9 to 16: Grapevine to the right for 4 counts, then grapevine to the left for 4 counts.
- Counts 17 to 24: Perform a gallop with a half-turn (partners are changing places).
- Counts 25 to 28: Jump backward sequence.
- Counts 29 to 32: Do the boogie walk forward toward your partner.
- Repeat the dance.

Closure

- What did you find challenging when working with a partner?
- Share with your partner which dance movement you felt the most confident performing.
- What helped you use stay on the correct count in each sequence? Did you count your steps? Did you rely on the skills cues from the teacher? Did you use the music to guide you through each sequence?

Look For

- How quickly students transfer from one step to the next.
- Students who can jump backward in unison.
- Students who can count and move the 4 counts during the boogie walk to a new partner without cues from the teacher.

How Can I Change This?

Adapt the dance into a mixer. Start with groups of eight (two contra lines of four). During the jump in the dance, students jump backward one time and pause, then they do the second jump to the left in each contra line so now they are facing a new partner, and then they perform the boogie walk toward the new partner. The last person in each contra line moves quickly to the back of the line during the boogie walk counts (see figure 10.6).

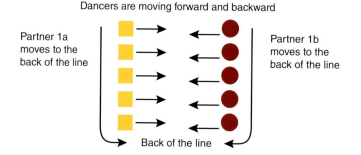

Figure 10.6 Movement of dancers in the hit man contra dance (mixer variation).

The original dance created by Gregg Montgomery, physical education teacher in New Jersey, was adapted by Susan Flynn.

Honky Tonk Line Dance

Grades

4 to 8

Outcomes

As a result of participating in this learning experience, students will be able to do the following:

1. Perform the five simple dance steps in a sequence to different tempos of music (psychomotor).
2. Choose their favorite part of the dance and share why it is their favorite with a classmate (cognitive and affective).

Organization

Students are arranged in multiple lines facing the front and facing the same direction.

Equipment Needed

This dance is choreographed for songs using a 12-bar blues beat. Suggested music:

- "Boot Scootin' Boogie" by Brooks & Dunn
- "Good Golly Miss Molly" by Little Richard
- "Blue Suede Shoes" by Elvis Presley
- "Roll Over Beethoven" by The Beatles

Introduction and Warm-Up

Today, we are going to learn a new line dance with a country flair. In a line dance, a group of people stand together in one or more lines, usually facing the same direction, and follow repeated sequences of steps. Typically, there is no physical contact in line dancing. Because steps are repeated throughout the dance, line dances are easy to learn and practice. There are also lots of opportunities to stylize the dance to add your own flair. Although the music used may vary, the major emphasis is on country and western music. The line dance we are learning today has five simple movements that can be practiced separately and then blended as a line dance. I think everyone is going to like this fast-paced, fun dance.

To get started, everyone spread out in the general space and make sure you have enough room around you to move forward, backward, and to both sides. The first 16 counts are the basic grapevine step, which we have practiced before. I am going to have my back to you so you can follow along and copy my movements. Let's get started. Let's practice the grapevine to the right and left a few times to warm up. The second step is the heel-cross-heel-stomp sequence. Begin by tapping the right heel forward for one counts. Next, cross your right foot over the left, then tap the right heel forward again and then stomp the right foot next to the left for a total of 4 counts. Let's try that again. Ready, 5, 6, 7, 8. [Cue "5, 6, ready, tap heel" and have the students practice a few times.] The next step is to repeat the 4 counts with the left foot, heel tap forward left, cross the left over the right, heel tap forward left, and stomp the left foot next to the right foot. Let's put all the heel taps together. [Have students practice the heel tap sequence, with the right and left foot and repeat.] Now let's connect the grapevine for 16 counts and the heel-cross-heel-stomp sequence for 16 counts. [Have students practice connecting the two sequences together to music so they can feel the tempo.]

To add to the dance, we will perform four gallops forward. Start with the right foot and then gallop with the left foot and repeat. You are now in position to jump backward toward your starting spot. To perform the backward scoots (jumps), put both of your feet together with your knees bent, then jump or scoot backward on the diagonal right, then left, then right, and then left for a total of 8 jumps. The jumps are quick and 1 count each. Try the gallops and jumps one more time for 8 counts each.

Let's practice all the dance movements connected. Looks like we are ready to add the music. [Have the students practice with you until they feel comfortable to perform the steps with the dance cues and then add the music.]

Movements

- Heel-cross-heel-stomp: Tap the right heel forward, cross the right foot over the left foot, tap the right heel forward again, and stomp the right foot next to the left foot (heel, cross, heel, stomp). Repeat with left foot.

- Grapevine.

- Gallop.

- Backward scoots: With the feet together and the knees bent, jump or scoot backward on the diagonal right, then left, then right, and then left in quick 1-count jumps.

- Twist: In place, bend knees and twist side to side for 8 counts.

Sequence of Dance Steps

- Counts 1 to 16: Grapevine.

- Counts 17 to 32: Heel-cross-heel-stomp sequence.

- Counts 33 to 40: Gallop forward leading with the right foot, then left foot.

- Counts 41 to 48: Backward scoots.

- Counts 49 to 56: Twist in place.

- Repeat the entire dance until the end of the song.

- To make the line dance a four-wall dance, have students jump turn to the right on the last jump of the backward scoot sequence.

Closure

Dance is a great way to improve your aerobic capacity and coordination. Which steps do you think helped improve your coordination? Were any steps challenging for you, and if so, which ones and why? Match up with a classmate and create a different step to perform instead of the grapevine. Practice for a few minutes, and then we will show our new dance move.

Look For

- How well students can perform the movements in segments of 16 counts.

How Can I Change This?

- Change the scoot jump backward to four power jumping jacks with the arms in bent in a T position and the fists clenched tightly.
- Perform the learning experience as a line dance without changing direction.
- Increase the intensity by using the song "Roll Over Beethoven" by The Beatles and keeping it a one-wall dance. Students can increase the pace of the steps.
- Students work in groups and blend four different songs to make a three-minute dance to perform the same steps to different tempos.

This learning experience is an adapted version by the authors based on a very popular line dance called boot scootin' boogie. The original 32-count, four-wall dance is designed for the song "Boot Scootin' Boogie" by Brooks & Dunn and choreographed by Bill Bader from Vancouver, Canada.

Honky Tonk Circle Dance

Grades

4 to 8

Outcomes

As a result of participating in this learning experience, students will be able to do the following:

1. Perform the honky tonk circle dance with one partner while maintaining the bandanna/scarf connection for each movement sequence (psychomotor, cognitive, and affective).
2. Perform the honky tonk circle dance by working with a partner to perform the forward gallop sequence in unison while maintaining the bandanna/scarf connection (psychomotor and affective).

Organization

Students form two circles, an inside circle and an outside circle (figure 10.7). The dancers face the line of dance, which means facing counterclockwise while standing shoulder to shoulder with a partner. In a double circle formation, rockers are on the inside of the circle and rollers are on the outside of the circle, holding a bandanna between themselves. The rocker holds the bandanna with their right hand, and the roller holds the bandanna with their left hand.

Equipment Needed

- Bandannas or scarves, one per couple
- Suggested music:
  - "Boot Scootin' Boogie" by Brooks & Dunn
  - "The Walker" by Fitz and The Tantrums

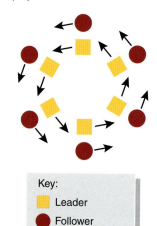

Figure 10.7 Formation for honky tonk circle dance.

Introduction and Warm-Up

Today's dance will be performed in a circle. Circle dances are common in many cultures and represent a strong community. You might remember learning some nursery rhymes with dances in a circle. Unlike line dancing, circle dances are often performed with a partner. The connection with a partner can be made by hand to hand, hands on shoulders, linking fingers, or other forms of connection. We will be using a scarf to connect with our partner in this dance. Circle dances also give us an opportunity to dance with many partners, so we will make this dance a mixer so you can greet a new partner in each sequence.

First, we need to practice the steps without a partner. To get started, find some space and face the front of the room. The first move is a grapevine. We have had many dances with this dance step. I will have my back to you so you can copy my direction and movements. [Perform grapevine with students copying for two grapevine sets, for a total of 16 counts.] Now we will perform the heel-toe-stomp sequence. I will continue to have my back to you so you can copy my movements with the same leg. Tap the right heel forward, cross the right leg over the left leg, and tap the right toe beside the left foot, then tap the right heel forward again, and stomp the right foot next to the left foot. Let's repeat all of that with the left foot. [Have students perform slower than tempo to develop confidence with the grapevine and heel-tap combination. Once they have grasped the steps, have them practice at tempo and add the music.]

The next step is the gallop. Gallop forward to the right, then left, then right, then left for a total of eight gallops, making 16 counts for the gallop sequence. [Practice the gallops again, but this time count the gallops to practice for the complete dance.] Now you are ready for the last dance move. After the last gallop, bend your knees, and twist down 4 counts, then twist back up to standing for 4 counts. Move back to your original spot, and practice all four movements in sequence. [Have students practice the three 16-count sequences and finish with the 8-count twist.] Now that we know the basic movements and have warmed up our bodies to dance, we are ready to try these movements with a partner and in a circle.

Movements

- Grapevine.
- Heel-toe-stomp: Tap the right heel forward, cross the right leg over the left leg, and tap the right toe beside the left foot, then tap the right heel forward again, and stomp the right foot next to the left foot. Repeat with the other foot.
- Gallop-twist: 8 gallops, then bend the knees and twist from side to side while bending down for 4 counts and up for 4 counts.

Sequence of Dance Steps

In a double-circle formation facing counterclockwise, dancers stand side to side, each holding one end of the bandanna. The partner on the outside of the circle (roller) holds one end of the bandanna in their left hand, and the inside partner on the inside of the circle (rocker) holds the other end of the bandanna in their right hand.

- Counts 1 to 16: Grapevine sequence for 16 counts. The roller takes a 4-count grapevine to the inside of the circle, passing in front of their partner who's still holding the bandanna. The partner on the outside of the circle (roller) holds one end of the bandanna in their left hand, and the partner on the inside of the circle (rocker) holds the other end of the bandanna in their right hand. The grapevine with a partner and a scarf takes some practice. The key to the success of the partner grapevine movement is for the partners to lift their scarves above their heads and then perform the grapevine. The outside dancer (roller) will grapevine by moving in front of their partner, and the inside dancer (rocker) will grapevine behind their partner while still holding onto their scarf. Repeat the grapevine to move back to the starting position.
- Counts 17 to 32: Heel-toe-heel-stomp sequence for 16 counts.
- Counts 33 to 48: Gallop forward.
  - Counts 33 to 40: Holding the bandanna and moving in a counterclockwise direction, do 4 gallops forward while alternating feet.

- Counts 41 to 48: The roller on the outside of the circle lets go of their bandanna and gallops 4 times (8 counts) forward to meet a new partner. The rocker on the inside of the circle keeps their bandanna and marches in place while clapping 8 counts or lassos the bandanna 360 degrees in place and then greets a new partner.
- Counts 49 to 56: Do a twist sequence for 8 counts. With a new partner, the dancers hold bandannas and face each other, then twist down for 4 counts and up for 4 counts.
- Repeat the dance until the end of the song.

Suggestions for sequence:

- Circle individual dance: Have students perform the dance movements in one large circle, then add music. Dance cues: "Ready, 5, 6, grapevine, go" for a total of 4 counts; heel-toe stomp for 4 sets; 8 gallops forward, and twist 4 counts down and 4 counts twist, then face the line of dance to dance again.
- -After the students have completed the circle partner dance or mixer to music, see if they can perform the dance to a new song without teacher cues.

Closure

- Which dance step did you find the most challenging?
- Was it hard to manipulate a bandanna between you and your partner while dancing?
- Do you think the dance would be successful without using a partner connection?
- Why do you think it is important to make a dance into a mixer?
- What does the mixer offer the dancers?

Look For

- Students cooperating and relating to each other positively when they change partners.
- Students accurately reproducing the dance movements when performing them both side by side face-to-face with a partner.
- Students lifting the bandanna and performing the grapevine with a partner at the correct timing.

How Can I Change This?

- Perform the mixer with a new song, such as "The Walker" by Fitz and The Tantrums. To make the music work with the dance, students need to choreograph an extra 8 counts after the twist. Students could repeat the twist sequence for another 8 counts or choreograph another movement for the extra 8 counts, such as a do-si-do or partner elbow swing.

Rockin' Shuffle

Grades

3 to 12

Outcomes

As a result of participating in this learning experience, students will be able to do the following:

1. Perform the 32-count line dance as a four-wall dance by making a quarter turn on the twist step to face a different wall (psychomotor).
2. Perform the 32-count, four-wall dance in unison on the teacher's cues (psychomotor and cognitive).

Organization

Students are arranged in multiple lines facing the front and facing the same direction, completing this four-wall dance.

Equipment Needed

Suggested music:

- "Cupid Shuffle" by Cupid
- "Sugar, Sugar" by the Archies
- "Wavin' Flag" by K'naan

Introduction and Warm-Up

Do you remember when we learned the grapevine slide dance? Today's dance is a party favorite and a staple that gets everyone moving in sync. The rockin' shuffle dance we are learning today can be performed as a line dance or a four-wall dance. This dance is similar to the cupid shuffle created by rapper Cupid.

First, let's warm up by practicing each step separately to give you an opportunity to stylize your movements to your comfort level and match the tempo of the music. Spread out in the space and make sure you have enough room to move, and everyone should face the front of the room. We will practice each movement a few times, and then we will blend the steps together. [Have students perform individual movements, and then add music so they feel the tempo.]

I am going to face you so you can mirror my movements as we warm up. The dance steps are simple, and you can stylize the movements with different arm movements as we perform each dance movement.

The first step is a moving step touch. Step to the right, bring your left foot next to the right foot, and repeat those three more times while moving to the right for 8 counts. Then perform the moving step touch to the left for 8 counts. Combine the 16-count sequence two times. (Step touch move to the right for 8 counts and to the left for 8 counts.) As we practice the movement to music, bend your knees a little more and add your own unique but simple arm movements.

The next dance movement is called small kicks. [Face the students so they can mirror your movements.] Tap your right heel forward or perform small kicks while alternating the right foot and left foot for four kicks, for a total of 8 counts. Arm movements are optional. Practice the 8-count kick sequence two times.

Let's connect the first and second movements. Everyone face forward, and make sure you have enough space to move. I will dance facing you and move in the direction you are supposed to move. "Ready, 5, 6, 7, 8. [Cue "Step right," instead of saying the numbers 7 and 8.] Let's practice the two movements with music a few times.

The third movement is a small 8-count march with a quarter turn to face a new wall. Let's dance together. Ready, 5, 6, 7, 8. [Counts 7 to 8 cue the movement "March."] Let's try the march movement to complete a 360-degrees turn so that we go back to facing the wall where we started. As we practice all the movements together, stylize the arm movements during the march.

Now we are ready to put the warm-up movements together with music.

Movements

- Moving step touch: Step your right foot out to the side, then bring your left foot to meet it. Repeat that in the same direction with four step touches one each side. Then repeat the move to the left side four times by stepping the left foot out to the side and bringing the right foot to meet it.

- Step kicks: Do small heel-tap kicks forward by alternating the right foot and left foot for four kicks. Step right, then kick left, then step left, then kick right for a total of four kicks.

- March with a turn: Do small marches as you do a quarter turn to the right for a total of 8 counts.

Sequence of Dance Steps

- Counts 1 to 16: Moving step touch (arm movements are optional)
- Counts 17 to 24: Step kicks
- Counts 25 to 32: March with a turn

Closure

- Did you feel successful completing the rockin' shuffle dance? What led to your success?
- Does anyone want to share how they stylized one of their dance movements? You can use this dance in the future when you attend school dances and weddings.

Look For

- Students performing the quarter turn in unison with their classmates.
- Students performing the four-wall dance steps in unison on your cues.

How Can I Change This?

- Have students add a hop or a bounce to the step-touch movement.
- Instead of performing the step touch, have students perform a smooth slide to each side.
- Ask students to stylize the movements by adding choices such as a sway to their hips or arm movements during each portion of the dance.
- Ask students to create fun movements with their bodies, such as snapping the fingers, shimmying the shoulders, or place their hands on their hips for some of the movements.
- Changing the music can spark interest. Have students split into three groups and work together to choreograph the same dance steps to match three different tempos of music and share them with the class as a performance.
- Have students listen to the suggested songs and ask them to change the tempo of the movements to fit the music while still maintaining the basic steps. (Using the song "Wavin' Flag" by K'naan, students will slow the step-touch rhythm to two-step touches on each side.)

Rock This Party Line Dance

 Visit **HK*Propel*** to see students demonstrating the rock this party line dance.

Grades

K to 5

Outcomes

As a result of participating this learning experience, students will be able to do the following:

1. Perform the basic five movements to different music without verbal teaching cues (psychomotor).
2. Perform the basic five movements to two different songs and match the movements to the tempo of the songs (psychomotor and cognitive).

Organization

Students are arranged in multiple lines facing the front and facing the same direction, completing the dance.

Equipment Needed

Suggested music:

- "Rock This Party (Everybody Dance Now)" by Bob Sinclar and Cutee B.
- "Stomp to the Beat" by Js-16
- "La La La (Brazil 2014)" by Shakira

Introduction and Warm-Up

[This learning experience offers 32 counts of five different dance moves that the students can stylize to their comfort level. The 32 counts are repeated throughout the song, and intensity can be added to each dance move to improve cardiorespiratory health.]

For today's lesson, we will warm up by practicing the five movements from the dance we are learning. We will practice the movements to build confidence and offer you an opportunity to add creative arm movements to the simple movements. Starting with the grapevine, let's move in unison on my count to the right and to the left. As we warm up by practicing the grapevine, add different arm movements to each 8-count movement. Now, let's march in place while you pump your arms. Make your arms into a broken-T formation with the arms bent at the elbows and the fists facing each other. Pump your arms forward and backward as you march. Now lunge to the right with your arms straight in front of you and swing them up and down for 4 counts to the right and 4 counts to the left. Your heart rate should be increasing as you move your arms. Keep marching or pivot around in a small circle with your arms alternating and pumping up and down. Let's combine the movements one more time to warm up for eight counts so we can continue to elevate our heart rates. Okay, now we are warmed up and ready to learn the new dance.

Movements

- Grapevine.
- T march: March in place for 4 counts and pump the arms forward in a broken-T formation.
- Pump lunge arms: Hold a lunge to the right with the arms straight out in front, and move the arms up and down for 4 counts. Repeat that to the left.
- Pump around: Pivot around in a circle on the right foot, pushing off the left foot for 4 counts to complete the turn. Alternate pumping the arms above the head while performing the pivot.
- Rocking movement forward and backward: Step forward with the right foot and the knees bent, keeping the weight on the right foot. Sway the arms right and left as you lean forward for 4 counts, then move your body back to a standing position for 4 counts while swaying the arms at the same time.

Sequence of Dance Steps

- Counts 1 to 8: Grapevine (or step touch).
- Counts 9 to 12: Broken-T march.
- Counts 13 to 16: Pump lunge arms to the right.
- Counts 17 to 20: Pump lunge arms to the left.
- Counts 21 to 24: Pump around.
- Counts 25 to 32: Rocking movement forward and backward.
- Have the students perform the dance movements for two different songs, and ask them to stylize their movements to match the tempo of the songs.

Closure

- Share your favorite move and how you stylized the movement with the classmate next to you.
- What movement did you like the best and why?
- How did the dance movements help keep your heart rate elevated?
- What component of fitness does this dance enhance?

Look For

- Students performing the dance movements at tempo and in rhythm with the verbal dance cues.
- Students demonstrate the grapevine with a variety of arms movements they choreographed to stylize their dance.

How Can I Change This?

- Adapt the dance into a four-wall dance by turning a quarter turn to the right on the rocking 8-count movement. This could happen by rocking and turning on the movement back to the center for 4 counts.
- Add intensity by making the grapevine a slide in each direction, changing the rocking forward and backward step into two jumping jacks forward, and then doing a quarter turn while performing two jumping jacks for the total of 8 counts. (These changes work best with the "Stomp to the Beat" song because it is a quicker-paced song.)

Fitness Dances

Baba Hou Fitness Dance

Grades

6 to 12

Outcomes

As a result of participating in this learning experience, students will be able to do the following:

1. Perform three sets of 16-count sequences and increase the intensity within each sequence by increasing jumping power and lifting their arms above their head on the heel jacks (psychomotor).
2. Move in unison with others to the same rhythm (psychomotor and affective).
3. Share with a classmate at least two movement adaptations that can be used to increase heart rate and intensity during the dance (cognitive and affective).

Organization

Students are arranged in multiple lines facing the front and facing the same direction.

Equipment Needed

Suggested music: "Last Night" by Chris Anderson and DJ Robbie

Introduction and Warm-Up

Today, we will focus on improving our aerobic strength with a high-energy, upbeat fitness dance. Fitness dances are designed to increase cardiovascular endurance and improve bone and muscle strength. The baba hou dance we are going to learn offers simple and repetitive movements with creative variations.

Chapter 10   Learning Experiences in Popular, Fitness, and Social Dances   241

We will infuse the FITT principle by creating ways to increase aerobic intensity in each dance movement. During the lesson, we will refer to an intensity chart to perceive our heart rate and the difference we can make in our heart rate by increasing the intensity of our movements. Let's warm up by practicing each movement in our space. The grapevine movement is a staple for many dances, including this one, so let's practice doing a grapevine to the right for 4 counts and a grapevine to the left for 4 counts. Continue to warm up the grapevine, but as you move from side to side, explore what movements you can add to increase the intensity of the movement, such as sliding side to side or pumping your arms above your head as you move right to left. As we perform the movements, make your arm movements powerful. [Have the students share their ideas for all to try.]

Skipping is included in this learning experience, so let's warm up the skip by skipping forward for 8 counts and skipping backward for 8 counts. We are going to practice the skip movement again for 16 counts, but this time when you skip, pump your arms and lift your knees as high as you can. Try the 16 counts of skipping again two more times and try to pump your arms harder to increase your intensity. Look at the intensity rating chart, and choose a rating for how your body is feeling based on the description, to rate your perceived exertion. [Have students share their rating with a classmate and discuss the intensity rating chart.] (See figure 10.8.)

The last movement we should warm up is called heel jacks. Start with 10 jumping jacks to warm up the arm movements and continue to increase your heart rate. To change the jumping jack movement to heel jacks, jump on one foot with the other leg tapping a heel (it does not make a difference to the dance which heel the student uses first for the heel jack) and alternating that tap on each jump. The heel jumps replace the straddle part of a jumping jack. Let's perform eight heel jacks, pumping your arms above your head to increase your heart rate. Try eight more heel jacks, and if you feel confident, try performing the heel jacks in a small circle while still pumping your arms above the head.

Understanding something called the FITT principle can help you work effectively and efficiently in all workouts and in fitness dance as well. Each part of the FITT acronym has a purpose:

- *Frequency:* how often a person performs the activity
- *Intensity:* how hard a person exercises during an activity period
    - Use the target heart rate or a rating of perceived exertion (RPE) scale
    - Target heart rate = (220 - age) × 0.60
- *Time:* how long the activity is maintained
- *Type:* what kind of activity a person chooses to perform in each area of health-related fitness

In dance, increasing intensity by adding arm movements or making a movement faster, for example, helps raise the heart rate and improve cardiorespiratory endurance. [Post the FITT principle with each component for students to refer to.] Now that we have warmed up, we are ready to learn the fitness dance.

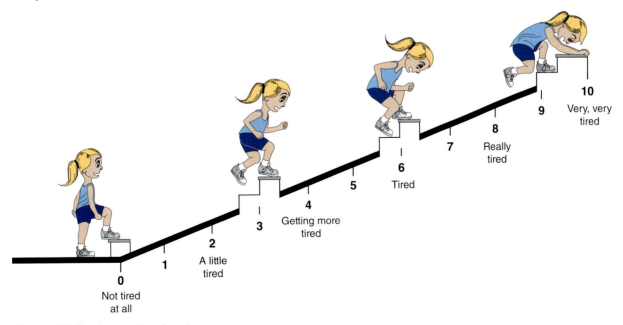

Figure 10.8   Intensity chart.

Movements

- Grapevine: Perform the typical grapevine with a new arm movement. On the fourth count, lean in the direction you are moving and punch the right elbow out to the side and the left arm straight out to the left side.
- High knee skip roller coaster: Skip four times while lifting the knees up high. On the fourth skip, straddle the legs shoulder-width apart, link the fingers together in front of the chest, and move the arms left and right like a roller coaster or a snake movement in the wrists for 4 counts.
- Heel jacks: This movement is a variation of a jumping jack. As you jump, land on the right foot and put your left heel out to the side. Then jump on the left foot and put your right heel out to the side. The arms move up over your head for each heel jack.

Sequence of Dance Steps

- Counts 1 to 4: Grapevine to the right.
- Counts 5 to 8: Grapevine to the left.
- Counts 9 to 16: Repeat the grapevines to the right and to the left.
- Counts 17 to 24: High knee skip roller coaster traveling forward.
- Counts 25 to 32: High knee skip roller coaster traveling backward.
- Counts 33 to 48: Jumping jacks or heel jacks.
- Show students the intensity rating chart and remind them that the goal is to increase their heart rate by increasing the intensity of the movements. Have students repeat the entire dance to music and then check the intensity rating chart to perceive heart rates.

Closure

- Share with a classmate what you perceived as your intensity for the dance based on the intensity rating chart. How could you change the movements to increase your intensity?
- What part of the FITT principle did this dance focus on?

Look For

- Students who change at least one dance step to increase the intensity of the movements (examples include bigger arm movements, adding jumps to movement, and increasing the pace and power of the dance movements).
- Students who can complete the entire dance to one three-minute song without stopping due to fatigue.

How Can I Change This?

- Add music with different tempos, and have the students perform the same dance sequence to match the music.
- Encourage students to explore the movement possibilities to increase the power, energy, and intensity of the movements.

T Fitness Dance

Grades

3 to 12

Outcomes

As a result of participating in this learning experience, students will be able to do the following:

1. Perform the jump sequence with a quarter turn on the last three jumps of each sequence (psychomotor).
2. Continue the jumping dance continuously for 2.5 minutes without stopping (psychomotor).

Organization

Students are arranged in multiple lines facing the front and facing the same direction.

Equipment Needed

- Each student needs a T formation of tape or lines on the floor. Rubber + or Ts made from equipment companies work very well for this dance.
- Suggested music:
  - "The Bunny Hop" by Ray Anthony
  - "Popcorn" by Crazy Frogs (or remix by DJ Yoshi)
  - "Freedom" by Pharrell Williams

Introduction and Warm-Up

Today's fitness dance is going to be performed using the T boxes designed with the blue tape in front of you. This dance was first performed in 1952. Students from Balboa High School in San Francisco, California, created a conga-line type dance to the big band version of the "The Bunny Hop" by Ray Anthony. The dance was considered a wedding party novelty dance. Then in 2020, during the COVID-19 pandemic when physical education was taught virtually, Sandy Hagenbach, a physical educator from Heritage Elementary School in Wisconsin, created a unique learning experience using the same steps from "The Bunny Hop" while having the students perform the steps in their own space with a T or + sign on the floor. We are going to warm up with jumping jumps to practice using the T (made from tape) before we try this new fitness dance. Everyone, please find a T box, stand at the top of the T, and face the front to warm up.

First, practice jumping forward and backward over the top of the T without touching the tape lines. [Have students practice this on their own.] Now, we are going to jump with a quarter turn to the left, trying to land straddled over the top of the T. Continue to do a quarter turn, and this time, you should be facing the back of the room with your feet straddling the line of the T, then do another quarter turn to straddle the top of the T again. Now, practice the three quarter turns a few more times to develop the rhythm. Now you are ready to learn the dance.

Movements

- Heel taps: Standing behind the top of the T, tap the heels forward four times while alternating your feet by doing a heel tap forward, then bringing it back to meet the other foot, and repeating alternating heel taps. (Starting with either foot works.)
- Jumps forward and backward: Jump forward one time for 2 counts and backward one time for 2 counts over the cross of the T.
- Jumps with a quarter turn: Jump and do a quarter turn to the right, then to the right again, and one more time for a total of three jumps, each time doing a quarter turn as you move to each side of the T.

Sequence of Dance Steps

- Counts 1 to 8: Heel taps.
- Counts 9 to 12: Jump forward and backward.
- Counts 13 to 15: Jumps with a quarter turn.
- Count 16: Pause.
- Repeat the entire sequence for the entire song. [Encourage students to reach their arms above their heads on each jump.]
- Have students perform the T fitness dance to "The Bunny Hop" song and then assess their perceived exertion using the intensity rating chart. Then have students perform the T fitness dance to one of the other songs, and ask them to increase the intensity of the basic movements to increase their heart rates. Have students reassess their perceived exertion using the intensity rating chart. Have students demonstrate the basic movements to a variety of music to continuously maintain the movements for 2.5 minutes.

Closure

- How did you do performing the jumping quarter turns around the T lines? Were you able to avoid jumping on the lines?
- Which song made the dance interesting?
- Were you able to increase your intensity in your movements. If so, how? Did your perceived exertion change between the two different songs?

Look For

- Students jumping and turning simultaneously for three consecutive jumps.
- Students using their arms to increase the intensity of each movement.

How Can I Change This?

Use a variety of music that interests the students and will help motivate them to continue the T fitness dance movements to improve their agility and cardiorespiratory health.

Adapted by permission from Sandy Hagenbach.

Cha-Cha Plank Fitness Dance

 Visit HKPropel to see students demonstrating the cha-cha plank fitness dance.

Grades

6 to 12

Outcomes

As a result of participating in this learning experience, students will be able to do the following:

1. Maintain a plank while performing a variety of dance movements in a plank position for a three-minute fitness dance (psychomotor).
2. Move in unison with others to the same rhythm, all while moving in the correct direction (psychomotor and affective).
3. Create a new version of the plank dance with other classmates to the same song or a new song (psychomotor, cognitive, and affective).

Organization

Students are arranged in multiple lines facing the front and facing the same direction, in a plank position.

Equipment Needed

Suggested music:

- "Cha Cha Slide" by DJ Casper
- "Get Ready for This" by The DJs of Euro Trance
- "Me Too" by Meghan Trainor

Introduction and Warm-Up

Dancing is and always has been a fun way to improve one's cardiorespiratory fitness, flexibility, and agility. Thanks to both easy-to-follow line dances like the cupid shuffle and the cha-cha slide and to creative fitness enthusiasts, we now have new ways to practice these line dances to improve muscular endurance and muscular strength. Today, we are going to reinforce the physical fitness components of muscular endurance and muscular strength during the fitness plank dance. The fitness dance will be a fun way to gain strength.

To warm up the dance, we will practice a few different plank holds and new fitness moves. Spread out in your own space facing the front of the room, and make sure you have enough room to your right and to your left. Most of this fitness dance will be performed in a plank. The plank is a total body isometric exercise done to strengthen the core. The plank helps stabilize the lower-back spine area, the core, and it works the shoulder stabilizers.

First, let's review the plank position. Start in the prone position, facing forward, and push up with arms straight and the shoulders over the wrists while tightening the core and glutes. To modify the plank, you can lower to your knees while still maintaining a straight back.

To develop our muscular endurance and practice the fitness moves in the dance, we will perform the following moves for 16 counts each.

The first movement is plank shoulder taps. In the plank position, alternate crossing your arms to tap your right hand to the left shoulder and then your left hand to the right shoulder for 8 counts. Let's practice again for another 8 counts. Sit back in the yoga child's pose position to rest and stretch your shoulders for 16 counts. Child's pose is designed to rest the body and mind. Start in the kneeling position, touch your big toes together while sitting on your heels, and keep your knees in line with your hips. Bend forward with your torso against your thighs, stretch your arms forward with the palms down on the floor to provide a shoulder stretch along with a rest for your hips and back.

The second move we will practice is a moving plank. Rise into plank position to practice marching planks. In plank, lift first one foot then the other in a marching pattern while maintaining a straight back and straight arms with a head neutral. Practice for 16 counts. Then rest again in child's pose for 16 counts.

Our third fitness plank movement is called a walking plank. Maintaining a straight back and arms in plank position, move to the left by walking your hands and feet to the left for 2 counts, then hold for 2 counts, and move to the right by walking your hands and feet to the right for 2 counts, and hold for 2 counts. Let's warm up the walking plank by performing the movement in unison and move each count to the clap. [Clap for each count to have students perform the walking plank for 32 counts.] Let's add to the walking plank with a backward and a forward walking pattern. In plank, walk backward for 2 counts, hold for 2 counts, then walk forward for 2 counts, and hold for 2 counts. Practice again. [Offer a rest if needed.]

Are you ready to try a new challenge? This move is called the frogger. In plank, jump your feet forward out of plank then backward into plank, and hold for 2 counts. Practice the frogger a few more times.

The next warm-up movement is called the cross-cross jumps. In plank, with your feet shoulder-width apart in a straddle, jump and crisscross your legs, then go back to a straddle, then jump and cross again. Practice this a few more times. Now rest in child's pose.

Let's try one more plank movement before we learn the fitness dance. This movement is called the cha-cha mountain climber. In plank, bring the right knee up to the chest, then alternate with the left, completing eight cha-cha mountain climbers.

We are now ready to use these warm-up moves to put together a challenging fitness dance to improve our muscular strength and endurance. [When using the cha-cha slide song, listen to the words and perform the movements that match the words of the song. If using a different song, follow the sequence of steps in the order given in this learning experience and repeat the sequence of fitness movements for the entire song.]

Movements

- Plank shoulder taps: Start in plank position with the arms straight and the shoulders over the hands. The right hand lifts off the ground to tap the left shoulder and then is placed back on the floor. Repeat with the left hand lifting to tap the right shoulder.
- Plank walking sequence: In a plank, walk your hands and feet to the left for 2 counts. Hold 2 counts. Then walk backward for 2 counts. Hold 2 counts.
- Frogger: In plank, jump your feet forward, then go back to plank and hold for 2 counts.
- Plank stomp: In plank, tap the right foot to the side and then replace back to plank. Then tap the left foot to the side and then replace back to plank.
- Cha-cha mountain climber: In plank, bring the right knee up to the chest, then alternate with the left to complete 8 counts.
- Holding plank: Hold a plank for 4 counts.
- Crisscross: In plank with the legs straddled shoulder-width apart, push off the toes to crisscross the legs, then go back to straddle. Hold for 2 counts.
- Cross-knee taps: In plank position, reach across under the body with one arm to cross tap the opposite knee. Put hand and foot back down on the ground. Repeat alternating hand taps to the opposite knee.
- Marching plank: In plank position, lift the right foot straight up, put it back down, then lift the left foot straight up, then put it back down. Continue alternating marching your feet while in plank position.

Sequence of Dance Steps

Sequence for cha-cha slide music

- Counts 1 to 16: Do a marching plank or just hold a plank.
- Counts 17 to 32: Do plank shoulder taps.
- Counts 33 to 36: Holding plank.
- Counts 37 to 44: Plank walking sequence
- Counts 45 to 48: Frogger.
- Counts 49 to 56: Plank stomp.
- Counts 57 to 64: Cha-cha mountain climber.
- Counts 65 to 68: Holding plank.
- Counts 69 to 76: Plank walking sequence.
- Counts 77 to 80: Frogger.
- Counts 81 to 88: Plank stomp.
- Counts 89 to 96: Cha-cha mountain climber.

For the remainder of the song, follow the directions to match DJ Casper's movement cues:

- Do a walking plank to the right by moving 2 counts and holding 2 counts.
- Do a walking plank to the left by moving 2 counts and holding 2 counts.

- Do a walking plank backward by moving 2 counts and holding 2 counts.
- Do two frogger jumps for a total of 8 counts.
- Do a plank stomp.
- Do a walking plank to the left by moving 2 counts and holding 2 counts.
- Do a walking plank to the right by moving 2 counts and holding 2 counts.
- Do two crisscrosses two times for a total of 8 counts.
- Do a cha-cha mountain climber for a total of 8 counts.
- Do a holding plank.
- Do a walking plank sequence.
- Do two frogger jumps for a total of 8 counts.
- Do a plank stomp.
  - Do cross-knee taps for a total of 16 counts.
  - Holding plank.
  - Do cha-cha mountain climbers for a total of 8 counts.
  - Holding plank.
- Finish the cha-cha plank fitness dance when students have been in the plank position long enough to engage in increased heart rate or can no longer physically hold their plank.

Closure

- Do you feel stronger just by trying the fitness plank dance?
- What muscles do you feel you worked the most?
- Do you know what muscles the plank is designed to strengthen? The plank specifically strengthens the core and the back. Do you remember the two fitness components that are enhanced from the plank exercises? Correct, the plank improves muscular endurance and muscular strength.
- Set a daily goal to perform a plank, and time yourself to see how long you can hold it, then increase the time each day, and you will develop core strength.

Look For

- Students who may not be able to hold a plank: They can modify the plank by dropping to the knees, still working to keep the back flat and/or moving the knees closer to the chest.
- Students using correct form in the plank position: Shoulders and wrists are in line and the shoulders are not leaning forward or too far backward.

How Can I Change This?

- Students can modify the plank to perform the movements on their knees for those students who can't hold a full-body plank for the duration of the time required.
- Students can perform the plank dance to differently paced music.

Circle Jam Fitness Dance

 Visit HK*Propel* to see students demonstrating the circle jam fitness dance.

Grades

6 to 12

Outcomes

As a result of participating in this learning experience, students will be able to do the following:

1. Perform the fitness steps to the dance in a sequence repeated for the entire song (psychomotor).
2. While performing the kick movements, punch their arms forward and up above the head for each kick (psychomotor).

Organization

Students are arranged in a large circle for the two-wall dance.

Equipment Needed

Suggested music: "Club Can't Handle Me" by Flo Rida

Introduction and Warm-Up

Today, our fitness dance will give you an opportunity to increase your heart rate with power kicks, vertical jumps, and strong arm movements. This learning experience is designed to be performed in a circle working individually, giving you the freedom to add your energy to each movement while still having the feel of a group performance. Let's warm up by jogging in our space, and then I will add some movements to the jog to get us ready for the dance. Spread out and start jogging, and change direction each time after 16 counts. Count on your own, and change your direction every 16 counts to jog forward, then right, then left, then diagonally.

You should feel warm now, so let's add the vertical jump. You will jog while moving forward for 7 counts, then stop and perform a vertical jump with your arms reaching up above your head for count 8. Change direction, and continue to jog and jump.

Now, let's add a powerful kick movement. Everyone will jog toward the front of the room for 3 counts, and on count 4, kick your left leg forward (right, left, right, kick left). Turn around to face the back of the room, and practice the kick movement again. Turn to the front, and perform the kick movement again, making an effort to punch one arm forward and up above your head with power, then repeat to the back of the room. Arm movements increase the intensity of the movement and they also increase your heart rate.

In the learning experience, we also need to be able to walk or jog backward and kick backward. Let's try the kick forward again but a little slower this time so we can add the backward kick sequence. Step forward to the right, then left, then right, then kick left with your right arm punching forward. Now, place your left foot back behind you, step right and backward, step left and backward, and then kick your right foot backward with one arm punching forward and up. Let's try this again with a little more speed. Continue to practice the kicking sequence forward and backward, adding more intensity to the kick and arm punch every time.

Now that you are warmed up, check the intensity rating chart (see figure 10.8) and see where your heart rate is now. During the dance, as we become comfortable with the movements, our intensity ratings should increase.

Movements

- Walk and kick sequence (8 counts): Walk forward to the center of the circle for counts 1, 2, 3 (right, left, right), and on count 4, kick your left leg forward while your arms move in opposition as the right arm punches forward. Place your left foot back behind you, step right and backward, step left and backward, and then kick your right foot backward with one arm punching forward and up.
- Sticky pump (slow walk) (8 counts): Sticky pump is 4 slow steps as if your foot is stuck to the floor for each step. Each step is 2 counts. Step right, then step left, then step right, then step left. Your arms are at your sides, pumping down and up to waist height with two arm pumps per step.
- Drop-step pivot (quarter turn and half turn) (4 counts): Pivot on the right foot by dropping the left foot backward with a quarter turn counterclockwise. Then pivot on the left foot clockwise by dropping the right foot for a half turn.
- Jumps (4 counts): Jump around for 4 counts to face the outside or inside of the circle. You can turn in any direction and should end up facing the opposite direction of how you were just facing. For example, if you started facing the inside of the circle, the 4 count jump results in your facing the outside of the circle.

Sequence of Dance Steps

This song has a long lead-in and can be used for the warm-up by having the students perform a step touch to the beat and rhythm of the song. Model for the students how to clap to the beat and change levels with their claps by clapping low and then high above the head as they step touch.

- Lead-in: Students step touch with a clap for the beginning of the song.
- Counts 1 to 8: Walk and kick sequence.
- Counts 9 to 16: Repeat the walk and kick sequence.
- Counts 17 to 24: Sticky pump.
- Counts 25 to 28: Drop-step pivot.
- Counts 29 to 32: Jumps.
- Repeat all the steps for the entire song.

Closure

Look at the intensity rating chart (see figure 10.8) and see how you feel. Did your heart rate increase after the warm-up rating? What part of the FITT principle did we focus on? That is correct, intensity. Tell a classmate what movements you made in the fitness dance to increase your heart rate.

Look For

- Students kicking in the correct direction for the forward and backward movements.
- Students facing the correct direction when they finish the jump counts. (They should be facing out of the circle or back into the circle together.)

How Can I Change This?

- Have students increase the intensity of the movements by punching the arms forward and backward during the walk/kick fitness step.
- During the jump steps, have students pump their arms above their heads to increase the intensity.

Tabata Dance

Grades

4 to 12

Outcomes

As a result of participating in this learning experience, students will be able to do the following:

1. Perform 8 to 10 different dance movements, doing each dance step for 20 seconds and then resting for 10 seconds (psychomotor).

2. Create strategies to increase the intensity of the different dance movements and increase their heart rates (psychomotor and cognitive).

Organization

Students are arranged in multiple lines facing the same direction or in a circle.

Equipment Needed

- Props that work well with Tabata are scarves, paper plates, ribbon sticks, drumsticks, and half-size swimming noodles
- Suggested music:
  - "House Tabata (featuring Coach)" by Tabata Songs, Volume 1
  - "Animals" (Remix by Global Inc.) by DJ Kevin
  - "Cups" (Remix by Chapter One) by Golden Flowers
  - Additional Tabata music apps are also available.

Introduction and Warm-Up

Tabata is a type of high-intensity interval training (HIIT) we will try today for our fitness dance. The exercises we perform will involve both aerobic and anaerobic training and will improve our muscular endurance for many muscles. In this learning experience, we will complete eight sets of fast-paced exercises or dance moves, performing for 20 seconds then resting for 10 seconds. The fitness dance will provide us with lots of activity, so let's warm up with some basic stretches to prepare our bodies for the workout. [Warm up with general dynamic and static stretching.]

Movements

Dance movements that work well in a Tabata workout include the following:

- March: Steady walk in-place with a high knee lift and the arms pumping in a consistent rhythm.
- Wave: Standing with the feet shoulder-width apart, put the arms out to the sides and alternately move them up and down while swaying the hips or marching.
- Sway: In your own space while marching with small steps in place, sway the body from the right to the left.
- Skips.
- Step touch.
- Twist: The twist is performed by standing with the feet approximately shoulder-width apart. The torso may be squared to the knees and the hips or turned at an angle so that one foot is farther forward than the other. The arms are held out from the body, bent at the elbow. Twist your knees from side to side while moving your arms in the opposite direction. You can also do these movements while changing levels.

- Vertical jump: Push off with both feet, using an upward arm swing to lift the feet off the floor, and then land on both feet with the knees bent to absorb the shock and help with balance.
- Kick ball change: Kick the left foot forward ("one"), place the foot back in place ("and"), slightly push off the floor with the ball of the left foot (partial weight transfer), and step with the right foot ("two").
- High kicks: Step and alternate kicks forward in place with the opposite arm reaching to touch the toes.
- Cross jumping jacks: Cross the feet and arms above the head on each jumping jack.
- Lateral jumps: Jump two feet from side to side, as though you are jumping rope.
- Skaters: In this plyometric cardio exercise, you hop from one foot to the other from side to side, creating a skating stride. The arms move in a running formation.
- Plank taps: In a plank position, alternate tapping the hands forward and backward.
- High knee lifts: Lift the knee up toward the chest as high as possible and then place back down on the ground under the body. Repeat with the opposite knee.

Sequence of Dance Steps

The movement choices are limitless. This Tabata fitness dance provides a simple way to introduce moving the body to show basic dance movements and build confidence and competence. Pick a sequence of basic dance movements, and have the students perform them for 20 seconds, then rest for 10 seconds. Have the students raise their arms out to the sides and up over their heads as they inhale deeply. Below is an example dance sequence using some of the described movements :

- Counts 1 to 20: Step touch
- Counts 21 to 30: Rest
- Counts 31 to 50: High knee lifts
- Counts 51 to 60: Rest
- Counts 61 to 80: Twists
- Counts 81 to 90: Rest
- Counts 91 to 110: Skaters
- Counts 111 to 120: Rest
- Counts 121 to 140: Plank taps
- Counts 141 to 150: Rest
- Counts 151 to 170: High kicks
- Counts 171 to 180: Rest and finish

Closure

Tabata is a great way to exercise the whole body. What was your favorite exercise we tried today? What muscles do you feel you worked the most? What movements raised your heart rate the most, and why do you think that is? What movements would work well in a dance? Do you have any other ideas for props we can use for Tabata?

Look For

- Students who can elaborate on the basic movements with more upper-body movements or engagement with props.
- Students who are hesitant with the dance movements can move any way they feel comfortable while maintaining the basic movements.

How Can I Change This?

- Students work in teams, using a variety of equipment to create dance movements they have seen in music videos.
- Use various props throughout the dance to make the movements more challenging or exciting. If using a scarf, students can wave the scarf above, beside, or below the body. For example, they can wave the scarf above their head while completing the step touch or pass under their knee from hand to hand during high knee lifts. With a pool noodle, students can hold the noodle in front of their body during high knee lifts or place it on the ground and tap with alternating hands during plank taps. If using paper plates, students can try to touch their toes with the plate while completing high kicks or place under their toes during planks and alternate sliding the toes to the side and back to center.

Social Dances

Salsa

Visit **HK*Propel*** to see students demonstrating the salsa.

Grades

6 to 12

Outcomes

As a result of participating in this learning experience, students will be able to do the following:

1. Perform the dance sequence for 32 counts with each partner in a two-hand hold position (psychomotor).
2. Work with a partner to create a salsa sequence of three different salsa steps to perform to music (psychomotor, cognitive, and affective).

Organization

Students spread out in their own space to learn the basic steps. Students dance in the general space, facing a partner once the basic steps are demonstrated successfully.

Equipment Needed

Suggested music:

- "Sin Salsa No Hay Paraiso" by El Gran Combo de Puerto Rico
- "Cali Pachanguero" by Grupo Niche

Introduction and Warm-Up

Today, we are going to learn about social dance and try some basic movements working with a dance partner. We will start with a social dance called salsa that works well with popular and Latin music. Has anyone tried salsa dancing? Does anyone have family members who know how to salsa dance? Salsa dancing is huge around the world, especially in Miami, New York City, Puerto Rico, Cuba, and many more places. Salsa has a lot of hip and body action, plus turns and fancy footwork that provide a lot of opportunity to be creative in your movements. There is a lot of joy in dancing, and salsa is one of the types of dances that lifts your spirits with its fun movements. This dance is also a great way to dance with many different partners.

First, let's warm up with some basic movements to feel the rhythm and beat of the music. Everyone stand up and find some space. I am going to play some different music, and you will walk around in the general space, weaving around your classmates and feeling the rhythm of the music. Walk 8 counts in one direction, and then change your direction for the next 8 counts. Continue to change direction every 8 counts. Now, add some movement in your shoulders as you walk. Roll the shoulders forward and backward, and try alternating shoulder rolls as you walk. Now, add hip movements, moving side to side as you walk. Combine the hip and arm movements as you walk around in general space. Now that we are warmed up, let's learn the basic steps and how to dance and turn with a partner.

Movements

Practice by first learning the leader steps and have students add arm and hip motions as they feel comfortable with the foot movements.

- Basic salsa step for the leader (see figure 10.9): The salsa step is only three steps and is made for every four beats with one step to each beat and the fourth beat paused. Step the left foot forward, then lift the right foot and put it back down, then step the left foot next to the right foot (counts 1 to 4: quick, quick, slow; or rock, step, replace), then step the right foot backward, lift the left foot and put it back down, and put the right foot back next to the left foot (counts 5 to 8). These steps are small and quick.

- Basic salsa step for the follower: The follower completes the same three step movements as the leader, but in reverse order. The follower would step the right foot backward, lift the left foot and put it back down, and put the right foot back next to the left foot (counts 1 to 4). Then they would step the left foot forward, lift the right foot and put it back down, then step the left foot next to the right foot (counts 5 to 8).

- Basic salsa side step for the leader: Step to the side with the left foot, lift the right foot, put the right foot back down, then put the left foot next to the right foot (counts 1 to 4). Perform the same steps on the other side, starting with the right foot (counts 5 to 8). Hips sway from pressing through from toes to heels when stepping each foot.

- Basic salsa side step for the follower: The follower completes the same side step as the leader but in reverse order. Step to the side with the right foot, lift the left foot, put the left foot back down, then put the right foot next to the left foot (counts 1 to 4). Then repeat to the left side (counts 5 to 8).

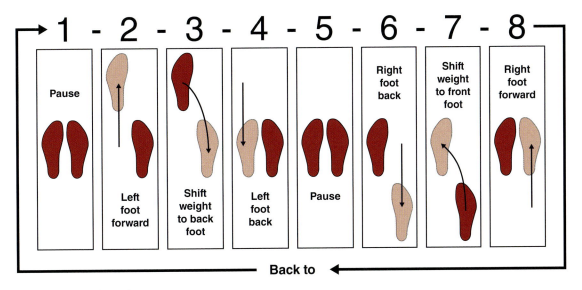

Figure 10.9 Basic salsa steps.

When students have mastered the salsa steps on their own, begin the partner work.

- Two-hand hold: The leader places their arms in front of their body, shoulder-width apart, with the elbows bent at a 90-degree angle and the palms up. The follower, with their arms similarly positioned, places their hands palms down on top of the leader's hands. [Teach beginner steps with this open-hold position or no hold to practice the movements.]

- Basic salsa with a partner: Standing with both feet together, the leader steps forward and to their left to perform a basic salsa step. [The follower does the natural opposite, starting by stepping back and to the right to perform the basic salsa step.]

- Basic salsa side step with a partner: Standing with both feet together, the leader steps to the side. The follower does the natural opposite, stepping to their right.

- Under-arm turn for the leader: The leader does a forward basic step and, as they perform the forward motion of the basic step, they lift their left hand to indicate to the follower to do a turn, and let go of their partner with their right hand (counts 1 to 4). As the follower turns, the leader continues to finish the basic step by stepping back on the right foot, lifting the left foot, and then bringing the right foot back next to the left (counts 5 to 8). The leader should grab their partner's hand with their right once the turn is completed.

- Under-arm turn for the follower: The follower performs the first part of the basic step by stepping backward, at which time the leader indicates the turn by lifting the follower's right hand (counts 1 to 4). Instead of completing the front portion of the basic step, the follower will turn under the lifted right arm by stepping left, right, left in a full 360-degree circle and finish with both feet together, facing their partner (counts 5 to 8).

Sequence of Dance Steps

Have students practice the basic steps individually and then face a partner in a two-hand hold position.

- Counts 1 to 16: Two basic salsa steps.
- Counts 17 to 32: Two basic salsa side steps.
- Counts 33 to 40: One basic salsa step.
- Counts 41 to 48: One under-arm turn.
- Counts 49 to 56: One basic salsa step.
- Repeat the sequence.

Play a variety of salsa music and have students perform the dance sequence above for the 56 counts with each partner in the two-hand hold position. Each time the music switches, the partners should switch.

Closure

You are now a ballroom dancer. Knowing how to dance unlocks many opportunities. You might not see them right now, but you can use these skills for a lifetime. Ballroom and Latin dancing can be done socially and competitively at any age.

Look For

- Students cooperating with each partner by holding the two-hand hold with respect and courtesy.
- Students who can smoothly connect the salsa basic with the side breaks without breaking the rhythm.
- Leaders lifting the follower's arm for the under-arm turn on the correct count.

How Can I Change This?

- Salsa basic with a partner in a variety of different handholds often leads to creative movements. Have students try the half-open right to left hold. (Leaders reach their right hand out with palm up, and followers place their left hand palm down in their partner's hand.) Try the salsa basic with the handshake hold. (Partners face each other with the right hand holding the right hand.) Have students research the many different handholds and explore the salsa basic and the side break with different handholds. During the under-arm turn, leaders can also turn immediately following the follower's under-arm turn. As the leader steps forward onto their left foot, they turn under their own arm to the right by stepping onto their left foot and rotating 180 degrees, then they step forward onto their right foot, continuing to turn to the right and rotating 180 degrees, finishing by bringing their feet together and shifting their weight back to the left foot so that their right foot is free to step back into the second half of the salsa basic.

- Form two parallel lines across from a partner and perform the basic sequence, then rotate to the right in both lines to perform the sequence with a new partner. Continue until all students have danced with many different partners.

- Have all students practice the role of a leader and a follower so they understand the roles each has when partner dancing.

Swing

Grades

6 to 12

Outcomes

As a result of participating in this learning experience, students will be able to do the following:

1. Perform two basic turns and an under-arm turn with a partner in the two-hand hold position (psychomotor and affective).
2. To keep a bounce in the swing step, dancers can keep their heel up in the rock step (psychomotor).
3. Work with a partner to create a swing sequence combining the basic dance step with an under-arm turn to music (psychomotor and affective).

Organization

Students dance individually in the general space to learn the basics, and then in parallel lines across from a partner.

Equipment Needed

Suggested music:

- "Dance With Me Tonight" by Olly Murs
- "Boogie Woogie Bugle Boy" by Andrews Sisters
- "(We're Gonna) Rock Around the Clock" by Bill Haley & His Comets
- "Swing the Mood" by Jive Bunny and the Mastermixers

Introduction and Warm-Up

Has anyone watched the show *Dancing with the Stars* or seen a movie with swing dancing? Today, we are going to learn how to do basic swing steps. Swing dance is a fast-paced partner dance that can be danced to any style of music but is best when used in a combination of jazz, blues, and funk-type music. Swing is characterized by swinging, flipping, and partner-tossing dance moves. This dance is unique because it combines multiple genres, is upbeat, and is a lot of fun. Once mastered, you will be able to combine the basic rock step with all kinds of turns and spins. Before we start swing dancing, let's warm up with some basic static and dynamic stretches. [Lead students through stretches.]

Movements

Swing dance typically follows a 6- or 8-count rhythm. The basic count is a rock step (1, 2), a triple step (3, 4), and another triple step (5, 6). The rock step has two full weight changes completed in two 2 of music. The triple steps are faster movements with three weight changes in the 2 beats of music. Before students work with a partner, it is important that the basic can be danced solo. Students should learn the footwork for both a leader and a follower. Leaders perform on the left foot first, and followers dance on the right foot first.

- Two-hand hold: The leader places their arms in front of them, shoulder-width apart, with their elbows bent at a 90-degree angle and the palms up. The follower, with their arm similarly positioned, places their hands palms down on top of the leader's hands. The leader's left hand and the follower's right hand hold at about hip level to create space to rock backward.

- Triple rock step side basic: This name refers to the rocking action done during the move. The weight is a transfer from one foot to another and then back again. Dancers stand with both feet together. The leader performs a rock step by stepping backward on the left (keeping the heel off the floor), then lifting the right foot, then transferring the weight back to the right foot (counts 1, 2). Then the leader performs a triple step left, then right, then left (counts 3, 4) and a triple step right, then left, then right (counts 5, 6). The follower does the natural opposite. Standing with both feet together, the follower steps backward on their right foot (keeping the heel up), then lifts the left foot, and then transfers the weight back to left foot, creating a rock step movement. Then the follower performs a triple step by stepping right, then left, then right (counts 3, 4) and a triple step left, then right, then left (counts 5, 6).

- Triple rock step forward and back basic: Leaders complete the rock step by stepping back on the left foot and replace the right foot forward-, then dancing three quick steps while moving forward by stepping left, then right, then left. Next, the leaders do three quick steps moving backward by stepping right, then left, then right. The count is 1, 2 (rock step), 3, 4, 5, and 6 (triple step). The followers complete the rock step by stepping back on the right and then stepping forward on the left, then dancing three quick steps while moving forward by stepping right, then left, then right. Next, the followers do three quick steps while moving backward by stepping left, then right, then left. The count is 1, 2 (rock step), 3, 4, 5, and 6 (triple step).

- Under-arm turns (natural and reverse) leader's footwork: The leader's footwork does not change. As they side step onto their left foot, they raise their left hand, indicating that the follower should turn in a clockwise direction. Then the leader lowers their hand slightly on their next rock step and raises it again on the side step left, indicating that the follower should turn counterclockwise. Then they regain the dance hold. The rotations happen in the slow-slow movement.

- Under-arm turns (natural and reverse) follower's footwork: Followers complete one basic step, standing slightly off to the leader's right side. The leader lifts the follower's right hand, indicating that the follower should side step onto their right foot to turn 180 degrees to the right in a clockwise direction under the leader's arm, then step onto their left foot and turn another 180 degrees so that they are slightly offset but once again facing the leader. Then they do their rock step back onto the right foot, staying in place. As they rock step, the leader lowers the follower's right arm slightly. As the follower steps onto their right foot, the leader once again raises the follower's right hand, and this time just the follower turns to the left, essentially unwinding from their last turn. As the follower steps onto their right foot, they turn 180 degrees to the left, then step onto their left foot and continue to turn left 180 degrees until they are once again facing their partner. Dancers regain the dance hold and continue with the basic step.

Sequence of Dance Steps

- Swing dancing is characterized by a 6-count circular basic step, or swing out step, and it emphasizes improvisation.

- Students practice the basic steps individually.

Chapter 10 Learning Experiences in Popular, Fitness, and Social Dances **257**

- Students practice the basic steps while facing a partner in a parallel handhold.
- Dance sequence: Once students master the beginner rock step or the triple rock step and the under-arm turn, they should practice the steps together in a sequence or combination to perform with different partners.
  - Perform two basic steps.
  - Perform two under-arm turns.
  - Repeat these steps.
  - Play a variety of swing music and have students perform the dance sequence with different partners.
  - Have students research other swing dance moves and choreograph the new moves into a partner dance.

Closure

Ask students to share what they enjoyed about swing dance. What were the challenges? What rock step did they feel most comfortable with, the beginner basic or the triple step rock step?

Look For

- Respect and courtesy shown by dancers as they work with a partner holding the parallel two-hand hold.
- Students smoothly connecting the swing basic step with at least two different creative movements.
- Leaders lifting the follower's arm for the under-arm turn on the correct beat to turn their partner smoothly after the basic step.

How Can I Change This?

- The leader can turn and rotate around the follower to change places during the second (reverse) turn. Immediately after the follower steps onto their right foot and rotates 90 degrees, the leader, who has side stepped onto their left foot, rotates 90 degrees to their right, under their own arm, to essentially swap places with the follower as they finish their basic step.
- During the under-arm turn, leaders can turn immediately after the follower's under-arm turn. As the leader steps forward onto their left foot, they turn under their own arm to the right by stepping onto their left foot and rotating 180 degrees, then stepping forward onto their right foot, continuing to turn to the right and rotating 180 degrees, and finishing by bringing their feet together and shifting their weight back onto the left foot so that their right foot is free to step back into the second half of the basic step.
- The class forms two parallel lines with each student standing across from a partner, and they all perform the basic sequence, then they rotate to the right in both lines to perform the sequence with a new partner. Continue until all students have danced with many different partners.
- It is also helpful to have students be both a leader and follower so they understand the roles each have when partner dancing.

258 Teaching Children Dance

Cha-Cha

Grades

6 to 12

Outcomes

As a result of participating in this learning experience, students will be able to do the following:

1. Perform the dance sequence for 32 counts with each partner in a dance hold or a two-hand hold position (psychomotor and affective).
2. Work with a partner to create their own cha-cha sequence of steps to music (psychomotor, cognitive, and affective).

Organization

Students dance individually in the general space to learn the basics and then in parallel lines across from a partner.

Equipment Needed

Suggested music:

- "Familiar" by J. Balvin and Liam Payne
- "Corazon Espinado" by Santana featuring Mana
- "Havana" by Camila Cabello

Introduction and Warm-Up

Today's dance is called the cha-cha. It is a fun, upbeat partner dance that uses a rock step as the base for the dance. The cha-cha dance was developed from a Latin or Cuban beat and has a 4/4-time signature with a rhythm count of 2, 3, 4, 1. The basic cha-cha steps can be danced to a variety of musical styles including Latin pop or Latin rock. What is great about this dance is that current popular music can be used to entice students to participate. We will warm up with combinations of marching steps and stretches. Spread out in the general space and face the front of the room. As you march in place, move your hips from side to side. Now, as you march with hip movements, add subtle arm movements. Next, march in place for 2 counts and then take three quick marching steps in place. That's called a triple step. The three quick steps present as three weight changes in 2 counts. Let's extend this basic marching movement using the rhythmic step pattern for the cha-cha. Step forward on the left and take a backward step on the right in what is called the break step, and then perform the triple step (three quick weight changes: left, right, left, which are also called the cha, cha, cha) in place. There is a pause after the third quick step. Let's practice a few more times and then try the basic step with a backward to forward step and then the triple step. [Continue to practice this basic step with music.] Do you feel warmed up and ready to learn this fun, upbeat dance?

Movements

- The forward-backward cha-cha basic (4 counts): The basic cha-cha step can be executed when traveling individually forward and backward or from right to left directions to develop the rhythmic pattern. The basic step combines a break step (two weight changes in 2 counts) with a triple step (three weight changes in 2 counts). Practice the counts as 2, 3, 4, and 1, or slow, slow, quick, quick, slow (pausing on the last cha). This counting best matches the music.
  - Dancers stand with both feet together. The leader performs a rock step by stepping forward on the left foot, then lifts the right foot, then transfers weight back to the right foot, creating a rock step movement (counts 2, 3, step, replace or slow, slow).

Chapter 10 Learning Experiences in Popular, Fitness, and Social Dances **259**

- Step left to perform a triple step left, right, left (counts 4 and 1, side, together, side or quick, quick, slow).
- Next, step backward on the right foot, then lift the left foot, then transfer weight back to right foot (counts 2, 3, step, replace or slow, slow).
- Then step right to perform a triple step: right, left, right (counts 4 and 1, side, together, side or quick, quick, slow).
- The follower does the natural opposite. Standing with both feet together, the follower rocks back on their right foot, then lifts the left foot, then transfers weight back to the left foot, creating a rock step movement (counts 2, 3, step, replace or slow, slow). Then the follower steps to the right to perform a triple step: right, left, right (counts 4 and 1, side, together, side or quick, quick, slow). Next, the follower steps forward with the left foot, lifts the right foot, and transfers weight back to right foot (counts 2, 3, step, replace or slow, slow). Then the follower steps to the left to perform a triple step: left, right, left (counts 4 and 1, side, together, side or quick, quick, slow).

- Crossover cha-cha step:
    - Leader's footwork:
        - Step the left foot 90 degrees to the right (count 2, slow).
        - Transfer the weight back to the right foot (count 3, slow).
        - Swing the left leg to step left, right, left (counts 4 and 1, quick, quick, slow).
        - Step the right foot 90 degrees to the left (count 2, slow).
        - Transfer the weight back to the left foot (count 3, slow).
        - Swing the right leg to step right, then left, then right (counts 4 and 1, quick, quick, slow).
    - Follower's footwork:
        - Step the right foot 90 degrees to the left (count 2, slow).
        - Transfer the weight back to the left foot (count 3, slow).
        - Swing the right leg to step right, then left, then right (counts 4 and 1, quick, quick, slow).
        - Step the left foot 90 degrees to the right (count 2, slow).
        - Transfer the weight back to the right foot (count 3, slow).
        - Swing the left leg to step left, then right, then left (counts 4 and 1, quick, quick, slow).

- Under-arm turn
    - Dancers use one-hand hold or a high-five hold.
    - Under-arm turn leader's steps: The leader performs a forward back basic step. Halfway through the basic, as they are finishing their triple step to the left, the leader lifts the left arm, indicating that the follower will perform an under-arm turn, as the leader rock steps back onto the right foot and then replaces their weight to their left foot. (The follower performs the under-arm turn as the leader rock steps backward over counts 2, 3.) Partners regain frame after the completion of the leader's back rock step and follower's under-arm turn, as they triple step to the leader's right, follower's left (over the cha, cha, cha).
    - Under-arm turn follower's steps: Follower performs a basic step; as they are finishing their triple step to the right, the leader will raise the follower's right hand to prepare for the under-arm turn. The follower completes the under-arm turn or pivot by crossing their left foot across and in front of their right foot (instead of directly in front of them for the rock step). The follower transfers weight to the left foot and rotates right and clockwise 180 degrees under their raised right arm, pivoting on the toes. Follower replaces the weight back on the right foot, then continues to turn to face their partner. The turn takes place over counts 2, 3, and the leader and follower regain dance hold as they complete the follower's triple step to the left, 4 and 1. (Cha, cha, cha, to side together, side.)

- Spot pivot turn
  - Perform a half basic cha-cha step. Leaders step forward to the left, and followers' step back to the right. After the side cha-cha, both leaders and followers perform a crossover.
  - Spot pivot turn leader's steps: Leaders cross the right foot over the left foot. Then they pivot on both toes, turning counterclockwise. Put the weight back on the left foot. Side, together, side.
  - Leaders cross the left foot over the right foot. Then they pivot on both toes, turning clockwise. Put the weight back on the right foot. Side, together, side.
  - Spot pivot turn follower's steps: Followers cross the left foot over the right foot. Then they pivot on both toes, turning clockwise. Put the weight back on right side. Side, together, side.
  - Followers cross the right foot over the left foot. Then they pivot on both toes, turning counter-clockwise. Put the weight back on left side. Side, together, side.
  - One-hand hold: Use the one-hand hold position for the spot pivot turn. Leaders use their left-hand hold first for the basic and first pivot turn, then drop the hold. Followers use the one-hand hold on the other hand for the second pivot turn. Once the crossover step is performed, leaders put a little pressure on the follower's palm to indicate the pivot turn.
  - Two-hand hold: The leader places their hands in front of them, shoulder-width apart, with the elbows bent at a 90-degree angle and the palms up. The follower, with their arms similarly positioned, places their hands palms down on top of the leader's hands. [Teach beginner steps with this open hold position or no hold to practice the movements.]
  - One-hand hold open facing position or high-five handhold: Facing their partner, leaders hold their left hand up and out to the left with their fingers facing up and an open palm. The followers place their right hand on their partner's open hand with the fingers facing up and an open palm.

Sequence of Dance Steps

Once the basic cha-cha steps and turns are mastered, connect the steps in a sequence or combination for students to perform and present.

- Four forward and backward basics
- Perform one under-arm turn sequence.
- Perform four crossover basics.
- Perform the pivot turn sequence.
- Repeat all those steps.

Students show their competence with the basic cha-cha steps to a variety of different cha-cha songs, while dancing across from a partner.

Closure

- Who can share where the cha-cha dance originates from?
- What turn did you feel the most comfortable with: the pivot turn or the under-arm turn?
- Share with your partner what made the dance easy to learn.

Look For

- Students cooperating with every partner as they rotate to a new partner after every set of four basics and respectfully dancing in a two-hand hold.
- Students smoothly connecting the forward and backward basic steps with the triple step while moving from side to side.

How Can I Change This?

- Form two parallel lines, with students standing across from a partner, and perform the basic forward and back sequence, then rotate to the right in both lines to meet and greet a new partner and perform the sequence again. Continue until all students have danced with many different partners.
- Have students be both a leader and follower so they understand the roles each have when partner dancing.

Create Your Own Fitness Dance

Grades

3 to 12

Outcomes

As a result of participating in this learning experience, students will be able to do the following:

1. Demonstrate the basic composition of most popular dances including musical and facing components (cognitive).
2. Collaborate as a group to create a dance and perform it together (psychomotor, cognitive, and affective).
3. Perform the complete dance without the teacher's assistance (psychomotor and cognitive).

Organization

Students create a dance that can be performed individually by standing in a line next to other dancers or in a circle facing other dancers.

Equipment Needed

Suggested music: music with a steady beat and repetitive sections (instrumental or lyrics will work, depending on the age group).

Introduction and Warm-Up

Today, we are going to review some of the basic exercises we have learned in class so we can create a dance using the exercises. Let's start by naming all the bone-strengthening, muscle-strengthening, and cardio exercises we know and doing them together. [Have students name as many exercises as they can. Either list them on a board and then physically do them together, or do several of each as they are called out. Exercises may include items such as jumping jacks, planks, sit-ups, or running in place.]

Now, let's think about how a dance is a little bit different than doing the exercises that we just did in our warm-up review. In a dance, there is usually a smooth transition and a certain number of steps we have to do in an order that never changes. For example, let's all try to run in place four times and then perform two jumping jacks. Since it is a dance, we should all be in unison and do it at the same time. Here we go, 5, 6, 7, 8. Jog, 2, 3, 4. Jacks, 6, 7, 8. Okay, we are going to take a deep breath and do it one more time, just like we should practice a dance several times so we remember the sequence. Now that we have tried my version, let's try another way to combine some exercises to choreograph a dance with three different exercises. [Have students name three different exercises and work as a class to find a way to put them together that transitions smoothly like a dance. Practice once or twice.]

Movements

Everyone is going to be put into small groups to work on creating their own fitness dance. The goal of this dance is to put some of the different exercises we have learned together in a seamless sequence to a song. This way, we can have fun while building our strength and endurance. There is no right or wrong way to put your fitness dance together, but there are some basic elements of a dance you should remember when you are working. First, just like a story, there should be a beginning, a middle, and an end to your dance. You should know when it starts and then have a final move or shape to signify the finish. You also want to connect the movements so that it feels smooth and never really stops. This might be difficult when you think about how some exercises are standing up and some are done down on the floor. Think about how you can move from one to the other without stopping the dance. Also, be sure to use 6 out of the 10 exercises listed at some point in your dance. I will give you time to work with your group to create and practice your fitness dance before we share. [Make sure specific criteria for the dance is listed or posted somewhere for the students to follow. This could be a teacher-created or student-created list of specific exercises to include in the fitness dance.]

Closure

All the groups are going to perform their fitness dance together at the same time so we can practice our dances before sharing. [Play a song for the students to complete their fitness dance, counting them in with cues 5, 6, 7, 8 so they all begin at the same time.] Now, we are going to take turns sharing our fitness dances with each other. As you watch, I want you to see if you can name the different exercises each group is using. [Have other students sit to watch, silently or verbally naming exercises they see performed. You can also repeat this by having other groups attempt to copy and learn each group's dance.] Are there any sequences from the dances that were fun and successful to copy? Why were they successful? What were some challenges in making a dance from fitness movements?

Look For

- How students are progressing in the use of any specific criteria given for the creation of their fitness dance.
- Groups that need help to collaborate, share ideas, and practice together.
- Clear use of exercises in the fitness dance, ensuring students are using the body anatomically correctly and not injuring themselves in the process.

How Can I Change This?

- Instructors can use this format to create their own fitness dance to teach students, rather than having students come up with a fitness dance. It can also be beneficial for students—particularly younger students—to learn various fitness exercises and see how an instructor puts them together into a dance first, before being asked to create their own.

- Give the students a specific song or exercise goal to focus on for completing the dance. This could mean only part of a specific song, since a fitness dance may not last for the duration of a whole song, especially when it comes to younger students.

- Using the jigsaw method, have small groups of students each create a 16-count (minimum of two exercises) part of the fitness dance, and then work as a class to put it together to create one entire class fitness dance. This could last an entire song once all the parts are put together, and it would be unique to this specific class. The class could use it in the future for warming up or for reviewing certain exercises.

- Make the criteria as specific or as broad as you choose, depending on the age group and experience level of students. For example, younger students might need a very short list and specific exercises to include, such as running, skipping, and jumping jacks, but you can let them choose the order or amount. You can also have a longer list but prescribe a specific amount of time for each exercise, such as 4 or 8 counts of each exercise before adding on to the next step. Older students can have

Chapter 10 Learning Experiences in Popular, Fitness, and Social Dances **263**

more freedom in their choices and likely create longer dances, but they still might enjoy using a list of criteria to work from.

- In addition to formal or previously learned exercises, students can be told to create a new exercise movement somewhere during their fitness dance. They should name the step and be able to describe what it is and how it helps with the fitness process. This exercise will likely be more successful for middle school students.

Create Your Own Popular Dance

Grades

3 to 12

Outcomes

As a result of participating in this learning experience, students will be able to do the following:

1. Demonstrate how to use everyday movements and abstract them to create a dance (psychomotor and cognitive).
2. Apply the elements of dance to create movement variations (cognitive).
3. Create movements for the basic composition of most popular dances, including musical and facing components (psychomotor and cognitive).
4. Collaborate as a group to create a dance and perform it together (psychomotor, cognitive, and affective).
5. Perform the complete dance without the teacher's assistance (psychomotor and cognitive).

Organization

Students create a dance that can be performed individually by standing in a line next to others, or in a circle where all dancers face each other or face a partner.

Equipment Needed

Suggested music: music with a steady beat and repetitive sections (instrumental or lyrics will work, depending on the age group).

Introduction and Warm-Up

Today, we are going to create our own popular dances that the rest of the class can follow along and learn. What are some popular or line dances that are easy for us to remember and dance to? [Have students name various popular and line dances that they may have done in class or know from their personal lives. If students are willing, they can demonstrate the movements of the dance they name.] Let's think about what makes these dances popular and memorable. I noticed some similar movements in the dances you named a moment ago. Let's use some of these familiar steps to do our warm-up today so we can begin thinking about steps we might use in our own popular dance. [Begin the warm-up by playing a song with a steady and repeating beat.]

Begin warming up with me by following along with the basic steps I do. Let's step and touch to each side. Add in the arm movements you feel comfortable with as you step and touch. Can you clap each time you touch your foot? What about changing the location of the clap to over your head or behind you? Let's switch to the grapevine. Don't forget about your upper body. Add in upper body shapes and movements, like going up and down with your shoulders. Maybe you bob your head from side to side as you walk, or twist your spine right and left. [Keep adding in new steps you know or feel comfortable with as the instructor, maintaining the beat and keeping the movements simple and repetitive. With older students, you can also ask someone to volunteer another common step that the class can repeat.]

Movements

Now that you have reviewed and practiced some common steps in popular and line dances, let's think about how we can create a new popular dance no one has ever done before. We already discussed how popular dances are easy and repetitive, which is why they catch on so quickly. Maybe we can find some other ways of moving that would be easy to catch onto. First, let's work as a class to discover some new movements. Let's think of something all of us do every day, like eating. Using your upper body, show me movements that demonstrate eating. [You can play music while the students experiment with movement and encourage them to try out multiple ideas. You may even copy various students' choices you see to acknowledge the different choices being made.] Now, let's see if we can add in lower body movement. Remember, keep it simple and repeat it just like the other popular dances we have done before. Can you do the same upper body movement you were doing to show eating while also moving your lower body? Can you show me a different way someone might use their body to eat? Think about the different actions that happen when you are eating to think of new movements: using a fork, using a knife, chewing, swallowing, putting food on your plate, sharing with others, smelling the food, blowing on something hot, or even taking a sip of your drink. Find your favorite way of moving for this exercise and continue to repeat it. It could be just one count of movement or several counts, like Jeremiah's movement where he set down his plate and sliced his food. I also saw Mariah pretending to sit down at a table and then stand back up. Now that we have explored several ways to take a simple, everyday movement and make a dance out of it, you are going to create your own popular dance. You should take something you do every day, and make it the focus of your new popular dance. The goal is to create a dance that is simple, fun, and repetitive so others in the class can easily learn and repeat it. You can use common steps from other popular dances we have learned, such as the grapevine or the step touch. You can also create new movement with your upper or lower body that can easily be performed by others. [Put the students into small groups to work together to create this dance. You can give the students a specific length of time the dance must last, certain body parts or movements that must be used, or a specific song the dance must fit to. Allow students time to create and rehearse their dance.]

Closure

Each group performs its own dance creation for the rest of the class. The rest of the class can either sit as an audience to watch for the criteria given, or they can follow along to try to learn the dance, since the goal is to be fun, simple, and repetitive for others to learn.

Look For

- How students are progressing in the use of any specific criteria given for the creation.
- Groups that need help to collaborate, share ideas, and practice together.
- Clear use of everyday motions turned into more abstract ideas, especially for older students who are capable of more abstract thinking.

How Can I Change This?

- For younger or less experienced students, you may begin the lesson by working as an entire class to create a line dance together. This could be a separate day's lesson, before giving students the ability to create a dance on their own.
- To further guide students toward creating their own dance, provide a certain number of dance movements you as the teacher created that must be included in the dance, in addition to a certain number of steps the students must create and include. For example, you might have three specific steps or movements that the students must include while they must also create five movements of their own. These numbers can vary depending on the age and experience of the students as well as the complexity of the dance they are attempting to create.

- The dance could be centered around a specific theme of everyday movements from which students generate ideas. For example, younger children may focus on using wake-up-in-the-morning movements to guide their ideas. These may include movements of yawning, brushing their teeth, or eating breakfast. Older students may still appreciate a focused theme, but it can be more abstract or broad in nature. For example, they might use school or friendship as basic ideas from which movement ideas such as raising hands or giving hugs are generated to jump-start the abstraction process.

SAMPLE RUBRICS

For many of the dances in this chapter, the goal is to teach a lifetime skill of movement and physical literacy for students to continue as they grow. However, it is also important for instructors to assess learning in the classroom, and adjust teaching strategies when necessary, and ensure that all students are learning to dance to their fullest potential. Chapter 6 provides a fuller explanation and examination of assessing student learning in dance and why it is important. Figures 10.10 and 10.11 show two basic sample rubrics that could be used and adapted for any of the dance lessons taught in this chapter. These rubrics could be used by the teacher as part of a formative or summative assessment or used by the student to do self- or peer assessments as part of the learning process.

Figure 10.10 Basic Movement Performance Rubric for Grades K to 8

	Beginning (1 point)	Developing (2 points)	Accomplished (3 points)	Exemplary (4 points)
Knowledge of Steps	Does not know steps of the dance; stops and/or watches others the entire time	Somewhat knows the steps of the dance; has to constantly watch others to remember; messes up and stops several times	Mostly knows the steps of the dance; keeps going even if messing up; barely watches others for guidance	Knows the steps of the dance; does not hesitate or have to watch others
Performance Quality	No energy or effort shown; no facial expressions; seems bored or tired	Few moments of effort and energy; could be more full-out or full bodied while dancing	Mostly dances with effort; a few slips when unsure or not confident about movement choices; trying to best of ability	Dancing entire time to fullest ability; demonstrates energy and effort through movement and facial expressions
Musicality	No concept of time, beat, or rhythm; has difficulty doing steps with the music given	Some understanding of the music, but body and dancing often does not match the given beat; has trouble doing basic steps, like walking to the beat of the music	Mostly demonstrates an understanding of the given music with minimal errors of matching the music (possibly due to nerves or to one or two wrong steps)	Demonstrates understanding of the music and matches dancing with the given beat of the music at all times

Figure 10.11 Dance Movement Rubric for Grades 6-12

	Beginning (1 point)	Developing (2 points)	Accomplished (3 points)	Exemplary (4 points)
Recall and Memorization	Rarely able to demonstrate dance terms, positions, steps, and directions; has many errors; always watches others; could not perform by self; few steps performed accurately; looks overwhelmed or gives up	Sometimes able to demonstrate dance terms, positions, steps, and directions with some errors; watches others often; could not perform clearly by self; performs some steps accurately, struggles often	Mostly able to demonstrate dance terms, positions, steps, and directions with few errors; watches others at times; accurately performs most dance steps; struggles at times	Always able to demonstrate dance terms, positions, steps, and directions with no errors; understands and follows terms given; accurately performs all steps with ease
Energy, Articulation, and Expression	Demonstrates below-average range of movement qualities; limited ability to communicate ideas/feelings through movement	Demonstrates average range of movement qualities; makes attempts to articulate movement through smaller body parts; average ability to communicate feelings/ideas through movement	Demonstrates a wide range of movement qualities; ability to move with subtlety and intensity; above-average ability to communicate feelings/ideas through movement	Demonstrates full range of movement qualities; could easily change qualities when asked; above-average ability to move with subtlety and intensity; advanced ability to communicate ideas/feelings through movement
Musicality	Unable to consistently match body movements with beat of music; appears to struggle to dance in rhythm; limited ability to repeat complex rhythmic patterns	Matches body movements with beat of music at times but not consistently; struggles at times with dancing in rhythm; able to repeat complex rhythmic patterns with support or practice	Able to consistently match body movement with beat of music; reflects beat/rhythm in whole body; repeats complex rhythmic patterns with few errors	Able to consistently match body movements with beat of music; reflects beat/rhythm in whole body; demonstrates keen sense of time and rhythm in performance; repeats complex rhythmic patterns precisely

CHAPTER 11

Learning Experiences in Folk and Cultural Dances

Students in classrooms across the United States have roots in many different cultures and heritages, and teaching folk and cultural dances is a great way to help them learn about these cultures. Teaching folk and cultural dances expands the learning and understanding of dance, allowing integration of history, music, and other content areas to bring an appreciation of diversity into the classroom. Folk and cultural dance has sustained its importance in many countries around the world, preserving elements of a country's history and representing the livelihoods that would otherwise lose their significance over time. When learning folk and cultural dances in the physical and dance education settings, students are allowed an opportunity to learn about ancestors, native songs, traditional work or dress, as well as the value of a country's people.

Folk and cultural dance forms represent the values, beliefs, traditions, and different ways people live, as expressed through their dance movements, rhythms, and formations. Sometimes referred to as world or ethnic dances, these dances occur in many variations. For the purposes of this book, we refer to these dances as folk or cultural dances since many originated with everyday people and represent the heritage of the people who perform them (Rovegno and Bandhauer 2017). Through these dances, students learn about what is important to the people in a specific culture, such as their history, language, rituals, occupations, and values, and how these dances are passed down from one generation to the next.

Generally speaking, most folk and cultural dances represent some aspect of the daily life, activities, or culture of the people who perform the dance and can be danced almost anywhere (Kassing and Jay-Kirschenbaum 2021). The dances are often a combination of simple locomotor steps or movements in repeatable patterns with changes in formations or floor pathways (Rovegno and Bandhauer 2017). These dances can also be easily modified to meet the varying levels of physical activity needed in classrooms of all ages.

Each dance learning experience in this chapter is outlined in 10 sections, which identify outcomes and suggested music, equipment and formation, and a detailed description of how to implement the introduction and warm-up, the development of movement sequences, and the closure. Many of the basic steps used in the folk and cultural dances in this chapter are also used in the previous chapter on social, popular, and fitness dances. We suggest learning and understanding some of those basic steps before learning more complicated patterns in the folk and cultural dances. Additional ideas and suggestions are included for varying the dance lessons.

The description of each dance learning experience lesson follows this format:

267

- Title
- Grades
- Outcomes
- Organization
- Equipment needed (including suggested music)
- Introduction and warm-up
- Movements

- Sequence of dance steps
- Closure
- Look for
- How can I change this?

The instructions for each dance learning experience provide you with guidance and instructions to teach the dances successfully. To facilitate your selection of learning experiences, we have summarized each one in table 11.1.

Table 11.1 Index of Learning Experiences in Folk and Cultural Dances

Name of dance learning experience	Description of dance learning experience
American square dance (U.S.) (Grades 4 to 12)	Square dance teaches inclusion and cooperation where everyone is part of the dance and everyone helps to make it work.
Bele kawe (African-Caribbean) (Grades K to 6)	This traditional folk dance originated in West African and Caribbean cultures. This learning experience tells a story of two women who are having a friendly competition for a man's attention. This dance can be performed in multiple lines or in a circle.
Appalachian big circle (U.S.) (Elementary version) (Grades 3 to 6)	An American folk dance that uses square dance movements with the dancers in one large circle instead of the traditional square formation. In this way, all the dancers are together in one big circle sharing and socializing. The elementary version modifies some of the movements in the circle and does it with partners to make it more accessible for younger or beginning level dancers.
Appalachian big circle (U.S.) (Secondary version) (Grades 6 to 12)	Similar to the elementary version, this American folk dance uses square dance movements in a circle formation rather than a traditional square and includes some partner movements to provide challenges for more advanced dancers.
Kinderpolka (Germany) (Grades K to 2)	A children's dance from Germany that mocks the adults scolding finger and uses a clap and slap pattern.
La raspa (Mexico) (Grades K to 3)	This learning experience originated in Veracruz, Mexico. It is performed at festivals.
Mayim, mayim (Israel) (Grades 4 to 8)	*Mayim* means water in Hebrew, the language spoken by many people in Israel. This learning experience is one of the earliest dances of Israel. The country is very dry, and the dance was created to express the joy of finding water.
Samoan sasa (Samoa) (Grades 3 to 12)	An energetic Samoan dance with many variations of movement. The dancers' movements reflect activities from their daily life, such as paddling, cracking a coconut, making nets and rope, climbing trees, making food, and more. This version is one that was created using some of the traditional movements.
Tanko bushi (Japan) (Grades 3 to 5)	In this learning experience the movements reflect the movements of coal miners at work.
Tinikling (Philippines) (Grades 3 to 12)	Pronounced *tin-ick-ill-ing*, this dance originated from Leyte (an island in the Philippines) and depicts the flight of the tikling bird as it travels through the rice fields, avoiding bamboo traps made by the farmers. Some dancers click poles in rhythm while others dance movements around the props or use jump bands.
Virginia reel (U.S.) (Grades 3 to 12)	Named after the state of Virginia, this learning experience is a fun and easy way to focus on both the enjoyment and socialization of dancing as a group.

American Square Dance

 Visit HK*Propel* to see students demonstrating the American square dance.

Grades

4 to 12

Outcomes

As a result of participating in this learning experience, students will be able to do the following:

1. Develop an understanding of how square dance represents the American values of community and democracy (cognitive).
2. Perform the traditional square dance steps with a partner and group when the step is announced by the caller (psychomotor).

Organization

Students should first learn the steps individually while spread out in space or in one large circle, facing the inside center. Once they understand the steps, students will make a traditional square formation with eight dancers completing one square, having two pairs on each of the four sides (see figure 11.1). Students will need to learn the difference between their partner and their corner partner. The partner is the person directly next to them on their side of the square. The corner partner is the person on their other side who makes up a different side of the square.

Equipment Needed

- Pictures or artifacts of American symbols
- Books, costumes, and pictures of people square dancing
- Suggested music:
    - "Fiddlin' Rag" by Tommy Jackson
    - "Oh! Susanna" by Eight Hands String Band

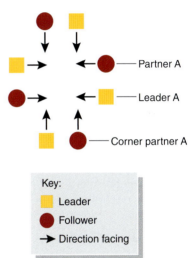

Figure 11.1 Square dance formation.

Introduction and Warm-Up

Today, we are going to learn about American square dancing. Square dance was designated as the national folk dance of the United States of America in 1982 by a Senate joint resolution signed into law by President Ronald Reagan. The resolution stated that square dancing demonstrates the democracy and etiquette of the American people. Can you think of some reasons why or how square dancing may demonstrate these ideas? [Students may name ideas such as working together in a big group, facing each other in the dance, or the use of bows or taking turns when dancing the steps.] Are there other symbols or activities you can think of that you believe represent America? [Have students list and name various ideas. Use pictures, artifacts, and books to help guide discussion as necessary.] Keeping these ideas in mind, I want us to focus on the social and community aspect of folk dancing as we learn today's American square dance steps. We are going to start with a simple warm-up to learn some of the steps before we put them together into a sequence we will perform later. Let's start by spreading out into one large circle, facing the center, with enough space on our left and right so we can all move safely.

We are going to start our warm-up by marching to the beat of the music. [Play a song with a medium tempo for students to practice staying on beat during all the warm-up steps.] Make sure to move your arms forward and backward as you march to have your upper and lower body move and warm up. Now, I want you to practice changing the direction of your marches as I call them out. One aspect of square dance is the use of the caller, who is the person telling the dancers what steps to complete. You will have to listen carefully to what directions and steps I tell you to do. First, I want you to march toward the center of the circle for four steps and then march backward for four steps. Ready? 5, 6, 7, go! [Guide the students to march forward and backward several times. If using silence or playing a drum, you can change the tempo for an added challenge.] Now, march in place until I tell you to turn to your right or left. When you do that, you will be facing the back of someone's head and you will march in a circle, similar to how you might walk in a line down the hallway. Turn to your left and march, 5, 6, 7, 8. Now, turn around and go to the right. [Repeat this sequence, having students march in a circle to their left or right for various amounts of counts. They can march in place when you are ready to move on to the next step.]

Now, let's try some of these steps while holding hands. Carefully grab the hands of the dancers to your right and left and continue to march in place. I am going to call out some new directions and steps, so be ready to change to the next step. March forward to the center four times, and now march backward four times. [Repeat and guide as needed.] Now, I want you to slide or gallop to your right for 8 counts. March in place. Get ready; we are going to slide or gallop to the left for 8 counts. Ready, 5, 6, 7, 8. Next, we are going to try to grapevine to our right while still holding hands for 8 counts. Then we will go to the left. [Guide students to transition back and forth between these various steps of marching forward, backward, galloping right and left, and grapevine stepping right and left. Be sure to call out a few counts before you want students to begin moving.] You may let go of both dancers' hands and give them a small bow as a thank-you before we begin learning our sequence for the American square dance.

Movements

- *March forward and back:* Stand tall with your back straight and arms at your sides, elbows bent at 90-degree angles. Lift the right and left knees alternately while simultaneously pumping the arms forward and backward to take four steps forward into the circle and then four steps backward out of the circle.

- *All circle:* All dancers hold hands and while still facing the center point, circle to the left or right. There are multiple movements students can do depending on their ability level. These include marching, running, galloping, or grapevine.

- *Greet partner:* Dancers bow toward their partner who shares the same side of the square with them. The person on the left of the pair is considered the leader, and the person on the right is considered the follower.

- *Greet corner partner:* Dancers bow toward the person on the other side of their body who does not share the same side of the square with them. This means leaders will bow to the follower on their left side, while followers will bow to the leader on their right side.

- *Do-si-do:* This 8-count sequence requires dancers to march past their partner and then return to their beginning spot without turning their body around. Dancers face their partner and march 2 counts past each other with the right shoulders passing. Then they march two steps to their right side with their backs to each other. Next, they march backward with the left shoulders passing. Finally, they march two steps to their left side and end up back in their beginning locations, facing each other.

- *Elbow swing:* Partners hook elbows and circle for 360 degrees. This can be done with both left elbows or both right elbows. Dancers can march or skip while connected to their partner.

- *Promenade around the ring:* In this move, partners stand side by side and act as a single unit while following other pairs around the circle ("around the ring"). The leader stands to the left of their partner, and all pairs turn to face the right side of the circle, creating a follow-the-leader effect. This places the leaders closer to the center of the circle, while the followers are on the outside of the circle. Partners hold hands while marching and following the other pairs around the ring. Beginning students can simply connect inside hands (leader's right and follower's left). More advanced students can reach their arms across their waist toward their partner, connect both left hands together, and place the leader's right hand across the top of the follower's left arm to connect to the follower's right hand.

Sequence of Dance Steps

- Sequence 1
  - Counts 1 to 4: Greet your partner.
  - Counts 5 to 8: Greet your corner partner.
  - Counts 9 to 24: All circle to the right for 16 counts.
  - Counts 25 to 40: All circle to the left for 16 counts.
  - Counts 41 to 56: Everyone march forward and backward two times.
- Sequence 2
  - Counts 1 to 4: Partners swing elbows.
  - Counts 5 to 8: Corner partners swing elbows.
  - Counts 9 to 16: Repeat partners and corner partners swing elbows.
  - Counts 17 to 24: Partners do a do-si-do.
  - Counts 25 to 32: Corner partners do a do-si-do.
  - Counts 33 to 36: Partners swing elbows.
  - Counts 37 to 40: Corner partners swing elbows.
  - Counts 41 to 48: Repeat partners and corner partners swing elbows.
- Sequence 3
  - Counts 1 to 16: All partners promenade around the ring. The goal is to get back to the beginning position by count 16.
  - Counts 17 to 20: Partners swing elbows.
  - Counts 21 to 24: Corner partners swing elbows.
  - Counts 25 to 40: Everyone march forward and back (2 times).
- Repeat sequences 1, 2, and 3 until the music ends, with the teacher as the caller providing a cue for each upcoming step. Beginning students may need to complete one sequence several times in a row before adding on a second and third sequence. Advanced students can work toward repeating the sequences without the aid of a caller.

Closure

Discuss with your partner which part of the dance you felt the most comfortable performing. Why? What sequences were easier with your partner, and which were a struggle? [Have students share their answers with the whole group.] As a group, discuss the successes and struggles while dancing in a larger group.

Look For

- Those who feel comfortable enough with the movements to serve as a caller for an upcoming set.
- A group of eight dancers who can maintain their square formation after the circular movements.
- Students who remember the differences between the three sets of sequences.

How Can I Change This?

- Usually, there is a pattern to the calls, but the teacher can serve as the caller and challenge students by calling out various movements while in the square formation without having previously practiced the sequence.
- Dancers can use cooperative calling, meaning that each dancer in the square has an opportunity to make a call. Cooperative calling traditionally follows an order in the square for all dancers to

get a chance to play this role. Number off the pairs in each square. Then, the sequence for each call would follow as: leader in pair 1, follower in pair 1, leader in pair 2, follower in pair 2, and so on. Each person makes one movement call before it goes to the next person. Students can repeat the order of callers for several rounds, if the music continues.

- If the group does not divide evenly into groups of eight, have students find ways to adjust, including using imaginary partners or a group of three rather than a pair. The dance can also be completed in one large circle for younger or beginning groups of students rather than in separate squares.

- For students who still struggle with hand holding, scarves can be included in the dance. Students can each have one scarf to share and hold on to.

Bele Kawe

Grades

K to 6

Outcomes

As a result of participating in this learning experience, students will be able to do the following:

1. Perform the three dance steps each for 16 counts (psychomotor).
2. Perform the basic steps while traveling safely through the space (psychomotor).
3. Explain how the three dance steps relate to the story of the dance (cognitive).

Organization

Students are arranged in lines to begin learning the sequence, before moving to do the sequence in a circular formation. All dancers face the inside center of the circle.

Equipment Needed

- Pictures of African and Afro-Caribbean dancers or artifacts from Africa and the Caribbean, such as clothing, drums, sculptures, or artwork
- Suggested music:
  - African and Afro-Caribbean music or drumming music
  - "Slow Tribal" by Godfrey Mgcina
  - "Welcome to Africa" by African Drums

Introduction and Warm-Up

Today, we are learning about a traditional folk dance that originated from West African and Caribbean cultures called bele kawe. This dance tells a story of two women who are having a friendly competition for a man's attention. The first part of the dance represents the women trying to get the man's attention, while the last part represents the warding off of any bad spirits that may be standing in the women's way. Can you think of a time when you were trying to get someone's attention? What did you do to get them to notice you? While staying in your personal space, can you show me some of the movements you may have done to get someone's attention? I see some of you jumping up and down, waving your arms wildly in the air, and some of you are doing strong body shapes. Let's think about the second part of the dance that represents warding off bad spirits. What are some movements you have made when you want something to go away or you want negative things out of your space? Think about the words *stop, no, go, shoo,* or *away* as you demonstrate the different types of movement you may do. [Students demonstrate different movement choices.]

There are many different versions of bele kawe, and it can be performed in multiple lines or in a circle. The legs remain bent during the whole dance, and the body has a feeling of being grounded, which means connected to the earth or floor. The upper body should move freely, and the whole dance should have a feeling of energy or vibrancy. Let's practice some of these movements as we continue to warm up our bodies. Move yourselves into a circle so we can see each other, and stand with your knees bent. When you hear the drumming music, I want you to march in place while moving your hips. [Students try the march.] Now, I want you to march for 3 counts and then jump on count 4. Ready, go! [Students march and jump for several sequences in a row.] Now, I want us to practice having our upper body moving freely. While keeping your knees bent and marching, I want to see you really swing your arms forward and backward. This should be like when you are walking, but with even bigger and looser movements. [Students try for several counts.] Now, let's see if we can move our arms in different ways. First, let's practice tapping our heels out in front of us and then placing them back down underneath our body. Then switch to the other foot, tap the heel, and bring it back. [Practice this a few times with just the feet.] Keep that rhythm of your feet going, and swing your arms to the left and right as you tap each foot, making a big U-like shape in front of your body as you swing from side to side. Remember to go right and left. [Practice several times in a row.] Finish your last tap with me. Ready, 1, 2, 3, and freeze. Now that we have practiced some of the steps, let's begin learning the choreography for bele kawe.

Movements

- *Forward shuffle (traveling rock step):* Step forward with the right foot, placing a significant amount of weight onto the ball of the foot (this is the area where the toes meet). While stepping forward with the right foot, the left foot behind you should slightly lift off the floor, and you should feel your upper body rock in this forward direction. Then place the left foot back down on the ground to shift your weight again while the right foot slightly lifts off the floor. Step the right foot down, still in front of your body. Then repeat this step by first stepping forward on your left foot, lifting the right foot behind you slightly, and then placing the right foot back down while the left foot lifts slightly off the floor. Step the left foot down, still in front of your body. As you step forward to begin each step, travel your body forward in the space, and it will appear as though your feet are shuffling as you walk. Each shuffle or rock step is counted 1 and 2.

- *Heel taps:* Tap the right heel out to the right front diagonal, digging your heel into the floor while your toes point toward the sky. While stepping, reach both arms and swing up to the right side of the body. Step the right foot back to the center of the body, but place it slightly behind yourself so you can travel backward. Repeat the step to the left by tapping the left heel out to left front diagonal while swinging both arms up to the left side of the body. Step the left foot back, but place it slightly behind yourself to continue traveling backward.

- *Four-step turn:* Traveling to the right side of the body, turn clockwise by stepping right, then left, then right, and finish by touching the left foot next to the right foot. This should take 4 counts. While turning, reaching your arms out to the sides. Repeat the turn, traveling left by turning counterclockwise while stepping left, then right, then left, and touching the right foot next to the left foot.

Sequence of Dance Steps

- Counts 1 to 16: Forward shuffle.
- Counts 17 to 32: Heel taps.
- Counts: 33 to 48: Four-step turn four times: right, left, right, left.
- Repeat the dance until the end of the song.

Closure

Find a partner and demonstrate your favorite move of this dance to them. [Pair up the students and give them time to share.] Explain to your partner why this was your favorite move of the dance. What part of the dance's story do you think your favorite move is related to?

Look For

- Dancers who can complete the rock step and heel taps while simultaneously traveling.
- Dancers who can move their arms in unison with the heel-tap movements.
- Dancers turning in the correct clockwise or counterclockwise direction during the four-step turn.

How Can I Change This?

- Have the dancers perform the dance with a scarf in each hand or while holding on to a skirt they are wearing to add movement and challenge to the dance.
- Have the dancers complete each dance step to different music, and change each set of steps from 16 counts to 8 counts.
- Make the dance a four-wall line dance by adding an extra quarter turn on the last four-step turn so students face the wall with their left shoulder.
- Have students do the dance in lines facing the same wall, in one large circle, in contra lines (two parallel lines facing each other), or in contra circles (two circles facing each other).
- Add extra movement to count 4 of the four-step turn, such as a loud stomp, clap, or jump.
- Remove the traveling in the forward shuffle and the heel taps for younger or beginning groups, and keep the dance stationary in a single spot.

Appalachian Big Circle (Elementary Version)

Grades

3 to 6

Outcomes

As a result of participating in this learning experience, students will be able to do the following:

1. Work together holding hands in a circle, walk to the left for 8 counts, and walk to the right for 8 counts (psychomotor and affective).
2. Play patty-cake with the person to their left and the person to their right at the same time for 4 counts (psychomotor and affective).

Organization

Students warm up individually while spread out in the space. Then they learn the sequence in a circle formation, facing the inside center. Younger or beginning groups can complete the warm-up in one large circle, while older or more advanced groups can complete the warm-up in smaller circles of four to six dancers.

Equipment Needed

- Traditional square dance or fiddlers' music
- Suggested music: "Buffalo Girls and Boys" by The Backyardigans

Introduction and Warm-Up

Today, we are going to learn a dance called the Appalachian big circle. This learning experience is an American folk dance and uses square dance movements. However, instead of dancing in a square, we are going to dance together in a circle. Can you think of a reason why a folk dance would be danced in a circle instead of in lines or spread out in space? [Students should name ideas, such as being able to see others, sharing the space, socializing or community, or working together.] Today's dance is a simple version with just a few steps put together that we will repeat several times. First, we are going to warm up together before we learn the steps and come together in a circle. Spread out in the space so you can move freely and safely.

In your personal space, begin marching in place. [Play music or a drum to keep the dancers on a steady beat.] You can swing your arms forward and backward as you march to get your upper body ready to dance too. Now, I want everyone to march to their right for 8 counts when I say go. Ready, set, go. March in place, and when I say go this time, I want you to march to your left and end up back where you started. Ready, set, go. Let's try that again, but this time I want to see you sliding instead of marching when we travel to the right. We will march in place once we get to count 8. Ready, 5, 6, 7, 8. Now, let's slide to the left side, and 5, 6, 7, 8.

For the next part of the warm-up, we need to make sure our upper body is ready to dance. Keep your feet still in your personal space, and show me how you can slap your thighs on the beat. [Play music or a drum for a steady beat while dancers slap thighs.] Now, I want you to clap your hands together while staying on the beat.

For the last part of the warm-up, we are going to practice our movements in a circle. Everyone march on the beat, and make one circle in the space. [Give dancers time to travel, connect, and make one circle. If they were holding hands, ask them to let go.] Let's practice our thigh slaps and hand claps on the beat again while in our circle. [Guide students to slap thighs and clap hands, switching between the two as needed.] Now, I want you to look to your right and to your left, and notice that you have a person on each side, since we are in a circle. I want you to play patty-cake with both of these people at the same time by giving them each one of them a high five on the beat. Let's try eight patty-cakes in a row. [Count until the students complete all eight patty-cake movements. Repeat as needed.] Give both of your partners a quick bow as a thank-you before we start learning today's movement sequence.

Movements

- Patty-cake sequence: Slap the thighs two times; clap two times; slap the hands of the person to the right and to the left of you in the circle at the same time for 4 counts, doing a total of 8 counts.
- Circle right and left: Students hold hands and walk in a circle to the right for 8 counts and then to the left for 8 counts (16 counts total).

Sequence of Dance Steps

- Counts 1 to 8: Patty-cake sequence.
- Counts 9 to 24: Circle right and left.
- Repeat the two sequences until the music ends.

Closure

Ask the students, "Can you name the dance steps in the correct order? What part of the dance did you enjoy dancing most? Why did you like that part?"

Look For

- Students circling to the right and left for 8 counts each with smooth transitions from right to left.
- Dancers playing patty-cake for the 8 counts with correct timing.

How Can I Change This?

- Have the students perform the dance movements in smaller groups of six to eight dancers.
- Use a slower-paced song to accommodate younger students or a faster-paced song to challenge more advanced groups.
- Have dancers complete the circle right and left with different movements instead of walking. Examples include skipping, sliding, galloping, or grapevine.

- The learning experience can be performed using a scarf instead of holding hands. The students would need to hold the scarves with their thumb and forefinger in order to still play the patty-cake sequence.
- Have the students work as a team in smaller groups to create a new patty-cake sequence that would work in the dance.

Appalachian Big Circle (Secondary Version)

Grades

6 to 12

Outcomes

As a result of participating in this learning experience, students will be able to do the following:

1. Work together in groups of 8 with a partner and a corner partner to perform the first sequence to the timing of the caller (psychomotor and affective).
2. Work together in a large circle of 16 students to complete all sequences to music, following the caller (psychomotor and affective).

Organization

Students first learn the steps individually while spread out in space or in one large circle, facing the inside center. Once they understand the steps, students pair up and place themselves in one large circle. Although the dancers are in a circle, they still use the concept of partners and corner partners outlined in the American square dance. In this scenario, their partner is the person they paired with to make the circle, while their corner partner is the other person next to them (see figure 11.2).

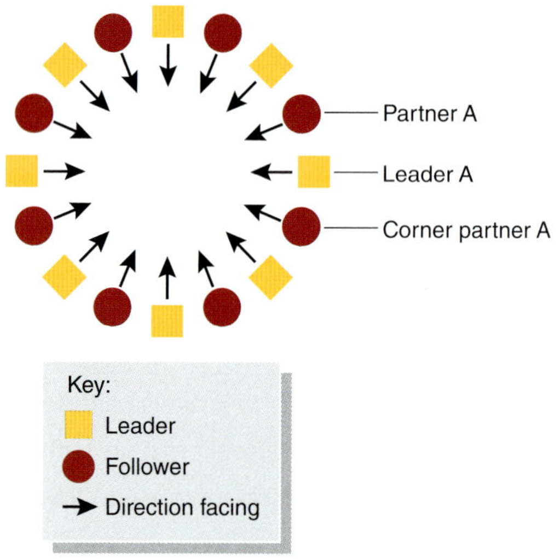

Equipment Needed

- Traditional square dance or fiddle music
- Suggested music: "Return to Fraser Canyon" by SecondAttack

Introduction and Warm-Up

Key:
- ◼ Leader
- ● Follower
- → Direction facing

Figure 11.2 Formation for Appalachian big circle.

Today, we are going to learn an American folk dance called the Appalachian big circle. This dance is a more difficult version and uses square dance movements. However, instead of dancing in a traditional square, we are going to dance in one large circle. Can you think of a reason why a folk dance would be danced in a circle instead of in lines or spread out in space? Why might we dance in a circle instead of a square? [Students should name ideas, such as being able to see others, sharing the space, socializing or community, or working together. They may also discuss how a square requires several small groups, while a circle can be one large group.] Keeping these ideas in mind, I want us to focus on the social and community aspect of folk dancing as we learn today's harder version of the Appalachian big circle. We are going to start with a simple warm-up to learn some of the steps before we put them together into a sequence we will perform later. Let's start by spreading out into one large circle, facing the center, with enough space on our left and right so we can all move safely.

We are going to start our warm-up by marching to the beat of the music. [Play a song with a medium tempo for students to practice staying on beat during all the warm-up steps.] Make sure to move your

Chapter 11 Learning Experiences in Folk and Cultural Dances **277**

arms forward and backward as you march to have your upper and lower body move and warm up. Now, I want you to practice changing the direction of your marches as I call them out. One aspect of square dance is the use of the caller, who is the person telling the dancers what steps to complete. You will have to listen carefully to what directions and steps I tell you to do. First, I want you to march toward the center of the circle for four steps, and then march backward for four steps. Ready? 5, 6, 7, go! [Guide the students time to march forward and backward several times. If using silence or playing a drum, you can change the tempo for an added challenge.] Now, march in place until I tell you to turn to your right or left. When you do that, you will be facing the back of someone's head, and you will march in a circle, similar to how you might walk in a line down the hallway. Turn to your left and march, 5, 6, 7, 8. Now, turn around and go to the right. [Repeat this sequence, having students march in a circle to their left or right for various amounts of counts. They can march in place when you are ready to move on to the next step.]

Now, let's try some of these steps while holding hands. Carefully grab the hands of the dancers to your right and left and continue to march in place. I am going to call out some new directions and steps, so be ready to change to the next step. March forward to the center four times, and now march backward four times. [Repeat and guide as needed.] Now, I want you to slide or gallop to your right for 8 counts. March in place. Get ready; we are going to slide or gallop to the left for 8 counts. Ready, 5, 6, 7, 8. Next, we are going to grapevine to our right while still holding hands for 8 counts. Then we will go to the left. [Guide students to transition back and forth between these various steps of marching forward, backward, galloping right and left, and grapevine stepping right and left. Be sure to call out a few counts before you want students to begin moving.] You may let go of both dancers' hands and give them a small bow as a thank-you before we begin learning our sequence.

Movements

- *Grand right and left:* Dancers face their designated partner, grab their partner's right hand, and walk past each other, slightly pulling each other forward before letting go of hands. They will now be facing a new partner. They grab this person's left hand, walk past, and let go. Then another new partner appears, and the right hand is grabbed. This pattern continues until the original partners meet. Each grab and walk past takes 2 counts.

- *Do-si-do:* This 8-count sequence requires dancers to march past their partner and then return to their beginning spot without turning their body around. Dancers face their partner and march 2 counts past each other with the right shoulders passing. Then they march two steps to their right side with their backs to each other. Next, they march backward with the left shoulders passing. Finally, they march two steps to their left side and end up back in their beginning locations, facing each other.

- *Seesaw:* This 8-count sequence is just like the do-si-do where partners march past each other and return to their beginning spot without turning their body around, but it starts by passing the left shoulders. Dancers face their partner and march 2 counts past each other with the left shoulders passing. Then they march two steps to their left side with their backs to each other. Next, they march backward with the right shoulders passing. Finally, they march two steps to their right side and end up back in their beginning locations, facing each other.

- *Elbow swing:* Partners hook elbows and circle for 360 degrees. This can be done with both left elbows or both right elbows. Dancers can march or skip while connected to their partner.

- *Wrist turn:* Partners face each other and hold their partner's right wrist with their right hand (like a handshake, but up on the arm a bit higher for a stronger hold). To turn, partners walk around in a circle, following each other. This can be repeated holding the left wrist and walking in the opposite direction for the turn.

- *All circle:* All dancers hold hands, and while still facing the center point, they circle to the left or to the right. There are multiple movements students can do depending on their ability level. These include marching, running, galloping, or grapevine.

- *March forward and back:* Stand tall with your back straight and arms at your sides, elbows bent at 90-degree angles. Lift the right and left knees alternately while simultaneously pumping the arms forward and backward to take four steps forward into the circle and then four steps backward out of the circle.

Sequence of Dance Steps

- Sequence 1
  - Counts 1 to 8: All circle for 8 counts to the left.
  - Counts 9 to 16: All circle for 8 counts to the right.
  - Counts 17 to 24: Do-si-do your partner.
  - Counts 25 to 32: Seesaw your corner partner.
  - Counts 33 to 40: Do-si-do your partner.
  - Counts 41 to 48: Seesaw your corner partner.
- Sequence 2
  - Counts 1 to 8: March forward and backward.
  - Counts 9 to 16: March forward and backward again.
  - Counts 17 to 24: Right elbow swing your partner.
  - Counts 25 to 32: Left elbow swing your corner partner.
  - Counts 33 to 40: Right elbow swing your partner.
  - Counts 41 to 48: Left elbow swing your corner partner.
- Sequence 3
  - Counts 1 to 8: Grand right and left until your back is to your partner. (Counts will vary depending on the circle size.)
  - Counts 9 to 16: Right wrist turn your partner.
  - Counts 17 to 24: Left wrist turn your corner partner.
  - Counts 25 to 32: Right wrist turn your partner.
  - Counts 33 to 40: Left wrist turn your corner partner.
  - Counts 41 to 48: March forward and backward.
  - Counts 49 to 56: March forward and backward.
- Repeat the three dance sequences until the end of the song.

Closure

Discuss with your partner which part of the dance you felt the most comfortable performing. Why? What sequences were easier with your partner, and which were a struggle? [Have students share their answers with the whole group.] As a group, discuss the successes and struggles while dancing in a larger group.

Look For

- Dancers who can stay on count for each movement and transitioning easily into the next movement.
- Dancers showing that they know the difference between a partner and a corner partner when performing the dance.

How Can I Change This?

- Have the dancers perform the dance movements individually by following the calls made by the teacher without a set sequence.
- Perform the dance in smaller circles throughout the space.
- Have the dancers work in smaller groups (six to eight dancers) to put the dance movements into a different sequence and then perform them for the class.
- Have everyone dance holding a scarf instead of hands. Each dancer would receive one scarf.

Chapter 11 Learning Experiences in Folk and Cultural Dances   279

- Have advanced students take turns being the caller and demonstrate the ability to follow the same sequence of steps made by the teacher or create their own sequence while giving clear directions to their peers.

Kinderpolka

 Visit HK*Propel* to see students demonstrating the kinderpolka.

Grades
K to 2

Outcomes
As a result of participating in this learning experience, children will be able to do the following:
1. Perform the dance movements to the rhythm and tempo of the music (psychomotor).
2. Perform the patty-cake sequence with their partner on tempo (psychomotor and affective).
3. Work as a unit with their partner throughout the dance to recall and perform the sequence of steps (psychomotor and affective).

Organization
Students first learn the movements individually while spread out in the space. Once they have mastered the movements, they can practice facing a partner. After students are comfortable with their partners, they create one large circle while facing their partner to learn the sequence of movements. The circle will have children facing their partner and holding hands while back-to-back with the partners on either side of them (see figure 11.3).

Equipment Needed
- Map of Germany
- Suggested music:
  - "Kinderpolka" by Bow Tie Music
  - "Kinderpolka" by Denise Gagne and Carmen Bryant

Figure 11.3 Formation for kinderpolka.

Introduction and Warm-Up
Today's kinderpolka dance comes to us from Germany. [Show students the map of Germany.] In German, *kinder* means *children*. Have you ever heard any other words that sound like kinderpolka? [Discuss the word *kindergarten*, which students have likely heard.] The word *polka* means a lively or fast dance with a partner. If we put those two words together, that means that today we are learning a children's version of a couple's dance. There are some movements that require us to be connected to a partner and work as a team, but first we are going to warm up individually so we are ready to work with our partners when it is time. Let's spread out in the space so we can move safely in our own dance space.

First, I want us to warm up our feet and demonstrate stomping on beat. Stomping is one of our moves in the kinderpolka dance. You can keep your arms still or move them any way you want to while we practice stomping. [Play a drum or music with a steady tempo, and have students practice stomping on the beat.]

Now, we are going to make sure we can make other sounds on the beat of the music. Let's slap our thighs to the beat. [Have students slap their thighs on tempo with a drum or recorded music.] Next, I want you to clap your hands together on the beat. Finally, I want you to extend your arms out in front of you on beat, like you are giving an imaginary partner a high five. Let's do that eight times. I think you are ready to put several of those steps together and show me that you can stay on beat with the music at the same time. You are going to slap your thighs two times, then clap your hands two times, and then give your imaginary partner three high fives in a row. We are going to do it altogether. Ready, set, and go. [Count the students through the sequence and repeat several times.]

Now that you know how to do several steps on beat, we are going to travel our feet side to side to practice another step from the dance. Make sure we are all facing the same wall together so we can practice our side steps. Step your right leg open, then bring your left foot together, then step the right foot out again, and finish with your left foot together. Try that one more time before we switch sides. [Have children repeat the side stepping to the right. When ready, repeat the motion, but begin with the left foot. Repeat this several times with the children, switching between the right and left feet.] Since you all know the sidestep now, we are going to add in stomping in-between. That means after we step-together-step-together, I want to hear you stomp three times on the beat of the music. Let's try it together before I watch you do it. [Demonstrate the movement to the children. Have them repeat it several times, moving both to the right and to the left with stomping in-between.]

Finally, we are going to learn a turn that happens in our kinderpolka. This turn requires you to spin clockwise, meaning toward your own right shoulder, while taking three steps. Watch me first before you try. [Demonstrate for the dancers, then have the children try it several times with a pause in between each turn attempt.] Just like we did with our side stepping, I want to see you add in stomping after you finish your turn. We are going to spin to our right for 4 counts, and then we are going to stomp right, then left, then right, and pause on count 4. I will know you stayed on beat if I hear silence on count 4. Let's try it together. [Practice several times using a drum or recorded music to help students practice staying on beat.] Now that you are experts on several dance movements, we are going to try some of them with a partner. [Have students pair up. Students can be spread out in the space or in two parallel lines with their partners. Go through the same sequence of steps, but have the students hold hands while completing them. These include stomping feet, slapping thighs, clapping hands, giving a high five, side stepping, and letting go to turn around.] We look like we are ready to create one big circle and put our dance movements together for the kinderpolka.

Movements

- *Side step and stomp:* Partners holding hands facing each other, with their shoulders facing the middle of the circle and their backs facing the backs of other pairs in the circle. Partners move together toward the center of the circle, moving sideways, with a step-together-step-together motion for 4 counts. Then they stomp three quick stomps and pause, right, left, right for 4 counts. This is also repeated by moving sideways with a step-together-step-together motion in the opposite direction, away from the center of the circle.

- *Patty-cake sequence:* Each dancer slaps their thighs twice, claps their hands twice, and claps both hands against their partner's hands three times, followed by a pause for a total of 8 counts. The cues are, "Slap it, clap it, and one, two, three."

- *"No, no, no" shake:* Looking at your partner, shake your right index finger three times, then shake your left index finger three times (8 counts) and say, "no, no, no" as you shake your finger every time.

- *Spin and stomp:* Each dancer performs a three-step turn in place, turning clockwise and stomping right, then left, then right, and finishing with the turn for a total of 8 counts.

Sequence of Dance Steps

In one large circle, children begin by facing each other and holding hands with their shoulders facing the middle of the circle.

- Counts 1 to 8: Side step and stomp to the inside of the circle.
- Counts 9 to 16: Side step and stomp to the outside of the circle.

- Counts 17 to 32: Repeat counts 1 to 16.
- Counts 33 to 40: Patty-cake sequence.
- Counts 40 to 48: Repeat the patty-cake sequence.
- Counts 48 to 55: "No, no, no" shake.
- Counts 55 to 62: Spin and stomp.
- Repeat the dance sequence several times or until the music ends.

Closure

Conduct a discussion about how the patty-cake sequence and the "no, no, no" shake represent some everyday experiences a child might have, like playing with a friend or having an adult tell them "no." Brainstorm ideas about other everyday experiences students might have, which they could turn into simple dance movements. Have students create and share their ideas with the class.

Look For

- Children performing the dance movements to the rhythm and tempo of the music.
- Children respectfully hold hands with their partner to move as a unit during the step-touch movement.

How Can I Change This?

- To simplify the side step and stomp, students can take one large sliding step, put their feet together, and then stomp one time. This makes the movement slower and does not require them to travel as far.
- Make the dance a mixer by having students work with different partners throughout the dance. Instead of spin and stomp, students shake hands with their partner for 2 counts, step out to their left for 2 counts, and move forward for 2 counts to greet their new partner by grabbing hands for 2 counts (8 counts total). The dance then repeats with these new partners.
- Have partners create their own patty-cake sequence for the 8 counts and then try the new patty-cake sequence while dancing to music. Older or more advanced students can teach their sequence to others or try multiple patty-cake sequences throughout the dance.

La Raspa

Grades

K to 3

Outcomes

As a result of participating in this learning experience, children will be able to do the following:

1. Perform the bleking step with a partner in unison to the tempo of the music (psychomotor and affective).
2. Perform a smooth transition from the right elbow swing to the left elbow swing with their partner (psychomotor).

Organization

Students learn the movements individually while spread out in the space. Once the movements are mastered, they practice facing a partner.

Equipment Needed

- World map showing the location of Mexico
- Artifacts for the dance, including items like a picture of the Mexican flag or costumes traditionally worn for the dance
- Handheld drum or tambourine
- Suggested music:
  - "La Raspa" by Mariachi Mexico de Pepe Villa
  - "La Raspa" by Shenanigans

Introduction and Warm-Up

Today, we are learning a dance called la raspa. The term *la raspa* translates in English as *the rasp* or *the scratch*. The name may come from the scratching sound of the instrument in the song or the sound the feet make on the floor. La raspa originated in the state of Veracruz, Mexico. [Show students a world map and point out Mexico and the state of Veracruz.] It is typically danced by children and performed at festivals, such as Cinco de Mayo. [Show students any other pictures or artifacts related to Mexico or the dance.] It is a dance of fast and slow rhythms and is performed with a partner. The dance is often inaccurately confused with the Mexican hat dance, or el jarabe tapatio. To learn the la raspa dance, we are going to spread out individually in the space to warm up. Then we will learn the steps and work with a partner to do it together.

Once you are spread out and have enough space to dance, we are going to start by walking in place to the beat of the drum. If I play faster or slower, I want to see you go faster or slower with my beat. [Play a steady beat on a handheld drum or tambourine. Go faster or slower, and watch for students stepping down on each hit of the instrument.] Now that you can walk in place on the beat, I want to see you walk in a circle on the beat, just like you will have to do in the dance. When you hear the drum, I want you to walk in a circle around yourself to the right. Once we finish, we will switch to the left. [Play a steady tempo, and have students walk to the right in a circle on the beat. Then repeat, and have students walk to the left in a circle.] The next thing we are going to try is skipping in place, just like we did with walking. Be sure to listen to the beat of the instrument and match my tempo. [Have students skip in place while playing a beat on the instrument. Go faster and slower to make sure students can stay on the beat of the music.] As skipping experts, now we are going to try skipping in a circle around ourselves for 16 skips to our right. Then we will switch to our left for 16 skips. Make sure you are counting so you know when to switch. [Play a beat on the instrument, and have students make the right and left circles. Repeat as necessary.] It looks like we are ready to learn the steps of la raspa. Remember to stay on the beat with the music, just like you did in the warm-up.

Movements

- *Elbow swing:* Partners hook elbows and circle for 360 degrees. This can be done with both left elbows or both right elbows. Dancers can walk or skip while staying connected to their partner.

- *Clap:* Both hands come together, with one hand's fingers and palm striking the palm of the other to make a clap sound.

- *Bleking step:* This step is similar to heel taps but includes hopping in place while tapping the foot out. Hop in place on the left foot, and touch the right heel forward with the toes pointing up. Jump by pushing off both feet and switch to touching the left heel forward with the toes pointing up. Then jump one more time to switch to the right heel touching forward. This takes 3 counts with the feet holding still and silent on count 4. The step can then be repeated by jumping to touch the left heel forward, then the right, and then the left, followed by a hold on count 4.

Chapter 11   Learning Experiences in Folk and Cultural Dances   **283**

Sequence of Dance Steps

- Sequence 1 (32 counts)
  - Counts 1 to 3: Do the bleking step.
  - Counts & 4: Clap two times.
  - Repeat the bleking step and two claps seven more times, for a total of eight sequences. Students should be facing a partner during this bleking step to be prepared for the partner work in sequence 2.
- Sequence 2 (32 counts)
  - Counts 1 to 16: Elbow swing to the right.
  - Counts 17 to 32: Elbow swing to the left.
- Repeat sequences 1 and 2 several times or until the song ends, to complete the dance.

Closure

Ask students to recall facts about the la raspa dance, including where it was created, when it is often danced, and what the words *la raspa* mean in English. Students can discuss which sequence, 1 or 2, they thought was the easiest or hardest to do and explain why.

Look For

- Students listening to the music to change from the partner elbow swing to the bleking step.
- Students cooperating and relating to each other positively while performing the dance with a partner.

How Can I Change This?

- Less experienced students can walk or march instead of skipping during the elbow swing portion.
- If connecting with a partner is difficult, students can dance in one large class circle. Instead of completing a partner elbow swing, students can walk or skip around themselves individually like they did during the warm-up exercise, or they can hold hands in one large circle to walk or skip to the right, then to the left as one large group.
- Experienced students can make the elbow swing harder by switching every 8 counts instead of every 16 counts, making the elbow swing 8 counts right, 8 counts left, 8 counts right, and 8 counts left. These more experienced dancers could also change partners during the last 8 counts of the elbow swing and then repeat the sequence with their new partner.
- Students can hold hands during the bleking step and pause for the & 4 counts instead of clapping.
- Soccer sports connection variation: Give each student a ball and have them stand in a stationary position with the ball at their feet. The students perform the bleking step by tapping the ball for the bleking rhythm. During the skipping portion of the song, students perform controlled soccer dribbles in the general space and stop the ball for the bleking dance portion.

Mayim, Mayim

 Visit HK*Propel* to see students demonstrating mayim, mayim.

Grades

4 to 8

Outcomes

As a result of participating in this learning experience, students will be able to do the following:

1. Dance together in a circle while holding hands, performing the mayim step in sync as they move in a circle to the left for 16 counts (psychomotor and affective).
2. Remain on tempo throughout the song and remember to clap on the correct counts in the sequence (cognitive and psychomotor).

Organization

Students learn the steps individually as a whole class. Then they perform in a single circle formation with all dancers facing the inside center of the circle while holding hands, as traditionally done in the mayim, mayim dance.

Equipment Needed

- Scarves (if using scarves instead of holding hands): one fewer than the total number of students dancing
- World map and flag from Israel as well as any pictures or videos of dancers in the traditional costumes
- Suggested music:
  - Mayim music composed by Emanuel Amiran-Pougatchov
  - Mayim by Music Express and John Jacobson
  - "Lo Ahavti Dai" by Yankale Levy
  - "Hora Nirkoda" by Yoav Ashrid
  - "Mocher Prachim" by David Swisa

Introduction and Warm-Up

The folk dance we are learning today comes from the country of Israel. [Show students a map and flag of the country.] It is called mayim, mayim. The word *mayim* means *water* in Hebrew, which is a language spoken by many people in Israel. The country is very dry, and the dance was created to express the joy of finding water. It is one of the earliest Israeli dances, and various stories exist about how it was originally created. This may explain why you might see different variations of the dance performed at festivals or concerts. Today, we are going to learn a simple version of the dance. To get started, we are going to do some basic locomotor steps to warm up. Let's start by finding an individual spot in the room to dance.

    Now that you have space to move, we are going to do different locomotor, or traveling, movements in both our own personal space as well as the general space around us, taking care not to run into any other dancers. This will prepare us for when we dance together in our circle later. Let's start with some running in place at a medium tempo. [Play music or use a drum to keep students moving at the desired tempo.] While being mindful of the other dancers, I want you to keep running at this tempo, but move to a new spot in the room. You have 16 counts to get there. In this new spot, let's practice jumping on two feet while remaining on tempo. Now, I want you to take eight jumps into the general space to find a new spot. Let's stop and take two deep breaths together in this new spot. This time, we are going to practice hopping in place. Remember, hopping means to be on only one foot. Can you switch to hopping on the opposite foot from the one you started with? Instead of traveling while hopping, I want you to try to tap the non-hopping foot from side to side as you hop. Can you switch and try it with the opposite feet? This is good practice for one of the steps in our dance. To finish our warm-up, let's practice walking forward and backward in the space. You have 4 counts to go forward and then 4 counts to go backward. Let's try it altogether several times. It looks like we are ready to learn the steps for the mayim, mayim dance.

Movements

- *Mayim step:* The mayim step is similar to the grapevine step found in many other dances, and it takes 4 counts to complete. Step the right foot to the left, crossing it in front of the left foot. Step out to the left with the left foot. Step the right foot to the left, crossing it behind the left foot. Step the left foot out to the left again.

- *Forward and backward step:* Lean forward and walk or run forward toward the center of the circle with the arms down by the sides for count 1, and then straighten and raise the arms up over the head for counts 2, 3, 4, then clap on count 5, and walk backward for the last 3 counts while bringing the arms back down. Dancers hold hands except for the clap on count 5.

- *Celebration step:* Walk or run to the left for 4 counts while holding hands in the circle. Then, letting go of your partners' hands, hop on the left foot while tapping the right foot across the body to the left on one hop, and then tapping out to the right on the next hop, for a total of 8 counts. The foot-tap sequence will be across-out-across-out-across-out-across-out. Switch to hopping on the right foot while tapping the left foot across the body to the right, and then out to the left for a total of 8 counts. The foot-tap sequence is again across-out-across-out-across-out-across-out. Dancers should clap on every odd count, when the left foot is tapping across the front of the body.

Sequence of Dance Steps

- Counts 1 to 16: Mayim step four times in a row.
- Counts 17 to 24: Forward and backward step.
- Counts 25 to 32: Forward and backward step.
- Counts 33 to 52: Celebration step.
- Repeat the dance from the beginning until the song ends.

Closure

As a class, discuss with the students if they thought the dance felt like a celebration and why. Have them discuss with a partner why this dance was created and what other types of celebrations a dance could be created for. Have them name examples of specific celebration dances, if they know any.

Look For

- Dancers who can perform the mayim step by always starting with the right foot and crossing it in front of the left as they move around the circle to the left.
- Dancers who can count the forward and backward steps and can all clap on count 5 together.
- Smooth transitions between each of the step sequences.

How Can I Change This?

- The dance can be done with dancers holding hands, without holding hands, or with a scarf held between the dancers. If using a scarf, dancers would omit the clap and could instead use a vocal rhythm (such as the word "hey") to keep them on beat with the music.

- Change the mayim step to include moving together in a circle with the hands joined together above the dancers' heads.

- Instead of one large class circle, have the class form smaller circles of six to eight dancers.
- During the forward and backward step, instead of letting go to clap, students can remain connected by walking forward for 3 counts, hopping on count 4, walking backward for 3 counts, and then hopping on count 8.
- During the celebration step, students can create their own movements in their space using hops, kicks, and claps to demonstrate their version of a celebration step.
- During the celebration step, instead of walking four times to the left, beginner dancers can clap on beat for 4 counts and then begin the hopping and clapping portion of the celebration step.

Samoan Sasa

 Visit HK*Propel* to see students demonstrating the Samoan sasa.

Grades

3 to 12

Outcomes

As a result of participating in this learning experience, students will be able to do the following:

1. Demonstrate at least three of the movement sequences with the same timing as a partner (psychomotor and affective).
2. Name the various sequences of the dance in order without cues from the teacher (cognitive and psychomotor).

Organization

Students are sitting with their legs crossed and their hands on their thighs, spreading out in the space and facing the front wall.

Equipment Needed

- World map showing Samoa
- Flag or picture of the Samoan flag
- Videos or photos showing the possible variations of the dance
- Drumsticks with a bucket or drum to provide a beat
- Suggested music:
  - "Bongo Song" by Safri Duo
  - "On the Drums" by Eric Sneo

Introduction and Warm-Up

Did you know that in the United States the month of May is Asian American and Pacific Islander Heritage Month? One way to celebrate Asian American and Pacific Islander heritage is to learn about various aspects of the culture in one or more countries. Today, we are going to talk about Samoa, an island country in the South Pacific. [Show the map and flag of Samoa, along with any other artifacts found to represent the country.] In Samoa, rhythm, dancing, singing, and music are integral to the culture. The sasa is an energetic Samoan group dance performed with a variety of unique hand movements. The dancers' movements reflect activities from their daily life, such as paddling, cracking a coconut, making nets and rope, climbing trees, making food, and more. This version is one that was created using some of the traditional movements. In this dance, the clapping and slapping movements create the sounds for the dance. We will also have a drum beating to add a more traditional sound to the dance.

Let's begin learning and warming up by sitting down with our legs crossed to practice our clapping movements. Our goal is to make sure we can stay on beat as a group as we practice clapping, just like we will need to do in the dance. Make sure to listen to my drumbeat and match the tempo I play as you clap. [Play the drum and have students clap along, getting faster or slower as the tempo changes.] Now, we are going to do some call and response, which means you listen as I play a rhythm on the drum, and then you respond by clapping that rhythm back to me. [Play a 4-count rhythm, and have students clap it back. Repeat several times with various rhythms.] Let's add in some other body rhythms by slapping our thighs and the floor to make new sounds and rhythms. We are going to continue our call-and-response pattern, but I am going to perform the rhythm first on my body, and then I want you to copy it. Make sure to watch and listen. There will be different patterns each time. [While sitting and facing the students, create a 4-count pattern of clapping, slapping thighs, or slapping the floor in any order you choose. Have students respond back. Repeat several times with varying rhythms and varying orders of body parts used. For example, one rhythm could be clap-clap-slap thighs-slap floor.] It sounds like we have the hang of using our bodies in different ways with different rhythms, so I think it is time for us to learn a sequence. Remember, this is just one version of the sasa we are learning, as there are many variations that exist.

Movements

- *Pati clap:* Clap the fingers from one hand on the palms of the other hand.

- *Po clap:* Clap with the hands cupped, which creates a lower sound.

- *Flick:* Put the hands at shoulder height with the palms facing your face. Roll or flick the wrist outward with a quick, light movement to have the palms face away from the face. This might resemble throwing something away from your face or body.

- *Floor slaps:* Using both hands, slap the floor with the palms. This can happen to the right side, the left side, or center of the body.

- *Thigh slaps:* Using both bands, slap the thighs with the palms. The right hand should be slapping the right thigh while the left hand slaps the left thigh.

- *Handshake sequence:* This sequence is a total of 8 counts. The right arm reaches out to the right side at shoulder level and does two handshakes, or twists of the wrist, while the left hand touches the left side of the head with the left elbow lifted for a total of 2 counts. Then the left arm reaches out to the left side at shoulder level and does two handshakes, while the right hand touches the right side of the head with the right elbow lifted for 2 counts. Then the right and left arms reach in front of the body and do two handshakes for 2 counts. Clap once, and then raise the arms above the head saying "Talofa" for 2 counts. *Talofa* means *greetings* or *hello* in the Samoan language.

- *Butterfly slap sequence:* This sequence is a total of 8 counts. Crisscross the arms in front of the chest while holding them away from the body and parallel to the floor. Slap the hands on opposite elbows, with the right hand on the left elbow and the left hand on the right elbow, while the hands are held at chest height. Slap both elbows twice in a row for 2 counts. Then slap the backs of the hands together at chest height, like you are clapping with the backs of your hands instead of your palms for 2 counts while keeping elbows in place. Then repeat the elbow slaps followed by the backhand slaps for 4 counts.

- *Cracking the coconut:* This sequence is a total of 8 counts. With the left hand, pretend to scoop up a coconut for 2 counts. Pretend you are chopping to open a coconut, striking it twice with the right hand while holding the pretend coconut in the left palm for 2 counts. Hold the right fist over the left fist, and do a wringing action as if you are squeezing coconut milk out through the string remnants of the coconut husk for 2 counts. Throw away the husk with the right hand by tossing it over the right shoulder for 1 count, and hold for 1 count.

- *Elbow slaps, pati clap, and thigh slap sequence:* This sequence is a total of 4 counts. Hold the left elbow up at a 90-degree angle, and slap the inside of the left elbow with the right hand for 1 count. Repeat with the left hand slapping the right elbow for 1 count. Then do one pati clap and one thigh slap for 2 counts.

Sequence of Dance Steps

- Counts 1 to 4: Pati clap four times.
- Counts 5 to 8: Po claps four times.
- Counts 9 to 32: Repeat the sequence of four pati claps followed by four po claps three times.
- Counts 33 to 36: Pati clap, po clap, flick, and thigh slap.
- Counts 37 to 48: Repeat the sequence of pati clap, po clap, flick, and thigh slap three times.
- Counts 49 to 56: Flick, floor slap right, flick, floor slap left, flick, floor slap center, pati clap, and po clap.
- Counts 57 to 80: Repeat the sequence of flick, floor slap right, flick, floor slap left, flick, floor slap center, pati clap, and po clap three times.
- Counts 81 to 112: Do the handshake sequence four times.
- Counts 113 to 120: Do the butterfly slap sequence one time.
- Counts 121 to 128: Pati clap, po clap, pati clap, po clap, pati clap, po clap, pati clap, po clap.
- Counts 129 to 160: Crack the coconut sequence four times.
- Counts 161 to 176: Do the elbow slaps, pati clap, and thigh slap sequence four times. On the last sequence, shout "Chew" at the end.

Closure

Have students partner up and share with a classmate which hand movement sequence was their favorite and why. Allow students to share with the entire class after sharing with a partner, and ask them to explain what they think their favorite hand movement sequence might represent.

Look For

- Dancers who can complete sequences at the tempo of the drums and stay in rhythm with their classmates.
- Dancers who can identify the different movement sequences by name and remember the correct order without teacher cues.

How Can I Change This?

- There are many variations of the sasa dance, and the sequence or steps can be modified as needed for different groups of students. Depending on the grade level, you may only need to practice a few sequences or counts of the dance, then repeat them several times to develop competence in the dancers.
- Dancers can work with a partner or in groups of three to four and create their own 8 count sasa sequence that can be repeated four times for a total of 32 counts. Emphasize the use of everyday movements, such as slaps using different body parts, foot stomps, or other movements that can be added to the sequence. Although the sequence provided required sitting the entire time, the sasa dance can involve standing and movements in personal space.
- Dancers can pick their favorite three sequences and perform the dance in a small group or a large class circle.
- More advanced dancers can perform the entire dance while facing a partner. If working with a partner and creating their own sequence, they can also consider creating movements that require connecting with their partner, such as high-five claps or elbow taps.

Tanko Bushi

Grades

3 to 5

Outcomes

As a result of participating in this learning experience, children will be able to do the following:

1. Demonstrate the correct pattern of the dance without cues from the teacher (psychomotor and cognitive).
2. Perform the dance in a circle, in unison with other dancers, moving counterclockwise around the circle (psychomotor and affective).

Organization

Children move individually as a whole class, learning the steps before moving into a single circle to perform the movement sequence.

Equipment Needed

- Map of the world
- Flag of Japan
- Pictures of Japanese kimono dancers wearing traditional costumes
- Pictures of the coal mine and workers to help dancers understand the coal miner's job
- Suggested music:
  - "Tanko Bushi" by Isaku Kageyama
  - "Tanko Bushi" by Otomaru

Introduction and Warm-Up

Today, we are taking a trip in our classroom to Japan to learn a dance called tanko bushi that was first recorded in 1932. [Show map and flag of Japan.] In Japanese culture, this dance is one common example of a bon odori, a dance that occurs during the Bon festival to celebrate ancestors. Just as in other folk and cultural dances, the choreography communicates and celebrates the unique struggles and triumphs of a group of people. The tanko bushi dance pays tribute to the spirits of departed ancestors, and the dance movements reflect the coal miners' work movements relating the dance to the common people (Gilbert 2018). [Show images of the dancers in their traditional wear.] The actions in this dance will look like working in a coal mine with actions such as digging, carrying a bucket, and pushing a shovel. [Show images of the coal miners and the work they do.]

To begin, we are going to do some basic movements in our space to warm up our body for this dance. I am going to call out some everyday things you might do at home or at school, and I want to see you move like you are completing this action. This will be similar to the miming-type movements we will do in tanko bushi. Let's start by showing how you might yawn as you wake up in the morning. You might stretch out your arms and legs, or maybe twist your spine from side to side. You could move your head right and left as you imagine stretching your body in your bed. I might even see a couple of yawns actually happen with your mouths. Next, let's imagine we are getting ready for school and getting dressed. Show me the different movements you might make when you are putting on your clothes. Remember, you have two sleeves on your shirt and two legs for your pants. Let's repeat your movements of putting on your clothes three times to make it feel like a dance sequence. Next, let's try moving like we are eating our breakfast. I want everyone to do 4 counts of a breakfast-eating movement so we can repeat it several times. Here we go. [Count the sequence through, and have students repeat it several times.] For our last warm-up movement, I want to see your movement for traveling to class. Maybe you are imagining walking down the hallway and then opening a door. After you open a door, you could walk to your desk and sit down. Let me see how you move to get to your imaginary classroom. Try it one more time from the beginning. [Have students repeat their getting-to-class movement to finish.] Now, I want you to make a circle to begin learning the tanko bushi dance.

Movements

- *Cho-chon-ga-chon clap sequence:* Clap fast twice, pause, and clap (2 counts, counted as "1 & [pause on 2] &").

- *Dig step:* Two steps in place with the right foot only while the hands pretend to hold a shovel and perform a shoveling motion two times to the right. Repeat the same action with the left foot only and shovel to the left. This sequence is a total of 4 counts.

- *Throw the dirt:* Take one step (walk) forward on the right foot, and with both hands together, pretend to throw dirt over the right shoulder. Repeat the same action with the left foot. This sequence is a total of 2 counts.

- *Wipe the sweat:* Step backward (walk) on the right foot, and wipe with the right hand across the forehead as if you are wiping the sweat from your forehead. Repeat the same action with the left foot and the left hand. This sequence is a total of 2 counts.

- *Push the cart:* Step forward on the right foot, and push both hands forward to represent pushing a cart. Repeat this by stepping forward on the left foot and pushing both hands. This sequence is a total of 2 counts.

- *Brush the dirt:* Step forward with the right foot, placing a significant amount of weight onto the ball of the foot. While stepping forward, the left foot behind you should slightly lift off the floor, and you should feel your upper body rock in this direction. Then, place the left foot back down on the ground to shift your weight again. Place the right foot back together, next to the left foot. As you complete the rock step with your feet, reach your arms out at chest height and pretend to brush dirt out to the sides, away from the center of the body. This sequence is a total of 2 counts and should be counted as "1 & 2" to match the rhythm of the rock step.

Sequence of Dance Steps

- Counts 1 to 2: Perform the cho-chon-ga-chon clap sequence.
- Counts 3 to 6: Do the dig step.
- Counts 7 to 8: Throw the dirt.
- Counts 9 to 10: Wipe the sweat.
- Counts 11 to 12: Push the cart.
- Counts 13 to 14: Brush the dirt.
- Repeat the sequence until the song ends. The cho-chon-ga-chon clap sequence will begin as soon as both feet are together at the end of the brush the dirt step.

Closure

Have students partner up and discuss which step was their favorite to perform. Students can share with the class or explain to another student why this step was their favorite. Have the students brainstorm other jobs a dance might celebrate and name any dances they already know that show a specific job or type of work someone might do.

Look For

- Dancers who can stay on the beat of the music with each dance move.
- Dancers who can perform the correct dance movement without cues from the instructor.
- Dancers who can move smoothly and calmly through the space as they complete each step.

How Can I Change This?

- Traditionally, the dancers should stand in a circle facing the back of the person in front of them to travel around the circle as they dance the sequence. Beginner students can perform the dance in lines, all facing the same wall, and move forward and backward on the walking steps.
- Perform the dance in contra lines across from a partner.
- Ask dancers to work with partners or in small groups of three to four to create a new 8-count movement sequence representing what coal miners might do in their job. Examples might include items such as extracting coal from mines, operating machinery, drilling, chopping, scraping, and collecting coal. Have students add to the original tanko bushi dance as a new section of the dance or perform it separately from the original.

Tinikling

Grades

3 to 12

Outcomes

As a result of participating in this learning experience, students will be able to do the following:

1. Demonstrate teamwork between strikers and dancers to complete the jump pattern for 10 consecutive sequences while staying on beat (psychomotor and affective).
2. Complete the basic dance sequence for 32 counts (psychomotor).

Organization

- Students are arranged in small groups scattered around the dance area, using bamboo poles, jump bands, or lines on the floor to complete the dance.
- If using bamboo poles, two dancers are the strikers who beat the poles and two to four dancers perform the steps.
- If using jump bands, two dancers have the bands around their ankles and are the rhythm jumpers rather than the strikers, jumping two times in straddle position and one time with the legs together. The other two to four dancers perform the dance variations in and out of the jump bands.
- If using lines on the floor, only use two to four dancers standing next to the lines.

Equipment Needed

- 10- to 12-foot bamboo poles or PVC poles and a 2-foot wood beam that is 2 inches by 4 inches (The equipment is organized into sets that include two poles and two wood beams for each group of two to four dancers. If using jump bands, each group needs two bands instead of poles.)
- Drum or metronome to keep the tempo
- Suggested music (to perform the tinikling strike rhythm and basic step, it is best to dance to music with a three-quarter time):
  - "Tinikling" by Bayanihan Philippine Dance Company
  - "We Will Rock You" by Queen
  - "Hey Ya!" by Outkast
  - "Beat It" by Michael Jackson

Introduction and Warm-Up

The tinikling (tin-ick-ill-ing) dance originated from Leyte island in the Philippines and depicts the flight of the long-necked, long-legged tikling bird as it travels through the rice fields, avoiding bamboo traps made by the farmers. Tinikling is traditionally performed with two bamboo poles managed by two people called *strikers*, one holding each end of the poles. The bamboo poles serve as a percussion instrument and are also part of the dance choreography.

To warm up, we are all going to practice being strikers first to understand the rhythm and timing of the dance. All dancers need to sit on the floor with their legs crossed. We are going to practice the striker pattern by tapping our hands on the floor, just past our knees, for 2 counts. On count 3, I want you to clap. The rhythm should be tap-tap-clap. [Demonstrate for students while saying the rhythm out loud.] Let's try this pattern together for several repetitions in a row. I will tell you when to stop. The hard part is to make sure we do not speed up or slow down as we continue. [Students should repeat the tap-tap-clap pattern several times in a row. Listen for consistency in the tempo. If students need help maintaining the tempo, using a metronome or beating a drum can help keep the pace.] Now, I want us to try the same pattern of tap-tap-clap but in faster and slower tempos. I am going to play a tempo, either faster or slower than you just heard, and when I say "5-6-7-8," I want you to show me the tap-tap-clap pattern at that tempo. Be sure to listen carefully. [Play a steady tempo on a drum or with a metronome. Count students in, and have them repeat the rhythm several times before stopping and repeating the process with a different tempo.]

Now that we understand the striker's role and rhythm, we are going to continue warming up by practicing the dancer's portion. In tinikling, there are many different patterns of hopping and jumping, which we will learn when we get to the choreography. For now, we are going to practice two different patterns with our feet. Standing in your own personal space, I want you to jump in what is called a *straddle*, meaning your feet are shoulder-width apart as you jump up and down. You are going to jump twice with your feet in this straddle, or what I will call as "out." On count 3, you will jump your feet together so the legs are touching under your hips to what we will call "in." The jumping pattern will then continue with you jumping back out to the straddle on count 1. The pattern is out-out-in. Let's practice this several times and make sure we are all placing our feet in the correct spots. [Have students practice this pattern several times, and watch for students staying in unison.] Next, I want us to reverse the pattern and jump in-in-out. Remember, a jump is on two feet, and you want to jump with both feet under you going out to the straddle on the third count. Let's try it several times in a row. [Have students practice the pattern multiple times in a row.] To finish off our warm-up, let's add in a hop, which is like a jump but on one foot instead of two. Go back to the out-out-in pattern, and now when we say "in," land only on one foot. For now, it does not matter if it is your left or right foot. We are focused on being able to switch from two feet to one foot. [Students should jump in a straddle position for out-out and then hop onto one foot for the in. Repeat this pattern multiple times, looking for a unison switch.] Now that you have the first pattern with a hop and jump, we are going to switch to the second pattern of in-in-out. This means you will hop-hop-jump. Again, it does not matter which foot you hop on for now. [Have students practice this pattern multiple times, looking for unison switches between one and two feet.] With the striker and dancer rhythms learned, we can now put them together as a team to learn a tinikling dance.

Movements

- *Hopping:* Hopping is a springing up in the air and back down to the ground on only one foot while the other foot is lifted.

- *Jumping:* Jumping is a springing up in the air and back down to the ground with both feet starting and ending on the floor equally.

- *Jump straddle:* Jumping action involves rebounding from both feet to land in a straddle with the legs apart.

- *Tinikling striking rhythm using bamboo poles:* The strikers sit on the floor on their knees or with their legs crossed. In front of their feet is the beam (small wooden block), and on top of the beam are the ends of the poles. The strikers sit behind the beam, holding the poles, with one striker at each end of the poles. Strikers hold the poles in their hands and perform the 3-count rhythm. On counts 1 and

2, the poles are tapped on the beam about two feet apart, and on count 3, the poles strike together in the air and off the beam. The cue is tap-tap-strike or open-open-close. The strikers maintain a steady tempo throughout the dance.

- *Dancers' basic tinikling step:* The dancer begins by standing on two feet with their right side next to the poles. As the strikers perform the open-open-close rhythmic pattern, the dancer hops on the right foot between the poles on the first tap open, then switches to a left foot hop on the second tap open while still between the poles, and then hops on the right foot to the right and lands outside of the poles on the close of the poles. The dancer's cue is in-in-out or right in, left in, right out. The dancer should hold their left knee up, ready to hop in on the next beat. This basic step is repeated, beginning with the left side next to the poles (left hop between the poles, right hop between the poles, and left hop to the outside left of the poles).

Sequence of Dance Steps

There is no set pattern for tinikling. Once students develop the basic striking pattern and the basic tinikling dance step, they can learn or create variations to connect with the basic steps. Here are some sample variations to add to the basic dance step:

- *Pattern A (jump-jump-straddle):* Dancers start by standing between the poles or jump bands that are in the open position. Dancers jump two times in the middle of the poles, while strikers tap two times. Then the dancers perform a straddle jump outside each of the poles or bands as the strikers tap close or the band jumpers jump together. Repeat this several times (see figure 11.4).

- *Pattern B (jump-jump-side jump):* Start on either side of the poles or jump bands. Jump two times between the poles with both feet on open-open, and then jump to either the right or left side with both feet on close. Repeat this pattern and change landing from right to left, or continue to jump to only one side of the poles.

- *Pattern C (front jump):* Face the poles or jump bands, and jump forward in the middle two times on tap, tap and back out of the poles or bands on strike (see figure 11.5). Dancers can jump backward out of the poles, back to their beginning spot, or they can jump forward out of the poles on strike, but they will have to jump backward to get back between the poles to repeat the pattern.

- *Pattern D (crossover step):* Each time dancers hop in and out, use a crossover step. Start with your right foot outside the poles or bands. Cross the left foot over the right as you step the left foot inside, then step the right foot inside.

- *Pattern E (jump-jump-straddle turn):* Dancers start standing between the poles or jump bands that are in the open position. Dancers jump two times in the middle of the poles, while the strikers tap two times. Then the dancers perform a straddle jump with a half turn to face the opposite direction, straddling outside each of the poles or bands as the strikers tap close or the band jumpers jump together. Repeat this several times.

- *Pattern F (three-step turn):* After one repetition of the basic step to the right, the dancers do a three-step half turn on the outside of the poles, moving backward, so the right side is next to the poles but on the opposite end of where they stepped out. When this step variation is repeated several times, the dancers end up moving in a circular pathway, always leading with the right foot. The cue is in-in-out, back-back-back, in-in-out, back-back-back.

- *Sample sequence:* Due to tinikling being best danced in three-quart time, counts are in sets of 3.
  - Counts 1 to 18: Dancers do a basic tinikling step, repeating it six times.
  - Counts 19 to 36: Repeat pattern A six times.
  - Counts 37 to 54: Repeat pattern B 6 times.
  - Counts 55 to 66: Dancers do a basic tinikling step, repeating it four times.
  - Counts 67 to 78: Repeat pattern F four times.
  - Students can then repeat the same sequence, but switching roles as strikers and dancers.

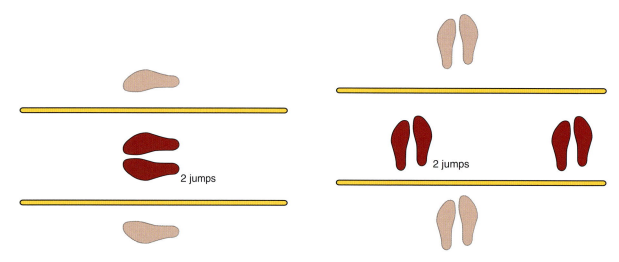

Figure 11.4 Sample tinikling step pattern A.   **Figure 11.5** Sample tinikling step pattern C.

Closure

Have students partner up and demonstrate their favorite tinikling step variation learned during the lesson. Students should be able to explain why this variation is their favorite. Have some students share with the entire class and discuss any other variations they can imagine that were not yet taught or demonstrated.

Look For

- Teams who can work together to practice the rhythm and verbalize the cues to develop a successful dance.
- Dancers and strikers who can develop consistency with the tempo and rhythm.
- Dancers who can complete the basic steps on the right and left without breaking the rhythm.

How Can I Change This?

- Dancers can do the steps together but enter from opposite sides of the poles or bands.
- Two dancers can face each other, hold hands, and perform pattern A (jump-jump-straddle).
- Two dancers can perform the basic tinikling dance step together and also add in patty-cake or other hand motions to match the rhythm.
- Have students create their own variations on the jump pattern. Students can also work with the strikers to change any variations in the striking rhythm and make the choreography more difficult or interesting.

Virginia Reel

 Visit HK*Propel* to see students demonstrating the Virginia reel.

Grades

3 to 12

Outcomes

As a result of participating in this learning experience, students will be able to do the following:

1. Perform three basic movements of the dance with a partner for 8 counts each (psychomotor and affective).
2. Perform a sequence of dance movements based on the cues from the caller of the dance (psychomotor).

Organization

Students first learn the movements individually as a whole class, or while in pairs. Then the dancers learn the sequence in the traditional contra formation, which is when dancers are paired and face each other in two parallel lines. Lines of six to eight partners are best. One set of partners, called the head partners, are traditionally those who are closest to the music, while a pair at the opposite end of the line is called foot partners (see figure 11.6).

Equipment Needed

- Suggested music:
  - "Virginia Reel" by Wongawilli (upbeat version)
  - "Virginia Reel" by Shenanigans (with dance calls)
  - "Durang's Hornpipe" by Adam Steffey

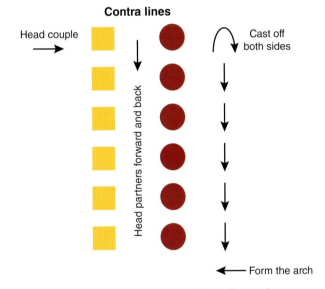

Figure 11.6 Formation for Virginia reel.

Introduction and Warm-Up

Today, we are learning a dance called the Virginia reel, which is a folk dance from the 1700s. Although there is conflicting information regarding the true origins of the Virginia reel, the dance likely began as a variation or tribute to the Scottish reels of medieval times in which two or more couples danced in a circle formation, changing partners as they weaved in and out, all while dancing on tiptoe (Kassing 2017). Some sources claim the Virginia reel originated as an Irish and Scottish dance that evolved into the English version called Sir Roger de Coverley. English colonists brought the dance to America, creating their own version and naming it the Virginia reel, and many additional versions of the dance have been created over time. Can you think of any other dances that have been influenced by different cultures and have many versions? [Students name various folk, social, or cultural dances they may know that have variations and changes over time.] The tricky part about the Virginia reel is the teamwork involved throughout the dance, because it is all about dancing with a partner while also being aware of the entire group. We are going to warm up today by working with a partner so we are ready for learning the sequence later. [Pair the students or have them find a partner.] I want you to face your partner so we can begin. Be sure you are spread away from other partners and have plenty of space.

First, we are going to practice honoring our partners so we know how to walk on the beat of the music and stay aware of our space. Back up from your partner so you have space to walk toward them, and then take a bow in 4 counts. Let's try that slowly together. [Have students walk toward each other for 4 counts, bowing on count 4.] Now, you are going to walk backward, back to your beginning spot, in 4 counts without a bow this time. Ready, go. Now that we know how to safely honor our partner, let's practice that movement several times. I want you to focus on your spacing and staying on beat. [Play a drum or a song with a steady tempo, and have students practice this forward and backward motion several times.]

Now that you are experts in working with your partners, we are going to practice a few more partner movements. The first two are called right hand through and left hand through. Let's try the right hand through first. I want both partners to reach their right arms out to their partner and carefully grab hands. Once you are connected, walk in a circle and end up back in your beginning spot on count 8. Let's try that together. Ready, 5, 6, 7, 8. [Count the students or use music to keep the beat for walking 8 counts.] Now let's try the left hand through. You do the exact same movement, but this time you grab left hands and your circle will be in the opposite direction. Remember to stay on beat and finish in your beginning spot. Ready, set, and go. Let's practice going back and forth between the right and left sides several times. Be ready to change when I call it out. [Have students practice both circles, calling out the switch every time.] This time, I want you to complete your circle, but connect both hands together. This is called a two-hand circle. You still need to end up back in your beginning spot by the final count. [Have students try the movement and look for students ending in unison on the final count of 8. Then have students try the three variations of right, left, and two hands while calling out the changes.] Let's finish our warm-up with a final sequence of honoring our partner to thank them for working with us. Face your partner and be ready to walk forward. Ready, 5, 6, 7, walk! [Have students honor forward and backward a few times. End the warm-up, and then begin learning the sequence.]

Movements

- *Honor your partner:* Partners walk four steps forward toward each other and bow on the fourth step for a total of 4 counts. Partners walk four steps backward away from each other and back to their place for a total of 4 counts.

- *Right hand through:* Partners walk forward toward their partner, take each other's right hands, walk clockwise in a circle, and return to their place for a total of 8 counts. This can be used interchangeably with a right elbow swing.

- *Left hand through:* Partners walk forward toward their partner, take each other's left hands, walk counterclockwise in the circle, and return to their place for a total of 8 counts. This can be used interchangeably with a left elbow swing.

- *Two-hand circle:* Partners walk forward toward their partner, grab both hands, walk counterclockwise in the circle, and return to their place for a total of 8 counts.

- *Do-si-do:* This 8-count sequence requires dancers to march past their partner and then return to their beginning spot without turning their body around. Dancers face their partner and march 2 counts past each other with the right shoulders passing. Then they march two steps to the right side with their backs to each other. Next, they march backward with the left shoulders passing. Finally, they march two steps to the left side and end up back in their beginning locations, facing each other.

- *Seesaw:* This 8-count sequence is just like the do-si-do where partners march past each other and return to their beginning spot without turning their body around, but it starts by passing the left shoulders. Dancers face their partner and march 2 counts past each other with the left shoulders passing. Then they march two steps to the left side with their backs to each other. Next, they march backward with the right shoulders passing. Finally, they march two steps to the right side and end up back in their beginning locations, facing each other.

- *Head partners down and back:* Head partners face each other, then perform eight slides moving toward the foot partners of the set and eight slides back to the head of the set for a total of 16 counts. Partners can hold hands or slide without touching, with their arms stretched out to the sides.

- *Reel the set:* Head partners do a right elbow swing for 4 counts. After the right elbow swing, the head partners swing the left elbows with the person on the opposite side of the line, facing whoever is next in the line, for a total of 4 counts. Head partners meet in the middle of the parallel lines and swing the right elbows for 4 counts. Next, the left elbows swing with the next person in the line who is on the opposite side, for a total of 4 counts. Head partners meet in the middle of the lines and swing the right elbows for 4 counts. Continue the reel until the head partners have performed the left elbow swing with each person in the opposite-facing line, always meeting their partner for a right elbow swing in-between.
- *Elbow swing:* Partners hook elbows and circle for 360 degrees. This can be done with both left elbows or both right elbows. Dancers can march or skip while connected to their partner.
- *Slide back up:* When the head partners get to the end of the line, they slide back up to the head of the line for a total of 8 counts.
- *Cast off:* Also called "peel the banana," "hit the highway," or "strip the willow." Head partners face the front of the line, away from the rest of the dancers, and all the other dancers face the head partner in a single-file line. At the same time, the head partner on the left turns to the left and walks toward the foot of the line, and all the dancers follow. The head partner on the right turns to the right and walks toward the foot of the line, and all the dancers follow. This is done for a total of 16 counts.
- *The arch:* When the head partners reach the foot of the line, they face each other and form an arch by holding their hands raised up high. The other dancers, now led by the second set of partners, walk under the arch and slide together to the start position, followed by all other partners. The second set of partners now becomes the new head partners, and the dance begins again.

Sequence of Dance Steps

- Part 1
  - Counts 1 to 8: Honor your partner
  - Counts 9 to 16: Right hand through
  - Counts 17 to 24: Left hand through
  - Counts 25 to 32: Two-hand circle
  - Counts 33 to 40: Do-si-do
  - Counts 41 to 48: Seesaw
- Part 2
  - Counts 1 to 16: Head partners down and back
  - Counts 17 to 48: Reel the set (counts may vary depending on the size of the group)
  - Counts 49 to 56: Slide back up
  - Counts 57 to 64: Cast off
  - Counts 65 to 97: The arch (counts may vary depending on the size of the group.)
- The dance repeats sequences one and two until all partners have had an opportunity to be a head partner.

Closure

- Share with a classmate your favorite part of the dance as well as which part of the dance was the most challenging.
- Discuss with a classmate when you think the early colonists in Virginia performed this dance as a community.

Look For

- Dancers who can perform the correct dance movements in the right order.
- Dancers being respectful of their partner and holding hands when required for a dance movement.
- Dancers moving in rhythm to follow the leaders in the cast-off dance movement to form the arch in 16 counts.

How Can I Change This?

- Change the right hand through and left hand through movements to elbow swings.
- Instead of performing both sets of right hand and left hand through movements, remove them and only use the two-hand circle.
- To simplify the dance for elementary-school-aged children, eliminate the reel the set sequence.
- Have students choreograph different locomotor movements with their partner to perform during the head partners down and back sequence.

References

Ambrosio, N. (2003). *Learning about dance: Dance as an art form and entertainment* (3rd ed.). Kendall/Hunt

Anderson, L.W., and Krathwohl, D.R. (Eds.). (2001). *A taxonomy for learning, teaching, and assessing: A revision of Bloom's taxonomy of educational objectives*. Longman.

ASCD. (2015). "The whole child." www.wholechildeducation.org/about

Assessment Work Group. (2019). *Student social and emotional competence assessment: The current state of the field and a vision for its future*. Chicago, IL: Collaborative for Academic, Social, and Emotional Learning. https://casel.org/casel-gateway-student-sel-competence-assessment

Axelrod, A., and McGinley-Nally, S. (2005). *Pigs in the corner: Fun with math and dance*. Aladdin.

Ball, D., and Forzani, F. (2011). Teaching skillful teaching. *Educational Leadership, 68*(4), 40-45.

Barone, T., and Eisner, E.W. (2012). *Arts based research*. SAGE.

Benzwie, T. (1987). *A moving experience: Dance for lovers of children and the child within*. Zephyr Press.

Benzwie, T. (2000). *More moving experiences: Connecting arts, feelings and imagination*. National Dance Education Organization.

Benzwie, T. (2002). *Alphabet movers*. National Dance Education Organization.

Benzwie, T. (2011). *Numbers on the move: 1 2 3 dance and count with me*. Temple University Press.

Bertills, K., Granlund, M., and Augustine, L. (2019). Inclusive teaching skills and student engagement in physical education. *Frontiers in Education, 4*(1), 1-13. https://doi.org/10.3389/feduc.2019.00074

Bevans, K.B., Fitzpatrick, L-A., Sanchez, B.M., Riley, A.W., and Forrest, C. (2010). Physical education resources, class management, and student physical activity levels: A structure-process-outcome approach to evaluating physical education effectiveness. *Journal of School Health, 80*(12), 573-580. https://doi.org/10.1111/j.1746-1561.2010.00544.x

Bilitza, M.S. (2021). Being the facilitator: A brief research report on the motivation of the choreographer and dance maker to work with heterogeneous groups in a community dance setting. *Frontiers in Psychology, 12*(1), 1-6. https://doi.org/10.3389/fpsyg.2021.601033

Boynton, S. (1993). *Barnyard dance*. Workman.

Boynton, S. (2021). *Woodland dance*. Workman.

Brady, K., Forton, M., and Porter, D. (2011). *Rules in school: Teaching discipline in the responsive classroom*. Northeast Foundation for Children.

Brehm, M., and McNett, L. (2015). *Creative dance for learning: The kinesthetic link*, 2nd ed. Princeton Book Company.

Brookfield, S. (2017). *Becoming a critically reflective teacher* (2nd ed.). Jossey-Bass.

Buckley, J. (2021). *It's a numbers game! Baseball: The math behind the perfect pitch, the game-winning grand slam, and so much more!* National Geographic Kids.

Buckley, S. (2018). *Advocacy strategies and approaches: Overview*. Association for Progressive Communications. www.apc.org/en/advocacy-strategies-and-approaches-overview

Bucura, E., and Brashier, R. (2021). Transformational learning strategies for the secondary general music classroom. *Journal of General Music Education, 35*(3): 6-11. https://doi.org/10.1177/27527646211061495

Bugler, B., and Bechtel, M. (2018). *My first book of basketball: A rookie book*. Sports Illustrated Kids.

Burk, R. (2021). *Stomp, wiggle, clap, and tap: My first book of dance*. Rockridge Press.

Carle, E. (1996). *Little cloud*. Philomel Books.

Chaud, B. (2015). *The bear's surprise*. Chronicle Books.

Cleary, B., and Prosmitsky, J. (2001). *To root, to toot, to parachute: What is a verb?* Carolrhoda Books.

Cone, T. (2000). Off the page: Responding to children's literature through dance. *Teaching Elementary Physical Education, 11*(5), 11-34.

Cone, T. (2002). *Off the page: Children's creative dance as a response to children's literature*. Unpublished doctoral dissertation, Temple University.

Cone, S., and Cone, T. (2002). Using sport themes in creative dance. *Strategies, 16*(1), 9-12.

Cone, S., and Cone, T. (2003). Dancing, learning, creating, knowing. *Teaching Elementary Physical Education, 14*(5), 7-11.

Cone, T, and Cone, S. (2005). *Assessing dance in elementary physical education*. National Association for Sport and Physical Education.

Cone, T., and Cone, S. (2011). Strategies for teaching dancers of all abilities. *Journal of Physical Education, Recreation and Dance, 82*(2), 24-31.

Cone, T., Werner, P., and Cone, S. (2009). *Interdisciplinary elementary physical education: Connection, sharing, partnering*. Human Kinetics.

Cook, J. (2008). *It's hard to be a verb*. National Center for Youth Issues.

Davey, O. (2019). *Fanatical about frogs*. Flying Eye Books.

Davies, B., Nambiar, N., Hemphill, C., Devietti, E., Massengale, A., and McCredie, P. (2015). Intrinsic motivation in physical education. *Journal of Physical Education, Recreation, and Dance, 86*(8), 8-13.

Dean, J. (2013). *Pete the cat: Pete at the beach*. HarperCollins.

de Mille, A. (1991, April 7). Measuring the steps of a giant. *New York Times*.

Department of Justice: Disability Rights Section of the Civil Rights Division. (2011, March 8). *Appendix 2: Summary of requirements*. www.ada.gov/regs2010/RIA_2010regs/ria_appendix02.htm

Dervent, F. (2015). The effect of reflective thinking on the teaching practices of preservice physical education teachers. *Issues in Educational Research, 25*(3), 260-275. www.iier.org.au/iier25/dervent.pdf

DiPasquale, S. (2022). Reframing movement modifications: Integrative dance in a collegiate environment. *Journal of Dance Education, 22*(1), 51-57. https://doi.org/10.1080/15290824.2020.1773471

Dixson, D.D., and Worrell, F.C. (2016). Formative and summative assessment in the classroom. *Theory in Practice, 55*(2), 153-159. https://doi.org/10.1080/00405841.2016.1148989

Doan, R.J., MacDonald, L.C., and Chepko, S. (2017). *Lesson planning for middle school physical education: Meeting the national standards & grade-level outcomes.* Human Kinetics.

Donnelly, F. (2002). Make learning an electric experience! *Teaching Elementary Physical Education, 13*(2), 25-27.

Double, K.S., McGrane, J.A., and Hopfenbeck, T.N. (2019). The impact of peer assessment on academic performance: A meta-analysis of control group studies. *Educational Psychology Review, 32*(2), 481-509. https://doi.org/10.1007/s10648-019-09510-3

Drake, S.M., and Reid, J.L. (2020, July 14). 21st century competencies in light of the history of integrated curriculum. *Frontiers in Education Vol 5: Policy and Practice Reviews.* https://doi.org/10.3389/feduc.2020.00122

Eddy, M. (2016). Dancing solutions to conflict: Field-tests somatic dance for peace. *Journal of Dance Education 16*(3), 99-111. https://doi.org/10.1080/15290824.2015.1115867

Ensanian, K.D. (2021). *I can make a water dance.* Equus Potentia.

Faber, R. (2018). Opportunity-to-learn standards for dance. National Dance Education Organization. www.ndeo.org/Portals/NDEO/Standards%20Documents/NDEO_Opportunity_to_Learn_Standards_2-22-18(1).pdf?ver=i_1yJxa3GvB3rC5pMi5eYw%3d%3d

Farrington, C.A., Maurer, J., McBride, M.R.A., Nagaoka, J., Puller, J.S., Shewfelt, S., Weiss, E.M., and Wright, L. (2019). *Arts education and social-emotional learning outcomes among K–12 students: Developing a theory of action.* Ingenuity and the University of Chicago Consortium on School Research.

Fencl, M.J. (2014). Fun and creative unit assessment ideas for all students in physical education. *Journal of Physical Education, Recreation, and Dance, 85*(1), 16-21. http://dx.doi.org/10.1080/07303084.2014.855589

Fleming, D. (1993). *In the small, small pond.* Holt.

Gardner, H. (2011). *Frames of mind: The theory of multiple intelligences* (3rd ed.). Basic Books.

Gerstein, M. (2007). *The man who walked between the towers.* Square Fish.

Gilbert, A.G. (2002). *Teaching the three R's through movement experiences.* National Dance Education Organization.

Gilbert (2018). *Brain-compatible dance education* (2nd ed.). Human Kinetics.

Gilbert, A.G. (2015). *Creative dance for all ages* (2nd ed.). SHAPE America.

Goodway, J.D., Ozmun, J.C., and Gallahue, D.L. (2019). *Understanding motor development: Infants, children, adolescents, adults.* Jones & Bartlett Learning.

Graham, G., Elliott, E., and Palmer, S. (2016). *Teaching children and adolescents physical education* (4th ed.). Human Kinetics.

Grant, C.N. (2021). *Oodles and oodles of noodley noodles.* Cynthia E. Grant.

Hanna, J. (1987). *To dance is human: A theory of nonverbal communication.* University of Chicago Press.

Hood, S. (2016). *Leaps and bounce.* Little, Brown Books for Young Readers.

Hutchinson Guest, A. (2006). *The movement alphabet.* Language of Dance. www.lodc.org/what-is-lod

Jenkins, C. (2013). *The lost (and found) balloon.* Aladdin.

Johnson, I. (2002). Liven up those line dances. *Teaching Elementary Physical Education, 13*(1), 30-32.

Jönsson, A., Balan, A., and Hartell, E. (2021). Analytic or holistic? A study about how to increase the agreement in teachers' grading. *Assessment in Education: Principles, Policy & Practice, 28*(3), 212-227. https://doi.org/10.1080/0969594X.2021.1884041

Joven, C.C. (2017). *Baseball buzz.* Capstone Press.

Kaittani, D., Kouli, O., Derri, V., and Kioumourtzoglou, E. (2017). Interdisciplinary teaching in physical education. *Arab Journal of Nutrition and Exercise, 2*(2), 91-101. https://doi.org/10.18502/ajne.v2i2.1248

Kane, K. (1998). *Move and learn: A kaleidoscope of creative movement activities for literacy development.* Instructional Fair TS Denison.

Karin, J., and Nordin-Bates, S.M. (2020). Enhancing creativity and managing perfectionism in dancers through implicit learning and sensori-kinetic imagery. *Journal of Dance Education, 20*(1), 1-11. https://doi.org/10.1080/15290824.2018.1532572

Kassing, G. (2017). *History of dance* (2nd ed.). Human Kinetics.

Kassing, G., and Jay-Kirschenbaum, D. (2021). *Dance teaching methods and curriculum design: Comprehensive K-12 dance education* (2nd ed.). Human Kinetics.

Kaufmann, K., and Dehline, J. (2014). *Dance integration: 36 lesson plans for science and mathematics.* Human Kinetics.

Krasnoff, B. (2016). Culturally responsive teaching: A guide to evidence-based practices for teaching all students equitably. Region X Equity Assistance Center at Education Northwest. https://educationnorthwest.org/sites/default/files/resources/culturally-responsive-teaching.pdf

Laban, R. (1976). *Modern educational dance* (3rd ed.). Macdonald & Evans.

Leisen, M. (2022, April 1). Make your rubric more than a wall of words. Association for Supervision and Curriculum Development. www.ascd.org/el/articles/make-your-rubric-more-than-a-wall-of-words

Lester, A. (2014). *Run like a rabbit.* Allen & Unwin.

Lewis, P. (2015). *National Geographic Book of nature poetry: More than 200 poems with photographs that float, zoom, and bloom.* National Geographic Kids.

Locker, T. (2003). *Cloud dance.* HHM Books for Young Readers.

Maloney Leaf, B., and Ngo, B. (2017). The importance of "downtime" for democratic dance pedagogy: Insights from a dance program serving Asian American youth. *Journal of Dance Education, 17*(2), 65-72. https://doi.org/10.1080/15290824.2017.1280323

McCarthy-Brown, N. (2017). *Dance pedagogy for a diverse world: Culturally relevant teaching in theory, research and practice.* McFarland & Company.

McTighe, J. (1997). What happens between assessments? *Educational Leadership, 54* (4), 6-12.

Medina Rosas, J. (2017). *ABC pasta: An entertaining alphabet.* Viking Books for Young Readers.

Mosston, M., and Ashworth, S. (2008). *Teaching physical education: First online edition.* Spectrum Institute for Teaching and Learning.

Murray, R.L. (1963). *Dance in elementary education* (2nd ed.). Harper & Row.

National Coalition for Core Arts Standards. (2014). *National core arts standards.* State Education Agency Directors of Arts Education (SEADAE). www.nationalartsstandards.org

National Dance Education Organization. (2018). *Opportunity-to-learn standards for dance.* www.ndeo.org/Portals/NDEO/Standards%20Documents/NDEO_Opportunity_to_Learn_Standards_2-22-18(1).pdf?ver=i_1yJxa3GvB3rC5pMi5eYw%3d%3d

National Dance Society. (2020). *National dance education standards framework.* Human Kinetics.

Ndoye, A. (2017). Peer/self assessment and student learning. *International Journal of Teaching and Learning in Higher Education, 29*(2), 255-269. https://files.eric.ed.gov/fulltext/EJ1146193.pdf

Nelson, H. (2009). High-quality arts programs can contribute to the intellectual, physical, and emotional well-being of children. *Principal*: 14-17.

Newman, J., and Feinberg, M.P. (2015). *Move to learn: Integrating movement into the early childhood curriculum.* Gryphon House.

Norworth, J. (2016). *Take me out to the ball game.* Charlesbridge.

Nurmi, A., and Kokkonen, M. (2015). Peers as teachers in physical education hip hop classes in Finnish high school. *Journal of Education and Training Studies, 3*(3), 23-32. https://doi.org/10.11114/jets.v3i3.659

Ostersmith, S., and Jeffs, K. (2023). *Interdisciplinary arts.* Human Kinetics.

Overby, L., Post, B., and Newman, D. (2005). *Interdisciplinary learning through dance: 101 moventures.* Human Kinetics.

Payne, H., and Costas, B. (2021). Creative dance as experiential learning in state primary education: The potential benefits for children. *Journal of Experiential Education, 44*(3), 277-292. https://doi.org/10.1177/1053825920968587

Pernice, C. (2014). *Circus girl.* Simply Read Books.

Rovegno, I., and Bandhauer, D. (2017). *Elementary physical education: Curriculum and instruction* (2nd ed.). Jones & Bartlett Learning.

Sarrazin, N. (2016). *Music and the child.* Open SUNY Textbooks.

Sayre, A.P. (2017). *Full of fall.* Beach Lane Books.

SHAPE America. (2013). *National standards for K-12 physical education.* Author. www.shapeamerica.org/standards/pe/upload/Grade-Level-Outcomes-for-K-12-Physical-Education.pdf

SHAPE America. (2019). *Crosswalk for SHAPE America national standards & grade-level outcomes for K-12 physical education and CASEL social and emotional learning.* Author.

Silverstein, S. (1974). *Where the sidewalk ends.* Harper & Row.

Silverstein, S. (1981). *A light in the attic.* Harper & Row.

Slepcevic-Zach, P., and Stock, M. (2018). ePortfolio as a tool for reflection and self-reflection. *Reflective Practice, 19*(3), 291-307. https://doi.org/10.1080/14623943.2018.1437399

Society for Health and Physical Educators. (2010). *Opportunity to learn: Guidelines for elementary, middle & high school physical education. A side-by-side comparison.* www.shapeamerica.org/upload/Opportunity-to-Learn-Guidelines.pdf

Square Dance Legislation Collection. (2004). Library of Congress American Folklife Center. www.loc.gov/folklife/guides/squaredance.html

Stauffer, K. (2019). Reclaiming creativity through objects, collaboration, and site-specific work. *Art Education, 72*(1), 6-12. http://dx.doi.org/10.1080/00043125.2019.1534442

Steinglass, E. (2019). *Soccerverse: Poems about soccer.* Wordsong.

Stinson, S. (1988). *Dance for young children: Finding the magic in movement.* National Dance Association/American Alliance for Health, Physical Education, Recreation and Dance.

Tanis, C.J., and Hebel, S.L. (2016). Emergency action plans in physical education. *Strategies: A Journal for Physical and Sport Educators, 29*(4), 3-7. https://doi.org/10.1080/08924562.2016.1181589

Taylor, A., and Fritz, N. (2021). *The crab dance.* Bookbaby.

Tomlinson, C. (2014). *The differentiated classroom: Responding to the needs of all learners* (2nd ed.). Association for Supervision and Curriculum Development.

Torzillo, M., and Sorin, R. (2018). Dancing toward each other: Dance in the primary school classroom. *The International Journal of Interdisciplinary Educational Studies, 13*(2), 31-48. https://doi.org/10.18848/2327-011X/CGP/v13i02/31-48

United States Department of Health and Human Services. (2018). *Physical activity guidelines for Americans* (2nd ed.). https://health.gov/sites/default/files/2019-09/Physical_Activity_Guidelines_2nd_edition.pdf

United States Department of Justice. (2010). *Final regulatory impact analysis of the final revised regulations implementing titles II and III of the ADA, including revised ADA standards for accessible design.* www.ada.gov/regs2010/RIA_2010regs/ria_appendix02.htm

Vischer, F. (2011). *Fuddles.* Aladdin.

Wall, J., and Murray, N. (1990). *Children and movement: Physical education in the elementary school.* Brown.

Wallace, A., and Nhin, M. (2021). *Never EVER dance with a Dracula.* Grow Grit Press.

Wells, H., Jones, A., and Jones, S.C. (2014). Teaching reluctant students: Using the principles and techniques of motivational interviewing to foster better student-teacher interactions. *Innovations in Education and Teaching International, 51*(2), 175-184. http://dx.doi.org/10.1080/14703297.2013.778066

West, W., and Capaldi, G. (2012). *Square dance! A ruckus in the barn.* CreateSpace Independent Publishing Platform.

Wiggins, G., and McTighe, J. (2005). *Understanding by Design* (2nd ed.), Association for Supervision and Curriculum Development.

Winner, Y., and Oliver, T. (2003). *Frogs sing songs.* Charlesbridge.

Wright, J.P. (2012). *Social dance: Steps to success* (3rd ed.). Human Kinetics.

Yi, S. (2021). *Cat & cat adventures: The quest for snacks.* HarperAlley.

Zakkai, J. (1997). *Dance as a way of knowing.* Stenhouse.

Zoehfeld, K.W. (2019). *Adventure cat! And more true stories of amazing cats.* Recorded Books.

About the Authors

Susan Flynn, MA, teaches in the School of Education, Health, and Human Performance at the College of Charleston, South Carolina, training students in sport pedagogy and preK-5 teacher education. Flynn specializes in the areas of rhythms and dance in the PE curriculum, adapted physical education, and elementary methods. She has also taught at Purdue University and in public schools in Maryland.

Flynn developed the Perceptual Motor Development Clinic at the University of Toledo and was director for 10 years. She also organized Pete's Pals, a mentoring initiative at Purdue University offering aquatic and motor therapy for children with disabilities. Currently, she conducts a similar program at the College of Charleston called FitCatZ Aquatic and Motor Therapy.

Emily Enloe, EdD, is a dance educator at Oakbrook Middle School in Charleston, South Carolina. In addition to teaching, Enloe was the graduate mentor for the Dancers Connect program housed through the University of South Carolina's dance education program from August 2010 to May 2014. Work with this program earned Enloe the 2012 Elsa Posey Graduate Student Scholarship from the National Dance Education Organization. She earned her MEd in early childhood education from the University of South Carolina in August 2013, and she continues to present at workshops and both state and national conferences in addition to teaching. Dr. Enloe is past president of the South Carolina Alliance for Health, Physical Education, Recreation and Dance as well as the South Carolina Dance Association. She graduated from Charleston Southern University with an EdD in leadership in May 2022.

Stephen L. Cone, PhD, is a professor emeritus in the department of health and exercise science at Rowan University in New Jersey. Dr. Cone is past president of the American Alliance for Health, Physical Education, Recreation and Dance (AAHPERD; now SHAPE America) and received their Honor Award in 2000. He is also a member of the New Jersey AHPERD, the Alliance for Arts Education New Jersey, and numerous other professional organizations. He has written dozens of articles for physical education publications and was coauthor of *Interdisciplinary Teaching Through Physical Education* (Human Kinetics, 1998) and the three previous editions of *Teaching Children Dance*.

Theresa Purcell Cone, PhD (1950–2019), was a physical education and dance teacher at Brunswick Acres Elementary School in Kendall Park, New Jersey, where she also directed a children's dance company. She was an adjunct professor at Rowan University in New Jersey and a teacher and choreographer at the Princeton Ballet School. Dr. Cone was a past president of the National Dance Association and was named its first Dance Educator of the Year. She was also a member of the National Dance Education Organization, the Alliance for Arts Education New Jersey, and numerous other professional organizations. Dr. Cone was coauthor of *Interdisciplinary Teaching Through Physical Education* (Human Kinetics, 1998).

In 2004, Dr. Cone was awarded a Presidential Citation by the American Alliance for Health, Physical Education, Recreation and Dance. She also was awarded the Margie R. Hanson Distinguished Service Award by the National Association for Sport and Physical Education. Dr. Cone received her doctorate in dance from Temple University.